Hostage to the Devil

Books by Malachi Martin

The Scribal Character of the Dead Sea Scrolls
The Pilgrim (under the pseudonym Michael Serafian)
The Encounter
Three Popes and the Cardinal
Jesus Now
The New Castle
Hostage to the Devil
The Final Conclave
King of Kings
The Decline and Fall of the Roman Church
There Is Still Love
Rich Church, Poor Church
Vatican
The Jesuits

HOSTAGE TO THE DEVIL

The Possession and Exorcism of Five Living Americans

Malachi Martin

PERENNIAL LIBRARY

Harper & Row, Publishers, New York
Cambridge, Philadelphia, San Francisco, Washington
London, Mexico City, São Paulo, Singapore, Sydney

All of the men and women involved in the five cases reported here are known to me personally; they have given their fullest cooperation on the condition that their identities and those of their families and friends not be revealed. This stricture has, of necessity, been extended to the publisher who has therefore not verified the book's contents other than the author's personal assurance, and the publisher's own verification from independent sources that exorcisms have been and continue to be performed currently in the United States. All names and places and any other elements that could conceivably lead to the possible identification of the people involved in the cases reported here have been changed. Any similarity between the cases reported here and any others that may have occurred is unintentional and purely coincidental.

A hardcover edition of this book was published by Reader's Digest Press. It is here reprinted by arrangement with the author.

First PERENNIAL LIBRARY edition published 1987.

Library of Congress Cataloging-in-Publication Data

Martin, Malachi.
  Hostage to the devil.

  Reprint. Originally published: New York, N.Y.:
Reader's Digest Press, 1976.
  Includes index.
  1. Exorcism—Case studies. 2. Demoniac possession—Case studies. I. Title.
[BX2340.M35 1987]   265′.94   86-46207
ISBN 0-06-097103-7 (pbk.)

89 90 91 MPC 10 9 8 7 6 5 4 3

Contents

How are you fallen from Heaven,
Lucifer! Son of the Dawn!
Cut down to the ground!
And once you dominated the peoples!

Didn't you say to yourself:
I will be as high as Heaven!
I will be more exalted than the stars of God!
I will, indeed, be the supreme leader!
In the privileged places!
I will be higher than the Skies!
I will be the same as the Most High God!

But you shall be brought down to Hell,
to the bottom of its pit.
And all who see you,
will despise you. . . .

—Isaiah 14:12–19

. . . "Lord! In your name, even evil spirits are under
our control!"

And He said to them: "I saw Satan falling like
lightning from Heaven.
You know: I gave you power . . .
over all the strength of Satan. . . .
Nevertheless, don't take pride in the fact
that spirits are subject to your control,
but, rather, because you belong to God . . .
The Father has given Me all power. . . ."

—Luke 10:17–22

The Fate
of an Exorcist

Michael Strong—
Part I

When the search party reached the disused grain store known locally as *Puh-Chi* (One Window), the bombing of Nanking was at its height. The night sky was bright with incandescent flares and filled with explosions. Japanese incendiaries were wreaking havoc on Nanking's wooden buildings. It was December 11, 1937, about 10:00 P.M. The Yangtze delta all the way down to the sea was in Japanese hands. From Shanghai on the coast to within two miles of Nanking was a devastated area on which death had settled like a permanent atmosphere. Nanking was next on the invaders' list. And defenseless. December 13 was to be its death date.

For one week the police of a southern Nanking city precinct had been looking for Thomas Wu. The charge: murder of at least five women and two men in the most horrible circumstances: Thomas Wu, the story was, had killed his victims and eaten their bodies. At the end of one week's fruitless searching, Father Michael Strong, the missionary parish priest of the district, who had baptized Thomas Wu, sent word unexpectedly that he had found the wanted man in the barnlike *Puh-Chi*. But the police captain did not understand the message Father Michael had sent him: "I am conducting an exorcism. Please give me some time." °

° This is the only exorcism reported in this book for which I have no transcript and could not conduct extensive interviews. My sole source was Father Michael himself, who recounted these events to me and allowed me to read his diaries.

The main door of *Puh-Chi* was ajar when the police chief arrived. A small knot of men and women stood watching. They could see Father Michael standing in the middle of the floor. Over in one corner there was another figure, a young, naked man, suddenly ravished by an unnatural look of great age, a long knife in his hands. On the shelves around the inner walls of the storehouse lay rows and rows of naked corpses in various stages of mutilation and putrefaction.

"YOU!!" the naked man was screaming as the police captain elbowed his way to the door, "YOU want to know MY name!" The words "you" and "my" hit the captain like two clenched fists across the ears. He saw the priest visibly wilt and stagger backward. But, even so, it was the voice that made the captain wonder. He had known Thomas Wu. Never had he heard him speak with such a voice.

"In the name of Jesus," Michael began weakly, "you are commanded . . ."

"Get outa here! Get the hell outa here, you filthy old eunuch!"

"You will release Thomas Wu, evil spirit, and . . ."

"I'm taking him with me, pigmy," came the voice from Thomas Wu. "I'm taking him. And no power anywhere, anywhere, you hear, can stop us. We are as strong as death. No one stronger! And he wants to come! You hear? He wants to!"

"Tell me your name . . ."

The priest was interrupted by a sudden roaring. No one there could say later how the fire started. An incendiary? A spark carried by the wind from burning Nanking? It was like a sudden, noisy ambush sprung by a silent signal. In a flash the fire had jumped up, a living red weed running around the sides of the storehouse, along the curved roof, and across the wooden floor by the walls.

The police captain was already inside, and he gripped Father Michael by the arm, pulling him outside.

The voice of Wu pursued them over the noise: "It's all one. Fool! We're all the same. Always were. Always."

Michael and the captain were outside by then and turned around to listen.

"There's only one of us. One . . ."

The rest of the sentence was drowned in a sudden outburst of flaming timbers.

Now, the glass rectangle of the single window was darkening over with smoke and grime. In a few minutes it would be impossible to see anything. Michael lurched over and peered in. Against the window he could see Thomas' face plastered for an instant of fixed, grinning agony. It was a horrible picture, a Bosch nightmare come alive.

Long, quickly lashing tongues of flame were licking at Thomas' temples, neck, and hair. Through the hissing and crackling of the fire, Michael could hear Thomas laughing, but very dimly, almost lost to the ear. Between the flames he could see the shelves with their gray-white load of corpses. Some were melting. Some were burning. Eyes oozing out of sockets like broken eggs. Hair burning in little tufts. First, fingers and toes and noses and ears, then whole limbs and torsos melting and blackening. And the smell. God! That smell!

Then the fixity of Thomas' grin broke; his face seemed to be replaced by another face with a similar grin. At the top speed of a kaleidoscope, a long succession of faces came and went, one flickering after the other. All grinning. All with "Cain's thumbprint on the chin," as Michael described the mark that haunted him for the rest of his life. Every pair of lips was rounded into the grinning shape of Thomas' last word: *"one!"* Faces and expressions Michael never had known. Some he imagined he knew. Some he knew he imagined. Some he had seen in history books, in paintings, in churches, in newspapers, in nightmares. Japanese, Chinese, Burmese, Korean, British, Slavic. Old, young, bearded, clean-shaven. Black, white, yellow. Male, female. Faster. Faster. All grinning with the same grin. More and more and more. Michael felt himself hurtling down an unending lane of faces, decades and centuries and millennia ticking by him, until the speed slowed finally, and the last grinning face appeared, wreathed in hate, its chin just one big thumbprint.

Now the window was completely black. Michael could see nothing. "Cain . . ." he began to say weakly to himself. But a stablike realization stopped the word in his throat, just as if someone had hissed into his inner ear: "Wrong again, fool! Cain's father. I. The cosmic Father of Lies and the cosmic Lord of Death. From the beginning of the beginning. I . . . I . . . I . . . I . . . I . . ."

Michael felt a sharp pain in his chest. A strong hand was around his heart stifling its movement, and an unbearable weight lay on his chest, bending him over. He heard the blood thumping in his head and then loud, roaring winds. A dazzling flash of light burst across his eyes. He slumped to the ground.

Strong hands plucked Michael away from the window just in time.

The storehouse was now an inferno. With a tearing crash, the roof caved in. The flames shot up triumphantly and licked the outside walls, burning and consuming ravenously.

"Get the old man away from here!" screamed the captain through the smoke and the smell. They all drew back. Michael, slung over the shoulder of one man, was babbling and sobbing incoherently. The captain could barely make his words out:

"I failed . . . I failed . . . I must go back. Please . . . Please . . . must go back . . . not later . . . please . . ."

When they got Michael to the hospital, his condition was critical. Apart from burns and smoke inhalation, he had suffered a minor heart attack. And until the following evening, he continued in a delirium.

Before the fall of Nanking, he was smuggled out by the faithful police captain and a few parishioners. They made their way north-westwards, barely escaping the tightening Japanese net.

On December 14, the Japanese High Command let loose 50,000 of their soldiers on the city with orders to kill every living person. The city became a slaughterhouse. Whole groups of men and women were used for bayonet and machine-gun practice. Others were burned alive or slowly cut to pieces. Rows of children were beheaded by samurai-swinging officers competing to see who could take off the most heads with one sweep of the sword. Women were raped by squads, then killed. Fetuses were torn alive from wombs, carved up, and fed to the dogs.

All told, over 42,000 were murdered. Death enveloped Nanking as it had the entire Yangtze delta. Animals and crops died and rotted in the fields.

It was as though the spirit that Michael had tangled with in the microcosm of Thomas Wu's grisly charnel house in the suburbs of Nanking—"the Cosmic Lord of Death"—had been let loose over all the lands. In the world-shaking events of the war years, some special viciousness had been given free rein, had impressed itself on hundreds of thousands with the sting of absolute and irresistible authority. Death was the strongest weapon. It settled all disputes over who was master. And eventually it claimed all as its victims, putting everyone on an equal level. In war, where death was the victor, you tried to have it on your side.

Back in Hong Kong, where Michael was finally brought in the late summer of 1938 after a considerably roundabout journey, the realists knew it was a matter of time before the Japanese winners took all.

On Christmas Day 1941, Hong Kong became a Japanese possession. During the years of occupation Michael lived quietly at Kowloon, teaching a little in the schools, doing some pastoral work. He was slow in recuperating.

During that time, everyone was under a strain. Food was scarce. Harassment by the occupying Japanese was extreme. And all lived with the sure knowledge that, barring miracles, if the Japanese had to evacuate the city, they would massacre everyone; and if they stayed on, they would eventually kill all they could not enslave.

Still, Michael took all the physical hardship with greater ease than those around him. He suffered two more heart attacks during the Japanese occupation, but they did not diminish his spirit in any way. He did not feel, as his colleagues did, the intolerable uncertainty, the strain of waiting for death at Japanese hands or for liberation by the Allies. As some of his acquaintances noticed, his sufferings were not chiefly in his body or his mind or his imagination. He had come from the interior of China broken in a way neither rest nor food nor loving attention could mend.

To the few who knew his story, it was clear that he had paid only part of his price as an exorcist. He frankly told them of that price. And of his failure. Both they and he realized he would have to liquidate his debt sooner or later.

His waiting creditor fascinated Michael, was always on his mind. For instance, toward the end of the Japanese occupation of Hong Kong, he and a friend were watching a flight of American bombers progress imperturbably like enchanted birds through a rain of Japanese antiaircraft fire. They deposited their bomb loads, and then departed unharmed over the horizon. As the explosions and fires in the harbor continued, Michael muttered: "Why does death make the loudest noise and the brightest fire?"

Some weeks later, a man-made light brighter than the sun mushroomed over Hiroshima. A new human record: more people were killed and maimed by this one human action than by any other ever recorded in the story of man.

I was not to learn of Michael for some years—or of the special price he paid day by day until his death, for his defeat in that strange exorcism at *Puh-Chi.*

A Brief Handbook
of Exorcism

The recent vast publicity about Exorcism has highlighted the plight of the possessed as a fresh genre of horror film. The essence of evil is lost in the cinematographic effects. And the exorcist, who risks more than anyone else in an exorcism, flits across the screen as necessary but, in the end, not so interesting as the sound effects.

The truth is that all three—the possessed, the possessing spirit, and the exorcist—bear a close relation to the reality of life and to its meaning as all of us experience it each and every day.

Possession is not a process of magic. Spirit is real; in fact, spirit is the basis of all reality. "Reality" would not only be boring without spirit; it would have no meaning whatsoever. No horror film can begin to capture the horror of such a vision: a world without spirit.

Evil Spirit is personal, and it is intelligent. It is preternatural, in the sense that it is not *of* this material world, but it is *in* this material world. And Evil Spirit as well as good advances along the lines of our daily lives. In very normal ways spirit uses and influences our daily thoughts, actions, and customs and, indeed, all the strands that make up the fabric of life in whatever time or place. Contemporary life is no exception.

To compare spirit with the elements of our lives and material world, which it can and sometimes does manipulate for its own ends, is a fatal mistake, but one that is very often made. Eerie sounds can be produced by spirit—but spirit is not the eerie sound. Objects can be made to fly across a room, but telekinesis is no more spirit than the material object that was made to move. One man whose story is told in this book made the mistake of thinking otherwise, and he nearly paid with his life when he had to confront the error he had made.

The exorcist is the centerpiece of every exorcism. On him depends everything. He has nothing personal to gain. But in each exorcism he risks literally everything that he values. Michael Strong's was an extreme example of the fate awaiting the exorcist. But every exorcist must engage in a one-to-one confrontation, personal and bitter, with pure evil. Once engaged, the exorcism cannot be called off. There will and must always be a victor and a vanquished. And no matter what the outcome, the contact is in part fatal for the exorcist. He must consent to a dreadful and irreparable pillage of his deepest self. Something dies in him. Some part of his humanness will wither from such close contact with the opposite of all humanness—the essence of evil; and it is rarely if ever revitalized. No return will be made to him for his loss.

This is the minimum price an exorcist pays. If he loses in the fight with Evil Spirit, he has an added penalty. He may or may not ever again perform the rite of Exorcism, but he must finally confront and vanquish the evil spirit that repulsed him.

The investigation that may lead to Exorcism usually begins because a man or woman—occasionally a child—is brought to the notice of Church authorities by family or friends. Only rarely does a possessed person come forward spontaneously.

The stories that are told on these occasions are dramatic and painful: strange physical ailments in the possessed; marked mental derangement; obvious repugnance to all signs, symbols, mention, and sight of religious objects, places, people, ceremonies.

Often, the family or friends report, the presence of the person in question is marked by so-called psychical phenomena: objects fly around the room; wallpaper peels off the walls; furniture cracks; crockery breaks; there are strange rumblings, hisses, and other noises with no apparent source. Often the temperature in the room where the possessed happens to be will drop dramatically. Even more often an acrid and distinctive stench accompanies the person.

Violent physical transformations seem sometimes to make the lives of the possessed a kind of hell on earth. Their normal processes of secretion and elimination are saturated with inexplicable wrackings and exaggeration. Their consciousness seems completely colored by the violent sepia of revulsion. Reflexes sometimes become sporadic or abnormal, sometimes disappear for a time. Breathing can cease for extended periods. Heartbeats are hard to detect. The face is strangely distorted, sometimes also abnormally tight and smooth without the slightest line or furrow.

When such a case is brought to their attention, the first and central problem that must always be addressed by the Church authorities is: Is the person really possessed?

Henri Gesland, a French priest and exorcist who works today in Paris, stated in 1974 that, out of 3,000 consultations since 1968, "there have been only four cases of what I believe to be demonic possession." T. K. Osterreich, on the other hand, states that "possession has been an extremely common phenomenon, cases of which abound in the history of religion." The truth is that official or scholarly census of possession cases has never been made.

Certainly, many who claim to be possessed or whom others so describe are merely the victims of some mental or physical disease. In reading records from times when medical and psychological science did not exist or were quite undeveloped, it is clear that grave mistakes were made. A victim of disseminated sclerosis, for example, was taken to be possessed because of his spastic jerkings and slidings and the shocking agony in spinal column and joints. Until quite recently, the victim of Tourette's syndrome was the perfect target for the accusation of "Possessed!": torrents of profanities and obscenities, grunts, barks, curses, yelps, snorts, sniffs, tics, foot stomping, facial contortions all appear suddenly and just as suddenly cease in the subject. Nowadays, Tourette's syndrome responds to drug treatment, and it seems to be a neurological disease involving a chemical abnormality in the brain. Many people suffering from illnesses and diseases well known to us today such as paranoia, Huntington's chorea, dyslexia, Parkinson's disease, or even mere skin diseases (psoriasis, herpes I, for instance), were treated as people "possessed" or at least as "touched" by the Devil.

Nowadays, competent Church authorities always insist on thorough examinations of the person brought to them for Exorcism, an examination conducted by qualified medical doctors and psychiatrists.

When a case of possession is reported by a priest to the diocesan authorities, the exorcist of the diocese is brought in. If there is no diocesan exorcist, a man is appointed or brought from outside the diocese.

Sometimes the priest reporting the exorcism will have had some preliminary medical and psychiatric tests run beforehand in order to allay the cautious skepticism he is likely to meet at the chancery when he introduces his problem. When the official exorcist enters the case, he will usually have his own very thorough examinations run by experts he knows and whose judgment he is sure he can trust.

In earlier times, one priest was usually assigned the function of exorcist in each diocese of the Church. In modern times, this practice has fallen into abeyance in some dioceses, mainly because the incidence of reported possession has decreased over the last hundred years. But in most major dioceses, there is still one priest entrusted with this function—even though he may rarely or never use it. In some dioceses, there is a private arrangement between the bishop and one of his priests whom he knows and trusts.

There is no official public appointment of exorcists. In some dioceses, "the bishop knows little about it and wants to know less"—as in one of the cases recorded in this book. But however he comes to his position, the exorcist must have official Church sanction, for he is acting in an official capacity, and any power he has over Evil Spirit can only come from those officials who belong to the substance of Jesus' Church, whether they be in the Roman Catholic, the Eastern Orthodox, or the Protestant Communions. Sometimes a diocesan priest will take on an exorcism himself without asking his bishop, but all such cases known to me have failed.

It is recognized both in the pre-exorcism examinations and during the actual exorcism that there is usually no one physical or psychical aberration or abnormality in the possessed person that we cannot explain by a known or possible physical cause. And, apart from normal medical and psychological tests, there are other possible sources for diagnosis. However rickety and tentative the findings of parapsychology, for example, one can possibly seek in its theories of telepathy and telekinesis an explanation of some of the signs of possession. Suggestion and suggestibility, as modern psychotherapists speak of them, can account for many more.

Still, with the diagnoses and opinions of doctors and psychologists in hand, it is often discovered there are wide margins of fluctuation. Competent psychiatrists will differ violently among themselves; and in psychology and medicine, ignorance of causes is often obscured by technical names and jargon that are nothing more than descriptive terms.

Nevertheless, the combined medical and psychological reports are carefully evaluated and usually weigh heavily in the final judgment to proceed or not with an exorcism. If according to those reports there is a definite disease or illness which adequately accounts for the behavior and symptoms of the subject, Exorcism is usually ruled out, or at least delayed to allow a course of medical or psychiatric treatment.

But finally, reports in hand, all evidence in, Church authorities judge the situation from another, special point of view, formed by their own professional outlook.

They believe that there is an invisible power, a spirit of evil; that this spirit can for obscure reasons take possession of a human being; that the evil spirit can and must be expelled—exorcised—from the person possessed; and that this exorcism can be done only in the name and by the authority and power of Jesus of Nazareth. The testing from the Church's viewpoint is as rigorous in its search as any medical or psychological examination.

In the records of Christian Exorcism from as far back as the lifetime of Jesus himself, a peculiar revulsion to symbols and truths of religion is always and without exception a mark of the possessed person. In the verification of a case of possession by Church authorities, this "symptom" of revulsion is triangulated with other physical phenomena frequently associated with possession—the inexplicable stench; freezing temperature; telepathic powers about purely religious and moral matters; a peculiarly unlined or completely smooth or stretched skin, or unusual distortion of the face, or other physical and behavioral transformations; "possessed gravity" (the possessed person becomes physically immovable, or those around the possessed are weighted down with a suffocating pressure); levitation (the possessed rises and floats off the ground, chair, or bed; there is no physically traceable support); violent smashing of furniture, constant opening and slamming of doors, tearing of fabric in the vicinity of the possessed, without a hand laid on them; and so on.

When this triangulation is made of the varied symptoms that may occur in any given case, and medical and psychiatric diagnoses are inadequate to cover the full situation, the decision will usually be to proceed and try Exorcism.

There has never been, to my knowledge, an official listing of exorcists together with their biographies and characteristics, so we cannot satisfy our modern craving for a profile of, say, "the typical exorcist." We can, however, give a fairly clear definition of the type of man who is entrusted with the exorcism of a possessed person. Usually he is engaged in the active ministry of parishes. Rarely is he a scholarly type engaged in teaching or research. Rarely is he a recently ordained priest. If there is any median age for exorcists, it is probably between the ages of fifty and sixty-five. Sound and robust physical health is not a characteristic of exorcists, nor is proven intellectual brilliance, postgraduate degrees, even in psychology or philosophy, or a very sophisticated personal culture. In this writer's experience, the 15 exorcists he has known have been singularly lacking in anything like a vivid imagination or a rich humanistic training. All have been sensitive men of solid rather than dazzling minds. Though, of course, there are many exceptions, the usual reasons for a priest's being chosen are his qualities of moral judgment, personal behavior, and religious beliefs— qualities that are not sophisticated or laboriously acquired, but that somehow seem always to have been an easy and natural part of such a man. Speaking religiously, these are qualities associated with special grace.

There is no official training for an exorcist. Before a priest undertakes Exorcism, it has been found advisable—but not always possible or practical—for him to assist at exorcisms conducted by an older and already experienced priest.

Once possession has been verified to the satisfaction of the exorcist, he makes the rest of the decisions and takes care of all the necessary preparations. In some dioceses, it is he who chooses the assistant priest. The choice of the lay assistants and of the time and place of the exorcism is left to him.

The place of the exorcism is usually the home of the possessed person, for generally it is only relatives or closest friends who will give care and love in the dreadful circumstances associated with possession. The actual room chosen is most often one that has had some special significance for the possessed person, not infrequently his or her own bedroom or den. In this connection, one aspect of possession and of spirit makes itself apparent: the close connection between *spirit* and *physical location*. The puzzle of spirit and place makes itself felt in many ways and runs throughout virtually every exorcism. There is a theological explanation for it. But that there is some connection between spirit and place must be dealt with as a fact.

Once chosen, the room where the exorcism will be done is cleared as far as possible of anything that can be moved. During the exorcism, one form of violence may and most often does cause any object, light or heavy, to move about, rock back and forth, skitter or fly across the room, make much noise, strike the priest or the possessed or the assistants. It is not rare for people to emerge from an exorcism with serious physical wounds. Carpets, rugs, pictures, curtains, tables, chairs, boxes, trunks, bedclothes, bureaus, chandeliers, all are removed.

Doors very often will bang open and shut uncontrollably; but because exorcisms can go on for days, doors cannot be nailed or locked with unusual security. On the other hand, the doorway must be covered; otherwise, as experience shows, the physical force let loose within the exorcism room will affect the immediate vicinity outside the door.

Windows are closed securely; sometimes they may be boarded over in order to keep flying objects from crashing through them and to prevent more extreme accidents (possessed people sometimes attempt defenestration; physical forces sometimes propel the assistants or the exorcist toward the windows).

A bed or couch is usually left in the room (or placed there if necessary), and that is where the possessed person is placed. A small table is needed. On it are placed a crucifix, with one candle on either side of it, holy water, and a prayer book. Sometimes there will also be a relic of a saint or a picture that is considered to be especially holy or significant for the possessed. In recent years in the United States, and increasingly abroad as well, a tape recorder is used. It is placed on the floor or in a drawer or sometimes, if it is not too cumbersome, around the neck of an assistant.

The junior priest colleague of the exorcist is usually appointed by diocesan authorities. He is there for his own training as an exorcist. He will monitor the words and actions of the exorcist, warn him if he is making a mistake, help him if he weakens physically, and replace him if he dies, collapses, flees, is physically or emotionally battered beyond endurance—and all have happened during exorcisms.

The other assistants are laymen. Very often a medical doctor will be among them because of the danger to all present of strain, shock, or injury. The number of lay assistants will depend on the exorcist's expectation of violence. Four is the usual number. Of course, in remote country areas or in very isolated Christian missions, and

sometimes in big urban centers, there is no question of assistants.
There simply is none available, or there is no time to acquire any. The
exorcist must go it alone.

An exorcist comes to know from experience what he can expect by
way of violent behavior; and, for their own sakes, possessed people
must usually be physically restrained during parts of the exorcism. The
assistants therefore must be physically strong. In addition, there may
be a straitjacket on hand, though leather straps or rope are more
commonly used.

It is up to the exorcist to make sure that his assistants are not
consciously guilty of personal sins at the time of the exorcism, because
they, too, can expect to be attacked by the evil spirit, even though not
so directly or constantly as the exorcist himself. Any sin will be used as
a weapon.

The exorcist must be as certain as possible beforehand that his
assistants will not be weakened or overcome by obscene behavior or
by language foul beyond their imagining; they cannot blanch at blood,
excrement, urine; they must be able to take awful personal insults and
be prepared to have their darkest secrets screeched in public in front
of their companions. These are routine happenings during exorcisms.

Assistants are given three cardinal rules: they are to obey the
exorcist's commands immediately and without question, no matter
how absurd or unsympathetic those commands may appear to them to
be; they are not to take any initiative except on command; and they
are never to speak to the possessed person, even by way of
exclamation.

Even with all the care in the world, there is no way an exorcist can
completely prepare his assistants for what lies in store for them. Even
though they are not subject to the direct and unremitting attack the
priest will undergo, it is not uncommon for assistants to quit—or be
carried out—in the middle of an exorcism. A practiced exorcist will
even go so far as to make a few trial runs of an exorcism beforehand,
on the old theory that forewarned is forearmed—at least to some
degree.

Timing in an exorcism is generally dictated by circumstances. There
is usually a feeling of urgency to begin as soon as possible. Everyone
involved should have an open schedule. Rarely is an exorcism shorter
than some hours—more often than not ten or twelve hours. Sometimes
it stretches for two or three days. On occasion it lasts even for weeks.

Once begun, except on the rarest occasions, there are no time outs, although one or other of the people present may leave the room for a few moments, to take some food, to rest very briefly, or go to the bathroom. (One strange exorcism where there was a time out is described in this book. The priest involved would have preferred one hundred times going straight through the exorcism rather than suffer the mad violence that caused the delay.)

The only people in an exorcism who dress in a special way are the exorcist and his priest assistant. Each wears a long black cassock that covers him from neck to feet. Over it there is a waist-length white surplice. A narrow purple stole is worn around the neck and hangs loosely the length of the torso.

Normally, the priest assistant and the lay assistants prepare the exorcism room according to the exorcist's instructions. They and the exorcee are ready in the room when the exorcist enters, last and alone.

There is no lexicon of Exorcism; and there is no guidebook or set of rules, no Baedeker of Evil Spirit to follow. The Church provides an official text for Exorcism, but this is merely a framework. It can be read out loud in 20 minutes. It merely provides a precise formula of words together with certain prayers and ritual actions, so that the exorcist has a preset structure in which to address the evil spirit. In fact, the conduct of an exorcism is left very much up to the exorcist.

Nevertheless, any practiced exorcist I have spoken with agrees that there is a general progress through recognizable stages in an exorcism, however long it may last.

One of the most experienced exorcists I have known and who was in fact the mentor of the exorcist in the first case related in this book, gave names to the various general stages of an exorcism. These names reflect the general meaning or effect or intent of what is happening, but not the specific means used by the evil spirit or by the exorcist. Conor, as I call him, spoke of *Presence, Pretense, Breakpoint, Voice, Clash,* and *Expulsion.* The events and stages these names signify occur in nine out of every ten exorcisms.

From the moment the exorcist enters the room, a peculiar feeling seems to hang in the very air. From that moment in any genuine exorcism and onward through its duration, everyone in the room is aware of some alien *Presence.* This indubitable sign of possession is as unexplainable and unmistakable as it is inescapable. All the signs of possession, however blatant or grotesque, however subtle or debatable, seem both to pale before and to be marshaled in the face of this *Presence.*

There is no sure physical trace of the *Presence*, but everyone feels it. You have to experience it to know it; you cannot locate it spatially— beside or above or within the possessed, or over in the corner or under the bed or hovering in midair.

In one sense, the *Presence* is nowhere, and this magnifies the terror, because there *is* a presence, an *other* present. Not a "he" or a "she" or an "it." Sometimes, you think that what is present is singular, sometimes plural. When it speaks, as the exorcism goes on, it will sometimes refer to itself as "I" and sometimes as "we," will use "my" and "our."

Invisible and intangible, the *Presence* claws at the humanness of those gathered in the room. You can exercise logic and expel any mental image of it. You can say to yourself: "I am only imagining this. Careful! Don't panic!" And there may be a momentary relief. But then, after a time lag of bare seconds, the *Presence* returns as an inaudible hiss in the brain, as a wordless threat to the self you are. Its name and essence seem to be compounded of threat, to be only and intensely baleful, concentratedly intent on hate for hate's sake and on destruction for destruction's sake.

In the early stages of an exorcism, the evil spirit will make every attempt to "hide behind" the possessed, so to speak—to appear to be one and the same person and personality with its victim. This is the *Pretense*.

The first task of the priest is to break that *Pretense*, to force the spirit to reveal itself openly as separate from the possessed—and to name itself, for all possessing spirits are called by a name that generally (though not always) has to do with the way that spirit works on its victim.

As the exorcist sets about his task, the evil spirit may remain silent altogether; or it may speak with the voice of the possessed, and use past experiences and recollections of the possessed. This is often done skillfully, using details no one but the possessed could know. It can be very disarming, even pitiful. It can make everyone, including the priest, feel that it is the priest who is the villain, subjecting an innocent person to terrible rigors. Even the mannerisms and characteristics of the possessed are used by the spirit as its own camouflage.

Sometimes the exorcist cannot shatter the *Pretense* for days. But until he does, he cannot bring matters to a head. If he fails to shatter it at all, he has lost. Perhaps another exorcist replacing him will succeed. But he himself has been beaten.

Every exorcist learns during *Pretense* that he is dealing with some force or power that is at times intensely cunning, sometimes supremely intelligent, and at other times capable of crass stupidity (which makes one wonder further about the problem of singular or plural); and it is both highly dangerous and terribly vulnerable.

Oddly, while this spirit or power or force knows some of the most secret and intimate details of the lives of everyone in the room, at the same time it also displays gaps in knowledge of things that may be happening at any given moment of the present.

But the priest must not be lulled by small victories or take chances on hoped-for stupidities. He must be ready to have his own sins and blunders and weaknesses put into his mind or shouted in ugliness for all to hear. He must not make excuses for his past, or wither as even his loveliest memories are fingered by ultimate filth and contempt; he must not be sidetracked in any way from his primary intention of freeing the possessed person before him. And he must at all costs avoid trading abuse or getting into any logical arguments with the possessed. The temptation to do so is more frequent than one might think, and must be regarded as a potentially fatal trap that can shatter not only the exorcism, but quite literally shatter the exorcist as well.

Accordingly, as the *Pretense* begins to break down, the behavior of the possessed usually increases in violence and repulsiveness. It is as though an invisible manhole opens, and out of it pours the unmentionably inhuman and the humanly unacceptable. There is a stream of filth and unrestrained abuse, accompanied often by physical violence, writhing, gnashing of teeth, jumping around, sometimes physical attacks on the exorcist.

A new hallmark of the proceedings enters as the *Breakpoint* nears, and ushers in one of the more subtle sufferings the exorcist must undergo: confusion. Complete and dreadful confusion. Rare is the exorcist who does not falter here for at least a moment, enmeshed in the peculiar pain of apparent contradiction of all sense.

His ears seem to *smell* foul words. His eyes seem to *hear* offensive sounds and obscene screams. His nose seems to *taste* a high-decibel cacophony. Each sense seems to be recording what another sense should be recording. Each nerve and sinew of onlookers and participants becomes rigid as they strive for control. Panic—the fear of being dissolved into insanity—runs in quick jabs through everyone there. All present experience this increasingly violent and confusing assault. But the exorcist is the one who rides the storm. He is the direct target of it all.

The *Breakpoint* is reached at that moment when the *Pretense* has finally collapsed altogether. The voice of the possessed is no longer used by the spirit, though the new, strange voice may or may not issue from the mouth of the victim. In Thomas Wu's case, the alien voice did come from the possessed's mouth; and that was why the police captain was so startled. The sound produced is often not even remotely like any human sound.

At the *Breakpoint,* for the first time, the spirit speaks of the possessed in the third person, as a separate being. For the first time, the possessing spirit acts personally and speaks of "I" or "we," usually interchangeably, and of "my" and "our" or "mine" and "ours."

Another very frequent sign that the *Breakpoint* has been reached is the appearance of what Father Conor called the *Voice*.

The *Voice* is an inordinately disturbing and humanly distressing babel. The first few syllables seem to be those of some word pronounced slowly and thickly—somewhat like a tape recording played at a subnormal speed. You are just straining to pick up the word and a layer of cold fear has already gripped you—you know this sound is alien. But your concentration is shattered and frustrated by an immediate gamut of echoes, of tiny, prickly voices echoing each syllable, screaming it, whispering it, laughing it, sneering it, groaning it, following it. They all hit your ear, while the alien voice is going on unhurriedly to the next syllable, which you then try to catch, while guessing at the first one you lost. By then, the tiny, jabbing voices have caught up with that second syllable; and the voice has proceeded to the third syllable; and so on.

If the exorcism is to proceed, the *Voice* must be silenced. It takes an enormous effort of will on the part of the exorcist, in direct confrontation with the alien will of evil, to silence the *Voice*. The priest must get himself under control and challenge the spirit first to silence and then to identify itself intelligibly.

As in all things to do with Exorcism of Evil Spirit, the priest makes this challenge with his own will, but always in the name and by the authority of Jesus and his Church. To do so in his own name or by some fancied authority of his own would be to invite personal disaster. Merely human power unadorned and without aid cannot cope with the preternatural. (It is to be remembered that when we speak of the preternatural, we are not speaking about what are known as polter-geists.)

Usually, at this point and as the *Voice* dies out, a tremendous pressure of an obscure kind affects the exorcist. This is the first and outermost edge of a direct and personal collision with the "will of the Kingdom," the *Clash.*

We all know from our personal experience that there can be no struggle of single personal wills without that felt and intuitive contact between two persons. There is a two-way communication that is as real as a conversation using words. The *Clash* is the heart of a special and dreadful communication, the nucleus of this singular battle of wills between exorcist and Evil Spirit.

Painful as it will be for him, the priest must look for the *Clash.* He must provoke it. If he cannot lock wills with the evil thing and force that thing to lock its will in opposition to his own, then again the exorcist is defeated.

The issue between the two, the exorcist and the possessing spirit, is simple. Will the totally antihuman invade and take over? Will it, noisome and merciless, seep over that narrow rim where the exorcist would hold his ground alone, and engulf him? Or will it, unwillingly, protestingly, under a duress greater than its single-track will, stop, identify itself, cede, retire, disappear, and be volatilized back into an unknown pit of being where no man wants to go ever?

Even with all the pressure on him, and in fullest human agony, if the exorcist has got this far, he must press home. He has gained an advantage. He has already forced the evil spirit to come out on its own. If he has not been able to until now, he must finally force it to give its name. And then, some exorcists feel, the exorcist must pursue for as much information as he can. For in some peculiar way, as exorcists find, the more an evil spirit can be forced to reveal in the *Clash* and its aftermath, the surer and easier will be the *Expulsion* when that moment comes. To force as complete an identification as possible is perhaps a mark of domination of one will over another.

It is of crucial interest to speculate about the violence provoked by Exorcism—the physical and mental struggles that are so extreme they can bring on death. Why would spirit battle so? Why not leave and waft off invisibly to someone or someplace else? For spirit itself seems to suffer in these battles.

Time and again, in exorcism after exorcism, there occurs that curious thing to do with *spirit* and *place*, the strange puzzle mentioned previously in connection with the room chosen for the exorcism. When Jesus expelled the unclean spirits, those spirits showed concern for where they might go. In record after record, as well as in several exorcisms recounted in this book, the possessing spirits wail in lament and questioning pain: "Where shall we go?" "We too have to possess our habitation." "Even the Anointed One gave us a place with the swine." "Here . . . we can't stay here any longer."

Evil Spirit, having found a home with a consenting host, does not appear to give up its place easily. It claws and fights and deceives and even risks killing its host before it will be expelled. How violent the struggle probably depends on many things; the intelligence of the spirit being dealt with and the degree of possession achieved over the victim are perhaps two one could speculate about.

Whatever determines the actual pitch of violence, once the exorcist has forced the invading spirit to identify itself, and sustained the first wordless bout of the *Clash*, and then invoked its formal condemnation and expulsion by the Exorcism rite, the immediate result is generally a struggle tortuous beyond imagining, an open violence that leaves all subtlety behind.

The person possessed is by now obviously aware in one way or another of what possessed him. Frequently he becomes a true battleground for much of the remainder of the exorcism, enduring unbelievable punishment and strain.

It is sometimes possible for the exorcist to appeal directly to the possessed person, urging him to use some part of his own will still free of the spirit's influence and control, and engage directly in the fight, aiding the exorcist. And at such moments no animal pinned helplessly to the ground struggles more pathetically against the drinking of its life's blood by a voracious and superior cruelty. The very nauseous character of the possessed person's appearance and behavior appears to be a sign of his desire for deliverance, a desperate sign of struggle, evidence of a revolt where once he had consented.

Increasingly what had possessed him is being forced into the open, all the while protesting its victim's revolt and its own expulsion. The violence of the contortions and the physical disfigurement of the possessed can reach a degree one would think he could not possibly withstand.

The exorcist, too, comes in for full attack now. Once cornered, the evil spirit seems able to call on a superior intelligence, and will try to lure the exorcist on to a field boobytrapped and mined with situations from which no human can extricate himself.

Any weakness in the religious faith that alone sustains the exorcist or any fatigue will allow the exorcist's mind to be flooded with a terrible light he cannot fend off—a light that can burn the very roots of his reason and turn him emotionally into the most servile of slaves desperate to be liberated from all bodily life.

These are only some of the dangers and traps that face every exorcist. His pain is physical, emotional, mental. He has to deal with what is eerie but not enthralling; with something askew, but intelligently so; with a quality that is upside down and inside out, but significantly so. The mordant traits of nightmare are there in full regalia, but this is no dream and permits him no thankful remission.

He is attacked by a stench so powerful that many exorcists start vomiting uncontrollably. He is made to bear physical pain, and he feels anguish over his very soul. He is made to know he is touching the completely unclean, the totally unhuman.

All sense may suddenly seem nonsense. Hopelessness is confirmed as the only hope. Death and cruelty and contempt are normal. Anything comely or beautiful is an illusion. Nothing, it seems, was ever right in the world of man. He is in an atmosphere more bizarre than Bedlam.

If, in spite of his emotions and his imagination and his body—all trapped at once in pain and anguish—if, in spite of all this, the will of the exorcist holds in the *Clash*, what he does is to approach his final function in this situation as an authorized human witness for Jesus. By no power of his, on account of no privilege of his own, he calls finally on the evil spirit to desist, to be dispossessed, to depart and to leave the possessed person.

And, if the exorcism is successful, this is what happens. The possession ends. All present become aware of a change around them. The sense of *Presence* is totally, suddenly absent. Sometimes there are receding voices or other noises, sometimes only dead silence. Sometimes the recently possessed may be at the end of his strength; sometimes he will wake up as from a dream, a nightmare, or a coma. Sometimes the former victim will remember much of what he has been through; sometimes he will remember nothing at all.

Not so for the exorcists, during and after their grisly work. They carry nagging doubts and bitter conflicts untellable to family, friend, superior, or therapist. Their personal traumas lie beyond the reach of soothing words and deeper than the sweep of any consoling thoughts.

They share their punishment with none but God. Even that has its peculiar sting of difficulty. For it is a sharing by faith and not by face-to-face communication.

But only thus do these men, seemingly ordinary and commonplace in their lives, persevere through the days of quiet horror and the nights of sleepless watching they spend for years after as their price of success, and as abiding reminders that, once upon a time, another human being was made whole, because they willingly incurred the direct displeasure of living hatred.

The following five case histories are true. The lives of the people involved are told on the basis of extensive interviews with all of the principals involved, with many of their friends and relatives, and with many others involved directly or indirectly in minor ways. All interviews have been independently checked for factual accuracy wherever possible. The exorcisms themselves are reproduced from the actual tapes made at the time and from the transcripts of those tapes. The exorcisms have necessarily been cut for reasons of length; all of the exorcisms recorded here lasted more than 12 hours.

I have chosen these five cases from among a greater number known and available to me because, both singly and taken together, they are dramatic illustrations of the way in which personal and intelligent evil moves cunningly along the lines of contemporary fads and interests, and within the usual bounds of experience of ordinary men and women. No fourteenth- or fifteenth- or sixteenth-century case, for all its possible romantic appeal, would have any relevancy for us today. On the contrary, it would remain a simple matter for us to dismiss such cases as fables made up to suit the fears or fancies of "more ignorant" people of "less sophisticated" times.

Each case presented here includes as an important element some basic attitude or attitudes popular in our own society. In the possessed person, it is pushed to a narrow and frightening extreme.

In the first case, *Zio's Friend and the Smiler*, the insistence is that there is no essential difference between good and evil, and ultimately no difference between being and nonbeing; that all values are subject only to one's personal preferences.

In *Father Bones and Mister Natch*, the compelling idea that was seized by Evil Spirit seemed to be that all mysteries can and are resolved in "natural" (i.e., rational or scientific or quantifiable) explanations; that there can be no relevance for the modern person in anything that cannot be rationally understood; and that there can be no truth important to man beyond what is rational.

In *The Virgin and the Girl-Fixer*, the battle concerned some of the great, deep, and mysterious "givens" of our very nature and our society—in this case, gender and human love. The priest in this case said to me a few months before he died, in one of the most profound conversations of my life: "A bird doesn't fly because it has wings. It has wings because it flies." We will ignore that mysterious truth in its applications to our sexuality and our gender only at our great peril, I believe.

In *Uncle Ponto and the Mushroom-Souper*, we have an example of what may be happening to many in our modern society—without their realizing it and without those around them taking cognizance of it. For it seems that there is an individualism, a purely personalistic interpretation of human life abroad today, which exceeds by far the bounds of what used to be known as selfishness and egotism. It has produced in thousands of people an aberrant and idiosyncratic behavior which is truly destructive.

In *The Rooster and the Tortoise*, the fatal confusion (and in this case it was literally almost fatal) was between spirit and psyche; between those parts and attributes of ours that are quantifiable, and yet through which spirit most easily makes itself known. If everything we have taken to be of spirit can be made to seem a product merely of the human psyche, with no meaning or significance beyond its factualness, then love can be made to seem only a chemical interraction, and love's paradigm is killed.

In each case, one basic note of possession is confusion. Sex is confused with gender. Spirit is confused with psyche. Moral value is confused with absence of any value. Mystery is confused with untruth. And, in every case, rational argument is used, not to clarify, but as a trap, to foster confusion and to nurture it as a major weapon against the exorcist. Confusion, it would seem, is a prime weapon of evil.

There is much more to be observed and said about the meaning of possession. Not everything can be covered in a single volume. But possession and Exorcism are not themselves mere fads with no interest beyond the bizarre and significantly frightening. They are tangible expressions of the reality which envelops the daily lives of ordinary people. No study of possession and Exorcism cases within the Christian optic would be adequate without a minimum of explanation —from the Christian point of view—about that reality: what takes place in possession, and how that degrading process develops in a particular individual. Such an explanation occupies the final section of this book.

This study makes no attempt to answer the ultimate puzzle of possession: why this person rather than that person becomes the object of diabolic attack which can end in partial or perfect possession. The answer certainly does not lie in psychological probings, in heredity, or in social phenomena. A final answer will include, as prime ingredients, the personal free choice which each individual makes and the mystery of human predestination. About free choice we know the essentials: I *can* choose evil for no other reason or motive than that I choose evil. Some apparently do. About predestination we know little or nothing. The puzzle remains.

All of the men and women involved in the five cases reported here are known to me personally; they have given their fullest cooperation on the condition that their identities and those of their families and friends not be revealed. Therefore, all names and places have been changed, and other possible pointers to identity have been obscured. Any similarity between the cases reported here and any others that may have occurred is unintentional and purely coincidental.

The
Cases

Zio's Friend
and the Smiler

Peter took one more breath of fresh air. He was reluctant to pull the open window shut against the uproar on 125th Street 15 stories below. It was the first time in history that a Roman Pope was driving through New York streets, and the very air was alive with excitement. The Pope's motorcade had already passed over Willis Avenue Bridge into the Bronx on its way to Yankee Stadium. The crowds were still milling around. Some nuns scurried about like frenzied penguins blowing whistles and marshaling lines of white-clad schoolgirls. Hot-dog vendors shouted their prices. A dowdily dressed young woman and her child peddled plastic little popes to passersby. Two policemen were removing wooden barriers. A garbage truck snorted and honked its way through the traffic. Father Peter closed the window finally, drew the curtains together, and turned back toward the bed.

The room was quiet again, except for the irregular breathing of twenty-six-year-old Marianne. She lay on a gray blanket thrown over the bare mattress. With her faded jeans, yellow body-shirt, auburn hair straggling over her forehead, the pallor of her cheeks, and the aging, off-white color of the walls around her, she seemed part of a tragically washed-out pastel. Except for a funny twist to her mouth, her face had no expression.

To Peter's left, with their backs to the door, stood two bulky men. One: an ex-policeman and a friend of the family, a veteran of 32 years on the force, where, he thought, he had seen everything. He was about to find out that he hadn't. Sixtyish, balding, clad in dungarees, his arms folded over his chest, his face was a picture of puzzlement. The other: the closest acquaintance of Marianne's father, whom the children called uncle, was a bank manager and a grandfather in his midfifties, red-faced and jowled, in a blue suit, his arms hanging by his sides, eyes fixed on Marianne's face with an expression of helpless fear. Both these men, athletic and muscular, had been asked to assist at the exorcism of Marianne K., to quell any physical violence or harm she might attempt. Marianne's father, a wispy man with reddened eyes and drawn face, stood with the family doctor. He was praying silently. Peter always insisted on having a member of the family present at an exorcism. As if in contrast to the others, the young doctor, a psychiatrist, wore a concentrated, almost studious look as he checked the girl's pulse.

Peter's colleague, Father James, a priest in his thirties, stood at the foot of the bed. Black-haired, full-faced, youthful, apprehensive, his black, white, and purple robes were a uniform for him. On Peter, with his tousled gray hair and hollow-cheeked look, the same colors melted into a veiled unity. James was dressed up ready to go. Peter, the campaigner, had been there.

On a night table beside James two candles flickered. A crucifix rested between them. In one corner of the room there was a chest of drawers. "Should have had it removed before we started," Peter thought. The chest, originally left there in order to hold a tape recorder, had become quite a nuisance. Probably would continue to be until the whole business was finished, Peter thought. But he knew better than to fiddle with any object in the room, once the exorcism had begun.

It was a Monday, 8:15 P.M., the seventeenth hour into Peter's third exorcism in thirty years. It was also his last exorcism, although he could not know that. Peter felt sure that he had arrived at the Breakpoint in the rite.

In the few seconds it took him to cross from the window to her bed, Marianne's face had been contorting into a mass of crisscrossing lines. Her mouth twisted further and further in an S-shape. The neck was taut, showing every vein and artery; and her Adam's apple looked like a knot in a rope.

The ex-policeman and her uncle moved to hold her. But her voice threw them back momentarily like a whiplash:

"You dried-up fuckers! You've messed with each other's wives. And with your own peenies into the bargain. Keep your horny paws off me."

"Hold her down!" Peter spoke peremptorily. Four pairs of hands clamped on her. "Jesus have mercy on my baby," muttered her father. The ex-policeman's eyes bulged.

"YOU!" Marianne screamed, as she lay pinned flat on the bed, her eyes open and blazing with anger, "YOU! Peter the Eater. Eat my flesh, said she. Suck my blood, said she. And you did! Peter the Eater! You'll come with us, you freak. You'll lick my arse and like it, Peeeeeeeeetrrrrr," and her voice sank through the "rrrr" to an animal gurgle.

Something started to ache in Peter's brain. He missed a breath, panicked because he could not draw it, stopped and waited, swaying on his feet. Then he exhaled gratefully. To the younger priest he looked frail and vulnerable. Father James handed Peter his prayer book, and they both turned to face Marianne.

PETER

Almost a year later, in 1966, on the day Peter was buried in Calvary Cemetery, his younger colleague, Father James, chatted with me after the funeral service. "It doesn't matter what the doctor said" (the official report gave coronary thrombosis as cause of death), "he was gone, really gone, after that last to-do. Just a matter of time. Mind you, it wasn't that he wasn't brave and devoted. He was a real man of God before and after the whole thing. But it took that last exorcism to make him realize that life knocks the stuffing out of any decent man." Peter had apparently never emerged from a gentle reverie after the exorcism of Marianne; and he always spoke as if he were talking for the benefit of someone else present. It was as exasperating as listening to one side of a telephone conversation.

"He was never the same again," said James. "Some part of him passed into the Great Beyond during the final Clash, as you call it." Then, after a pause and musingly, almost to himself: "Can you beat that? He had to be born in Lisdoonvarna° sixty-two years ago, be reared beside Killarney, and come all the way over here three times—just to find out the third time where he was supposed to die;

° A town in County Clare, Ireland.

and how, and when. Makes you think what life's all about. You never know how it's going to end. Peter did not become an American citizen, even. All that travel. Just to die as the Lord had decided."

Peter was one of seven children, all boys. His father moved from County Clare to Listowel, County Kerry, where he prospered as a wine merchant. The family lived in a large two-story house overlooking the river Feale. They were financially comfortable and respected. Their Roman Catholicism was that brand of muscular Christianity which the Irish out of all Western nations had originated as their contribution to religion.

Peter spent his youth in the comparative peace of "the old British days" before the Irish Republican Brotherhood (parent of the IRA), the Irish Volunteers, and the 1916 Rebellion started modern Ireland off on the stormy course of fighting for the "terrible beauty" that lured Patrick Pearse, James Connolly, Eamonn De Valera, and the other leaders into the deathtrap of bloodletting, where, 50 years later, in Peter's declining years, blood was still being shed.

School filled three-quarters of the year for Peter. Summers were spent at Beal Strand, at Ballybunion seaside, or harvesting on his grandfather's farm at Newtownsands.

One such summer, his sixteenth, Peter had his only brush with sex. He had lain for hours among the sand dunes of Beal Strand with Mae, a girl from Listowel whom he had known for about three years. That day, their families had gone to the Listowel races.

Innocent flirting developed into simple love play and finally into a fervid exchange of kisses and caresses, until they both lay naked and awesomely happy beneath the early-evening stars, the warmth undulating and glowing sweetly through their bodies as they huddled close together. Afterward, Mae playfully nicknamed him "Peter the Eater." To calm his fear she added: "Don't worry. No one will know how you made love to me. Only me."

For about a year afterward, he was interested in girls and particularly in Mae. Then early in his eighteenth year, he began to think of the priesthood. By the time he finished schooling, his mind was made up. Peter had told me once: "When we said goodbye, that summer of 1922, Mae teased me: 'If you ever leave the seminary and don't marry me, I'll tell everyone your nickname.' She never told a human soul. But, of course, *they* knew." Peter's sole but real enemies were the shadowy dwellers of "the Kingdom" whom he vaguely called "they." He gave me a characteristic look and stared away over my head. Mae had died in 1929 of a ruptured appendix.

Peter started his studies at Killarney Seminary and finished them at Numgret with the Jesuits. He was no brilliant scholar, but got very good grades in Canon Law and Hebrew, which he pronounced with an Irish brogue ("My grandfather was from one of the Lost Tribes"), acquired a reputation for good, sound judgment in moral dilemmas, and was renowned locally because with one deft kick of a football he could knock the pipe out of a smoker's mouth at 30 yards and not even graze the man's face.

Ordained priest at twenty-five, he worked for six years in Kerry. Then he did a first stint in a New York parish for three years. He was present twice at exorcisms as an assistant. On a third occasion, when he was present merely as an extra help, he had to take over from the exorcist, an older man, who collapsed and died of a heart attack during the rite.

Two weeks before he sailed home to Ireland for his first holiday in three years, the authorities assigned him his first exorcism. "You're young, Father. I wish you'd had more experience," was the way he recalled the bishop's instructions, "but the Old Fella won't have much on you or over you. So go to it."

It had lasted 13 hours ("In Hoboken, of all places," he used to say whimsically), and had left him dazed and ill at ease. He never forgot the statement of murderous intent hurled at him by the man he had exorcised. Through foaming spittle and clenched teeth and the smell of a body unwashed for two years prior, the man had snarled: "You destroy the Kingdom in me, you shit-faced alien Irish pig. And you think you're escaping. Don't worry. You'll be back for more. And more. Your kind always come back for more. And we will scorch the soul in you. Scorch it. You'll smell. Just like us! Third strike and you're out! Pig! Remember us!" Peter remembered.

But a two-week vacation in County Clare restored him to his energy and verve. "God! The scones running with salty butter, and the hot tea, and the Limerick bacon, and the soft rain, and the peace of it all! 'Twas great."

Most of Peter's wounds were not inflicted by the harsh realities of the world around him; but, deep within him, they opened as his way of responding to the evil he sometimes sensed in daily life.

Those who still remembered him in 1972 agreed that Peter had been neither genius nor saint. Black-haired, blue-eyed, raw-boned in appearance, he was a man of little imagination, deep loyalties, loud laughter, gargantuan appetite for bacon and potatoes, an iron constitution, an inability to hate or bear a grudge, and in a state of constant difference of opinion with his bishop (a tiny old man familiarly called "Packy" by his priests). Peter was somewhat lazy, harmlessly vain about his 6′ 2″ height, and a lifelong addict of Edgar Wallace detective stories.

"He had this distinct quality," remarked one of his friends. "You felt he had a huge spirit laced with cast-iron common sense and untouched by any pettiness."

"If he met the Devil at the top of the stairs one morning and saw Jesus Christ standing at the bottom," added another, "he wouldn't turn his back on the one in his hurry to get down to the other. He'd back down. Just to be sure."

In normal circumstances, Peter would have stayed on permanently in Ireland after his vacation of scones and soft rain. He would have worked in parishes for some years, then acquired a parish of his own. But there was something else tugging at his heart and something else written in his stars. When he left for New York at the outbreak of the Korean War in order to replace a chaplain who had been called up, he recalled the exorcism in Hoboken. "Third strike and you're out! Pig! Remember!"

He remarked jokingly to a worried friend who knew the whole story: " 'Tis not the third time yet!"

In January 1952, he was asked to do his second exorcism. His effectiveness in the first exorcism and the resilient way he had taken it recommended him to the authorities. The exorcism took place in Jersey City. And, in spite of its length (the better part of three days and three nights), it took very little out of him physically or mentally. Spiritually, it had some peculiar significance for him.

"It was a sort of warmer-upper for the 1965 outing," he told me in 1966. "The ceremony lasted too long for my liking, was hammer and tongs all the way, almost beat us. But there was no great strain inside here [pointing to his chest]." And he added with a significance that eluded me then: "Jesus had a forerunner in the Baptist. I suppose darkness has its own."

Looking back on his role as exorcist today, it is clear to me that the first two exorcisms prepared him for the third and last one. They were three rounds with the same enemy.

The exorcee that January was a sixteen-year-old boy of Hispanic origin who had been treated for epilepsy over a period of years, only to be finally declared nonepileptic and physically sound as a bell by a team of doctors from Columbia Presbyterian Hospital. Nevertheless, on the boy's return home, all the dreadful disturbances started all over again in a much more emphasized way, so the parents turned to their priest.

"They tell me you've a . . . eh . . . a sort of a way with the Devil, Father," said the wheezy, red-faced monsignor, grinning awkwardly as he gave the necessary permissions and instructions to Peter. Then, stirring in his chair, he added grimly as a bad Catholic joke: "But don't bring him back here to the Chancery with you. Get rid of him or it or her or whatever the devil it is. We have enough of all that on our backs here already."

It had gone well. The boy became Peter's devoted friend. Later he went to Vietnam and died in an ambush late one night outside Saigon. His commanding officer wrote, enclosing an envelope with Peter's name on it which the dead man had left behind. It contained a piece of bloodstained linen and a short note. Over a decade previously, just before his release from possession, in a final paroxysm of revolt and appeal, he had clawed at Peter's wrist, and Peter's blood had fallen on his shirt sleeve. "I kept this as a sign of my salvation, Father," the note said. "Pray for me. I will remember you, when I am with Jesus."

Peter was then forty-eight years old and in his prime as a priest. Yet in himself, he suffered from a growing sense of inadequacy and worthlessness. He felt that, in comparison with many of his colleagues who had attained degrees, qualifications, high offices, and acknowledged expertise, he had very little to show by way of achievement. "I have no riches inside me," he wrote to a brother of his, "just black poverty. Sometimes it darkens my soul." When his turn for a parish of his own came around, he was passed over. (Packy was dead already; but, some said, the dead bishop had made sure in his records that Peter would be passed over.)

Peter, in fact, was a maverick. The normal priest found him inferior in social graces but superior in judgment, lacking in ecclesiastical know-how and ambition but very content with his work. Sometimes his protestations of being "poor inside," of having "no excellent talents" sounded hollow when matched with his stubborn and opinionated attitudes. Anyway, the normal bishop would take one look into his direct gaze and decide that his own authority was somehow at stake. For Peter's stare was not insolent, but yet unwavering; it acknowledged the demands of worth but was devoid of any subservience. It said: "I respect you for what you represent. What you are is something else." Such a man was unsettling for the absolutist mind and threatening for the authoritarian bent of most ecclesiastics.

Beyond the occasional funny remark, such as "The higher they go, the blacker their bottoms look," Peter gave no outward impression of discontent or anxiety. A lack of self-confidence saved him from revolt or disgust. And he bore it all lightly. "Well, Father Peter," one bishop joshed him as he left to do a three-month stint in London parish work, "off you go to hell or to glory, eh?" Peter laughed it off: "In either case, bishops get the priority, my lord."

Had he raised protests and used the influential friends at his disposal, he would doubtless have retired in good time to the rural repose of a peaceful Kerry parish and the extraordinary autonomy of a parish priest. (A pope or a bishop approached any settled "P.P." with care. Only his housekeeper could make a frontal assault on a parish priest's autonomy. But, then again, Irish housekeepers were a race unto themselves.)

As Peter was and as he chose to remain—in strict dependence on ecclesiastical whims and never striking out to seek a fixed position—he was available to be tapped for a temporary visit to Rome and an accidental meeting that changed him profoundly.

After his second exorcism, there were ten more years of "helping out" in various dioceses, practically always on a temporary basis as substitute for other priests. And then a chance breakfast in late September 1962 brought him together with a West Coast bishop who, on his way to the opening of the Second Vatican Council in Rome, stayed a few days in New York. The bishop was well known for his sympathy with mavericks and his welcome for "hard cases." Like all the bishops who went to the council, he needed one or two experts in theology to be his advisors in Rome. He needed, in particular, a theologian counselor skilled in pastoral matters.

The next day Peter was aboard a TWA flight with the bishop enroute to the Eternal City. But for that trip, he probably would not have been at the side of Marianne three years later. And he certainly would never have come close to two men who had a sudden, deep influence on the rest of his life. In Rome, Peter performed his duties as a counselor during his ten-week stay there. But what mattered much more to him personally and affected him deeply were his experiences with Father Conor and with Paul VI, then Monsignor Montini.

Father Conor was a diminutive Irish Franciscan friar, bald-headed, sharp-eyed, and voluble, who taught theology at a Roman university. He wore rimless glasses, trotted and never walked, and spoke with a very strong brogue which made his Latin lectures all but unintelligible.

He held court for students, professors, foreign visitors, officials, and friends in his monastery room after siesta hour, three or four days a week. There, any bit of gossip in Rome could be learned, tested, and assessed for its rumor value. For half of Rome always feeds on rumors about the other half. And speculation is the stick which continually stirs the pool of rumor. "They till me, me frind, that . . ." was a frequent opening of Conor's conversation.

Conor spent his summers fishing around Lough Corrib, Ireland, was an expert on Waterford glass, and had a lifelong fascination for all politics, civil and ecclesiastical, a fascination that made Vatican Council II appeal to Conor as catnip to a cat. He had studied demonology ("Mostly ballyhoo," he pronounced in his thick brogue), witchcraft ("A lotta junk, if y'ask me"), Exorcism ("A mad bizniz"), and possession ("The divil's toe-rag"). He served as a consultant to one Roman office that dealt with cases of possession; and on 14 occasions he had conducted exorcisms (but always protested that he "wouldn't touch wan wid a barge pole, unliss they ordher'd me teh"). According to an in joke about Conor that always made him furious, he induced devils to leave the possessed by threatening to "send them back to Ireland."

Outside Roman clerical circles, Conor's activity as an exorcist was relatively unknown. Indeed, he was regarded by his fellow clergy in Ireland as a bookworm and by his lay friends as a "grand, simple, innocent man, slightly dotty about the Middle Ages."

Peter and Conor were approximately the same age. They shared a love of Ireland and a passion for Rome's ruins. And Conor sensed in Peter a mind never tarnished by the baser ambitions he saw eating into those who gyrated and jockeyed around him in Rome on the political treadmill. He also felt Peter's sense of his own worthlessness.

He found Peter's exorcism experiences enormously interesting. For Peter had "the touch," he used to say—a natural ability to weather exorcism's storms. On the other hand, Peter found in Conor a friend of practical experience and advice. Rambling in the Roman suburbs, sitting in the *cortile* of Conor's monastery, visiting the sights of Rome, sipping coffee in the Piazza Navona, they gradually assumed the roles of master and disciple. Peter put questions; Conor answered them. He explained. He theorized. He instructed. He warned. He corrected. He encouraged.

In the area of Exorcism, Conor had things reduced to a recognizable pattern of behavior: how the possessed behaved; how the possessing spirit acted; and how the exorcist should react and conduct the exorcism. During the long walks and talks with Conor, Peter crystallized his own first impressions and learned some valuable guidelines.

He had never realized the radical distinction between the perfectly possessed and the revolters. Nor had he understood the revolters as victims of possession who, partly with their own connivance, surely, had become hostage and were now trying, on the one hand, to give some sign, to summon help, but who in that struggle also became victims of a violent protest against such help—a protest made by the evil thing that possessed them.

Peter was able to adjust and correct his techniques immediately, even without conducting further exorcisms, once Conor explained that the major portion of every exorcism was taken up with shattering a pretense, dispelling a smokescreen; that the most dangerous period lay in the Breakpoint of that Pretense and in the clash of wills that followed at once between the exorcist and the thing that tortured the possessed; and that the "Grate Panjandhr'm" (Conor's epithet for the Devil) intervened only rarely.

In Conor's view, the world of evil spirits was like an autocratic organization: "Joe Shtaleen used to sind Molotov to do his dirty work. So the Grate Panjandhr'm sens his hinchmin."

Conor taught Peter tricks and ruses; and he gave him tags—phrases, words, numbers, concepts—to label perilous phases, capital moments and events in an exorcism. He made available to Peter some of his own practices: the use of "teaser texts," for instance. At certain awkward gaps in the exorcism, there was no way to contend head to head with the possessed and with what was possessing them. The possessing spirit literally hid behind the identity of the possessed. It had to be flushed out into the open. Conor had the habit of reading certain texts chosen from the Gospels, until such time as the spirit made mistakes or arrogantly threw aside its disguise.

Conor's advice was always concrete and vivid, and always in Peter's mind echoed with that warm, fresh brogue they both shared like a piece of common turf: "The t'ing is beyond yer mind. It's a sperrit agin yoors. The reel camuflin' starrts inside in yeh. And yeh'r just an ole toe-rag, unless Jesus is wid yeh."

But, above all else, Conor reconciled Peter to the inevitable drain on the exorcist. He explained in simple terms what wounds he could receive as an exorcist, what wounds he should avoid, and what wounds were incurable once inflicted on him. All these wounds were "internal" to spirit and mind and memory and will. Peter had received some minor ones already. He now realized what he could undergo.

Conor refined Peter's primitive idea of "the Devil" and of "Devils," expressing in simple terms what to most moderns is an enigma if not downright nonsense: how that which has no body can be a person, have a personality. And he dealt curtly with psychoanalysts: "Down the road a bit, they're goin' to find out that the whole thing is entoirely differr'nt; and then they'll put Siggy and company up on the shelves as histhoric'l lave-overrs, like Galen on bones or Arishtot'l on plants."

But it was not Conor who rid Peter of his lack of confidence. He could never give Peter a reason to trust his own judgment. It was the man who in two years would become Paul VI who made that change in him.

Peter never exchanged one sentence with Giovanni Battista Montini, then Archbishop of Milan. Montini had been relegated from the Vatican to the political wilderness of Milan by Pope Pius XII, had survived it, and now was back in Rome—"still listening to his voices" (as the Roman wags described the ethereal gaze of Montini and the impression he gave of having shutters over his eyes to hide the light within)—and was deeply involved in the council.

One of Montini's theologian-counselors was impressed with Peter's arguments at an evening meal. They met several times afterwards during Peter's stay. Once they went with Conor to a gathering of theologians who were discussing issues being hotly debated on the council floor. Such gatherings were frequent in those days; Archbishop Montini was the guest of honor at this particular meeting.

As Montini arrived and walked to his seat, Conor gossiped in a whisper with Peter: "They tell me, my frind, that Johnny [then Pope John XXIII] won't lasht long." Then with a nod in Montini's direction: "There's the nixt wan."

But Peter was not interested in future popes as such. For an inexplicable reason, he was fascinated by Montini. Everything about the man, his person, and his speech and his writings had a peculiar significance for Peter. As he remarked to Conor, "He seems to walk with a great vision no one else sees."

He set out to learn all he could about Montini, speaking with those who knew the archbishop, reading his sermons, frequenting Montini's familiars and employees. He even got to the stage of referring to Montini as Zio, a name used affectionately by those around the archbishop.

Peter came to share Conor's trenchant point of view on recent popes: "Pacelli [Pius XII] was loike a shliver of ice serrved up in an archangel's cocktail at the hivinly banquit," confided Conor wryly as they walked home one evening. "Awsteerr, arishtocratic, sometimes wid a dead-an'-dug-up look, y'know. Johnny [John XXIII], av coorse, is out on his own, a mountin uv sperrit. But this lil' fella [Montini] has an airr 'v thragedee."

Peter made a point of going to listen to Montini whenever he was billed to speak in public. It was on one of these occasions that he had his "Montini experience." Together with others present, he knelt to receive the archbishop's blessing at the end of his speech. As Montini raised his right hand to make the sign of the cross, Peter lifted his eyes. They locked with Montini's at the juncture point of the cross the archbishop traced in the air. As he looked, the "shutters" over Montini's eyes opened for an instant. Montini's gaze was momentarily an almost dazzling brilliance of feeling warmth, communication. Then the "shutters" closed again, as Montini's eyes traveled on over the heads of the others kneeling around Peter.

Afterwards, Peter knew that the empty feeling of diffidence had left him. For the first time in his life, he had no fears.

That was in mid-November of 1962. At the beginning of December, as the first session of the council ended, he was told that he had been freed from his obligations back in New York and that he could go home to Ireland for Christmas. After Christmas vacation in his home town, he worked in Ireland from January 1963 until August 1965.

He was winding up his summer vacation in July 1965 and preparing to return to work in Kerry, when he received a short note from New York telling him of Marianne K., a young woman, apparently a genuine case of possession. The note was urgent: the authorities felt he could best handle the affair. Could he come over immediately?

In mid-August he arrived in New York.

MARIANNE K.

Toward the spring of 1964, and thousands of miles away from the calm and fresh Kerry countryside where Peter was then living, the habitués of Bryant Park, in New York City, began to notice a skinny young woman of medium height wearing jeans, sandals, and a blouse, with a raincoat thrown over her shoulders. Her visits there were irregular; and she stayed for unpredictable periods of time, sometimes for hours, sometimes for ten or fifteen minutes, once for two days. The weather had nothing to do with the length of her stay; sunshine, rain, snow, cold made no difference. She looked clean; but those she passed got the rancid odor of unwashed hair and skin. She never spoke to anyone, and never stood or sat in exactly the same place twice. Always she had a fixed expression, a kind of frozen smile that was only on her mouth; her eyes were blank, her cheeks unlined, taut; her teeth were never visible through the fixed and smiling lips. Her blonde hair was usually unkempt. Those who frequently saw her nicknamed her the Smiler. Marianne K.

Her behavior was harmless, though erratic, at first. Some days she came, sat or stood without any motion to speak of. Then she departed suddenly as if on a signal. Other days, she arrived, gazed blankly around at every corner, then left precipitately. At other times she brought little wooden sticks which she ceremoniously stood upright in the earth, tying scraps of cloth with a single bow to their base. "Like little crosses upside down," was a description given later.

Only once in that early time did she cause any commotion. She came to Bryant Park one morning, sat down for a while, then stood up stock-still facing south, with what could have been taken as a beatific gleam in her eyes. Someone passed by carrying a radio blaring music. As the radio came level with her, suddenly she flung her hands to her ears, screamed, spun around like a top, and fell hard on her face, her body twitching. A score of people gathered around her. A policeman strolled over with the unspeed of the New York cop. "Turn that thing off, pal," he said to the owner of the radio.

Almost immediately a tall man was by the policeman's side. "She's Marianne. I will take care of her." He spoke in a voice of authority and very clearly.

"Are you a relative?" the policeman asked, looking up as he crouched on his haunches beside Marianne.

"I'm the only one she has in this world." The policeman remembered the man touched Marianne on the left wrist and spoke quietly. In a few seconds she awoke, and got quickly but unsteadily to her feet. Her face still had the smile. Together, she and the tall man walked slowly away towards Fifth Avenue.

"You needn't report it, Officer."

The policeman heard the words said evenly, confidently, over the man's shoulder. "I was sure they were father and daughter," he commented later in recalling the incident. "He looked old enough; and they both smiled in exactly the same way."

Nothing of a recorded public nature took place again in Marianne's case, even though she was already in a state of possession by an evil spirit.

No definite sign of that possession, unequivocal in itself, had been visible in her from her childhood days until well into the year following the incident in Bryant Park.

Marianne grew up with one brother a year younger than she. They spent their first years in Philadelphia. The family was then of lower middle income. It was strongly Roman Catholic and closely knit. Her parents, both of Polish origin and second-generation American, had no living relatives in the United States. Close friends were few. Neither of them had completed high school; and they had never found time for culture or much leisure for the finer things in life. Her mother was a quiet-spoken, firm woman who held a job and continually worried about bills. Her father was a bluff, down-to-earth character who grew up in the Depression, married late, was solidly faithful to his wife, never fretted about difficulties, and, outside his working hours, spent all his spare time at home.

Discipline was not rigid at home, and a good deal of fun and merriment ran through it all. Both children were reared to lead an orderly existence. Religion occupied a prominent place in their lives. Prayers in common were recited mornings and evenings. Family love and loyalty were based on religious belief. The Polish pastor was the ultimate authority.

In those early years there was such a strong resemblance between Marianne and George, her younger brother, that they were often mistaken for twins. When their mother or father called them, either of them could answer by mimicking perfectly the voice of the other. They had special signs and words of their own, a kind of private language they could use. Marianne relied on George to a great extent. She was left-handed, had begun to speak normally only at the age of six, and was very shy and obstinate.

This close companionship between the two children was broken when, around Marianne's eighth birthday, the family moved to New York, where her father had been reassigned by his company. His new position made the family financially secure and comfortable. Marianne's mother no longer worked at a job outside the home. Her brother was successful in school. He made friends easily, was a good athlete, and had a rollicking disposition. In New York he gradually sought the company of his peers, and so spent less and less time with his sister.

Marianne made few friends and was at ease only when at home. She never seemed to prefer one parent over the other. After finishing high school, she spent two years at Manhattanville College, where her academic interests were physics and philosophy. But her stay there was stormy and unhappy. She wanted the "full truth, to know it all," she told her teachers in the first flush of enthusiasm. But with time she seemed to get cynical and disillusioned, and gave the impression she believed they were evading the real problem and hiding the full truth from her.

She found particular difficulty with her metaphysics teacher, a certain Mother Virgilius, middle-aged, myopic, high-voiced, exigent, a disciplinarian and member of the "old school." Mother Virgilius taught Scholastic philosophy. She derided modern philosophers and their theories. Her arguments with Marianne were, from the start, bitter and inconclusive. The girl kept plying the older woman with questions, perpetually throwing doubt on any statement Mother Virgilius made, driving her back step by step until the nun rested desperately on her own basic ideas she had accepted but had never questioned. And Marianne was too clever and too tenacious for her, leaping nimbly from objection to objection and strewing difficulties and remarks to trip her up.

But clearly what Marianne was after seemed to be a trap of an odd kind in which to catch the nun. There didn't seem to be any desire on her part to find out something true or to deepen her knowledge, only a disturbing viciousness, a stony-faced cunning with words and arguments alternating with a sardonic silence and smirking satisfaction, all leading to confusion and curiously bitter derision.

Virgilius sensed this but could not identify it. She merely stood on her dignity. But this was no help to either of them.

It all came to a head one afternoon. The lecture concerned the principle of contradiction. "If something exists, if something *is*, then it cannot but exist. It cannot *not* be at the same time and under the same respect," concluded Mother Virgilius in her high pitch. "The table is here. While it *is* here, it cannot *not* be here. Being and nonbeing cannot be identified."

As she finished, Marianne's hand shot up. "Why can't they be identified?"

They had been over this ground interminably. The nun had no more answers and no more patience. "Marianne, we will discuss this later."

"You say that because you cannot prove it. You just presume it."

"First principles cannot be proven. They . . ."

"Why can't I have another first principle? Say: being and nonbeing are inseparable. The table is here because it isn't here. God exists because he doesn't exist at the same time."

A titter ran around the class.

Marianne rounded on her classmates: "It's no joke! We exist and we don't exist!"

The general amusement gave way to hostility and embarrassment. None in the room, Virgilius included, realized, as Marianne reflects today, that by some kink of inner impulse, her mind was running in little twisted gorges of confusion. She was guided by no clear ideas, was not commenting from a rich store of reflection and experience, but was only pulled by a peculiar fascination with the negative. Many a greater mind had fallen off a dark cliff somewhere along this same way or impaled itself in desperation on some sharp rocks.

Virgilius, feeling already tired, was humiliated. She got angry. "I told you, Miss, we will speak . . ."

But before she had finished the sentence, Marianne was on her feet, had swept up her books, glared at everyone, and was out the door.

Marianne refused to return to Manhattanville. To all questions as to why and to all entreaties that she give it another chance, she kept repeating: "They are trying to enslave my mind. I want to be free, to know all reality, to be real." She had nothing but contempt for her former teachers. But none of them could guess how far she had already gone in this contempt.

As she traces it now, her new path began when she decided that her teachers—Mother Virgilius among them—were phonies, that they merely repeated what they had been taught. There was nothing abnormal in this. Up to a certain level, Marianne had an emotional reaction rather normal in the adolescent. But she pursued it with a logic that was not normal for her years. And she was deliberately isolated: she did not communicate with her companions, nor did she discuss it with her parents. She was determined to work it out for herself.

Gradually she extended the same premise ("All authorities in my life are phonies, because they repeat what they are told and never inquire") to her parents, to the priests at the local church, to the religious teaching she had been given, and to the habits and customs of daily life. To everything.

Her parents knew nothing of philosophy. And when Marianne spoke darkly of "how good it is to see all the 'noes' side by side with the 'yesses' " or of "dirt on the nose of the Venus de Milo" or of "murder as an act of beauty as real as composing a sonata," they were bewildered. They only knew that they loved her; but manifestations of that love were taken by Marianne as chains thrown around her. "If only you could hate me, Mummy, just for five minutes, we would get along so well," she said once to her mother. At another time: "Why doesn't Daddy rape me or break my nose with his fist? Then I would see my beauty. And he would be real for me."

In the end, after much discussion and consultation, it was decided to send Marianne to Hunter College for the fall semester of 1954. Perhaps a purely secular school with good standards would satisfy what her parents could only take on the surface to be Marianne's urge to acquire knowledge.

Academically Marianne never had any difficulty during her three years at Hunter. But the rhythm of family life changed around this time. And she took a totally unexpected turn in character. George, her brother, had gone away the previous year to study oceanography. He had been the one human being with whom she communicated on an intimate basis. Her father was more frequently than ever out of town traveling for his company. Her mother, who had taken up working again in an advertising agency, lost any real contact with Marianne by the end of her first year at Hunter.

Her contemporaries at the college remember her as a rather plump, grave-faced girl who rarely laughed, did not smile easily, spoke in a low voice, had few friends, never dated boys, gave the impression of great stubbornness whenever an argument arose, and (as far as they were concerned) was a "homebody." But neither they nor her family knew anything about her first meeting with the Man.

During her first two years at college, Marianne used to go downtown and sit in Washington Square Park, reading her textbooks and making notes. One afternoon in 1956, as she was reading William James' *Varieties of Religious Experience*, she felt suddenly, but without any sense of shock, that someone was bending over her shoulder and looking at the pages of her book. She looked around. He was a rather tall individual whose face and clothes never impressed themselves on her memory. His left hand was resting on the back of the park bench. Her one clear memory is only of his mouth and the regular teeth she glimpsed behind his lips as he read repeatedly from the open page of her book the words: "When you find a man living on the ragged edge of his consciousness . . ." running all the words as one sentence several times over and over again without pause or stop. The mouth kept repeating and repeating: ". . . on the ragged edge of consciousness on the ragged edge of consciousness on the ragged edge of consciousness on the . . ." It was done softly. Without hurry. Without emphasis. Until the words became a slowly whirling carousel in her ears, and her mind moved in circles, bumping against them on all sides. She burst into tears.

The mouth said, still softly: "They are all pushing you along the ragged edge. Want to get off it?"

She remembers a few things. She said through her tears: "I don't want them to help me. Just to leave me alone."

He sat with her for about one hour. The left hand remained visible in her memory. And the mouth. She remembers nothing else of him, except that there were instructions: "Don't let any man touch you! You have a short time to reach your true self! Come and find me regularly!" And there was one peculiar instruction: "Seek those of the Kingdom. They will know you. You will know them."

It was from this time that her family and acquaintances noticed definite changes in Marianne. She disappeared from home for long mornings and afternoons, even when there were no lectures or lab work at college. She spoke rarely with her parents. Her meals at home grew less frequent. Her contemporaries at Hunter noticed that she became more introspective, more fearful of strangers, more reticent with those who knew her, and extremely shy.

Her mother became worried. After much persuasion, she induced

Marianne to see a psychiatrist. But after a couple of sessions, he dismissed her; he told her parents that, while she certainly needed more nourishment (she had been losing weight) and much love, he could detect nothing awry or dangerous in her psychology. She just wanted to be free; and this was, he said, the new generation. Anyway, he advised them, they should think of her age: rebellion and independence were normal for her age bracket.

Her father was satisfied. But her mother felt some deep apprehension.

"By the time they realized that I was in earnest about the change in me," says Marianne, "I had already accepted the authority of the Man in my life. I had changed profoundly. I mean: my inner life-style altered under his influence."

Marianne always refers to this figure as "the Man"; but nowadays it is impossible for her to determine if he was hallucination, deliberate figment of her own, a real person, or merely a metaphor and symbol of her initial revolt. Indeed, in Marianne's memory of the nine years between that first meeting with the Man and the exorcism of 1965, the Man keeps on appearing and reappearing in her recollections. But most of the time, especially the last four years, is nearly a total blank. Only a few searing experiences stand out starkly for her.

Having finished at Hunter, Marianne decided to follow postgraduate courses in physics at New York University. Her isolation now became complete. After a little over one year at New York University, she dropped out, took an apartment in the East Village, and started working as a sales clerk in a store on Union Square. Her behavior, according to the conservative Catholic standards of her parents, was unorthodox. Marianne never went to church any longer. She lived sporadically with various men, did not take care of her external appearance, and spoke disparagingly—sometimes very rudely and with four-letter words—of all that her parents held dear. She did not allow them to bother her.

For their part, her parents worried greatly; but, following the hopeful lead of the psychiatrist, they still thought that all this was a temporary phase of rebellion. They did worry in particular about her health: she shrank from 130 pounds to 95 pounds in a matter of months. But, in great anguish and confusion, her mother ceased leaving food packages at the door of Marianne's apartment, when the first one was delivered back smelling and dripping. Marianne had mixed excrement and urine with the fruit and sandwiches.

In her memory now, the next big step in her changing "inner life-style," as she terms it, concerned formal religion and religious belief. She took that step consciously, with the Man by her side, and on two particular occasions.

One occasion was on Palm Sunday. In the evening as she passed by a church, services were being conducted. Something about the lights in this particular church aroused her interest—"It was in the nature of a challenge," she recalls. She entered and stood among the people at the back of the church. Suddenly she felt the same disgust and rejection then as she had experienced toward her parents and teachers. As she turned to go, the Man beside her turned also. He had been there but she hadn't noticed him.

"Had enough, my friend?" he said quietly, jocularly.

She saw his smile in the half-darkness, and smiled back at him. He said: "The smile of the Kingdom is now yours." Then, as they left: "If you don't like it, you haven't got to lump it, y'know." They both smiled. That was all.

The second occasion took place the next week, at Easter. An illuminated cross was set up on the General Building on Park Avenue. She was viewing this from the corner of 56th Street and Park Avenue, when she heard the Man nearby say: "Seems one-sided. Shouldn't they turn it upside down also? Just in order to balance the odds? Same thing, really. Only in perfect balance." The Man smiled.

"For me," comments Marianne now, "it was a perfect smile. You hadn't to balance it up with a scowl. Perfect for me then."

At home that night, she found herself drawing inverted crosses side by side with upright crosses. But she could not bring herself to draw the crucified figure on either type of cross. Whenever she tried, "The pencil ran away into S-shapes and Z-shapes and X-shapes." From that time on, there started in earnest what she recalls as a "new color and form in my inner life-style." Her descriptions of it are confused and marked by expressions that one finds difficult to understand. But the overall meaning of what she says is chilling. The whole process was an acquisition of the "naked light" and her "marriage with nothingness," expressions she learned from the Man.

"I began to live exactly according to *my* belief. I mean, inside *myself, my* thoughts, feelings, memories, and all mental activity moved accordingly. I reacted to all things—people and things and happenings—as if they were one side of the real coin. And I rapidly found that all people have a powerful force in them—as humans. People, things, events, challenge us to respond. The *way* we *respond* gives the things we respond to a special quality. In a sense, we make them what they turn out to be for us.

"Let me give you an example that will also tell you to what an extent I pursued my idea. Once outside the Public Library on 42nd Street, on a sunny afternoon, a well-dressed woman passed by on the arm of a man. I was sitting on the steps, and she smiled at me. I found myself smiling back at them and saying by my smile (because I felt like that inside me): 'You like me. I like you. You hate me. I hate you. See! It is all the same!' She must have realized the same things, because the smile sort of froze on her face; but she went on smiling—as I did.

"Another day, I picked up a young man on Third Avenue. We went to his apartment and had intercourse. He was gentle; but when I was finished with him, he was a very frightened being. I guess I showed him a side of his character he never guessed existed. And I could see by his face that he was scared. I insisted he make coffee. Drinking it while still naked, I told him how much I hated him and how much he hated me really, and that the more he loved me and I, him, the more we hated each other. I can still see the blood draining from his face and the fear in the whites of his eyes. He was obviously afraid of some trouble. When he mumbled something about 'Hyde' and 'Jekyll,' I said: 'Oh no, man! Put the two in one with no switching back and forth, and you have it down pat. Jekyll-Hyde. That's perfect. See?'"

From now on, as she remembers it, Marianne's development went in two quick stages. The first stage was very rapid. It consisted of a total independence. Except insofar as she needed them for survival or pleasure, she no longer bothered about anyone or anything. She had no more decisions to make about being morally good or evil; whether life was good or bad, worth quitting or worth continuing; whether she liked or disliked; whether she was liked or disliked; whether she met her obligations or shirked them.

The second stage was more difficult and went by fits and starts. It began with a near-adoration of herself. It ended in her "marriage with nothingness" and the fullness of the "naked light." It became clear during her exorcism a few years later that these were terms that described her total subjection to an evil spirit.

She came to monitor her perceptions closely and scrupulously. At first she was fascinated by her perceptions; they came with a startling freshness, appearing to be utterly original in their source—her self. She became in her own eyes a genius with a single vision. She found the company of others exasperating and destructive. To talk with another softened the sharp edge of her perception; to do anything with another meant clothing herself in false clothes and not being wholly herself; to feel anything with anyone else meant she would feel only relatively, for she had to take account of them. Ideally, she believed, one should feel absolutely whatever one felt; whatever one thought one should think completely; whatever one desired one should desire totally. No concentration on self could be greater.

Before she achieved absolute isolation, whenever she returned from a conversation or a meal with others, or even after listening to a lecture or working in the laboratory, it was very difficult for her to regain "the inner space and the single vision" she had possessed before such contacts. She was left with a "double vision"; she was blurred, confused, and confusing in herself. She had to spend days "doing her own thing"—walking in the park (this she now did almost every day), sitting in her apartment writing page after page, which she immediately tore up and which she never reread; sitting or standing still for hours—until at last she was fully absorbed in the self that had been hiding. Then quite suddenly all the clamor would fade out. In the presence of that inner self all was naked again. And absolute. And secure. No longer was she interrupted or disrupted by the "bad flow" from others.

As she reached more and more permanent mastery of her isolation, she came to realize that the self she sought lay "beyond" and "beneath" and "behind" (to use her own expressions) the world of her psychophysical actions and reactions. Out of reach of the endless rhythm of responses, of recordings on her memory, of the fast-paced hip chatter of her companions, of blaring monologues by individuals. She became slowly more sensitive and expectant that she would find the self she sought, wrapped in semitransparent shadows. It was independent, she believed, of that distracting outer world, and of her inner psychic theater which was always at the mercy of that outer world and was so easily shattered by it. The restlessness of details had no place with the self. She came to believe that, if she could prevent the "bad flow" of others entering, she could achieve "perfection of personhood."

"One of my big realizations was that in any commerce with others—a conversation, working with them, even being in their presence while they talked and acted with others—there were two levels of 'flow,' of communication."

One, the "outer one," was—as Marianne perceived it—the one with which she heard, saw, touched, tasted, smelled, remembered in images, conceptualized, and verbalized. All of its functions could be duplicated by a skillfully built machine, a computer, for instance. A lot of it could be found in highly intelligent animals. But in human beings you couldn't have this "outer" level of communication without the second level.

The second level of communication was, Marianne believed, a "flow" or "influence" from each person to another. And whenever two human beings communicated, they did so on both levels simultaneously. And they did so even if they didn't know it or wouldn't admit it.

Marianne had very definite ideas on the *source* of that second level of communication. Her academic training and her avid reading had given a very sophisticated edge to her viewpoint:

"The source was not the subconscious, not a sixth sense or telepathy or any of those gimmicky tags," as she puts it. The source, she thought, was the self in each one. She said: "The self has a means of communication which does not need images or thoughts or logic or any particle of matter." Psychologists and physiologists, she knew, identified the self with brain circuitry and synaptic joints and the mechanisms of sensation. This was like saying that the violin was the source of the violinist's music. Religionists and spiritualists identified the self with "soul" or "spirit"—even with God, or a god. And both psychologists and religionists insisted you make choices. And so, in most people, that source and its "flow" were split into a kind of "black-and-white" condition. Most people were always choosing, responding, being responsible for their actions, saying yes or no, and thereby "fissioning the self's lively unity."

Rarely did Marianne meet anyone whose "flow" entered and left her without attempting to split up the self she had found within her. She remembers that the Man's "flow" was absolutely right, that he even helped her to reach "the place of semitransparent shadows." At other times, in the subway, on the streets, at shop windows, she would receive helpful influence from passersby. But she never managed to find precisely from whom it came. Her daily life became a series of efforts to resist the "flow" from all but those who, like her ideal, had the "perfect flow" and the "perfect balance," who had "nothingness within them."

She has vague memories of continuing to be instructed by the Man, of seeing him regularly, of listening to him talk, of obeying some dictates he gave. But one can glean nothing precise or detailed from Marianne about her instructions. Even an effort by her today to recollect such instructions of the Man produces sudden panics and fears that temporarily paralyze her mind. It is as if, today, remnants of the Man's influence cling somewhere in the deep recesses of her inner being, and any effort to recall those days of her possession is like peeling the scab off a healing wound.

The end of her striving came one day in Bryant Park. She had entered cautiously, feeling the "flow" of all present, ready to flee if any disturbance came her way. *He* was sitting languidly on a bench doing nothing in particular, staring vacantly into space.

Sitting down at the other end of the bench, Marianne gazed vacantly on the passing scene. In the morning sunlight, beneath a sky cleansed by a light breeze, the traffic hummed with the busy purposefulness of other human beings about their day's work. School children and office workers passed by on their different ways. The pigeons were feeding. It could not have been a more peaceful city scene.

Then, in a quick instant, some tremendous pressure seemed to fall all around Marianne from head to toe like a net. She shivered. And then some invisible hand seemed to have pulled a tightening cord, so that the net slipped through every inch of her body and outer self, tightening and tightening. "As the net contracted in size passing through my outer person, it gathered and compressed every particle of my self."

Marianne no longer saw or felt any sensation of sunlight or wind. The outer world had become a flat and painted picture neither fresh nor hot nor cold. And the movements of people and animals and objects were angular tracings with no depth and no coherent sound. All meaning was drained from the scene.

The only movement was within her. Bit by bit "the net, now like a sharp, all-surrounding hand, tightened, narrowing and narrowing all my consciousness." At every moment, under that pressure, she was "opening up every secret part of my self, saying, 'Yes,' 'Yes,' 'Yes,' to a power that would not take 'No' for an answer."

And none who saw her, a young girl sprawled motionless on the bench in the sunlight, could guess that Marianne was becoming a casement of possession.

Without any warning the pressure ceased. The net had been drawn tight. She was held invincibly, securely. And then she realized, like waking up from sleep, that some kind of mist or fog was lifting from her consciousness, allowing her a new sensation. She now knew that all along—all her life—she had been very near to "dusk, an accompanying darkness." Even as she once more saw the grass, trees, men, women, children, animals, sun, sky, buildings, with their indifference and innocence in her regard, she saw also this dusk everywhere.

The dusk crept into her, like a snake slithering easily and lazily into a favorite hole, bringing with it twilight rustlings of such "smoky transparencies," such "opaque light," and such "brightest shadows" that a thrill ripped through her whole being.

What entered her seemed to be "personal," to have an individual identity but of such seductive repulsiveness that the thrill she felt stung her with a "pain-pleasure" she had never dreamed possible. She felt her "whole being going quiet, self-aware, dissolving all the cobwebs." It was like falling in love with the open jaws of an alligator. Each splotch of its saliva, each hook of its teeth, each crevasse in its mouth "was animal, just animal, and personal."

All the while she kept on repeating "yes" silently as if answering a request for marriage or a demand for surrender. Time seemed to stand still, "as a bestiary of animal sounds and smells and presences" gradually flowed into her consciousness and mingled there with the sounds of children laughing, the tones of workmen nearby calling out jokes, or snatches of conversation from couples passing along the pathway. All the sounds that had enlivened the morning when she had entered Bryant Park now seeped with "a new odor of old and new corrupting things, of corruption." The cool snap of the air and the sound of the traffic were marinated in a fluid of "grunts, snarls, hisses, bellowings, helpless bleatings." The blue of the sky, the shining faces of the skyscrapers, the green of the grass, all the colors around her were, according to her memory, suffused in wreaths of black, browns, reds.

It was the "balance" she had always sought. "I have finally stepped into the locus of my self," she reflected. It had always been there, of course. This was the wonder and the awe of it all. And the core of that wonder was "finding it to be nowhere, in a room with an empty chair that did not exist, bare walls that faded into nothingness," and she herself "at last seen as a final illusion dissipated and annihilated into nothingful oneness."

She stood up to go, overjoyed with her newfound "thrill of balance." But she was whiplashed back to clamorous and unwanted sense by music from a portable radio on the arm of a passerby. The snake resting inside her had suddenly coiled like a whip cord and was lashing out at the attempted entry of any singular beauty or grace. She felt herself falling and whirling, falling and whirling. It was as if inside her head a little flywheel had broken loose and was whipping itself into a high-pitched scream as it sped faster and faster. The ground came up and hit her across the forehead. But the real suffering was deep inside her. "Never did I know such sadness and pain," she said.

"When I walked away with the Man's help, he said little. His words burned themselves into my memory: 'Don't fear. You have now married nothingness and are of the Kingdom.' I understood it all without understanding anything at all with my intellect or reason. I said, 'Yes! Yes! All of me belongs now.'

"Nothing was ever the same again, until after I was exorcised."

It was not so much what Marianne had learned. It was rather what she had become. "I was not another person. I was the same. Only I was convinced I had become free by being totally independent *and* by what had entered me and taken up residence inside me."

Just to confirm herself in her conviction, "at one point about twelve months before the exorcism, I did go to a psychiatrist—really to find out how far I had traveled from the ordinary idea of being normal. As he spoke, I realized that all he said, the terminology and concepts he used, and the theories he relied on were such claptrap, all this was only halfway house to where I had arrived. He was treating me as if I were a sick human animal—concentrating on the *animal* part of me. But he did not know anything about spirit; and so I knew then he could not understand the spirit part of me, could not understand *me*. He smothered me in words and methods. Even tried some amateur hypnotic business. He finished up talking more about himself than me.

"A second psychiatrist told me I needed to travel, to get away from it all—but this was at the end of a long session. Again, in this case, I found that nothing the therapist, a woman this time, nothing she did by way of accepted psychoanalytic methods (discussions, monologues on a couch, hypnosis, pharmacology, etc.) ever reached beyond the shallow level of my psychic acts and consciousness. I always saw the therapist as if she were stalking around me fascinated by images and surfaces and terminology; and I saw my psychic self, this partial, puny mechanism in me, responding to her. All along, the real me, my very self which doesn't deal in images or words at all, was untouched. Its area was never entered by the therapist. No psychiatrist could fit in through the doorway because of the load of images and emotions and concepts he carried about with him. Only the naked I enters and lives there."

From now on, as far as any outside observer could have assessed, Marianne's course was a deterioration. After the "marriage with nothingness" in Bryant Park, some fixed moorings seemed to have been severed.

She encouraged all forms of sexual intercourse with men and women, but never found anyone willing "to go the whole hog." Lesbians generally stayed at the surface, wishing to generate pleasure and satisfaction without the necessity of a male. Men with whom she had anal intercourse suddenly became appalled, and usually impotent, when she proceeded to act out anal intercourse "to its fullest extent," as she said. In her view, they wanted merely a novel experience but were quite unwilling "to achieve complete bestiality." They could only take "a little of the beast." They missed "the deliciousness of beauty bestialized and of beast beautified."

The few neighborhood people who saw her with any frequency began to think she was peculiar. She rarely spoke. In shops she would point to what she wanted to buy or hand it to the shopkeeper with a grunt. She never looked them in the eye. All had a vague feeling of threat or danger, some indefinable sense of an unknown fire in her, as long as she stood near them.

Her parents tried to see her several times, but could speak to her only through the locked door of her apartment. Her language to them was littered with obscenities.

Once the neighbors heard dull thuds and crashes for four to five hours. Finally overcoming the reluctance of East Village apartment dwellers to interfere with anyone, they called the police. The door had to be forced. The smell in the room was stomach-curdling. And they could not understand the freezing temperature, while outside New York sweltered in the fetid humidity of high summer.

The room was in chaos. On the floor around the bed and table, in the closets, bathroom, and kitchenette, there were thousands of torn sheets of paper covered with indecipherable scrawls. Marianne was lying across the bed, one leg bent beneath her, a little blood dropping from the corner of her mouth, her eyes open and sightless. She was breathing regularly.

An ambulance called by someone arrived just when Marianne

stirred and sat up. She took in the scene in one glance. Quickly her face changed; she spoke in a normal voice, and assured them that all was well. She had fallen, she said, from a chair while fixing the curtains. "Police don't want trouble," she comments in recalling the incident. "And anyway, I radiated too much power and self-confidence. The only thing I wanted to do was to shout obscenities in their faces: 'You missed it all! I've just been fucked by a big-bellied spider.' But there was no point in saying that." They left her alone.

During all this time, Marianne always smelled bad, and she seemed to have constant cuts and bruises on her shins and the back of her hands. She never displayed any emotion except when confronted with a crucifix, or someone making the sign of the cross, the sound of church bells, the smell of incense from a church door, the sight of a nun or a priest, or the mention of the name of Jesus (even when spoken as an oath or used in jest). Her brother, George, who later went around her familiar haunts, was told by many that at such moments she seemed to shrink inside herself like somebody under a rain of blows, and through the gap in her dreadful, constant smile they would hear growled gurgles of resentment.

Violence to others was rare. On one occasion a schoolgirl with a collection box for a local church cause, shook the box in her face asking for a contribution. Marianne screamed through her teeth, fell into a paroxysm of weeping, shielding her eyes with her hands and kicking violently at the girl's shins. On the front of the box, she still recalls, there was a crucified figure together with the name of Jesus.

On the other hand, she repelled threatening violence rather easily. In the dusk of one October evening, at the corner of Leroy Street, she was accosted by a mugger. She remembers clearly that he made his first move at her from behind. She turned her face deliberately to him, displaying the full extent of that twisted smile to him: "Yes, my brother?" He stopped as if he had run up against an invisible brick wall and stood staring; he seemed unexpectedly and painfully bruised. Then with a scared glance, he backed away from her and took to his heels.

About May 1965 things were brought to a head. Marianne's brother returned to New York for an extended visit. George was married by now and the father of two children. Visits back home were not easy to arrange. Their mother had kept him informed by letter of the rift between Marianne and her parents. But she had given no idea of the extent to which Marianne had changed.

Now he heard the full story. He talked with Marianne's most recent employers and the few people who came into contact with her—her landlord, the grocer, and a few others. He even went to the local police precinct. The news was bad right through. No one had a good word to say for his sister. George could not bring himself to believe the stories about the little Marianne he had been so close to. Some spoke disparagingly of her in a way that hurt him deeply. Others manifested a great fear and apprehension about her. One police sergeant went very far: "If I didn't know otherwise, son, I would say you're a bloody liar and not the brother of that one. This gal is bad, bad, bad news. And, besides, there's something mucky about her. Doesn't even look like a fine lad like you."

George finally decided to go and see his sister for himself. Their mother sat him down in the kitchen before he went. George recalls now that she warned him "what ails our baby is something bad, something real bad. It's not the body. And it's not her mind. She's gone away with evil. That's it. Evil."

George took most of this and much more of the same with a grain of salt: it was his superstitious and beloved mother speaking about her little baby. She gave him a crucifix and told him to leave it hidden in Marianne's room. She said: "You'll see, son. She won't stand for it. You'll see." To humor her, George took the crucifix, put it in his pocket, promptly forgot about it, and went downtown to see Marianne.

It was the first time George and Marianne had met in about eight years. And he was also the first of her immediate family she had consented to see in about six years. Marianne was visibly delighted to see him in her one-room apartment. But George, sitting and listening to her talking slowly in a soft, staccato voice, knew immediately that something was indeed wrong with his sister, that some very deep change had taken place in her.

She was still recognizable to him as his sister—the mannerisms he had known in their earlier years were visibly there. And she still had the "family face" which he shared with her. But, as George told it, she seemed "to have seen something which constantly filled her mind even while talking to me. She was speaking for the benefit of somebody else's ear, repeating what somebody else was telling her." He had a funny feeling that made him look foolish to himself: she was not alone, and he knew it. But he could not get the sense of it all. He was not only puzzled by her behavior, but by its effect on him: she frightened him. George normally did not frighten easily. And he never had felt fear with any of his immediate family.

He was slightly reassured when, several times during the conversation, he saw glimmers of the personality he had known in their young years when they were inseparable companions. But at those moments she seemed to be appealing for help or trying to overcome some obstacle he could not define and she could not tell him of. Then the wave of fear would come on him again. And he remembered his mother's voice as she spoke to him earlier that day: "You'll see. She won't stand for it." Partly out of curiosity, partly to satisfy his mother's request, he decided to hide the crucifix in the room as his mother had asked him.

When Marianne went to the bathroom, George placed the small crucifix under her mattress. No sooner had Marianne returned and sat on the edge of the bed than she turned white as chalk and fell rigidly to the floor, where she lay jerking her pelvis back and forth as though in great pain. In seconds the expression on her face had changed from dreamy to almost animal; she foamed at the mouth and bared her teeth in a grimace of pain and anger.

George ran out and called her parents on a pay phone. They arrived about three-quarters of an hour later, bringing the family doctor with them. That night they took Marianne back to their home in upper Manhattan.

There followed weeks of nightmare for her parents and George. They now had full access to her. She lay in what the doctor loosely described as a coma. She would, however, wake up irregularly, take a little nourishment, fall into paroxysms of growling and spitting, was always incontinent and had to be washed continually, and finally would lapse back into the strange comatose state.

Sometimes they would find her wandering around the room in the middle of the night, stumbling over the furniture in the darkness, her face frozen into a horrible smile. Drugs and alcohol were ruled out as causes of her condition. Hospitalization was considered and rejected. Although she was undernourished, their doctor and a colleague of his could find nothing organically wrong and no trace of disease or injury.

From the beginning, her father insisted that their parish priest come to their home where Marianne now lay, but each visit was catastrophic. It was as if she knew in advance the priest was coming. She had terrifying fits of rage and violence. She would awaken, endeavor to attack the priest, pour out a stream of obscenity, tear her own skin, try to jump out their fifteenth-story window, or start battering her head against the wall.

There were constant disturbances. The door of her room would never stay either open or shut; it was continually banging to and fro. Pictures, statues, tables, windowpanes, crockery were regularly fragmented and crushed. It was, finally, all this, plus the unbearable and constant stench, that sent her mother and brother to Church authorities. No matter how she was washed and deodorized, and the room scoured and cleaned, it always smelled of sodden filth and a putrefaction unknown to them. All this, together with Marianne's extreme violence when a rosary or a crucifix was put to her lips, convinced her family finally that her illness was more than physical or mental.

When Peter arrived in New York in mid-August, he was given a short briefing. He insisted on two preliminary visits and examinations; during these, there was surprisingly no violence. First, he accompanied two doctors, chosen by him, on a visit to Marianne. She cooperated fully with them. On the second visit, he had an experienced psychiatrist with him. This expert prolonged his examinations for two or three weeks, taking copious notes, tape-recording conversations, discussing the case with colleagues, questioning her parents and friends. His conclusion was that he could not help her. He recommended another colleague of his. After a hypnosis session, more lengthy conversations with Marianne, and relying as well on the results of drug therapy, his colleague pronounced Marianne normal within the definition of any psychological test or understanding.

It was the beginning of October before Peter felt he could be morally sure he had a genuine case of possession in Marianne, and that he could safely proceed with the exorcism. He planned to start it early on a Monday morning. Beforehand, he chose his assistants and then spent many hours schooling them as to how they should act, what to do, and what not to do during the ritual of Exorcism. Their chief function was to restrain Marianne physically. Peter had a younger priest as his chief assistant; he had to monitor Peter's actions, warn him if mastery of the situation were slipping from him, correct any mistakes he might make, and—in Peter's words—"poleaxe me and carry on in my place if I make the ultimate mistake." All the assistants were given one absolute rule: never say anything in direct response to what Marianne might say.

Late on the Sunday evening preceding his Monday morning appointment at Marianne's home, as Peter sat chatting after dinner with some friends, he received a frantic call for help from George. Marianne's condition was worse than ever before. She raged around the apartment, screaming Peter's name. There had been a series of disturbances in the house that still continued unabated. And they were beginning to spread beyond the family's apartment. Not only were the neighbors complaining; his parents had already been the victims of some freak accidents. The situation was getting out of hand.

Peter left immediately, and arrived at the apartment some time past midnight. He set about preparing for immediate start of the exorcism. His assistants had already arrived. He did not approach Marianne's room. Under his directions, they entered, stripped the bedclothes from the bed, placed Marianne on a blanket thrown on the mattress. She made no resistance, but lay on her back, her eyes closed, moaning and growling from time to time. They stripped the carpet from the floor, and removed all but two pieces of furniture. Peter needed a small night table for the candlesticks, the crucifix, and his prayer book. The tape recorder was placed in a chest of drawers. The windows were closed securely and the blinds drawn. It was after 3:30 A.M. before all was ready for the exorcism.

The four assistants gathered around Marianne's bed in the little room. The only light came from the candles on the night table. Around them wafted the stale stench that marked Marianne's presence; even the little balls of cottonwool dipped in an ammonia solution which they had placed in their nostrils did not kill that smell. Occasionally, the honking of a car or the scream of a police siren sounded in their ears from the streets below. None of them felt at ease. The centerpiece of this scene, Marianne, lay motionless on the bed.

When Peter entered wearing black cassock, white surplice, and purple stole, Marianne tried to turn away from where he stood at the foot of the bed, but two of his assistants held her down flat. There was no violence until he held up the crucifix, sprinkled her with holy water, and said in a quiet voice: "Marianne, creature of God, in the name of God who created you and of Jesus who saved you, I command you to hear my voice as the voice of Jesus' Church and to obey my commands."

Not even he and certainly not his assistants were prepared for the explosion that followed.

Catching them all unawares, Marianne jerked free, and sat bolt upright on the bed. Opening her mouth in a narrow slit, she emitted a long, wailing howl which seemed to go on without pause for breath and in full blast for almost a minute. Everyone was thrown back physically by the force of that cry. It was not piteous, nor was it of hurt or appeal. It was much more like what they imagined a wolf or a tiger would sound like "when caught and disemboweled slowly," as the ex-policeman described it. It was an embodiment in sound of defiance and infinite pain. It confused and distressed them. Marianne's father burst into tears, biting his lip to stifle his own voice; he wanted to answer her. "One moment it made you afraid," said Peter's young colleague in recalling the moment. "Another moment it made you cry. Then you were shocked. So it went. *It confused.*"

By the time she was silent, they had recovered and had her pinned down again. She did not resist. The smile was back on her mouth, twisting her lips into a corkscrew shape. She was very cold to the touch. Her body was still, relaxed. The first words that came from her were calm:

"Who are you? Do you come to disturb me? You do not belong to the Kingdom. Yet, you are protected. Who are you?"

THE SMILER

Father Peter looked up from the exorcism text. "Funny," he thought, "I should be sweating." His palms were dry, and his mouth. He glanced at the girl. Her eyes were closed, but her eyeballs were obviously moving beneath her lids as if she were caught in animated conversation. That smile still lay across her lips like a curled whip. Her head was now turned slightly to one side as if listening.

"Marianne!" He said it in a half-whisper, not finding his voice easily. No answer. Silence for about ten seconds. Then, this time commandingly: "Marianne!"

"Why curse your gentle heart"—Marianne's words were spoken softly—"I am now of the Kingdom. Didn't you know?" A pause. "So,

please hump off." Another pause. "With little Zio." A little laugh.
Then: "Betcha he doesn't know how to hump, fella!"

The edge of her teeth appeared like a white curve behind the lips.
The crow's-feet melted away from around her eyes. The whole
expression hardened. "Unless . . . unless . . . unless you want to play
socket to my hammerrrrrrr . . ." Her words had come out all slurred
and on one breath but with no noticeable lip movement. Peter could
hear the end of that lungful of air as the prolonged "r" died away like
an echo into nothingness.

The four assistants stirred and looked at each other. The bank
manager, now perspiring freely, felt for the waxen pads in his ears to
reassure himself they were still there. James, the younger priest,
caught his breath and was about to speak when Marianne spoke again,
this time in a husky voice.

"Sorry, Peter." She sounded just like a lover who had kissed a little
too violently, was sorry, but might bite again if disappointed.

"Marianne!" This time insistingly. The name acted like the pull of
invisible wires. Her body became rigid. Her head was flat on the bed,
face to the ceiling; the eyeballs turned up behind the eyelids were still;
the skin, marbleized and utterly smooth, looked ten years younger. For
all the world, this was a teenage student listening intently to her
professor. Except for the smile.

"*Lechah venichretha verith.*" ° The Hebrew words came off her lips
quite intelligibly to Peter. "A deal," she continued, "just you, Peter,
and me. Peter the Eater."

A window opened in Peter's memory releasing a small sharp panic
in him. It was like a bat zigzagging at him out of the night of memory.
And like a grain of grit thrown in his eye and stinging him to tears.
"Don't worry. No one will know it. Only me." Mae's face and voice
were back with him for an instant from that distant summer evening.
They were so dear in his memory. But Marianne's voice seaped the
memory to ashes.

"A deal, Peter! Let's talk of the Un in the All-Holy. Aleph. Beth.
Gimel. Daleth. Shin. Forget your Hebrew in all that hair and skin?"
The tone was level, throaty, neither male nor female, grittily mocking.
The grain of panic in Peter now became a boulder pushing him against
the bars of his mind, as he sought refuge. He remembered the neat
trap, and the words of old Conor: "Nivir discuss, me bhoy. Nick's a

° "Come! Let's make a deal."

pahst mahsther at it. He'll have yeh bet in wan tick uv a lamb's tail."

Peter made a new effort at mental control. His panic receded. "Marianne!"

But the Pretense continued. "Tschah! Peter! What's a little Hebrew between you and me?" The voice was less throaty now, appealing, even.

"In the name of Jesus, I command you, Marianne, to answer."

"Why can't we forget the past? You forget it. I forget it. So everybody's happy, Peter."

"Marianne, you belong to the Most High . . ."

"Forget it, Peter!" The hard note again. "Don't be a bore. This *is, is, is* Marianne. The real Marianne . . ."

"Marianne, we love you, and we know you. Jesus knows you. God knows you. Answer me in the name of Jesus who saved you."

"If you're thinking of that little pimply girl with no breasts and heavy glasses and her silver cross and her calloused knees . . ."

"Only love can save and heal, Marianne." Peter knew that confrontation was being avoided, and the voice of Pretense went on.

". . . and her no-mother-yes-mother-no-father-yes-father-bless-me-father-for-I-have-sinned. Forget it, Peter." The throaty tone had returned; but there was a silky snarl laced with contempt and, Peter felt, some tiny threat.

A sound caught Peter's ear. Marianne's father was shaking and looking at the chest of drawers. For the last 17 hours, that chest of drawers had never stayed in exactly the same place. This had not been too disturbing. But now it rocked back and forth at irregular intervals; the brass handles rattled.

"Throw some holy water on that thing," Peter whispered to his colleague. He heard some short hissing sounds like drops of water falling on a red-hot stove.

But—even as quickly as that—the initiative had been taken out of Peter's hands. He had been distracted by her father's reactions and his own whispered order.

"Peter? You okay?" She had a mocking solicitude in her tones. The rattling had ceased. "About that Un. What's the difference?"

Peter clenched his teeth and decided to be assertive. "The All-Holy," he said flatly, "is one."

"Ah! But to be complete, the All-Unholy goes with it."

"Dirt does not go with cleanliness."

"Without darkness, no light, Peter. No light."

"The All-Holy cannot go with the All-Unholy."

"Wrong, Peter pet, pet Peter."

Peter's mental grip weakened for an instant, as he felt the claws of argument closing around his mind. Fatally his logic rose. Conor's warning faded in a kind of cry to intellectual battle, and he blurted out: "Impossible—"

"Now, we're on the ball." Her voice rose, cut in triumphantly. "I know your fuddy-duddy medieval Principle of Contradiction. *Esse et non-esse non possunt identificari.*° Even know the Latin! But that's for now, Peter. See? Only for now. It can be different."

Peter forced himself away from argument.

"Marianne!"

"No, Peter . . ."

"In the name . . ."

"Of the All-Unholy and, if you wish, the All-Holy. No objection." Then that terrible little laugh. "Some day soon, your *esse* and your *non-esse* will go together like . . ."

". . . of Jesus, Marianne . . ."

". . . a cock in a cunt, like a hand in a glove. Mine do . . . did . . . will . . ."

Suddenly she vibrated in a high-pitched scream, shoulders, hips, thighs, feet, hands, all beating against the hands that held her down, like a woman driven to insanity with caresses but cut short of orgasm: "Will somebody fuck me, fuck the *esse* out of my ass, Peter. Put your *esse* in me and fuck me, fuck me." She ended in a forlorn wail.

Marianne's uncle gasped for air, as if throttled by a blow across the throat. Peter's eardrums ached from that scream. He almost felt the hot tears of her father, who was now crying quietly, biting his lips as he held his daughter down.

Peter knew: the Pretense was wearing thin; something had to give. But they were not yet in sight of the Breakpoint.

Suddenly Marianne went limp. The men relaxed their grip on her and stood back. A high color crept into her cheeks. The voice that came from her throat now was youngish, full of interest, calm, as though reciting a lesson, cascading with soft syllables. As she spoke, her head moved from side to side, eyes closed. The whip-smile was now a coy kitten playing around the corners of her mouth.

"I have been on a simple quest. You see. No harm to anybody. Not

---

° "Being and nonbeing cannot be one and the same."

even to myself. Only, I wanted to end all the painful choosing. Mummy and Daddy could not help me. Nor my teachers. Nor boyfriends. All of them were split with decisions. All of them tortured by their choices. Afraid. Yes. You see? They were afraid. Had fears. Like dogs yapping at their heels. Is this right? Is this happy? Is this possible? Is this impossible? Miles and miles of yapping mongrel questions. I knew if I found my real self, there would be no more need to respond to choices and therefore no more fear of error. No more guilt."

Peter understood there was no hope of arresting this flow of her speech. She was eluding him now by a stratagem of logical talk into which he could not enter without closing steel jaws around his mind. It would be all over. Fatally. The only way of "teasing" her out of this tricky stage of the Pretense was by an equally sustained flow of talk in direct contradiction to the sense of what she was saying.

For long minutes and at various stages, Peter and Marianne responded as if chanting antiphonal psalms, one taking up where the other left off. But there was no sequence or logical connection between what each was saying. The only point on which he endeavored to match her was the manner of speaking. When she whispered, he whispered. When she shouted, he shouted. When she murmured, he murmured. When she interrupted, he interrupted her. When she was silent, he fell silent. If one could have visualized their struggle at this phase, it would have been like a surrealistic slow-motion Olympic wrestling match in which the contestants strove with each other's shadow, while all colors and actions faded into blurry grayness, and scores were kept by a referee never seen or heard but felt as a sure and eerie presence.

"Possible and impossible," Marianne cooed, "make all human happenings impossible, posing suppurating distinctions and pat partisanships and perfunctory periods . . ."

"If a man has any love for me," Peter read, "he will be true to my word." He was battering against the confusion, the numbing use of words that lulled the mind toward nothingness. "And then he shall love my Father; and we will both come to him and make our abode with him . . ."

". . . in between us and our other halves," Marianne interrupted. "Saying to the Yin in me: Thou shalt not have thine Yang. Saying to the Yang in you: Thou shalt not have a Yin . . ."

Peter cut Marianne off again. "The branch that does not live on in the vine can yield no fruit of itself." The very simplicity of the words gave Peter new blood. His voice was calm. "No more than you . . ."

". . . making a male the creature of his dangling ganglions," screamed Marianne violently, "and a female the bed of her clit and her clots and her . . ."

". . . if you do not live on in me," Peter said at the top of his voice. "I am the vine; you, its branches; if a man lives on in me, and I, in him, then he . . ."

". . . tomby womb." Marianne was now snarling the words in a hoarse yell. "He out. She in. And never the twain shall meet except in sweat and groans. Ugh! For out's out . . ." Now Marianne blew out a great gust of air at the candles on the night table at the foot of the bed. The young priest shielded them with the cupped palms of his hands.

Peter would not disengage. He went on, still knifing at the confusion, the verbal expression of the stink in the room, using the words that kept him free. ". . . will yield abundant fruit; separated from me, you have no power to . . ."

". . . and in's in," she broke across him. "This cut-and-dried business started long ago with all that crap of master and slave, creature and creator, god and man. The whole cotton-pickin', mother-fuckin' . . ."

". . . anything," Peter continued imperturbably with his text. "If a man does not live on in me, he can only . . ."

". . . winners-and-losers game." She paused slightly for a moment, as if listening. "The fella in that white robe with that camp-following whore and her vaseline. And then for us . . ."

She broke off. Her eyes opened and she sat up in bed. The ex-policeman and the bank manager, fearing violence, reached for her arms. But there was none. Father James thought of the old lithograph of Jesus and Mary Magdalen that hung in the rectory.

"Yeah, my young eunuch. That's him and her," said Marianne, laughing and looking at James crookedly and conspiratorially.

But Peter's voice recalled the stunned James to reality.

". . . be like the branch that is cast off and withers away. Such a branch is . . ."

"Mother Mary Maidenhead Virgilius announced that the impossible can't be possible." Marianne was lying back once more on the bed. "You're telling us, we all chorused at her . . ."

Peter caught the sardonic tone. His voice went hard as he cut her off.

". . . useless and cast into the fire, to burn there. I pray for those who are to find faith in me through their word; that they may be all one; that they too may be one in us, as thou, Father, art in me, and I . . ."

". . . withered boobs and remembering her fallen womb and her pasty complexion at curse time every month." Marianne's voice was once again rising to a falsetto. "If only you had known, Mother dear! The impossible isn't . . ."

Marianne was chuckling. Peter kept the hard note in his tone, as he took up where she had cut him off: ". . . in thee; so that the world may believe that it is thou who has sent me."

Still talking, Marianne now turned over on her side, relaxed. While she spoke, the doctor took her pulse as he was supposed to do every quarter of an hour, when her movements didn't make this too difficult.

". . . possible unless the impossible is actual. Otherwise the impossible would be impossible. Must be really impossible, though. *Really*." Her tone was confidential. "For the possible to be possible, I mean. Must have both. Must have . . ."

Peter's voice sank low and vibrant: "This is my commandment that you should love one another, as I have loved you. This is the greatest . . ."

They all jerked to attention: Marianne's body had become rigid as a plank of wood. She was still talking: ". . . both." Now her words ran ahead of him. He looked up, listening and watching for any telltale sign that the Breakpoint was upon them. She continued feverishly.

"The real is real because of the unreal. The clean, clean because of the unclean. The full, full because of the empty. The perfume, perfume because of the smelly. The holy, holy because of the unholy." Then in an intense rush of words interspersed with grunts intent on hammering home contradictions, in an unholy pursuit of all that could confuse and confound human thought and open blankness in the mind: "Sweet sweet huh bitter. What is is huh what isn't. Life life huh death." Each grunt preceded an opposite and sounded as though Marianne were being punched in the stomach each time. "Pleasure pleasure huh pain. Hot hot huh cold." Then in a chain of words pasted together in a scream: "*Updownfatthinhighlowhardsoftlongshortlightdarknesstopbottominsideoutsidealleachalleachalleachchchchchchchch-ch* . . ." The piping voice died away on that long, coagulated mishmash as if choking on its breath. The effort had been so violent that Marianne seemed to be almost plucked off the bed, every part of her prone body straining upward.

Peter resumed his reading evenly. "I have no longer much time for conversation with you. One is coming, who has power over the world, but no hold over me. Now is the time when the Prince of this world is to be cast out . . ." He paused in the middle of the sentence and looked at Marianne.

She was still lying rigid, her legs apart, hands on her crotch. A low whispered growl started in her throat and parted her lips.

Peter started to whisper: "Yes, if only I am lifted up from the earth, I will attract all men to myself." He stopped, no longer hearing that growl.

Marianne's body relaxed. She rolled over jerkily on her other side. In a girlish voice, a seemingly instantaneous departure in a new direction: "Binaries, we need them, y'know? Yessir. Cybernetics has 'em. Before and after. Plus and minus. Odd and even. Negative and positive. Always to be with us. But just as far as that: with us. Not splitting us."

Peter would not be pulled aside or try to follow any sense of Marianne's words. That same trap, that constant, easy invitation to defeat. He took up again: "He who rules this world has had sentence passed on him already. The spirit will bring honor to me because it is from me . . ."

"He who is not with me," she took up, interrupting in a dreadfully mocking falsetto, "is against me, sez the Lord. No man can serve two masters, sez the Lord." Lowering her tone: "Ever see two pricks in the ass and cunt of one broad and she pumping back and forth servicing two masters?" Her father turned his face away and leaned on the policeman's shoulder.

Again the falsetto: "Whom do men say I am? sez he. Black and white, sez he." Now the falsetto rose to a howl that pierced the ears of Peter and the others, making them wince and grimace: "You're in, sez he. You're out, sez he. The Lord God of Ghosts. Sheep 'n' goats, sez he. Doves and devils, sez he. Golden clouds and bloody brimstone. Driving a nail in the heart. Opening up a gaping wound in my oneness." Then, raising her pelvis up and down rhythmically and shouting at the top of her voice: "Jeebum! Jeebum! Jeebum! Jeebum!"

". . . the Father belongs to me," said Peter calmly, finishing his interrupted sentence.

Marianne stopped as Peter said those words. Now he was standing by the window but facing into the room and watching Marianne on the bed. She whimpered piteously: "All I want is no more questions. No more challenges. No more choices. No more yesses and noes. Not even maybes. No thou-shalt-nots. In the Kingdom . . ." Then in a suddenly deep gurgle like a man who needs no air but speaks through gallons of water ". . . in the Kingdom in the Kingdom in the Kingdom . . ."

Every instinct in Peter drummed at him to put pressure on her. He felt that the Pretense was almost over, that Marianne's revolt *against* possession would break out now, and that the evil occupying her would be forced to fight openly to retain its hold.

Peter moved quietly to Marianne's side, still looking for the telltale signs on her face. If the Breakpoint were near, then all expression should be absent; and there should be queer and unnaturally crooked lines. Sure enough, the face was a frozen mask grained with stark lines. Silence.

"Father, is she going to come out of it?" It was Marianne's father.

Peter ignored the question. Put the pressure on, his instinct told him. Now! Fast!

"Jesus, Marianne. The name is . . ."

"Jeebum! Jesusass! Jeebum! Jesusass! Jeebum!" She was howling again. Peter wanted desperately to cover his ears against the slivers of pain that pierced his brain.

"Watch it!" he shouted to his assistants as he saw her two forefingers shoot into her nostrils and begin tearing at them. He jumped to her side again. "Pin her down!"

Every pair of hands clamped down on her. They held on. Each one had his own memory of some wild animal: a tiger in a zoo cage, a hyena lowering at another hyena, a sow fighting the hands at a slaughterhouse. The sides of Marianne's mouth were pulled back—it seemed the grimace stretched to her ears—baring teeth, gums, tongue. A grayish foam bubbled and seeped over her lower lip and down her chin. Her eyes were open but rolled up so far that they saw only white, red-streaked patches glistening wet. Two men pinned her arms to the bed; one leaned on her belly; another held her legs still.

It seemed no human being could survive what Marianne was going through. The doctor closed his eyes as his own perspiration stung into them.

"Hold on, for the love of God," Peter said.

The muffled "zheeeeeeeeeee" buzzing between her teeth died away to nothing. Her eyelids closed. "Stay put," muttered the ex-policeman, "she's still all tight." The doctor lifted one of Marianne's eyelids, then let it fall shut again.

Peter had won. The Pretense had failed. But it was many hours after the start, and only the end of round one. He recited the second part of the Exorcism ritual, while his assistants stood back watching.

As always before, the Breakpoint came at the precise moment Peter least expected it. It started with a sound difficult to describe. A horse whimpering. A dog whinnying. A man meowing. It was the very sound of pain. Of nature violated by unnature. Of deep agony. Of protest. Of helplessness. "Supposing a cadaver, after the death rattle and after the grimacing of the last breath was over, started to cry for help, what do you imagine it would sound like?" Peter asked later in an effort to describe this indescribable sound. "Or supposing when you were closing his dead eyelids with your thumb and forefinger" (he made the motion with spatular fingers) "and supposing you missed one eye, and it looked up at you still glassy and dead—you know how they look—and it filled with genuine tears. That's the feeling. Something reaching out from the middle of all the worms and putrid flesh and stink and body water and silent immobility of death, saying: 'I'm alive! Pull me out! For the love of Jesus, save me!' That was Marianne when the Breakpoint began. The tug of war for her soul that nearly broke me in two."

Now, Peter felt, he could appeal directly to Marianne and aid her. He started to read the first part of another "teaser text" slowly.

"Marianne. You were baptized in the name of the Father, the Son, and the Holy Spirit. You belong to Jesus. It was the sacrifice of his life that made it possible for you to belong to God. Whatever of beauty, of love, of kindness, of gentleness there was in you—all came from Jesus. He knows you, knows every fiber of your being, is more than a friend, nearer than your mother, more loving than any lover, more faithful to you than you yourself can be. Speak! Speak! Speak out! And tell me you are listening. Speak and tell me you want to be saved in the name of Jesus who saved you and in the name of God who created you. Speak!"

Looking over the top of the book, he could see her hands relaxing and being placed at her sides by his assistants. The ear-to-ear grimace faded. Her eyes were open but still turned up so far that you felt she was looking into her own eye sockets. The whites of her eyes glistened. There was complete silence. The doctor took her pulse. "She's as cold as ice." "Okay, okay," Peter answered the doctor, with a motion of his head, never taking his gaze off Marianne.

Marianne's whole body was limp now. It looked heavy, sodden with fatigue. A faint bluish coloration gave an eerie appearance to her hands, arms, feet, neck, and face. All was still. He heard breathing: his own, his assistants'. Marianne's he could not hear.

The doctor reported a faint pulse. "She's very low, Peter," he said. Peter held up his hand restraining further comment. The moments ticked by. Her father cleared his throat and brushed his eyes: "It's over, Father?" Peter silenced him with a quick, almost rude shake of his head. He watched, waiting for the slightest change. "If it's going to happen, it's now," he said half to himself, half-aloud; "Keep watching."

But with the intolerable strain of silence, he felt the muscles in his calves, back, and arms relaxing. His grip loosened on his book. His head began to straighten up. The younger priest unfolded his arms. A radio blared in a downstairs apartment. Gradually the silence took over as a welcome blanket wrapping itself around their ears and swaddling the entire room. It gave an uneasy feeling to find oneself getting lost in that silence after the shouting, the discordancy, and the lethal sound of the gurgling voice Marianne had used.

The pain began to ease in Peter's mind. Still gazing at Marianne's face, he thought of Conor in Rome, of Zio—now Paul VI—in New York. And he thought of sleep. He glanced at his watch. It was 9:25 P.M. Mass at Yankee Stadium should almost be finished. This ordeal in the room should also be finished soon. Soon, hopefully, they could all go home and sleep . . . sleep . . . sleep.

Sleep? Through the settling haze of his fatigue, the thought triggered Peter's memory. Hadn't Conor warned him that sleep, sleepiness, the desire to rest, sometimes came as a last trap, usually preceding a last onslaught of the Presence?

But he was a few moments too late. As Conor's phrase lit up like a red signal in his memory: "Moind the sleeperrr, lad. Moind the sleeperrr! Tis all up wid yah, if yeh fergit the sleeperrr!", it was already upon him.

It was sudden. And yet the Presence seemed as if it had been clutching at him for ages beforehand, already had a hold on the vitals of his being. His body shuddered as he whispered, "Jesus! Jesus!"

The others heard only a groan from him and thought that he had tried to say something without having cleared his throat.

"Okay, Father?" asked the doctor.

Peter gestured wearily with his hand. This fight was all his. The others would be unknowing witnesses.

The Presence was everywhere and nowhere. Peter fought off the instinct to step back or to look around or, most of all, to run far and fast. "Freeze yer moind," had been Conor's advice. "Freeze it in luv. Shtick there, lad." But, Holy Jesus! how? The Presence was all over him, inside him, outside him. A total trap of cloying ropes he couldn't see. He heard no word, saw no vision, smelled no odor. But his skin was no longer the protective shell of his mortality. *His skin didn't work!* It was now a porous interface that let the invisible filth of the Presence ooze in. Worst of all was the silence of it. It was soundless. Suddenly he had been attacked and caught; and he knew his adversary was superior and ruthless, that it had invaded deep into the self he always hid from others and hoped only God did know and would never show him until he was strong enough to bear the sight.

He could not discern where the struggle lay. His confusion of mind was like molasses oozing over spiders, paralyzing every effort at control and every natural movement. Sometimes it seemed his will was made of rubber twisted this way and that and cruelly snapping back at his mind like a wet towel smacking the face. Sometimes his mind was a sieve through which stinging particles tumbled, each one tabbed with a jeering name: Despair! Dirt! Smell! Puny! Mush! Misery! Mockery! Hate! Beast! Shame! . . . There was no end to them. At other times, he realized, his mind and will were only exits, sewage pipes; and his imagination was the recipient of what they vomited. Out through them were pouring the shapes of the real struggle that lay in another dimension of himself. Deep down? High up? Conscious? Unconscious? Subconscious? He did not know. But certainly somewhere in the depths of the self he was. All the hidden valleys of that self were red with his agony. Every high peak was a sharp slope of tumbling confusion. Each plain and corner was crammed with pressure and weight and sorrow. His imagination was now a cesspool swelling with gobs of repulsive images and twisted fears.

"I'm alone," he thought, covering his face with his hands for an instant.

"Yes! Alone! Alone! Alone! Alone!" came the answer in silent mockery.

It seemed to be himself answering himself with a blasphemy as primal as the scream of the first man who murdered another man, and as actual as the grunt of the latest mugger on that same October night driving his knife deep into the back of his victim on Lenox Avenue.

"Oh, God! Oh, Jesus!" Peter exclaimed within himself. "Oh, God! Oh, Jesus! I'm finished . . ."

Then, as suddenly as it had come, and for no reason he could discern, the Presence receded from him; but it did not leave altogether. Peter felt as if extended claws pricked themselves loose out of his flesh and mind and folded back unwillingly.

Without Peter's knowing, a small gale of consternation—a pale copy of his own agony—buffeted his assistants all this time as they kept troubled watch over Marianne.

Little patches of relief spotted Peter's consciousness. His eyes focused again. Over rims of tears, he could now see her. She was a body of trembling. It seemed that everything beneath her skin and hair and clothes was moving in unnatural agitation, arhythmically, but that her exterior remained somehow still. Her mouth opened a fraction. The lips moved wordlessly.

And then, for the third time in his life, Peter heard the Voice.

It came from nowhere. It merely sounded; it was audible to Peter and all present, but it did not come from any discernible direction. It was everywhere in the room, but nowhere in particular. It was level in tone, slow in speed, without any trace of breathing or any pause. Not high-pitched. Not deep. Not throaty. Not tinny or nasal. Not male. Not female. Accentless. Controlled. Peter had once seen a film about a talking robot; when the robot uttered a word, each syllable, as it was pronounced, was followed by eddies of gurgling echoes of itself. The echoes muddied the next syllable; and so it went on for the syllables of each word in a sentence.

The Voice was something like that, but *in reverse:* the eddying echoes of each syllable preceded the syllable itself. To the listener, it was excruciating to understand but impossible to blot out. It was distracting and dizzying. The effect was like a million voices stabbing the eardrum with nonsensical confusion and clamor, preechoing each syllable. You tried to pick out one voice, almost succeeded, then another piled on top of that; you tried to pick out another, but the first one came back at you. And so on, seeming scores of persistent voices exasperating you, confusing you, defeating you. Then the Voice pronounced the syllable; and your confusion was complete with frustration, for the syllable and the word were drowned in the general babel.

Like most people, Peter had acquired the knack of "reading" voices. We all develop such an instinct and have our own classification of voices as pleasant or unpleasant, strained or peaceful, male or female, young or old, strong or weak, and so on. The Voice fitted into no category Peter could think of. "Unhuman I suppose you'd call it," he said later. "But it was the same as in Hoboken and Jersey City. With the added touch, of course."

The "added touch" was his way of indicating the peculiar timbre of the Voice at each exorcism. In Hoboken as in Jersey City the timbre conveyed some violent and shocking emotion that aroused fear. But the timbre in the Voice that October night was different. "For all the world," said Peter, "as if the Great Panjandrum himself was speaking, and all the little panjandrums pronounced each syllable before he did. His precursors, if you wish."

The timbre, the "added touch," conveyed a single message: utter and undiluted superiority. It didn't hit the emotions, but the mind, freezing it with a realization that there was *no* possibility and could never be any possibility of besting it; that its owner knew this, and that he knew you also knew; and that this superiority was neither sweetened by compassion nor softened by an ounce of love nor eased by a grain of condescension nor restrained by one whit of benignity toward one of lesser stature. "If sound can be evil, with no human good in it all," said Peter, "that was it." It brought him up to the thin edge of nothingness and face to face with the *anus mundi*, the ultimate in excretion of self-aggrandizing sin.

Then the bedlam and confusion of the Voice died away as if into some middle distance.

The four assistants lifted their heads, as Marianne's own voice was heard speaking with heavy deliberateness, almost quietly, in comparison with the preceding uproar.

"Nobody mortal has power in the Kingdom. Anybody can belong to it." A short pause. "Many do." Each word had come out polished, precise, weighty, and clear as a newly minted gold dollar tossed onto a bar counter.

Time for the final assertion, thought Peter. His final shot. The trump card of every exorcism: the power of Jesus and his authority.

"By the authority of the Church and in the name of Jesus, I command you to tell me what I shall call you."

Peter kept his voice level as he issued the challenge. All his hopes rested on the acceptance of that challenge. Rejected, the challenge could only result in further distortions of Marianne. At this stage, Peter knew she could not take much more. But there could be no turning back now. And to break off was total defeat. He could feel the nervousness in his assistants: all and everything in the room reflected the tension of the moment. Peter knew, and each one present knew, he had issued a final challenge.

"You command!" Now Marianne sounded amused, as though Peter had told a joke. He kept reminding himself that this was not Marianne, but the spirit using her voice. Still his heart sank a little. "I am us," he heard her say. "We are me. Isn't is? Aren't are? What we are called is beyond human mind."

We! Peter was riveted by that key word. Only those of the Kingdom used it. Peter knew instantly that he was almost there and he had no intention of allowing the Presence to identify again with Marianne, so he broke in brusquely.

"There is no immunity for you and your kind in the universe of being."

The calculated and cold ruthlessness, a new note in Peter's interruption, brought the ex-policeman up sharp. Years of experience had given him a sixth sense for lethal threat and attack, for hatred and open disgust. He had heard many a cop speaking to arrested murderers in that tone, and many a killer behind bars telling of his hatred in as controlled a way as Peter was using now. He looked at Peter's face. It had changed. Something subtly merciless had lodged there.

Peter continued: "You, all of you, are . . ."

"*You,* you, you have no particular immunity, my friend." Marianne's emphasis was exact as she broke in. Nicely calculated. Just heavy enough to make one uneasy. Too light to betray any ripple of annoyance or fear.

A vague uneasiness ran through Peter's assistants; they moved spontaneously nearer him. The Presence was getting to them. For all his instructions to them before the exorcism began, he knew there was no way to prepare them for the shock, the fear, the onslaught.

Marianne's body was utterly still, her face pasty white, her lips barely open. After a pause, her voice continued with the merest edge of sharpness: "You may have polished your knee balls in a Confession Box"—this with a sneering inflection—"but you were not sorry, friend. Not always, anyway. So where is your repentance? And need I tell you, priest, without repentance, you have sins still? And you! You command the Kingdom?"

In his memory Peter heard Conor's caution: "What happened in pahst histhoree, happened. The recorrd shtands. Ferivir. Loike a shtone 'n a feeld, opin 'n' maneefist. Fer awl teh see, me bhoy. Incloodin' the Grate Panjandhr'm hissilf. No, don't deny it. Wallow in humilitee."

"How shall we call you?" Peter persisted.

"We?" Sarcastically, but calmly.

"In the name of . . ."

"Shut your miserable mouth . . ."—it was suddenly an animal growling the words. "Close it! Shut it! Lock it! Fuck it!"

". . . Jesus. Tell us: how shall we call you?"

Then a low, long cry came from Marianne's lips. All in the room held their breath as the Voice gurgled and they made out the words with difficulty: "I will take my toll. I will take our pound of flesh. All 142 pounds of him! I will take him with me, with us, with me!" Complete silence. Then Marianne's voice: "Smiler. I just smile."

Peter glanced at her face. The name was obvious, now he knew it. The twisted smile was back on her mouth. Now, he realized, he had to deal with the most ancient of man's tempters and enemies: the hater who deceived you with a smile and a joke and a promise.

The cleverness of it. How could you suspect or attack someone called Smiler? And if they just smile at anything you do, what *can* you do? The whole thing—God, heaven, earth, Jesus, holiness, good, evil—becomes a mere farce. And by the evil alchemy of that farce, everything becomes an ugly joke, a cosmic joke on little men who in their turns are only puny little jokes. And, and, and . . . the utter banality of all existence, the wish for nothing.

He wrenched his mind away from this dead blanket of depression and concentrated again. This was the meeting point with Marianne.

"You, Smiler, you will leave, you *shall* leave this creature of God . . ."

"This annoying affair has gone on long enough." The words had a smirking quality overlaid with pomposity. "Marianne has made her choice." Peter's inner reaction was: We are almost there. Marianne's voice continued: "You understand better than these oafs do. After all . . ."

". . . because love is all there is needed . . ." Peter continued.

"... her life is short, as is yours. She takes what she can, as you ..."

"Because love is all there is needed." Peter repeated himself. But the monologue by Smiler went on uninterruptedly.

"... take it with your arrogance."

"And you, Smiler, you rejected love." There was a sudden break in the exchange. For a split second Peter waited. "We came from love," he started again. But that was as far as he got.

"LOVE!!!" The word was fired out at him like a pistol shot. The assistants bent toward Marianne, expecting violence in the wake of that shriek. Peter straightened up, not in suspense, not as though expecting more. Conor had said never trade shouts but let outbursts run their course.

But there was no more shouting. It was the violence of the loathing in Marianne's voice that was physically painful to Peter, as it continued on studiously and quietly: "Yes ..." A trailing pause, as if ruminating. Then: "Ah! Sixty-nine. Right? A handy image!"

Peter winced at the tone and the mental picture. His memory was wilting his effort, and he prayed.

But Marianne went on with unruffled mercilessness as if reciting from a technical report. "And first the tongue, its apex like a single wet pink eye with a white iris, goes exploring: sliding its dorsum over each groin, every epithelial cell registering the ripples of the musculus gracilis, following the tautened adductor longus, summoning saliva to glisten its course toward the darkling mountain, the mons veneris. Her saphena majora rustles and tickles with rushing blood."

A retort rushed to Peter's mouth. He held it back.

Marianne continued. "Then, at the os pubis it lingers, all its papillae hungry, tensile, wet. Filiform cries to fungiform, fungiform to circumvallatae, circumvallatae to foliatae; 'On! Brothers! On!'

The doctor whistled through his teeth and glanced at Peter. But Peter was dangerously abstracted from the scene. He could hear Mae's sigh, that long-distant day in the sunshine, miles and decades apart from this evil encounter; he could see her lying on the slope of the sand dunes, felt one hand lying lightly on his belly. And then he had the wisping image of her lying in her coffin just before it was closed forever.

Inexorably the recital went on. "Amid his moans and her heaving, the tickling in his sacrum (ah! Resurrection Bone! Those rabbis had a word for it!), through his thighs; the corpus cavernosum fills up with thick red-black blood. The tongue stabbing within, and she closing around it, holding it.

Smiler was now using Marianne's voice in a soft, matter-of-fact tone. There was a short pause of seconds. Then, with a burst of fierce contempt:

"He is fucking her. And like the hyena with a dead deer"—the voice rose to a scream—"he starts with her anus, and she like a mother snake is swallowing her son. LOVE?????" A piercing, shattering scream. The voice fell to a sneer: "Cunni-cunni-cunni-cunni-cunni! Peter the Eater." Then casually, as one asks the time of day: "Tell us, Peter. Are you sorry? Do you miss it?"

Marianne's father had his face buried in his hands; his shoulders heaved with sobbing. The ex-policeman and the banker stared red-faced at Peter. His young colleague leaned on the night table, his face ashen. The tirade, like a great, sprawling canvas, had thrown a mass of screaming colors and nonsensical patterns of thought and feelings over them all.

The doctor reacted more quickly than the others: "Peter, can we pause?" He was apprehensive, seeing the bloodless color of Peter's face and a distracted look in his eyes. Peter gave no answer.

Smiler, the cosmic joker, smears and tears at everything, Peter was thinking to himself, as he ruminated and groped toward his next step. Smiler, who turns memories to dirt and chokes you with them. But then he's not subtle. And he's not clever. Peter thought: This is either a trap for us, or we have Smiler trapped. Which?

He found himself reacting by instinct: "Silence! Smiler! Silence in the name of Jesus! I command you to desist, to leave her. Tell me that you will obey, that you will leave her. Speak!"

The other men in the room glanced at Peter, surprised at the force in his voice. The verbal assault had left them raw, ashamed of something vague, with a feeling that they had been filthied. They had expected Peter to wilt, to have been crushed. They had been willing to lose hope.

But now they took something from him. They sensed what he knew, saw it on his face, and almost heard him telling them: "I may be engaged in this to my own humiliation. But Smiler is equally engaged in it and there is no escape for him. Just hold on."

Smiler spoke, but as if Peter had never spoken. "Well! Here we have a thing never seen in the Kingdom"—the voice calm again—"a little drop of sea water pulls a little membrane around it and rots for a million years on an ancient, forgotten shore, and sprouts little hair-trigger nerves and puny little earthen mechanisms, and stands up on two spindly limbs one day, and says, 'I am a man,' and lifts its snout to skies above and says again, 'I am so beautiful' . . ."

"Silence! Desist!"

"You ugly sod! You smelly little animal . . ."

"And let the soul of Marianne be beautiful once more with the grace of . . ."

"Beautiful?" For the first time, the voice was raised almost an octave higher. "Beautiful?" Now it was a shrill, high-pitched, and painful scream of questioning scorn. "You helpless, yelping, puking, licking, slavering, sweating, excreting little cur. You whipped mongrel. You constipated shit canister. You excuse for a being. You lump of urine and excrement and snot and mud born in a bed on bloody sheets, sticking your head out between a woman's smelly legs and bawling when they slapped your arse and laughed at your little red balls"—the scream of high-decibel invective ceased suddenly, followed by three syllables pronounced calmly and with loathing contempt—"You creature!"

"And so are you, too. You creature." Peter surprised himself at his own self-possession: his adversary had made a mistake, and Peter knew it. Peter also surprised himself with the contempt he found himself putting in to his riposte.

He continued: "Once nothing. Then beautiful. The most beautiful of all God made." The bitter taunt in Peter's voice turned every head but Marianne's in his direction. He went on lashing and provoking. "Then ugly with pride. Then conquered. Then thrown from the heights like a dying torch."

A low roar issued from Marianne's mouth.

Peter went on unabashed; he had his adversary exactly where he wanted him: "And expelled, and disgraced, and condemned, and deprived forever, and defeated forever."

Marianne's body quivered.

"Hold her down!" he muttered to his assistants. Just in time. She was shaking violently. The roar was now the bellow of a pig with a knife gouging out its jugular in gobs of blood.

Peter piled it on: "You, too, creature of God, but not saved by Jesus' blood."

Again the long, howling wail.

As its sound died away, Peter's whole body was electrified with fear.

At that instant the Presence launched its hate again. Like a physical thing, it attacked him. It sent stinging talons into his mind and will, stabbing deep at the root of his determination, at some inner sensitive, delicate part of him where all his pain and all his pleasure lived.

This was the Clash that Conor had analyzed so well for Peter. This was the climax of his one-to-one struggle. Peter made the sign of the cross. He knew: now one of them had to yield; one would be victor. He had to hold. He had to refuse to despair. Refuse disbelief. Refuse damnation. Refuse fear. Refuse. Refuse. Refuse. Hold on. These came like automatic commands to him from his inmost self.

His first desperate thrust was to switch his mind toward any lifeline—any beauty or truth he had known and experienced: the cry of seagulls off Dooahcarrig in Kerry; the rhythmic pattern of nimble feet at winter dances; Mae's smile; the security of his father's house; the calm summer evenings he had spent off the coast of Aran Island looking at the Connemara mountains behind Galway City, purple masses welling up in a shining gold vault of sky in haze.

But as quick as any image arose, it dried like a drop of water in a flame. All his internal images of loyalty, authority, hope, legitimacy, concern, gentleness shriveled and faded. His imagination was burning with an overheated despair and his mind could not help him. Only his will locked both mind and imagination into an immobility that pained and agonized him.

But then the Presence turned silently on his will in a slash of naked adversity. For the others present, there was little to go on: no sound except Peter's heavy breathing and the shuffling of their legs as they endeavored to keep their balance and hold Marianne down; no sensation beyond the straining of Marianne's body against their hands.

The attack on Peter was a fury beating like sharp hailstones on a tin roof, filling all his awareness with a ceaseless din of fears that paralyzed his will and mind. If only he could breathe more easily, he thought. Or if only he could pierce that contempt.

Dimly he saw the candles sputtering on the night table and glinting on the crucified figure on the cross.

"Rimimb'r, lad, his proide. That's his weak heel. His proide! Git him on his proide!"

With Conor's voice in his memory, Peter blurted: "You have been vanquished, vanquished, Smiler, by one who did not fear to be lowly, to be killed. Depart! Smiler! Depart! You have been vanquished by a bloodied will. You cheat. Jesus is your master . . ."

The others present heard him croaking the words as they held Marianne down on the bed. A babel set in: everyone was affected. The chest of drawers rocked noisily back and forth, its handles clanked discordantly. The door to the room swung and banged, swung and banged, swung and banged. Marianne's body shirt split down the middle, exposing her breasts and middle. Her jeans tore at the seams. Her voice rose louder and louder in a series of slow, staccato screams. Great welts appeared across her torso, groin, legs, and face, as if an invisible horsewhip was thrashing her unmercifully. She struggled and kicked and heaved and spat. Now she was incontinent, urinating and excreting all over the bed, filling their nostrils with acrid odor.

Peter kept murmuring: "He vanquished you. He vanquished you. He vanquished you . . ." But the pain in his will struggling against that will began to numb him; and his throat was dry. His eyes blurred over. His eardrums were splitting. He felt dirty beyond any human cleansing. He was slipping, slipping, slipping.

"Jesus! Mary! . . . Conor," he whispered as his knees buckled, "it's all lost. I can't hold. Jesus! . . ."

Seven thousand miles away across ocean and continent, in Rome, the doctor nodded to the nurse as he stepped out of Father Conor's room. He told the father superior there was no point in calling the ambulance. The damage was too massive this time. It would be a matter of mere hours.

It was Conor's third stroke. He had been fine all that evening. Then in the small hours of the morning, he had called his superior on the house phone from his room: "Fatherr, I'm goin' teh cause yeh throubel agin." When they reached Conor, they found him slumped over his desk, his right hand clutching a crucifix.

"Father, it's all right. It's me. It's all over."

Peter's younger colleague helped Peter to his feet. Peter had fallen on his knees and bent over until his forehead touched the floor. By the bed, Peter saw the doctor was listening to Marianne's heartbeat with a stethoscope. Her father was stroking her hand and talking to her through his tears: "It's all right, my baby. It's all right. You're through. You're safe, baby. It's all right."

The bank manager had gone outside to talk with Marianne's mother and brother. Marianne was quiet now, breathing regularly. The bed was a shambles. The ex-policeman opened the window, and the sounds of traffic entered the room. It was around 10:15 P.M.

"I must phone Conor early," Peter said to his colleague. Then, "I wonder what else happened today?" He looked over at Marianne again. "Zio's visit can't be all."

Father James looked at him dumbly, not catching the train of his thought. He would never understand exorcists, he felt.

Then Peter continued: "Is it because love is one throughout the world, and hate is one throughout the world?" Peter addressed the seeming vague question to no one in particular.

The younger priest turned away from the pain he saw on Peter's face; it was more than he could take just now. "I will get you some coffee," he said brusquely, feeling the hot tears at the back of his own eyes.

But Peter was looking out the window at the night sky. His mind was far away, his senses almost asleep with fatigue.

Down below Marianne's window, the crowds were returning from Yankee Stadium. Zio at that moment was standing in a darkened gallery of the Vatican Pavilion at the New York World's Fair, gazing at Michelangelo's *Pietà:* the dead Jesus in the arms of his mother. Television cameras carried his voice to millions that night: "We bless all of you, invoking upon you an abundance of heavenly blessings and graces."

Father Bones
and Mister Natch

The marriage was to take place at 8:00 A.M. on the Massepiq seashore, just around Dutchman's Point, New England. It was already a bright and sunny March day at 7:30 A.M. as the first guests arrived. A landward breeze, like the breath of the sun from the East, blew clusters of white clouds across the blue morning sky and juggled the sea with ripples. The tide, almost fully in and about to ebb, was like a formless giant exhaling and inhaling. It sent wave after wave in an unbroken flow to the long shoreline. Each one broke there with a sharp tap on the sand, spread out a running tapestry of whitened water with a rustling whisper, and then was sucked rasping back over sand and pebbles.

This music of the waters and the thin piping of the wind was a quiet but powerful rhythm that ebbed and flowed, uninterrupted by any other sound. As the guests came, they fell under its spell. It was the voice of a very ancient world that had always existed, always moved, and now seemed to be putting them, the intruders, on notice: "This is my world you have entered. But since this is the morning of man and woman, my children, I will pause a while. This is a new beginning."

It was, in fact, exactly the sort of morning that Father Jonathan had hoped for. Everything was natural. The only perfume was the air, crisp with a little chill, fresh with salt, exhilarating with light. The only sanctuary was the sharply shelving beach, with the sand dunes behind it, the sea in front of it, its roof the wide dome of the sky. The only altar was formed by the barefoot bride and bridegroom standing where the waters spread a constantly renewed carpet of foam and spindrift around their feet. The only music was the sounding sea and breeze. The only mystery was this beginning undertaken by two human beings in view of an unseen future.

Father Jonathan arrived last. Punctually at eight he began the ceremony. Barefoot like the bride and the bridegroom, wearing a white sleeveless shirt over his denims and a gold-colored stole around his neck, he stood at the edge of the tide, the sea to his right and the land to his left. In front of him stood Hilda and Jerome, the boy and the girl to be married, both in their early twenties. She, in a white ankle-length dress gathered at her waist by a belt woven of long grasses, her hair parted in the middle, falling down on her shoulders. He, wearing a white shirt over blue shorts. Their faces were quiet and calm, swept clean of any trouble.

Hilda and Jerome had their eyes fixed on Jonathan's as he began to speak in a loud and exulting voice which, bell-like, carried to the ears of the 40 or so people standing some yards away at the edge of the sand dunes. "Here on the sand by the sea, here where all great human things have always begun, we stand to witness another great beginning. Hilda and Jerome are about to promise each other to each other in the greatest of all human beginnings."

A pleasant sense of anticipation ran through the listeners. Athletic, bronzed, graceful, deliberate in his movements, taller than either the boy or the girl in front of him, golden hair touching his shoulders, Jonathan was in complete, even dramatic command of the situation. His eyes had the peculiar blue sheen you cannot believe to be natural until you see it. A fire of blue seemed to burn in them, giving off a hypnotic brilliance. They lacked the warm sentiment of brown eyes; but a burnished patina prevented you from reading them, and this created their mystery.

Only one thing marred Jonathan's appearance. As he gestured grandly and raised his hand in an initial blessing, some of the guests noticed it: his right index finger was crooked. He could not straighten it. But it was a little thing swallowed up in the golden-blue morning, in the blaze of Jonathan's eyes, in the lilt of the moving sea.

As Jonathan's voice rang out, and nature kept up its endless rhythm in apparent unison, only one person seemed incongruous. He stood at the back and to one side of the guests, staring intently through Polaroid glasses at the boy and girl. Lanky, clad in sweater and slacks, with both hands thrust in his trousers pockets, he was the only one wearing a hat, a black hat.

"Funny character. Wonder who *he* is?" Jerome's father whispered to his wife. But the parents forgot about him momentarily, and no one else particularly noticed him as Father Jonathan's sermon reached its climax before the actual vows.

". . . both are entering this mystery. And both are mirrors of nature's fullness—its womb, its fertility, its nurturing milk, its powerful seed, its supreme ecstasy, its nestling sleep, its mystery of oneness, and the long mysteries of the immortality it alone confers—if we are one with nature and participants in its sacrament of life and of death. As the perfect man, Jesus, our model, was."

The man in the black hat stirred uneasily, leaning forward to catch every detail, all the while his eyes on the boy and the girl.

Father Jonathan flung a smoldering gaze over the guests to his left. "Many have sought to rob him, our supreme example, of his human value for us." His voice throbbed with deep emotion. "To cap his glorious life with a weak, milk-and-water ending. What is all this dreadful chicanery of his supposed resurrection but a cheat? If he died, he died. Completely. Really. What sort of sacrifice and therefore what sort of love for us was there if he died to live again? Thus to rob the sacrifice of its very sting and its true glory and to rob him and us of all true human nobility—is not this the cruel joke of the happy ending they have attached to his heroic death? He, the supreme hero? Making a Grimm's fairy tale out of the greatest story ever told.

"You, Jerome and Hilda," again looking at them with pride, "you will love his mystery of human unity; and, in time, like him, you will face death as he did, human, noble, and go back to nature, to be cemented into its eternal oneness where Jesus went with bowed head but triumphant."

By now the man in the black hat had moved in front of the little crowd of guests.

Jonathan launched into the marriage ceremony proper. "Look now, Hilda and Jerome, all nature is going to pause for one brief instant to witness your vows." A sweeping gesture took in all the scene, the crooked index finger jabbing oddly askew. "All things, the wind, the sun, the sea, the earth, all will stop in their ways . . ."

Jonathan broke off. He seemed to be having difficulty in drawing his breath. He gulped. His face flushed with the effort to continue. Then he managed to take up again, dictating word for word to Hilda.

"With all my heart, I do take you . . ."

"With all my heart, I do take you," Hilda echoed in clear, confident tones.

"As my honored husband . . ."

"As my honored husband . . ."

"Within the mystery of nature . . ."

"Within the mystery of nature . . ."

"To have and to hold . . ."

"To have and to hold . . ."

"In life and in death . . ."

"In life and in death . . ."

"As God's womb and pleasure . . ."

"As God's womb and pleasure . . ."

"For the glory of our humanness . . ."

"For the glory of our humanness . . ."

"As Jesus before us . . ."

"As Jesus before us . . ."

"World of living and dead . . ."

"World of living and dead . . ."

"Amen."

"Amen."

Hilda slipped the ring onto Jerome's finger. The guests stirred. Some had become unaccountably tense and could not take their eyes off Jonathan. Afterward, some remarked that it was as if a disfigurement had begun to show through in him.

The man in the black hat, now in front of the dunes and apart from the crowd, still watched intently.

Jerome looked at Jonathan and waited for the words of his vow to Hilda. Hilda's eyes were on Jerome. All nature, indeed, had seemingly stopped for her. For the first time she felt at one with life, with the world, with her own body.

Jonathan was again struggling with some impediment. His body was stiff. His chest swelled. At last he was able to fill his lungs, and he started to dictate Jerome's words.

"With this ring . . ."

"With this ring . . ." Jerome took up the words.

"I do take you . . ."

"I do take you . . ."

"As my dearly beloved wife . . ."

"As my dearly beloved wife . . ."

"As you have given me . . ."

"As you have given me . . ."

"The wonder and the mystery . . ."

"The wonder and the mystery . . ."

Jerome waited for the next line. But Jonathan was suddenly again almost purple with effort. His blue eyes were bulging now, showing large, terror-ridden whites. His hands, which had been folded across his chest solemnly, now were tensed by his sides, opening and shutting convulsively. He opened his mouth and rasped: "Of being one with nature . . ."

"Of being one with nature . . ." Jerome repeated.

"And—and—and . . ." Jonathan stammered.

Hilda's head turned in alarm. Jonathan's voice was climbing on each syllable toward hysteria. It seemed that every other sound had died out, as everyone hung on Jonathan's words.

"And—of be-being one with Je-Jes-Jeeeesus"—Jonathan's voice broke into a screeching crescendo that split the air. "JESUS!" The name was a curse cracking on every ear. His face twisted into an ugliness that froze Hilda with horror.

In a flash Jonathan was on top of Hilda, his outstretched arms catching her under the arms. Now, in his onrush, he was carrying her out bodily into the water, groaning and muttering wildly to himself. He pushed her head down, keeping her face beneath the surface and straddling her body as she kicked and struggled.

The lightning speed of Jonathan's actions and their crazy incongruity had frozen everybody. For a split second they did not grasp what was happening. Then a woman screamed with the unmistakable, high-pitched warning of mortal danger.

Within seconds half a dozen men ran and tore Jonathan's hands away from Hilda, struck him across the neck, lifted him off her, and threw him full length on the beach. He lay there thrashing and kicking for a moment, then went still.

Jerome and Hilda's father lifted Hilda clear of the water; she was gasping for air and sobbing, her long dress trailing rivulets of sand and water. They laid her down on the high ground among the sand dunes, her head pillowed on her mother's lap. Gradually she recovered her breath, crying uncontrollably. Jerome knelt by her, dazed, his mouth open, his face utterly white, incapable of any word.

Down on the beach, Jonathan lay flat on the sand. He stirred and groaned, turning over on his side. Then, lifting himself up on one

elbow, he clambered slowly and fitfully to his feet and swayed
unsteadily. His back and side were caked with sand. The water still
dripped from his long hair and his clothes. His eyes were bloodshot.
His head was lowered. He blinked in the sunlight at the hard stares of
the guests ranged around him. He was at bay.

Nobody said anything at first. Then a sharp, metallic voice broke in.
"If you will allow me, sir," addressing Hilda's father, "I am in charge
here now, sir." The authority and confidence in that voice attracted all
eyes to the speaker. It was the strange man, his black hat off now,
revealing a lean, not quite youthful face full of lines, beneath a full
head of gray hair tousled by the wind. He removed his sunglasses and
with a limp came closer to Jonathan, looking steadily at him. Then he
said quietly: "You and I have an important appointment now, Father
Jonathan." He paused; then, with a fresh edge to his voice, "The
sooner the better." The black hat was on his head again. He stretched
out his hand to Jonathan.

No one spoke. No one objected. Perhaps all were relieved that
someone was taking over.

The man spoke again. "The sun will be high in a couple of hours.
We have work to do that will not wait. Come!"

Jonathan blinked for a moment. Then shakily he put the hand with
the crooked finger into the other man's open palm. They turned their
backs on the sea. Hand in hand, Jonathan stumbling and swaying, the
other man limping, they walked up over the dunes and across to the
dirt road where the cars were parked, and stopped by a station wagon.

They stood there for a moment. The guests could see the man
talking to Jonathan. Jonathan, half-bent and leaning on the door
handle of the station wagon, was listening, his head bowed. He nodded
violently. Then they both got in.

As the car moved off and the sound died away, someone spoke for
the first time. "Who was that?"

Hilda's father, his eyes filled with tears, watched the station wagon
as it disappeared down the road. "Father David," he muttered.
"Father David M. Everything is going to be all right now." He shook
his head, as if freeing his mind from an uncomfortable thought. "He
was right all along."

FATHER DAVID

At the time he led Jonathan stumbling away from the aborted seashore marriage in 1970, Father David M. ("Bones," as his students liked to call him) was a forty-eight-year-old priest, member of an East Coast diocese, professor of anthropology at a major seminary, and official exorcist for his diocese. He had already conducted four exorcisms himself and he had been assistant at five others. The first had been in Paris, where he had been assistant to an older priest; the others had been in his home diocese.

When David M. started his professional life as an anthropologist in 1956, he could not have dreamed that within ten years his knowledge of anthropology and his enthusiasm for prehistory would be the major reasons for his role as exorcist and later for his involvement in the bizarre case of Father Jonathan. Nor could he have dreamed even in that March of 1970, as the exorcism began, that it would lead him, first, to the most harrowing personal crisis of his life, and then to abandon anthropology as a study and a profession.

When David was born in Coos, New Hampshire's northernmost county, in 1922, the state, with a population of nearly half a million, was still a rustic farming community, very far removed from the sophisticated centers south in Boston and New York. Coos County in particular was still permeated with the Yankee traditions of hard work, thrift, sobriety; and it hearkened to the preaching of the evils of alcohol, the wisdom of paying cash for what you bought, of self-reliance, individual responsibility, and—as rock-bottom foundation of right living—the infallible, all-sufficient guidance and enlightenment of the Bible. Even today, when the central and southern tiers of the state have suffered from the malice of change, the land itself still carries for the mind the atmosphere of an ancient and undisturbed kingdom. In mountain, lake, cliff, and forest there is a repose as awesome as the naked weight of the Himalayas and the volcanic face of the Sinai Mountains.

David M. was the only child born of affluent Yankee Roman Catholic parents on both sides. He spent his early years on his father's farm, occasionally visiting the nearby town and, once in a while, traveling down to Portsmouth with his parents for a brief vacation.

The most abiding images David has of the world in his youth are of lakes, mountains, forests, cliffs, rock formations, valleys shaded by trees and crags, and the great, still stretches of land that surrounded his home. His ears still retain the harmonies riding in the place names of his home ground—Ammonoosuc River, Saco River, Franconia range, Merrimack Valley, and the lingering magic of Lake Winnipesaukee, whose 20 miles of length were clad in foliage, and the names of whose 274 islands he once learned to repeat by heart.

The Roman Catholicism of his parents was of a conservative kind and an intimate part of daily life. Both parents had been to college; his father had studied in Cambridge, England. Both had traveled in Europe. And their home was centered around the library and its large open fireplace, where they gathered after meals and where David spent long hours browsing through his parents' books.

Many of David's relatives lived in the surrounding countryside. His playmates were normally his cousins. His earliest memories of any intellectual awakening he traces to the influence of an uncle who, having taught history in Boston for 37 years, finally retired to live on the farm with his brother and sister-in-law, David's parents.

Old Edward, as they called him, personified for David the stability and permanence of his home; and he deeply influenced David's mental development. Edward spent most of his days reading. He stirred out of the house ritually twice a day; once, in the morning, to walk around the farm—rain, hail, or snow; a second time, after dinner, when he walked up and down in the shade of a little copse at the west end of the house, smoking his pipe and talking to himself.

David remembers going with Old Edward again and again to view the Great Stone Face, "The Old Man of the Mountain," high up on its perch above Franconia Notch. "No one knows how it came there, son," Edward used to remark. "It just happened. Man emerging from raw nature." It became a symbol in David's mind, and a preview of how he later came to think of man's origin.

Whenever David and his Uncle Edward visited the Great Stone Face, the ritual was always the same. Once in view of the "Old Man," they would sit down and eat lunch over a fire. Afterward, Edward would light his pipe and, staring at the pockmarked profile, start dawdling through the same conversational piece.

"Now, lad! Who do you think made it?"

"It just seems to come out of the earth and rock, sir," would be David's reply.

Sometimes Edward would bring a work of his favorite author,

Nathaniel Hawthorne. Having read an episode to David, he would discuss it with his nephew. *The Scarlet Letter* was his most frequent text.

"Why did Arthur die on the scaffold, lad, and with a smile on his lips?" he would ask.

After a while, David knew the expected answer: "Because, sir, he knew he had to pay for his sins."

And then: "Why did he sin, lad?"

"Because of Adam's Original Sin, sir," would be David's answer.

Once David ventured a question himself. "Why did Hester put the scarlet letter back again in her dress pocket, if it was a bad letter, sir?" The answer came with unerring relish: "She wanted to be romantic, lad. Romantic. That's what they called it." It was David's first introduction to romanticism, an issue that took very tangible and painful form for him later on. The evil spirit he exorcised in Jonathan had possessed Jonathan under the guise of pure romanticism.

When David was fourteen, he was sent to a prep school in New England but his vacations were all spent on the family farm in Coos County. His uncle still lived there; and together they went on several trips to New York, Philadelphia, Chicago, and Montreal.

It was, however, a trip to Salem, Massachusetts—made at his own request—that became of prime importance in David's mind. He was sixteen then. His uncle wanted to see the John Turner house, which had been immortalized by Hawthorne in *The House of the Seven Gables*. But David had been delving into a copy of Cotton Mather's *Ecclesiastical History of New England* that he had found in his father's library; and he was more interested in people such as Elizabeth Knapp, Anne Hibbins, Ann Cole, and other "witches" and "warlocks" of seventeenth-century Salem. So when they had visited the Peabody Museum and the Turner house, they spent an hour and a half in the "witch house" where Judge Corwin had examined the 19 men and women condemned and executed for witchcraft in 1692.

David realized later that his stay in and around the "witch house" had a special significance. As they moved around inside and outside the house, his uncle provided him with a running commentary on the 1692 trials.

All the while, David had a striking but not uncomfortable sensation or instinct that "invisible eyes," as he put it then to his uncle, or "spirits," as he puts it now, were present to him and communicating in an odd way. They seemed to be asking something. It was as if one part of his mind listened and recorded his uncle's commentary and the sights around him, while another part was preoccupied with other, intangible "words" and "sights."

Striking as the experience was at the time, it did not in any way obsess his thoughts in ensuing years. In fact, he never vividly recalled this Salem experience until 32 years later at Old Edward's death and again during the exorcism of Father Jonathan.

No one in David's circle of family and friends was surprised when he decided to enter the seminary in 1940. His father would have preferred an Army career for him; his mother had nourished a secret hope of grandchildren. But David had made up his mind.

After seven years, when he was ordained in 1947 at the age of twenty-five, the bishop asked whether he would be willing to go through some extra years of study. The diocese needed a professor of anthropology and ancient history. If he agreed, he would first earn a doctorate in theology: Roman authorities were chary of letting any young cleric loose in scientific fields without a special grounding in doctrine. It might not be easy or pleasant, because Rome did not think highly of American theologates. The whole program would take about seven more years of David's life.

In spite of the possible difficulties, David consented. The following autumn he started to follow theological courses in Rome; and then, in the autumn of 1950, he proceeded to the Sorbonne in Paris.

Like many others of that time, he had heard much about a French Jesuit named Pierre Teilhard de Chardin, but he had never been exposed to his thought. In Paris he fell under the direct influence of the ideas which Teilhard had generated. For postwar Catholic intellectuals, Teilhard was something of a phenomenon; and from the mid-1950s and on he enjoyed the reputation of a twentieth-century Aquinas, and evoked the type of personal devotion that only a Bonaventure and a Ramon Llul had attracted in earlier centuries.

French of the French, intellectual, ascetic, World War I hero, brilliant student, innovative teacher, mystic, discoverer of Pekin Man (Sinanthropos), pioneer excavator in Sinkiang, the Gobi Desert, Burma, Java, Kashmir, South Africa, Teilhard set out to make it intellectually possible for a Christian to accept the theories of Darwinian evolution and still retain his religious faith.

All matter, said Teilhard, is and always has been transfused with "consciousness," however primitive. Through billions of years and through all the forms of chemical substance, plant, animal, and finally human life, this "consciousness" had blossomed. It is still blossoming; and now, in this final stage of its development, it is about to burst forth in a final culmination: the Omega Point, when all humans and all matter will be elevated to a unity only dreamed by the visionaries and saints of the past. The key character of the Omega Point will be Jesus, asserted Teilhard. And so all will be gathered into all, and all will be one in the love and permanent being of achieved salvation.

By 1950, when David arrived in Paris, Teilhard and his doctrines had become too much for the Roman authorities with their long memories. Teilhard's critical eyes, his ready flow of language, his Gallic logic, his constant ability to answer inquisitorial questions with a flood of professional and technical details, his refusal to kowtow intellectually, and his very daring attempt to synthesize modern science with the ancient faith—all this frightened ecclesiastical minds. It was not only Teilhard's aquiline nose that reminded the authorities of his eighteenth-century ancestor, Descartes, whose ideas they still considered anathema. It was as well, and chiefly, Teilhard's attempt to rationalize the mysteries of Catholic belief, to "scientize" the Divine and make the truths of revelation totally explicable in terms of test tubes and fossil remains.

Teilhard: dedicated to the "clear and distinct ideas" of Descartes, the father of all modern scientific reasoning; fired inwardly by the personal ideals of Ignatius, father not only of all Jesuits but of all the lone and the brave; lured onward by the mystical darkness of wisdom celebrated by his favorite author, John of the Cross, whose pains he shared but whose ecstasy ever escaped him; honed and refined in intellect by the best scientific training of his day; Teilhard was the custom-built answer, the ready-made darling for the bankrupt Catholic intellectuals of his century and for thousands of Protestants caught in the heel of the hunt by the vicious clamps of that merciless reason they had championed as man's glory some four centuries previously. Teilhard was, at one and the same time, their trailblazer and their martyred hero. For the tired and besieged French and Belgians he produced shining shibboleths to cry and a new pride to wear. He fanned into a blaze the cold fire that slowly burned in the brains of innovation-hungry Dutch and Germans. He nourished the ever-latent emotionalism of Anglican divines, who by then were floating free of traditional shackles.

His new terminology (he was the author of many current neologisms), his daring thought, his scientific panoply, his international reputation, his refusal to revolt when silenced by chicanery, his long vigil, his obscure death, and finally the flashing wonder of his posthumous fame and publication, all this conferred on him, on his name, and on his ideas the efficacy once enjoyed by a Joan of Arc, a Francis Xavier, and a Simone Weil. When Rome would never canonize him, he was canonized by a new "voice of the people." He was a marvelous source of esoteric words and intricate thoughts for American pop theologians.

Very few realized that Teilhard's vision had ceased long before his death. He had provided Christians with only a respite between the long autumn of the nineteenth century and the winter that enshrouded everything in the late twentieth century. Teilhard was neither strong food to satisfy real hunger nor heavenly manna for a new Pentecost. He was merely a stirrup cup of heady wine.

Under Pius XII, the Roman Catholic Church of the post-World War II period was being constantly purged of "dangerous ideas." And Teilhard fell foul of the censors. He was silenced and exiled, forbidden to publish or lecture. Nevertheless, his ideas ran through the intellectual milieu of Europe and America like mercury. David with many others drank deeply of this wine of ideas and believed that they were on their way to a new dawn.

Of course, David knew from the start that he was destined for anthropology later on. Therefore, in Rome he concentrated on those theological questions which had a direct bearing on anthropology. He studied, in particular, the divine creation of the material world and of man, the Adam and Eve doctrine and that of Original Sin. He found that Church teaching was explicit: God had created the world, if not exactly in seven days, at least directly and out of nothing. There had been a first man, Adam, and a first woman, Eve. Both had sinned. Because of their sin, all other men and women—for all men and women who ever existed were descended from Adam and Eve—were deprived of a divine quality called grace. They were born with Original Sin. And this condition was only changed by the sacrament of Baptism.

David was troubled that doctrines stated in this way, even including all the refinements and modifications allowed, were extremely difficult to explain in the light of the theories of paleontology current in his time. And the greater the impact of science on the mind, the more dramatic the difficulty.

When the full weight of anthropological and cross-cultural studies was brought to bear on the question of human origins, a human being seemed to have a long and remote ancestry during which not merely his body was formed but what was called his mind and higher instincts were fashioned. And, of course, if you once admitted these beliefs and assumptions of "scientific" theory to be "facts," or even highly probable, the idea of God creating the human condition and sending his son, Jesus, to save it from its dire predicament, this central theme of all Christianity was up for auction to the highest bidder.

The genius of Teilhard was that his bid was as high as that of any non-Catholic or non-Christian in the field, to construct a bridge across such an impassable and impossible gap. And it was in view of this promise that David, along with a whole generation of men and women, adopted Teilhard's formulation.

But the fatal flaw was quick and sure. The creating god of Christians was no longer taken as divine. He became internal to the world in a mysterious and essential way. Jesus, as savior, was no longer the conquering hero irrupting into the human universe and standing history on its head. He was reduced to the peak of that universe's evolution, as natural an element in the universe as amino acids. The thrust that would finally bring forth Jesus in the sight of all men was an evolutionary accident—a kind of cosmic joke—that started over five billion years ago in helium, hydrogen gases, and amino acids of protean space. That thrust had no choice but to keep on thrusting until it gave birth to the refined and culminating flower of "full human consciousness" in the "latter days."

Like the Great Stone Face on Franconia Notch that David remembered so vividly from his visits with his uncle, Jesus now simply emerged from nature. The Omega Point. Only this would be the final hour of glory, the Last Day.

Neither David nor many others who spoke of the "greatest biological adventure of all time"—meaning human history—were alerted to the fact that, once the ancient beliefs of Christianity were interpreted in this fashion, it was a matter of time before other fundamental issues were affected, and very hard-nosed conclusions would have to be drawn. But present euphoria often beclouds later issues. Intellectual freedom has its own chains, its own brand of myopia. And a triumph of mere logic seems always to carry with it a neglect both of the human and of the essence of spirit.

In this ferment, David's mentality matured.

From those years spent in doctoral studies, David has two deeply personal memories. Both took place on the occasion of his Uncle Edward's death. It was during David's second last year at the Sorbonne that the old man, in his eighties by then, started to die. David had just arrived back in Paris from a field trip in southern France when he received a telegram from his father: Old Edward had not much time; he had asked for David repeatedly.

David caught a flight that evening. By the following evening he was back in Coos County on the family farm. Edward was sinking gradually, coming out of semicomatose states and lapsing back again.

Toward midnight of David's second day at home, he was sitting in Edward's room reading. His family had retired for the night. The room's only light came from the reading lamp on the desk where David sat. Outside all was quiet. A late wind sighed softly in the trees. Occasionally a very distant cry would echo from the surrounding countryside.

At a certain moment David raised his head and looked at Edward. He thought he had heard the sound of a voice. But the old man was lying still, breathing with difficulty. David went over, dipped a hand towel in a bowl of water, and mopped the perspiration from Edward's forehead. He was about to return to his chair when he again heard, or thought he heard, a voice—or voices—he was not sure. He looked at Edward: he was unchanged. Then he lifted his head and listened.

If he had not known better, he would have sworn that about half a dozen people were talking with low voices in the next room. But he knew that, except for his parents and one house woman, he was alone with Edward in the house.

Edward stirred uneasily and drew in a few quick breaths. His eyelids fluttered for a moment. He opened them slowly. His gaze traveled across the ceiling to the far corner of the room, then back again to David. "Can I help you, sir?" David asked. He had never addressed Edward in any other way. Edward gave a characteristic shake of his head which David knew so well from the past.

Almost immediately Edward went into a short death agony, inhaling long, deep breaths, exhaling laboriously, heaving his chest, and groaning. David pressed the bell to call his parents, knelt down by the head of the bed, and started to pray in a whisper.

But a motion of the old man's finger stopped him. Edward was trying to say something. David bent his ear down close to the dying man's mouth. He could barely hear the breathed syllables: ". . . prayed for them . . . I prayed for them . . . coming to take me home . . . you did not . . . lad . . . home . . . you did not . . . home . . ."

Those voices, David thought. Those voices. Men and women. When had he been with Edward and others when Edward had prayed for those others and he had not? Why would they need prayers? He could not get it out of his head that Edward had been talking about their visit to Salem. He did not see any connection. But he could not rid himself of the idea.

Edward expelled one long breath. His lips moved and twisted slightly. David heard a faint rattle in his throat. Then he found himself alone in that long, deadening, unbroken quiet when the dying is done. Edward's eyes opened to the glassy sightlessness of a dead man's look.

After they buried Old Edward, David stayed for a couple of days; then he went down to New York. He had one or two errands to do in the city, and he had a chance to meet Teilhard de Chardin. He brought with him a copy of Teilhard's *Le Milieu Divin* in the hope of an autograph.

The meeting with the French Jesuit was brief and poignant for David. The mutual friend who arranged the meeting warned David as they drove to meet Teilhard that the old man had not been well lately. "Let's make the visit brief. Okay?"

Teilhard was much thinner than David had expected. He greeted David affably but crisply in French, chatted for a few minutes about David's career as an anthropologist, then took the copy of his book from David's hands and looked at it pensively. As if making up his mind on the spur of the moment, he took a pen from his pocket and wrote some words on the flyleaf, closed the book, handed it back, and glanced at David. Teilhard's lips were pursed characteristically, his head slightly bent to one side and forward.

David noticed the strength of Teilhard's chin. But, much more, it was the expression in Teilhard's eyes that imprinted itself on David's memory. David had expected to see the long, deep look of a man who had traveled very far and thought very steeply of the deepest issues in life. Instead, looking at him across the humped curve of that aquiline nose, Teilhard's eyes were very wide open. They had no hint in them of memories or reflections, no remnants of Teilhard's own storms. There were no traces of any glinting intelligence. The old paleontologist was completely with David, totally present to him, taking in David's own glance with a personable expression and a direct simplicity that almost embarrassed the younger man.

After a few seconds, the older man said: "You will be true. You will be true, Father. Search for the spirit. But, even if all else goes, give hope. Hope."

Their looks held together for a moment more. Then they parted. Returning to the center of the city, David remarked to the friend who was driving: "Why in the end, or how in the end, did it become so simple for him?" His friend had no answer for him.

Suddenly, David remembered: what had Teilhard written on the flyleaf of his book? He opened it. Teilhard's dedication ran: "They said I opened Pandora's Box with this book. But, they did not notice, Hope was still hiding in one of its corners."

David was bothered for weeks after that meeting by a nagging idea that hope had become difficult for the seventy-three-year-old Jesuit. But after his return to Paris for the remainder of his courses at the Sorbonne, the sharpness of the incident faded temporarily to the back of his memory.

By the time David returned to the United States in June 1955, Teilhard had been dead for over two months.

When he did return to the United States, few of David's former associates and acquaintances could recognize the new intellectual man he had become. He was thirty-four by then, in robust physical condition. His six-foot frame was lean and well muscled. His friends did notice the premature grayness, the faint but definite lines of maturity around his mouth, the disappearance from his face of that youthful ebullience with which he had been clothed five years before when he set out for Europe.

Another look had replaced the ebullience: it was a certain "definitiveness," as one friend described it. David's eyes were fuller in meaning. He spoke just as pleasantly as before, but less casually and with an emphasis that conveyed more meaning than ever before. When he talked of deep matters, those around him felt that what he thought and said came from an inner wealth of experience and resources gathered carefully, marshaled in harmony, and kept bright and burnished for use. He had the "finished" look. And more than one elder colleague remarked, "One day, he'll be the bishop."

Before starting his lectures at the seminary, David spent one extra year in private study, visiting museums, and traveling to various parts of the world where paleontologists were working in the field. This extra year was invaluable to him; he had time to reflect on the condition of research, to catch up on his reading, to acquaint himself with professional colleagues in the field, and to examine the various diggings firsthand. Then, in mid-September 1956, he arrived home to Coos County for two weeks' vacation on the farm with his parents. The following October he started giving his first courses at the seminary.

The next nine years of his life passed uneventfully. From the beginning he was popular and highly thought of. The students conferred on him the nickname of "Bones" because of the fossils he kept in glass cases in his study.

In May 1965, he was again staying in Paris, attending an international convention. During the three weeks he was there, he was asked one evening by an old friend, a parish priest from a northern French diocese, to help out as a substitute assistant at the exorcism of a fifty-year-old man.

David had very little knowledge of Exorcism. Indeed, from his anthropological studies he was inclined to regard Exorcism as a remnant of past superstition and ignorance. Like any well-indoctrinated anthropologist, he could parallel the Roman Catholic Exorcism rite with scores of similar rites from Africa to Oceania and throughout Asia.

"No, Father David," the parish priest had answered him amicably when David had let the old man know that in his opinion Exorcism and satanic possession belonged to the world of invented myth and fable. "No, Father. This is not the way it is. Myths are never made. They are born out of countless generations. They embody an instinct, a deep community feeling. Fables are made as containers, fashioned by men deliberately to preserve the lessons they have learned. But this—satanic possession, Exorcism—well! come and see for yourself. At any rate, help me out."

In this exorcism David was substituting for a young priest who had fallen ill in the course of the rite. The exorcism had already lasted about 30 hours. "Just another couple of hours, and it is the end," the old parish priest had told him before beginning.

In fact, by the time David entered the case, the worst was over. After only two and a half hours more, the parish priest was about to complete the exorcism and expel the evil spirit. He asked David to hand him the holy-water flask and the crucifix.

At that point, and without warning, the possessed man became rigid. He screamed and jeered: "If you take it from him, Priest, we needn't leave. He has too many enemies. We needn't leave! He didn't help them when they asked him. We won't leave! We needn't leave!" Then a hideous, raucous laughter cackled at them all. The possessed man pointed a fine finger at David. "Hah-hah! Burnt. And he didn't pray for them . . . Father of hopelessness! Hah-ha!"

David's nerves were jangled. The parish priest took the crucifix and the holy-water flask himself and concluded the exorcism successfully. Afterward, he had a short chat with David. He calmed the young man, but added: "You have a problem. I don't know your life. I am sure God will solve it at home for you."

Back in his own diocese, David had a heart-to-heart talk with his bishop, who remarked on the change in David: no longer the self-confident, sometimes cocksure, always rather inaccessible intellectual he had known, David was now questioning and searching for internal peace, working through some puzzle he could not verbalize but which he felt entangling him.

David talked on, telling the bishop about the Paris exorcism and about his meeting with Teilhard years before.

"Well, have you some serious doubts about your orthodoxy as an anthropologist?" asked the bishop after a time. "Or rather, perhaps, I should phrase the question differently. Do you feel that the exorcism experience has opened something in you, some deficiency perhaps, which your anthropology and your intellectualism were only hardening and making permanent?"

"I honestly don't know," David answered. "There is the death of Old Edward. Why did I take his last words so seriously? I know they meant something personal to me. But I don't know exactly what."

"Look, David," the bishop finally said, "I will put you in touch with Father G., the diocesan exorcist. He has very little work, thank God. But he can help you one way or another—at least as far as the puzzle of that exorcism goes."

Father G. turned out to be a breezy character full of snappy little phrases and quick, jerky movements. "Okay, Father David, okay," was his comment on David's story. "You have a problem. I have no solution for problems except action. I'm not an intellectual. I failed every exam they gave me. But they needed priests in the diocese so they let me through. I can say a valid Mass and baptize babies at any rate, even if my Latin is awful. And I am a good exorcist. The next time we have a case of possession, I'll put you in the picture. Only concrete participation in this matter will help you."

True to his word, Father G. took David as his assistant exorcist in two cases of possession the following year. Both were relatively uneventful; at any rate, nothing personal to David occurred in either of them. David, however, underwent a continuing change within himself in the succeeding two years. His experience with the possessed man in Paris and with the two exorcisms at home had convinced him that, whatever was at stake in possession and exorcism, it was not a question either of myth or fable, or of mental illness. In addition, he had to keep struggling to make sense of his personal history. He kept stringing a few facts together, trying to make sense out of them.

There was, first of all, the dying conversation of his Uncle Edward about praying for "them" and their going "home," and David's own failure to pray for "them." Then there was Teilhard's "give hope" and his words on the flyleaf of the book. And, finally, there were the jeering words of the fifty-year-old man in Paris. On the face of it, he could not understand any of these things, and there seemed to be very little connection between them all. Yet David felt sure there was a connection, if he could only perceive it.

During a few vacations at home on the farm, he walked down to the cemetery where Edward was buried. He sat in the old man's bedroom. He hiked over to stand in the same place Edward and he had so often visited, and stood in full view of the "Old Man" of Franconia Notch. Once or twice after dinner, he strolled up and down the copse at the west end of the house and thought about Edward. He always felt calm and peaceful in that copse but could not understand why.

David's mother, who was always very close to her son and his moods, said briefly to him as he was departing for the seminary after one of those home visits: "David, some things take time. Time. Only time can help. Be patient. With yourself, I mean. And with whatever it is that is bothering you. Remember how many years it took Edward to arrive at his own peace."

David was grateful for these words and felt consoled. It was some sort of special message for him. But, again, there was the perplexing character of it: the consolation and the "message" character of her words yielded to no rational explanation. Just as the effect of the copse on him, or the significance of Edward's last words, or what precisely the possessed man in Paris had conveyed to him, or the strangeness he had discovered in Teilhard. The point was none of his knowledge and scholarship seemed to be of avail. The meanings of all these incidents seemed to flow from some source other than his intellect; they were foreign to his knowledge and his learning. And this disturbed him.

His students began to notice that the tone and, in part, the content of David's lectures changed. He was still as unrelenting as ever in his probings of traditional doctrines in the light of modern scientific findings. And he excused in no way traditional presentations of doctrines about creation and Original Sin.

But a new element caught their attention. "Bones" returned again and again to the data of anthropology and paleontology with phrases they had not heard him use before. "As long as we measure this solely with our rulers and our logical reasoning, we will find no cause for hope," he might say. Or: "In addition to the scientist's eye and the theologian's subtleties, we must have an eye for spirit." Once he ended a lecture on burial cults in Africa saying, in effect: "But even if you analyze all these data theologically and rationally, you have to be careful. You can do all that faithfully, and yet pass blindly by the one trace of spirit present in the situation." There seemed to be a note of regret in his tone at such moments.

Very few people—and this included his students, who generally got to know their professors intimately—very few knew that by this time David had been appointed diocesan exorcist. Father G. had been severely injured in an automobile accident and would never walk again.

David did not take his new post lightly. In his interview with the bishop when he accepted the post, he tried to get across a curious foreboding to his bishop. "I am changing," he said. "I mean I am slowly coming to a deep, very deep realization about what I have become over the years. It isn't that I have gruesome problems. Rather, it's as if I had neglected something vital and the time is coming when I will have to face it. Exorcisms have the effect of making this need more acute," he told the bishop.

"You, Father David, can never stop being useful to the diocese," was the bishop's remark.

"No. Of course not. That is, I hope not. But—" David broke off and looked past the bishop. He had the vaguest premonition. If only he could tie it down in words. "It may be, Bishop, that at the end of a couple of years . . ." He broke off again and stared out the window. Vaguely he saw the faces of two choices rising up. Yet they made no sense to him. He turned and looked at the bishop. "It may be that I will resign from my teaching job at the seminary."

"Let's take a chance on that," the bishop answered pleasantly, confidently.

JONATHAN

For three weeks in November 1967, David was on leave from the seminary. He was in New York dealing with the strange case of one of his own students, Father Jonathan, born Yves L. in Manchester, New Hampshire. By the time of his excommunication from the Roman Catholic Church, Yves had changed his name. He was fourteen years younger than Father David. Like David, he came from an affluent home and, for all practical purposes, was an only child.

Yves' father, Romain, was Catholic, French Canadian, originally from Montreal, and a doctor by profession. His mother, Sybil, a convert to Catholicism, was of Swedish parentage. Her first marriage, a childless one, had ended when she was twenty-seven years old, in the suicide of her husband.

Sybil was over forty and Romain was fifty-two years old when Yves was born. He had one half-brother, Pierre, by his father's previous marriage in Canada. Pierre's mother had died giving birth to him. When Yves was born, Pierre was twenty-eight, married, with children of his own, and living in New Jersey.

Before her first marriage, Sybil had taught in a private Swiss school. She had been educated at the University of Heidelberg, Germany, and had a doctorate in philosophy. She emigrated to Canada with her parents in the early 1930s. Yves' good looks obviously reflected his Swedish ancestry and particularly his mother's Nordic beauty.

His childhood was a happy one. Relations and friends who knew all three over many years always remembered how united they were as a family, though some remember the house as too adult and mind-oriented for a little boy. Under his mother's influence in particular, by the age of nine Yves was reading voraciously; and seven years later, at the year-end examinations, he astounded his school examiners by his detailed knowledge of English and American literature.

Yves' mother had a smoldering personality; she always conveyed the impression of deep and somber experiences within her. As with many converts, she was more Catholic than the Catholics themselves.

His father's religion was of a more popular and instinctual kind. His youth had been spent in northwest Canada. Later, David was to find out that the earliest images retained by Yves' father were more or less like David's own: of rugged nature, gargantuan proportions of sky and mountain and water, unbeatable and often cruel forces in the snow, the storm, the wind, and the inhospitable soil.

Yves' parents always remained devoted to one another, but sexual expression of that love stopped when Sybil underwent a hysterectomy after Yves' birth. Apparently a deep feeling of being wounded or deficient in her femininity took hold of her.

Romain, on the other hand, entered a religious crisis of acute pain during his wife's pregnancy. Partly because his wife's life was endangered by the pregnancy, and partly due to a fleeting affair he had during that time, he developed a constant fear that, because of the sins of his earlier years and the affair during his wife's pregnancy, he would lose his faith, die an unbeliever, and suffer the loss of eternal life in Heaven.

Yves never noticed any sign of his father's agonizing scrupulousness; and he did not realize until much later in life that the marital love of his parents had cooled very early in his childhood. Both parents were outwardly very loving in every way.

By the time Yves reached his teens, Sybil had become a kind, intelligent, and healthy woman. While no longer attached to what she called the mechanisms of sexuality, she was very aware of her love and sensuality, very graceful in her life, creative, but beyond ambition. Romain was a doctor known for his devotion and skill as well as for his sense of community duty. Father and mother had an unwritten pact of close companionship and intimate care for each other. It created a personal world of utter trust and undisturbed peace.

All in all, the atmosphere in which Yves grew up and in which he felt secure was an adult one permeated by values he felt more than he understood. Home life was inspired by sentiments he perceived and reproduced but which did not deeply express his own tastes and inclinations. Life with Sybil and Romain gravitated around unseen things that the immature Yves knew best by intuition but could not identify. There was an integrity of person and a graceful style in their living. There was strength of love and a solidity of judgment. But the viewpoint was narrow, too narrow.

Within that family Yves' values and personal ties—his parents, his school, his parish ambient, his friends—were held in place by solid moorings. He went to parish schools until he was eighteen. In retrospect, and as far as anyone can remember, there was no difference between him and the other boys of his acquaintance. He was excellent at sports and a very good dancer; he dated local girls, and moonlighted with another boy until they had put enough money together to buy a secondhand car.

He had only a few serious scrapes with the school authorities. It was never a matter of study—at that he was consistently beyond reproach. But now and then Yves would turn on one of his teachers in full view of the class in a fit of verbal abuse and uncontrollable rage.

He was always apologetic later, and his obviously sincere regret and winning smile generally had their effect; the school authorities forgave him easily. It probably did not hurt that his father was quite a prominent citizen, and that his mother was an active member of the parish, and that Yves won a state prize every year for his English essay, thus bringing honor to the school. He had a way with words and a touch of the poet that was beyond the ordinary. It helped him in his studies and in his scrapes.

By sixteen, Yves was an amateur painter, was writing poems to commemorate events at school and at home, was chosen to be his class valedictorian, and genuinely loved literature. By the time he was seventeen, he had decided to become a priest.

A final school essay written by Yves at the end of his last year reads today like a terrible prediction. In a precocious study of Shelley, Yves wrote: "But with all this beauty, no one can say what it would have done to the poet and the man had he lived beyond the age of thirty. Shelley pioneered a fresh idea of godliness. But it might—we will never know—have been a trap sprung by Job's Satan or Dante's Devil." Yves carried the essay around with him for many years, because he felt that in writing it he had perceived something very profound.

He owed his decision to become a priest largely to his parents' influence. Priesthood had been his father's first ambition in life; and he transmitted this frustrated wish to his son—not as a command or an obligation, but as an ideal. Yves knew from the age of seven that, in his father's eyes, the priesthood was the best, the highest, the most honorable profession. This is what his father conveyed by look, word, and attitude. His mother's influence was not so positive. It was more that, by looking down on any other occupation as secondary, she highlighted priesthood as the ideal and the goal.

The seminary Yves attended was the same one to which two years later Father David M. was posted. Yves was one of many seminarians and did not arouse any particular attention on David's part. His studies were, as usual, excellent. He had a very fine voice for chanting. He cut an impressive figure in ceremonial robes: over six feet in height, blond-haired, blue-eyed, with hands that were both masculine and beautiful. He was marked by a winsome grace and symmetry of movement; and, above all, he possessed a pair of eyes that radiated a striking luminosity and that had an almost hypnotic effect on people around him.

For all these reasons, Yves was the ideal actor in the liturgist's manual and the type for which every preacher's handbook was written. His knowledge of English and his good writing style helped him in the practice sermons he composed and delivered at the seminary.

In view of these talents, his interest in art and poetry was forgiven. In the atmosphere of any seminary during the 1950s, there was always a general suspicion of anyone interested in painting and literature—especially poetry. Roman Catholicism of that time regarded such things as "dangerous." The Church always had had difficulty in governing poets and painters; they sometimes were unwelcome prophets and discomforting commentators.

But Yves used his gifts well. He kept within the seminary mentality. He was careful, always careful.

One incident during his seminary years did disturb the authorities briefly. It was 1961. As always with Yves, he quickly overcame it. The occasion was Yves' final theological examinations, oral ones, conducted by three of his professors and presided over by a fourth, who would, if necessary, step in to arbitrate a dispute or cast a deciding vote in the assigning of grades. Generally, the moderator—as the fourth member of the examining board was called—had no part in the examinations and used the time to read a book or catch up with his correspondence.

This time the moderator was David. At one point in Yves' oral examinations, a heated dispute developed between one of the examiners, Father Herlihy, and Yves. Father Herlihy was questioning

Yves about the nature of the seven sacraments (baptism, confirmation, marriage, etc.), and he appeared to David to be angry. But it was Yves who drew David's closest attention—the handsome face drawn and haggard, mouth pulled tight in an obstinate grimace, perspiring forehead, eyes empty of their usual winsomeness. The change, so complete, so rapid, startled David and worried him. He could see none of the accustomed light, but only bitter resentment in Yves' eyes.

Yves finally was able to mumble out some sort of answer to Father Herlihy's questions, and ran quickly from the examination room as soon as time was up.

In his concern, David went along after the examination to Father Herlihy's study to discuss in greater detail exactly what had happened between him and Yves.

Apparently Yves had insisted at one point that all the sacraments were no more than expressions of man's natural unity with the world around him. According to accepted doctrine, this is heretical. The sacraments are believed to be the supreme means of union with God. Yves' words had implied that, after his death, Jesus had gone back to nature; and therefore the sacraments were our way of being one with Jesus in the earth, the sky, the sea, and the wide universe.

With his customary attention to detail, David wanted to know Father Herlihy's exact impression from Yves' words. "That was the funny part," Father Herlihy answered—and David never forgot his next words—"what he *said* was just foolish; but it was the peculiar *sense* he communicated to me; I seemed to be listening to something not quite human—I know it sounds foolish."

Afterward, David had deep qualms about the whole matter. In part, he blamed himself: he felt that his own lectures on creation and on the origin of man had something to do with Yves' reaction. Yves could have wrongly interpreted the Teilhardian doctrines David taught. With only a thin and fragile line between Teilhard's view and a total denial of divinity in Jesus, Teilhardian concepts were delicious mental playthings that could—David saw clearly for the first time—be used to exalt man as an animal, to make his world into a gilded menagerie, to reduce Jesus to the status of a Christian hero as grandly noble and as pitifully mortal as Prometheus in the Greek myth, and to picture God as no more than the very bowels of earth and sky and the spatial distances of the universe with all its expanding galaxies.

The incident continued to disturb David. Yves had conveyed merely by his looks during the exchange with Father Herlihy a sort of inner savagery and hate that David felt was out of kilter with Yves' normal demeanor. David had an instinctive suspicion of such sudden and dramatic breaks in the normal patterns of behavior. Perhaps it was merely a bad moment—and everyone has such moments. But if not, then that winning exterior and compatible behavior Yves ordinarily displayed must mask something else, some inner condition of spirit and bent of mind that no amount of seminary training had touched.

However, there the matter rested. The end of the school year was on them. Three weeks later Yves, with eleven others, was ordained to the priesthood. David himself was scheduled to leave for a vacation at home on the family farm, and then to proceed to Mexico City for an international conference of anthropologists. The incident was quickly forgotten for the time being.

When the summer was over, Yves was posted as assistant to an outlying parish of Manchester. He was near his hometown and within calling distance of his parents. For Yves' mother the new appointment was providential. Early in the new year, Yves' father, Romain, died suddenly from a heart attack. She would have been quite alone if Yves had not been posted to Manchester.

Yves' memory of the time span between September 1960 and January 1967 is clear and full of details. His recollections of 1967 are incomplete but still helpful in reconstructing what happened to him. From April 1968, when David made a first attempt to exorcise the evil spirit possessing Yves, until March 1970, when David concluded the exorcism, Yves' memory has large gaps. But his recollections, the notes and memories of David, together with the transcript of his exorcism contribute mightily to create a whole picture, a photomontage of how satanic possession started in one individual, gained ground, progressed continuously, and finally became as total as we can imagine it ever to be.

Possession by the spirit of evil proceeds along the structure of day-to-day life. In Yves' case, it used the priestly structure of his life, appearing first of all in the way he administered the Sacrament of Marriage, then in the way he said Mass, and finally in all his priestly activities.

In the Sacrament of Ordination, it is the whole man who is "priested." He does not simply acquire an extra function. He is not endowed with merely a new faculty or granted a rare permission. Rather, it is a new dimension of his spirit which necessarily affects all he does bodily and mentally. Any deformation of that dimension by the introduction of some antipathetic or utterly foreign element spells disturbance and trouble. The dimension of priesthood cannot be removed or replaced; it can be degraded, neglected, distorted.

Yves took up his duties in St. Declan's parish with apparent gusto. The work was not overwhelming. He had plenty of time for his own occupations. The parish bordered on the countryside; he had a view of the southeast from one window of his study and of the west from another. He rapidly became popular as a preacher in the parish, as a counselor for its younger members, and as a welcome visitor in the homes of the parishioners. At no time was there ever any question of his probity; he had no desire to accumulate wealth; he drank seldom; and those who knew him have always asserted that there was never in him the slightest deviation from his vow of celibacy. "A grand young priest" was the general judgment and impression.

When, after a couple of months, he had established a daily routine and found out what amount of time was needed for his official duties as an assistant, he started again to cultivate his two principal hobbies: painting and English literature. Once he made a trip to New York to talk with a publisher about a study of the poet, Gerard Manly Hopkins, and he returned home full of enthusiasm for the project.

It was toward the end of 1961, a little over a year after his arrival at St. Declan's, that the first traces of change became apparent in him.

On an average, Yves performed ceremonies of marriage three to five times every month. He seemed to add a special note of solemnity, joy, and celebration by his mere presence. His sermons on these occasions were beautifully delivered. And it thrilled everyone present to see this handsome and graceful young priest celebrating the love of the newlyweds within the purlieu of the Church's holiness and God's purity, and the Lordship of Jesus. For these were the themes on which Yves preached again and again in modulated tones and poetic language.

As time went on, however, Yves became more and more dissatisfied with the marriage ceremonial as prescribed in the *Roman Ritual*, the official handbook for priests that contains detailed instructions on how priests are to celebrate the various sacraments. He felt that the words and gestures assigned to the priest in performing a marriage ceremony were not merely outmoded, but that they did not convey what modern men and women thought and felt about marriage.

Above all, Yves found the actual words of the marriage vows more and more repulsive and irrelevant. Here he was, standing in front of two young people about to embark on a marvelous union and life together; and, as official representative of the Church, all he could tell them to do in the name of God and religion was to "stick it out," to stay together no matter what happened, until they were parted by death. Was that precisely what marriage partners promised each other? he asked himself.

In the beginning, he made no change in the words of the actual vows. But in his sermon at each marriage, he began to outline what the marriage partners did really promise to each other.

In the first sermons he insisted that the partners were giving each other what Jesus gave his Church. Jesus was the supreme model. Then, as he developed this theme, he began to say more explicitly what it was Jesus gave his Church.

Consciously now, Yves was drawing on what he had heard Father "Bones" say at the seminary and what he had thought out by his own reading of Teilhardian doctrines. Mixed with all he said were lines of poetry about Jesus which he applied to the bridegroom and the bride.

In these sermons Jesus was pictured by Yves as the summit of human development, the great Omega Point. He made all nature beautiful, including the bodies and the love of married people. Jesus was so dedicated to perfecting the material world that he was evolving as that world's peak of perfection. In the same total way that Jesus gave himself to this human world even to the point of dying like every living element in it, so the marriage partners should, Yves pointed out, adapt themselves to this world. They would find perfection primarily in each other, secondarily in other people around them, then in nature, in life, and finally in their dying and death.

All this was, of course, far from the normal teaching of Yves' Church, according to which Jesus does not depend on the material world in any way, and marriage is a sacrament which enables the partners to live their lives with supernatural grace and to achieve eternal life in heaven after death.

But the change in Yves' beliefs was not the strangest or most dramatic thing about this early "enigmatic stage" of his possession. What is relevant and striking is that Yves constantly found his thoughts and words "coming" to him. Sometimes, having spoken to the congregation in the church, he woke up to the fact that he had said this or thought that without having willed it or even been conscious of what he had done. It was not that his mind had wandered. It was a sort of "remote control."

In fact, Yves' first clear idea of what was happening within himself did not come because his clerical colleagues in the rectory and a few parishioners objected to some of his thoughts and expressions. They did, but this of itself did not bother Yves very much. He still relied on his charm and his words to get him out of any incidental difficulties.

That "remote control" which was to increase in him until it became paramount in his life—this was the first sign to him of something alien within him. It had become apparent to him at first during his free hours.

In his free time away from the church and his parish duties, Yves tackled painting and writing much as any other artist. He would be in the mood for painting or poetry. He would have some perceptions of color, line, form, or spatial dimensions. The perceptions burned in his imagination and inner sensibilities for some period of time. He would sit down to paint, for instance, while he thus burned inside with images, imaginings, flights of fancy and inner landscapes.

While doing initial drafts on canvas or paper, motivated by that not unusual activity of his imagination, he normally experienced a special inner perception which was always pleasurable. It was, Yves said, his mind and will gathering in and enjoying the fruits of his imagination. And there poured back into his imagination freshly burnished forms of what originally had entered through his senses.

It was these burnished forms he tried to depict on canvas or to express in his poetry. But even as he painted or wrote, he found his memory of past things reviving and lighting up like a panel, pouring assonances and shadings into his imagination. And his general effort suddenly expanded and became richer as he tried to reproduce the new form his experience had taken.

It was this rather normal creative routine that began to take a peculiar turn; and it was always in strict relationship to some exterior trouble or difficulty Yves had as a priest.

The most important occasion which he clearly remembers hinged upon a bit of unpleasantness with the senior assistant in his parish. In late September 1962, he had preached at a marriage. Afterward, the senior assistant of the parish, who had been present at the ceremony, admonished Yves about his sermon. "You are making marriage a merely human thing," he argued. "It is a sacrament, a channel of supernatural grace. The Lord Jesus is not going to evolve out of the earth or a woman's body or from gases in the upper atmosphere."

The rebuke was potentially serious, but Yves had talked his way out of it; the senior assistant was very firm, but he liked Yves, as everyone did. For his part, Yves wanted no trouble. He liked his post too much. But, afterwards, he had a deep surge of resentment about the whole matter.

The following day was his weekly free day. In the morning, while he was painting, the incident was still annoyingly in the forefront of his mind. But there was also a peculiarity which he was quick to notice and apparently powerless to prevent: he felt there were *two parts* of him or two functions going on at the same time in him, each of them *working in different directions*.

He went on painting, holding the brush, choosing colors, dipping, painting, standing back and returning to his easel and continuing to paint. All the while, the normal mechanism of his inner man was at work—imagination, memory, mind, will.

But all that while, too, another and parallel process was going on. His *imagination* was receiving data—images, impressions, forms—from some source other than the outside world. He knew this because they resembled nothing he had ever seen, heard, or thought. And then, too, it seemed to him that these images were not assimilated by his mind and will. Rather, they seemed to paralyze mind and will, to freeze them so that bit by bit they went fallow. An entire idea—he could not even make out its contours or details—was being "shoved" into his mind and forced into his will for acceptance.

He resisted the "push" of the idea; but it eventually invaded his mind and will through his imagination. And finally, as far as he could make out, he yielded. Then that grossly strange idea flooded back into his imagination with all its parts, reasons, and logic, there to be clothed in new images. His mind even supplied words for those images and sometimes, indeed, he found himself pronouncing these words in whole sentences.

After about an hour, on the first vivid and eerie occasion of this kind, he was shocked to discover that he was now painting in a strange and completely alien fashion compared to his normal way. His canvas had become a hodgepodge of his initial brushings, which he had intended to portray a street scene. On top of them was a crazy quilt of other forms and shapes—shadowy trees, rivers, irregular forms with legs, squares with ears, loops that ended in numerals.

When he resisted that inner "push" of ideas from that unknown source, his painting followed the normal course. But when he yielded, the hodgepodge started anew. He seemed to have become a means of translating into pictorial images some message or instructions or thoughts conveyed to him forcibly and not by his own choosing.

Yves felt alone and vulnerable. He was very disturbed. On an impulse he decided to drive out to see some friends in the country. But there was no letup. Along the way, he found he could no longer concentrate on his driving, so great and distracting was the force of all that was now pouring into him. He had to stop the car on the side of the road. He sat there and tried to keep his mind and will free of all those images and forms that were pounding at them from some source he could not identify.

But as he intensified his struggle, another element crept to the fore: his resentment about the previous day's argument with the senior assistant. When Yves yielded to the "push" of the idea being "shoved" into his mind, it brought with it some peculiar satisfaction in resentment. When Yves resisted, the resentment smoldered there and hurt him. In the brief pauses between these inner gyrations, Yves' mind dwelt on what he had said during the sermon and elaborated the ideas still further. He found intense satisfaction in this.

Eventually, as he sat beside the road, his planned visit with friends forgotten, he found himself yielding willingly to the "push" of the idea. And the moment he yielded, he felt immediate relief from an internal pressure and a deep conviction that his resentment against the senior assistant was justified: Yves had been right all along. He knew what was going on. Besides, he found his imagination and feelings once more chockful of inspiration which he knew would pour into his sermons, his painting, and his poetry.

Yves points to this experience as the moment "remote control" became a constant element in his life, because at that instant he accepted it willingly. It was, so to speak, the "consecration" of Yves' possession.

Once he voluntarily accepted it—and he insists today that he knew he was accepting some "remote" or "alien" control—he was suddenly inundated. He still had not moved from his car. All around him was soft-spoken countryside. But every sense—eyes, ears, taste, smell, touch—was saturated with a discordant medley of experiences. A riot of sounds, colors, odors, tastes, skin feelings washed over him. He could distinguish a certain rhythmic beat throughout this confusion and din. But he had no control and could not shake himself loose from these perceptions. Throughout, he felt a certain privileged awe, a secret pride. Then the storm in his senses gathered up inside him somewhere, absorbing utterly his imagination and memory. He now felt as if serpentine thoughts were touching the furthest reaches of his mind, and that fine tendrils were closing around each fiber of his will.

Slowly he began again to be conscious of the world around him. What had occurred had taken only moments, but for those moments he had been totally abstracted, walled up within himself.

Sound and light and shape now wafted back through the trellis of his senses, making him a newly aware observer of the world. He heard birds singing once more; he felt the sunlight on his face again. The coolness of the wind and the smell of morning-fresh grass and flowers became vivid for him. But now each lattice of sensation was filled by some coiling presence weaving slowly, possessively, with ease, lazily enjoying an acquired resting place in the shaded corners of his being.

For a brief instant, there was some echo of resistance in him. Some ancient voice protested in dim tones. Then it ceased. Yves "let go," and all tension fled. He was at peace for the first time in many years. And he felt renewed. There was a sudden ease throughout his body and an almost fierce, certainly overpowering calm flooding his thoughts.

He was never more conscious of being "visited." And every image he ever had of those who had been "visited" by "another" came tumbling from his memory: Moses at the burning bush; Isaiah catching sight of the flaming seraphs in the temple of Yahweh; Mary the Virgin in Nazareth bowing before Gabriel the messenger; Jesus transfigured with Moses and Elias on Mount Tabor and conversing with God; St. John in his Patmos cavern gazing at the Mystic Lamb in all his glory; Constantine galvanized by the Cross in the clouds; Joan of Arc in her prison cell tearfully hearing her "voices" in the depths of pain; John of the Cross in his prison cell piercing the Dark Night and embracing the Beloved; Teilhard fingering the bones of *Sinanthropos* and seeing Jesus, Omega Point, prefigured in those pathetic pieces. Yves had a clear sense of being destined, as all those had been, for a special revelation.

All this rushed by him and fell away as he raised his eyes and looked again at the fields, the trees, the sky. All was now moving in a new vision, animated by a life he had dreamed of, but never known. It was all, he now knew, a sacrament, a row of sacraments strung together as a lovely necklace around man's world. And his mind, will, and inner senses were permeated with a strange new incense consecrating him—as no bishop's hands could ever do—to the priesthood of a new being. He knew: always it had been so near him and yet so far. "Beauty, ever ancient, ever new! Too late have I known thee!" he murmured Augustine's quiet regret.

There was awe at the surprise of it all, humbleness at not having seen it all before. And, dominantly, an enthusiasm lush with passion. The coiling presence stirred in him; and he began to daydream.

"Hey, Father! Having any trouble?" The shout startled Yves. It was a local state trooper who had drawn alongside in his patrol car. Yves snapped his head around, angry at the interruption, his eyes blazing. But the genial smile of the trooper reassured him. They knew each other. "Just passing a few moments in peace, Pat," he said, recovering himself and reaching for the ignition key. "Give Jane and the kids my love."

With a wave of his hand he continued on his way to see his friends.

From then on, Yves became extremely careful. It was as if he had been put on his guard. He knew with an almost uncanny foresight when trouble was in store for him. At times he was forewarned about a particular person. "Someone" told him. At other times the warning concerned activities: a request to solemnize a marriage, a request for confessions, an invitation to dinner at a parishioner's house or with his fellow priests; or it might be a book or article in a magazine or a letter. The warning was silent, but clear and pithy: "Avoid it!" or "Don't do it!" or "Don't meet them!" Except for an occasional flourish in a sermon, his colleagues found no further reason to cavil at his ideas.

But when he spoke privately with parishioners, with an engaged couple about to be married, for example, it was different. Then he explained their union so poetically, and he dwelt so insistingly on the peculiarly earthly role of Jesus, that they always departed completely charmed by his counseling.

Yves himself clearly explains now how the entire purpose, meaning, and reason of marriage as a Sacrament had changed for him. It had become a Sacrament of nature for him. It had lost its dimension as a channel of supernatural grace, just as the senior assistant had warned him. It was something that united people with the natural universe. And this meant there had been some deep damage to Yves' own faith.

As time went by, and Yves introduced this same dark element to the other Sacraments, his own condition became far more extreme; and he himself began to sense more clearly the meaning of his voluntary commitment to a force he now could not control. The moment for possible resistance had passed.

In 1963, Yves' situation became critical for him. Saying Mass was a prime example. The servers and the people found that he began to take a longer time to say Mass. Peculiarly enough, it was only one part of the Mass that took the additional time. It was the most solemn section immediately preceding the Consecration that begins when the priest extends his hands, palms downward, fingers together, over the chalice and the bread. The ceremonial calls for complete silence, broken only by the tinkling of the Mass bell. Yves would now remain for abnormal lengths of time, with his hands outstretched—at first only three minutes, then ten, then fifteen, once thirty agonizing additional minutes, with congregation and attendants waiting and watching. Then he would take an abnormally long time to utter the actual words of Consecration. At an ordinary pace, all these ceremonial actions take no more than three to five minutes.

His colleagues thought he was going through a "mystical" period, or that he was suffering from "religious scruples," that he took too seriously each official prescription for the actions and words of the Mass. Some priests go through such a phase. They know that any deviation can result in venial or mortal sin. So they torture themselves, making sure they observe all the rules; they go back again and again repeating actions and words, to make sure they consciously do everything correctly.

But Yves neither was mystical nor was he paralyzed by religious scruples. He was undergoing what he now describes as the most agonizing whipping and thrashing of his inner self. It began one day when, as he tells it, from the moment that his hands were outstretched over the chalice and the bread, until after the Consecration, the "remote control" changed in force and in its "message."

"I fought every inch of the way," Yves recounts today, "and I lost every inch of that fight."

Instead of the officially prescribed words of the Mass and the concepts expressed in those words, Yves now found different concepts and different words. It was always and only key words that were changed. Every time, for instance, the word "saving" or "salvation" was ritually prescribed, he could only think and say "winning" and "triumph." "Saving" and "salvation" appeared to him like words scribbled on bits of torn paper and pinned to a wall out of his reach. To reach for them impotently was the source of intense agony and searing pain.

Similarly with "love" (this now became "pride"), "died" and "death" (now "returned home to death" and "nothingness"), "sacrifice" (now "defiance"), "sins" (now "myths and fables"), "bread" and "wine" (now "desire" and "pleasure"). So it went.

An additional agony ensued whenever a sign of the cross was called for by the ritual, when Yves would find only the index finger of his right hand capable of motion, and it could trace only a vertical line upward.

Throughout, his memory and reflexes propelled him to act according to the ritual. The substitute words and thoughts poured in. He recognized immediately that the sense and intent of the whole ceremony was changed utterly by those new words and thoughts. He fought with will and mind to retain the ritual. But each time it was the same: as long as he fought, some hard lump seemed to start expanding deep within him—not in his body, not in his brain, but in his living consciousness. "It was like remembering last night's nightmare and knowing that this reality was what frightened you then." As the lump expanded, it began to reduce in a sinister fashion the area of his very self.

At the excruciating limit of this inner pain, it began to have a physical and psychological ricochet: the blood roared in his ears and peculiar pains started—his hair, eyelashes, and toenails ached unbearably. Quick kaleidoscopic pictures of his entire life tumbled in front of his mind, always making him look ludicrous, smelly, contemptible, beyond help. He could hear himself beginning to form a scream, which, if it had emerged, would have been: "I'm drowning! I'm perishing! Save me!"

It never emerged. He stopped fighting. All agony ceased. And a marvelous exhilaration—not unmixed with relief—flooded him. The ease was almost painful in its contrast with the pain that had preceded it.

The final agony came one day when he started to pronounce the words of Consecration. Instead of "This is My Body" and "This is My Blood," other words echoed in his own voice: "This is My Tombstone" and "This is My Sexuality." As he pronounced these words while bending over the altar as prescribed by the ritual, all intent of authentic Consecration fled from him. His index finger bent into a hook shape, thrust itself into the wine, and then scratched a vertical red stain on the white wafer.

At that moment, Yves could not straighten up. His ears were filled with two different sounds. He was sure he actually heard them: a jeering laugh that echoed and echoed and echoed; and a faint keening, a muted wail or cry of protest which eventually died away in the reverberations of that heinous laugh. Then, as from that "remote control," he heard the syllables: "Jesus is now Jonathan," and "Jonathan is now Yves," and "Yves is now Jonathan and Jesus." And finally, "All is gathered into Mr. Natural."

It was some time before Yves realized that only he had heard all those profanities. But whether they heard those words or not, it was Yves' appearance after those painfully extended moments of inward battle that shocked the people who watched him. When he turned around finally to distribute communion, his face was terribly drawn, haggard, the color of chalk. His hair, cut short then, seemed to be standing on end. His eyes, normally so impressively clear and winning, were narrowed to slits; and he was muttering through clenched teeth. The whole impression was stark and lifeless.

He finished the Mass in a violent state of inner tension. Only after some time spent alone was he once more flooded with that strange peace and exultation. Finally, when he had recovered himself alone in the vesting room, he emerged smiling, composed, looking as he had always looked.

His yielding to the "control" at Mass had immediate and far-reaching effects. In baptizing infants, he changed the Latin words, which were unintelligible to the parents and bystanders. When he was supposed to say, "I baptize you in the name of the Father and the Son and the Holy Spirit," he said, "I baptize you in the name of the Sky, the Earth, and Water."

But the most momentous change in his performance both of Baptism and the other Sacraments (Extreme Unction, Confession) affected those parts which spoke of "Satan" or the "Devil" or "evil spirits."

At Baptism, instead of saying (in Latin), "Depart, Unclean Spirit" or "To renounce Satan and all his works" or "Become a child of God," he now said, "Depart, spirit of hate for the Angel of Light," and "To renounce all exile of Prince Lucifer," and "Become a member of the Kingdom."

In Confession, he stopped saying, "I absolve you of your sins in the name of the Father, of the Son, and of the Holy Spirit"; instead, he said, "I confirm you in your natural wishes, in the name of Sky, Earth, and Water." And when he administered the Sacrament of the Dying ("Extreme Unction" was its old name), he committed the dying person to the mercy and peace of "Sister Earth" and to the eternity of "Mother Nature."

Whenever he felt an initial repugnance to accepting what was "dictated" to him by the "remote control," that frightful inner lump grew sensitive; and Yves became a being of pure pain. He quickly obeyed, and he was rewarded always by a wild exultation. The sun was brighter. The blue of the sky was deeper. The coffee he drank was never so good. The blood coursed vigorously in his veins. And his head never felt clearer.

By the end of 1964, it became obvious to his colleagues there was something wrong with Yves that they could no longer explain by his artistic temperament, his French Canadian–Swedish ancestry, a mystical period of life, or religious scruples. It was all too peculiar. It frightened some. It repelled others. It angered still others. It left all with an eerie sense of something utterly alien in Yves. And to cap it all, Yves had begun to refer to himself as "Father Jonathan."

But it was always isolated things, and nobody ever put them all together into a definite pattern. When he turned around at Mass (as the priest did four or five times) to say *Dominus vobiscum* ("The Lord be with you"), one colleague swore he heard Yves say, *Dominus Lucis vobiscum* ("The Lord of Light be with you"). Others did not hear that single added word, but the faint glint in his eyes gave them a momentary shock. Once, as he touched the forehead of a baby he was baptizing, the baby went into violent hysteria and had to be rushed to the hospital for treatment.

All such incidents taken individually were susceptible of perfectly rational explanations. But his visit to a boy dying of bone cancer was the final incident that led ultimately to his abandonment of his post.

It was at the end of 1966. The boy, the fourteen-year-old red-haired son of Irish immigrant parents, was to be anointed: death was certain and imminent. Before the priest, Father Yves, arrived, the boy asked his mother to wash his face and hands and help him put on his favorite shirt and tie. He also asked his father to turn his bed toward the door, because, he said, there was a dark thing in the corner of the room.

When Yves arrived, all went normally until Yves endeavored to straighten the bed, making the boy again face the "darkened" corner. The boy started to scream: "No! Father! No! Please! Mother!" Then as his mother ran in and Yves, having straightened the bed, stood over toward that particular corner, the boy started to weep uncontrollably.

Yves does not remember all the boy said, but he does recall certain words and sentences: "darkness," "they smile at each other," "he hates Jesus," "save me," "I don't want to go with them."

Finally the boy's father apologetically requested Yves to leave and come back the next day. But his mother telephoned Yves' superior, the pastor of the parish. The pastor came an hour later, anointed the boy, and waited for the end, which came quickly.

The incident was the last straw. And now everything known and remarked about Yves for the previous three years was put together.

The pastor and his senior assistant said nothing to Yves, but they spent about three months gathering information and watching Yves closely. In addition to the peculiarities mentioned already, they received a puzzling report they could not make head or tail of. A man answering Yves' description periodically lived in a loft in Greenwich Village, New York. His appearances there always coincided with Yves' vacations and the free days when he was away from his home parish.

They found out that the loft was known as the Shrine of the New Being; that the man was called Father Jonathan; that he held services for all and sundry: said Mass, performed marriages, heard confessions, ordained men and women as priests of the Shrine, baptized infants and adults, went on call to homes and hospitals where the dying lay; and that he had one other specific rite, which he called the Bearing of the Light. Its initiated members were called the Light-Bearers. But no details about either members or their rites were available.

Just at the moment that a full written report was ready and about to be sent to the bishop, Yves seemed to have been alerted—however late—to the intentions of his colleagues. For about two months his behavior, as far as anyone could judge, was absolutely normal. He never went to Greenwich Village. He worked hard.

Then, in mid-June 1967, when all concerned were just about to dismiss the whole affair as exaggerated and irrelevant, Yves had his first terrible seizure. Predictably, perhaps, it was at Mass.

When he had stretched his hands out, palms downward over the chalice, he suddenly started to weep and groan and sway. One hand clamped down roughly over the chalice. The other fell resoundingly on the white wafer of bread. The servers called the pastor. He, together with the two other assistants, could not physically dislodge Yves' hands, or move the chalice, or stop Yves' weeping and groaning. He and the chalice and the bread were rooted physically to their place as if by rivets. He became incontinent on the altar.

By that time, the pastor had emptied the church and locked the doors. They were about to call a doctor when Yves suddenly let go of the chalice and the bread. He seemed to be flung backward, tumbling down the three steps of the altar and falling heavily to the marble floor of the sanctuary. He was unconscious when they reached him.

He awoke about an hour later. When the pastor spoke with him, Yves disclosed to him that his mother had been epileptic, and he pleaded with the pastor not to put him to shame publicly. He would go away in order to rest, follow a doctor's advice after a checkup, and all would be well.

But now the pastor believed the worst. In his eyes, Father Yves must be possessed. The pastor's conclusion was no more than a deep conviction based on his personal reactions. But even so, it was a serious matter, and it would not be dropped or postponed again until the pastor was sure one way or the other. A discreet inquiry revealed that Sybil, Yves' mother, was not epileptic. In a long Sunday morning interview, the bishop was told the whole story, including the pastor's worst fears. That was in June at the seminary, where the bishop was ordaining the new young priests.

The bishop called in Father David M. for consultation.

After his consultation with the bishop, Father David had an interview with Yves. He came away completely baffled. Not only did Yves cooperate fully with him, but whatever Yves said seemed to strike a sympathetic chord in David. The only two peculiarities he could not explain satisfactorily were Yves' constant use of his new name, Jonathan, and the condition of Yves' right index finger.

The name David could accept. After all, only ten years before, David had started to call himself, or at least to sign letters to his intimate friends, as "Pierre" (after Teilhard de Chardin); and he had taken a lot of leg-pulling from his colleagues about that. And the name "Bones" had stuck to David chiefly because David, once he heard the name, deliberately used it several times during his lectures; he liked it.

The finger was another matter. According to the doctor who had X-rayed it, no bone was broken and no nerve was shattered. The problem could in no way be traced to the supposed epileptic history of

Yves' mother. There was calcification in the finger; but the deformity could not be traced to a blow or injury; and no calcification could be found elsewhere in Yves' body. He was found not to be arthritic.

For the rest of it, David could not find much to be alarmed about. He had checked out Yves' mother: she had, indeed, been subject to some sort of seizures, but the doctors who examined her always ruled out epilepsy. That much left David relieved. But he still came away baffled. He was convinced that he had missed something essential; and he felt foolish without knowing why. His discussion with Yves had covered both the doctrine Yves professed as a priest and Yves' own spirituality. As far as David could make out, both doctrine and spirituality coincided more or less with his own.

"If Yves is in error," David told the bishop later, "then so am I. Now what do I do?"

The bishop eyed David speculatively for a while. Then he said softly: "I suppose if all this paleontology and de Chardin's teachings were to lead you to a point where you had to choose faith or de Chardin, you would choose faith, Father David."

It was a statement of fact, with an implied question. David glanced at the bishop, who was now looking out the window of his study with his back to David.

The bishop continued. "Tell me, Father. Is evolution as much a fact as, say, the salvation of us all by Jesus?"

David faced the question with its now distant echoes of the foreboding he had felt the day the bishop had named him to the post of exorcist. Today he says his first reaction to the question was surprise: "It's as if I had neglected something final, and the time was coming when I would have to face it." Deep in his mind, he realized, he had spontaneously said, "Yes."

To the bishop he answered by rising and saying something to the effect that it was like comparing apples and oranges. And the bishop apparently wanted only to put the question. He was far too old and wise a man always to expect precise answers.

After this interview with his bishop, David was not at peace. He made up his mind to see Yves the following day.

What he proposed to Yves was quite simple. After much thought, it seemed to David that they should conduct a ceremony in which they would say special prayers for the sick and against disease, and in which they would also go through the main parts of the Exorcism ritual. He,

David, would conduct a simple exorcism. The idea, he told Yves, was to satisfy the bishop and the pastor.

Yves saw no difficulty. He would like that, he said. Only Yves' pastor would be present; no trouble was anticipated.

They performed the exorcism in the private oratory of the seminary, all three men kneeling in the pews normally occupied by the seminarians. Yves answered in a low murmur all the questions put to him by David as exorcist. "Do you believe in God?" "Do you believe in Jesus Christ, Our Lord?" "Do you renounce the Devil and all his works and pomps?" and so on.

Yves kissed the crucifix; and, jabbing his crooked index finger into the holy-water font, he blessed himself.

David and the pastor rose to their feet at the end of the ceremony. Yves had not budged from his place where he knelt with his face in his hands. They both went out quietly, leaving him alone.

"That's that," said David with a sigh of relief.

"I did not hear one clear word from him," rejoined the pastor, "but I suppose I'd be as subdued as he was in the same circumstances."

In the oratory, Yves raised his face from his hands a few minutes later and looked around; he was alone; and he could not remember much. He remembered coming in with David and the pastor, kneeling down, and opening the ritual book. But that was all. For the 15 minutes of the exorcism ceremony he had completely blacked out. When he knelt down, it was as if a powerful sedative had been injected into him. He remembered nothing except a sudden compulsion forcing his lips to speak and his limbs to move.

He waited a moment now, then looked toward the altar. All was normal on the altar; but between him and it a bulky, formless shadow hung in the air blotting out all sight of the crucifix over the altar and of the stained-glass windows behind the altar. Then, abruptly but calmly, like a man remembering a decision he had made or some instructions from a superior, Yves rose and left the oratory. A seminarian he met at the door caught sight of Yves' face: it was glowing and laughing.

That evening, as David sat in his study, he could not concentrate on the work in hand. He was supposed to finish a paper for a conference on de Chardin's work at Choukoutien, China, where the Jesuit had unearthed the fossil of *Sinanthropos*. But David's mind kept going back again and again to the bishop's question: "Is evolution as much a fact as the salvation of us all by Jesus?" A foolish question, he told himself. No meaning to it at all. The bishop was of the old school. But still it kept bothering him.

He looked up at the glass cases where all his beloved fossils and paleontological treasures were exhibited. His eyes traveled over a chipped skull casing, the collection of anklebones, the pieces of ancient rock in which flora and fauna fossils were embedded, and the series of reconstructed busts: Solo Man, Rhodesian Man, Neanderthal Man, Cro-Magnon Man. His mind was playing tricks with him: not only were the plaster busts looking at him, he thought, but these dead and broken human bones seemed to be speaking without sound.

Then his head cleared. He got angry with himself. *Had* a choice to be made between evolution and Jesus? *Must* it be made? If Jesus were the culmination of it all, there was *no* such choice to be made. Jesus and evolution were one in some deep way or other.

He hung along the edge of these considerations for a while. Then on a sudden impulse he went over to the house phone and called to the guest room where Yves was spending the night.

"Hello, Yves—eh—Jonathan," he stumbled.

"Hello, Father," Yves answered in a calm and pleasant tone.

"I just had an idea, Jonathan. About evolution and all that, I mean. Supposing Teilhard was wrong all the time and his whole theory and evolution itself was irreconcilable with the divinity of Jesus, what would you say?"

There was a short pause. Then in a level voice with a certain note of hidden triumph, Yves said: "You seem to be asking this to yourself and for the first time, Father David!"

"But what do you say, Yves—Jonathan, excuse me," David insisted. "I am now asking *you.*"

"There can never be any such conflict, Father David"—David began to feel some relief—"for the simple reason that evolution makes Jesus possible. And only evolution can do that." Yves remembers the conversation very well. The "remote control" was on him again with a strong compulsion; he waited until the thoughts and words came to him. Then he continued quietly, but with the emphasis of one in possession of some superior or additional knowledge. "Father David, all I have become, you made me. My spirituality and my beliefs and my explanations all come from you. You also know that evolution makes it possible for us to believe in Jesus; it makes Jesus possible for us as rational men. Don't you, Father David?"

At the other end of the telephone, David caught his breath sharply. As Yves' words hit his ears, the thoughts and images they conveyed pushed past all his mental safeguards like rough visitors. He felt an invasion of himself such as he had never known before. He struggled for a moment: "Do you really think . . ."

"Father David, you have the testimony of your own conscience and your conscious mind." Then, with terrible deliberateness and a hard note in his voice that completely destroyed David's self-confidence: "After all, if I had to be exorcised, you also need it. Perhaps it is both of us who needed it. Or, perhaps—and this is a better idea—we are both beyond exorcism." The telephone clicked and went dead.

David was stunned. Within a few hours, he decided to telephone the bishop. Before he could say a word, he was given the latest news: Yves had gone to the bishop that evening, resigned from the diocese, and left with some friends for New York.

From that time onward until the marriage by the sea, David did not see much of Yves, though he heard about him constantly as Father Jonathan.

But now David had a problem of his own: had he in some way or other been contaminated? Had he yielded to the Evil One? Had he voluntarily, although under the veil of goodness and wisdom, admitted the influence of the Devil into his own personal life?

He thought back over the exorcism. Come to think of it now, Yves was not the only one who had mumbled the Latin words. He himself had mumbled them, his mind had been absent half the time thinking of other problems.

David did not realize it then, but he would not enjoy any peace until the exorcism of Yves had been accomplished some two years later.

When Father Jonathan, as Yves now called himself, came to stay in Greenwich Village, he chose at first to work among its inhabitants, seeking neophytes and converts for his cause. He hung around the popular discotheques and bars, joined the clubs, took part in several of the "happenings" organized by the various Village groups of the time. He became known for what he claimed to be: the founder of a new religion.

But after a year of this apostolate, Jonathan's emphasis changed. He no longer consorted with the ordinary denizens of the Village. He had a different mission: to create a new religious movement among the

well-heeled families of upper Manhattan. Initially he became good
friends with a few people he met by chance. As time went on, he
enlarged his circle. Soon he had enough voluntary contributions to
enlarge and decorate his Shrine of the Loft, as he called it. And there,
every Wednesday evening, he held services, administered the new
"Sacraments," and counseled the members of his "parish."

By the autumn of 1968, he had attracted a solid congregation who
found that Jonathan, far from being an iconoclast or a preacher of
strange doctrines, seemed to revive in them a new sense of religious
belief and a trust in the future. His message was simple. He couched it
in beautiful language. He strewed his addresses with a genuine
knowledge of art and poetry. And, most especially, he had a knack of
suffusing everything with esthetic values. He could preach on the
Missing Link, for example, or a picture of Neanderthal Man, and make
the entire idea of evolution from inanimate matter appear a glorious
beginning. For the future, Jonathan had a still more glorious outlook.
There was a new being in process now, he told his congregations; and
it would live in a new time. "New Being" and "New Time" became
his watchwords.

Jonathan's outlook and his intuition of the rather sinister "New
Being" came just in time to fill a vacuum felt by many people. The
vacuum had begun to appear many years before Jonathan's arrival; its
effects in theater, poetry, and art had been felt far and wide during
preceding decades. All—poetry, theater, and art—had constantly
lamented the fact that man's world had increasingly sacrificed
meaning for usefulness. And without any further meaning, without the
possibility of some transcendence, that world, however "useful,"
ceases to nourish the spirit of men and women and children. Without
that nourishment, the spirit of man must die.

In the area of religion and especially of Roman Catholicism, the
vacuum became widely visible and tangible in the late 1960s, when
the changes introduced by the Second Vatican Council had taken
effect. The new changes did away with much of the ancient
symbolism—its mystery and its immemorial associations. The changes
might have evolved into something worthwhile, except for the strange
vacuum that now seized Roman Catholics and religious people in
general.

Its effect seemed sudden. And it was numbing. For it was a vacuum
of indifference: to the external rites—words, actions, objects—proper

to religion; to the concepts of religious thought and theology; and to the functions and character of religious people—priests, rabbis, ministers, bishops, popes—to all of these was now applied the norm of "usefulness": form equals function; but, beyond practical use, there is meaning. The externals of religion no longer seemed to have any compelling significance. Increasing numbers of people laid them aside, or ignored them, or used them as mere social conveniences and conventional signposts.

Jonathan's message was simple and geared to this new situation. All the beauty of being human had, he said, been obscured by religious theorizing and institutional churches. But now is a new time, he preached: all is and always was really natural. Good meant natural. We did not need such artificial supports as organized religions had supplied. We must just rediscover the perfectly natural. Everywhere in the world around us there were natural sacraments, natural shrines, natural holiness, natural immortality, natural deity. There was a natural grace and overwhelming natural beauty. Furthermore, in spite of the chasm that institutional religion had dug between humans and the nature of the world, the world and all humans were one in some naturally mystical union. We came from that union and by death we went back into it. Jonathan called that natural union "Abba Father."

In effect, Jonathan made a fateful synthesis of Teilhardian evolutionary doctrines and Teilhard's idea of Jesus. And he permeated it with a deep humanism and had a knowing eye for the yawning indifference now gripping traditional Christian believers.

In Jonathan's outlook, "religious" belief became easy again. At one pole, one could accept the currently pervasive idea that man evolved from inanimate matter. At the other, one had no need to aim at believing in an unimaginable "resurrection" of the body. Instead, there was a return "to where we came from," as Jonathan used to say: a going back to the oneness of nature and of this universe.

All this allowed the clever use of the full range of vocabulary and concept about "salvation," "divine love," "hope," "goodness," "evil," "honesty"—all terms and ideas that were already so comforting and familiar to his congregation. But all these terms were understood in a sense completely different from the traditional one: minus a supernatural god, minus a man-god called Jesus, and minus a supernatural condition called "personal afterlife."

Jonathan's congregation was never very large—never more than about 150 people. But he drew deep satisfaction from it all; for in his mind, all this was a preparation for the glorious New Time which was just around the corner—at the Shrine of the Loft.

But there were deep consequences for Jonathan. As time went on, and the spring of 1969 approached, he found more and more that, in the literal sense of the words, "he was not his own man" any longer. Outsiders—his flock, his friends—noticed no difference beyond that he had let his golden hair grow longer, that he wore exotic clothes, and that his language became very exalted.

With the passage of time, however, Jonathan's "movement" seemed to be in danger of petering out—before the New Time started! He was getting no new followers. His doctrine and outlook did not easily accommodate the more flamboyant upheavals of the 1960s. He was no revolutionary in the political sense. The Shrine of the Loft was clearly on the wane before it had really taken off. He needed something new.

Meanwhile, Jonathan would wake up in the middle of the night and find his mind full of strange impulses coming from that "remote control." He kept finding himself packing a bag and preparing for a journey. He spent long hours alone in his Shrine; and later he did not know what he had been doing there all that time. The "remote control" was inexorable in its domination. He had to wait until he was told what to do. While waiting for that order, he performed marriages and birth celebrations for his few followers. He held weekly services. He dreamed constantly of starting a new priesthood and a new church that would sweep the ranks of Catholics and Protestants.

Toward the end of the summer of 1969, Jonathan's "instructions" started to come in earnest. He was invited to spend three weeks in the Canadian wilds with a party of friends who annually went there to hunt and fish.

Jonathan knew the moment he received the letter of invitation that this was it. Some inner voice kept telling him: "Go! Go! You will now find your mirror of eternity. Ordination to the supreme priesthood is at hand!" When asked if he heard an actual voice on this occasion, he denies this. It was an inner conviction coming with the same firmness of all his other "instructions" and exercising the same irresistible compulsion, far beyond the effect of mere words.

With Jonathan, the hunting party numbered 12 people. They lodged at a base camp. Each day they split up into groups. Each group departed for two- to four-day treks in the wilderness.

Apart from some fishing, Father Jonathan busied himself with painting and writing. But after the first week, he found himself venturing alone farther and farther from the base camp. He was looking for something or some place. When he came on it, he would recognize it, he knew. His walks always followed the course of a river on whose bank the base camp stood. He could easily find his way home by retracing his steps along the river.

It was on one of these forays that he found his *place*—as he called it later. That name, "my place," has now a grisly significance for Jonathan: there his final immersion in demonic possession was accomplished.

One day after lunch, he had been walking for about three hours in a southerly direction along the river. For those hours, the course of the waters had run fairly straight. At a certain spot, however, Jonathan noticed that the river entered between two high ridges of ground and that within them it described an S-shape. When Jonathan reached the farther curve of the S-shape, his whole body and mind suddenly became electrified with a sense of discovery. He stood stock-still, one Latin word—*sacerdos* (priest)—ringing like a clear bell in his ears. *Sacerdos!*

That was it! This was the place! Here he would be ordained truly as priest of the New Being and Bishop-Leader of the New Time. This was it! He felt full of gratitude.

The place was beautiful. The water in that corner was not more than a few feet deep. The center of the riverbed was a soft, shifting carpet of sand as white as salt. On each side, like rows of attendant black-cowled monks, there were tiers of boulders and rocks, rounded and smoothed by the overflow of water during the yearly flooding of the river. In the corners of the S-shape, on each bank, there was a small, shelving beach of that pure white carpet of sand sloping up out of the water to a rim of blue and black pebbles, then ferns and grass, then the pines, alders, sycamores, chestnuts. Everything burned in the sun, and silent shadows gloomed over rock and sand and river to make a patchwork of green half-darkness in the yellow light.

Jonathan could see a hundred summer suns mirrored in the green-gray water, and each of them gave off a fire that dazzled him. The river moved slowly, but not sluggishly, all the while singing a pervasive refrain of calm and constancy.

The place was Jonathan's "mirror of eternity," an opening in nature through which he could glimpse the strength of eternity, its softness and cleansing power, and the boundless spaces of its being.

Jonathan fell stunned and crying on the beach. Stretched out full length, face down, his hands digging into the sand, he kept shouting: "*Sacerdos! Sacerdos! Sacerdos! Sacerdos!*" His cries ricocheted off the rocks and the trees, each echo coming back fainter and fainter as if traveling away with his petitions and hopes, until he found himself listening silently.

The wetness of the sand soaked into his clothes, and the sun warmed his back. He began to feel a buoyancy all through his body: some mighty hand held him on its palm. He heard himself saying almost plaintively: "Make me . . . make me, please . . . make me . . . priest . . . priest-make . . ." Every word was spoken into the white sand beneath his face.

Now thoughts, emotions, imaginings, all seemed to be under the control of that hand. And he began to feel an emptying sensation. His past was being erased; his entire past, what he remembered and even what he had forgotten, all that had entered into the making of what he had been up to that moment, was being flushed from him. He was being emptied of every concept, every logical reasoning, every memory and image which his culture, his religion, his ambient, his reading had formed in him.

Then, under some inner impulse which he questioned no longer, he rose and went slowly into the water. He stood in midstream looking at the sky for a moment. Obeying the inner voice, he bent down; his hands groped at the base of a rock and sought to reach to where its roots went deep in water. The river swirled caressingly over his shoulders and back. His chin now was almost level with the surface.

"I was reaching for the veined heart of our world," he told me in one of our conversations, "to where Jesus, the Omega Point, was evolving and evolving, and was on the threshold of emerging."

It seemed to him that "only this world was forgiving and cleansing," it alone had "united elements." He had the impression that now at last he had "broken through," and that the revelation of all revelations had been granted him: the real truth, the real god, the real Jesus, the real holiness, the real sacrament, the real being, and the new time in which all this newness would inevitably take over.

He lost count of ordinary time, of the sun and the wind, of the river and its banks. The wind was a great rushing bird whose wings dovetailed into the green and brown arms of the trees on either side of him. The rocks became living things, his brothers and sisters, his millennial cousins, witnessing his consecration with the reverence that only nature had. And the water around him winked with gleaming eyes as it sang the song it had learned millions of years ago, from the swirling atoms of space, before there was any world and man to hear it. It was an irresistible ecstasy for Jonathan.

He began to chant to himself: "Jesus! Jesus! Jesus!" Then this became "Lord of Light! Lord of Light! Lord of Light!" Once again he had no control. Every fiber and sinew in his body and mind was flooded with a dusky power. Now he was chanting: "Lord of Light! Lord of Jesus and of all things! Your slave! Your servant! Your creature! Your priest!"

He felt a soft relaxation throughout himself; he had now no trace of tension, no anticipation, no forward-looking thought or emotion. All was wrapped up and contained in the now, the here-present.

He rose to his feet in the shallow water and faced the bank; his hands, bleeding from his efforts to dig for the bottom of that rock, hung by his sides. He looked at the scratches and tears in his fingers and palms, loving the gleam of blood in the sunshine on the background of his clean skin.

Slowly he walked up the beach. For no reason his pace quickened. He started to trot. Once past the sand and on solid ground, he ran zigzagging through the trees, propelled by the force within him. The ground sloped upward. Still running, he was out of breath as he reached the top of the slope. He began to falter and stumble.

He reached out for support. But on every side the tall, rough bodies of the pine trees, their branches many times his height off the ground, their heads lost in the sky, were the only things near to him; and they gave no help.

Through the haze of his sweat and weariness he saw on the ridge he was approaching a small tree with branches near the ground. He stumbled, fell, got up, and labored until he fell against the tree trunk, his outstretched arms falling on the short branches sticking out on either side. He leaned there a while, his cheek against the tree, his armpits resting on the branches, catching his breath and sobbing half syllables, waiting for his strength to return.

But he became aware that his face was lying against something smooth: this was no rough pine bark or knotty sycamore skin. He opened his eyes slowly, easing himself to a standing position and drew back from the tree wonderingly.

With a growing horror he could not control, he now saw it in clear outline: a bare tree trunk, stripped of all its bark, severed to a quarter of its original height by some force—a lightning bolt, a random axe, some accident. It was a withered tree trunk with only two stubby arms. Blood stained the putty-white surface of those mute cross-pieces and its withered trunk.

He was standing in front of a cross, he thought with a fierce horror and revulsion. There's blood on it. My blood? Or whose blood? His blood? Whose blood? The questions were hysterical cries of fear in his brain.

He started to shout. "Curse it! Curse him! Curse that blood! Curse that false Jesus!" The "remote control" was pouring the words into his brain, and he was echoing them with his lips. "Destroy it! Break those arms!" The instructions tumbled pell-mell.

He stretched out his hands, gripped one arm of the tree, and began to pull while he shouted. "Curses on you! Curses on you! I am free of you! Lord of Light! Save me! Help!" The arm of the tree broke. He seized the other arm with both hands and started pulling and shouting. It gave without warning, and its release sent him flying backward, tumbling down the slope toward the river, his world now a careening tunnel of lights and blows and bumps, until he fell against a tree trunk and lost consciousness.

The search party found him there a few hours later, just before sundown. He was semiconscious and weak, his two hands still holding a broken tree branch. They lifted him to a sitting position, his back resting against the tree that had broken his fall. He was facing the ridge. The sun was setting, but its last red-gold rays flowed thinly around the withered tree, its cross-arms now splintered stubs, its trunk stained with dark splotches.

Jonathan did not notice it for a while until his vision focused. Gradually he became aware of tall figures around him, of voices speaking, of hands that were putting a flask of whisky to his lips, and of other hands tending to his bruises. He heard the sounds of branches being cut with axes. But his gaze fell on the tree. Alarm bells sounded in him. He began to struggle to his feet, his eyes fixed on that tree.

The red light of the sun was rapidly fading to blue-black twilight, and the tree was dissolving into the ridge. One of the men in the search party saw Jonathan struggling to rise and noticed the fixity of his stare at the tree.

"Don't worry, Father," he said, "it's only a tree. A dead tree. It's all right, I tell you. Take it easy, will you, Father! It's only a tree, Father." He exerted pressure on Jonathan and prevented him from standing up.

Jonathan slumped back wearily and muttered: "Only a tree. Only a tree." Then he blacked out. They placed him on the makeshift stretcher they had fashioned and set off for the campsite.

The end was not far off for Jonathan; but he did not seem to realize it. After a few days' rest at the base camp, the party journeyed to Manchester, New Hampshire. Jonathan was taken to his mother's house.

He was extremely weak, suffered bouts of dizziness, had pains all over his body. He found it difficult to sleep at night and could not concentrate on reading or painting. The family doctor prescribed a two-month rest.

Jonathan spent the first few weeks in bed under sedation. He was tended by his mother and a day nurse. Gradually his strength returned. By October's end he was up and around the house. In November he was strong enough to walk around the garden, and he started to read and paint again.

His mother had been in touch with Father David at the seminary through her pastor. And the moment Jonathan (she also had to adopt his new name) was at all well, she telephoned David. He arrived one afternoon to see Jonathan.

The meeting was a disturbing one for David, but for Jonathan it seemed to be an occasion of new strength, an eerie triumph bathed him even in his misery. He addressed David as "my son," using a paternalistic tone of voice that affected David in an unexpected way. It was the first time in all his years as an adult that David had felt real fear.

With this atmosphere as a brooding backdrop to their conversation, David and Jonathan chatted about Canada. The common report brought back by his companions had been that either Jonathan had been attacked by a wild animal, or that for some other reason he had panicked, taken to his heels, and knocked himself unconscious while running. After a few minutes with Jonathan, David was certain that something much more significant than a mere accident had happened, but Jonathan would not open up to him.

After a while, Jonathan succeeded in shifting David's queries away from Canada and the recent trip. He began talking instead about his new apostolate and of his plans for a New York "mission." Then surprisingly, and in ways that seemed elusive to him, the conversation began returning to David himself. And once again David found that a whole part of his being was in total accord with all that Jonathan said. And again, in some other part of him, he felt a deep resistance.

Finally Jonathan rounded on him at one moment: "Father David, my son, eventually you too will find the light, and come out into the open and preach the New Time and the New Being."

David's conflict welled up full inside him, a welcoming chord for Jonathan's portentous words, and a hard, gripping fright. Supposing he could not stop himself going all the way into exactly what Jonathan was doing—whatever that was. What then?

David recalls vividly the slow and deep nausea that built up inside him as he sat in that sick room surrounded by a quiet countryside. It was disgust riven with fear. He had had a similar but not quite identical experience once before, descending into a mass grave in Africa, at the tomb of an ancient tribal chieftain. Over the piles of bones of people sacrificed to ensure a chieftain's safe passage to eternal happiness, he had felt the touch of independent and sovereign evil, almost heard its voice in the fetid darkness saying silkily to him: "Come into my domain, David! You belong here!" And it kept coming into his mind that those long-buried men had never known anything about Jesus or Christianity. Some obscure conclusions had started to run around his head as he had stood in the tomb. But his nausea had not permitted him to examine them clearly.

Now, trying to fathom the mystery, he looked at Jonathan. Who was possessed? Was either of them possessed? Was it all imagination? Jonathan, in spite of his illness, seemed erect, tall, the color back in his cheeks, his blue eyes gleaming, his long hair falling gracefully over his shoulders. All his strength and natural comeliness seemed restored. Facing him, David suddenly felt weak and puny and somehow dirty. A phrase of Jonathan's sent his courage reeling further.

"Not for nothing, my son, have I been named Jonathan. You are David. And in the Bible they were bound together in the divine work."

David turned away helplessly, fighting the floods of weakness and fear that engulfed him. He was seeking composure, but Jonathan's voice pursued, triumphant, resounding.

"What happens to me, happens to you, my son. Don't you see? It is all foreordained. We have entered the Kingdom of the New Time and the New Being."

David felt at the end of his resistance. The nausea was increasing.

He was enmeshed in a trap he had not suspected. He went to the door, opened it, and spoke over his shoulder in a weak voice:

"Jonathan. Let's agree on one thing. If you need help, I shall help. Is it a deal?" When there was no answer, he turned slowly around. "Jonathan! We have an appointment the day you—"

He broke off. Jonathan was standing in the middle of the room, his eyes closed, his body swaying back and forth as if buffeted by a strong wind.

"Jonathan! Jonathan! Are you all right?"

"Father David," the voice was almost a whisper and full of pain. "Father David, help me . . . not now . . . impossible now . . . too far . . . but at the moment . . . it's a deal . . . if . . ."

The rest was lost in a mumbling confusion. Jonathan turned away and then slumped down into an armchair. David noticed Jonathan's right index finger was held in his left hand.

The door opened. Jonathan's mother entered quietly, unhurriedly. Her face was a mask. "Don't worry, Father David," she murmured. "He will sleep now. And in the aftertime you can get back to him. Go and rest. You need it. You all need rest."

He chatted for a few minutes with her, then left. She would keep him posted on Jonathan's movements.

In the middle of December Jonathan left home again and went back to New York. For the next four months David followed Jonathan's activities. He was always available but never conspicuous, visiting New York regularly, keeping informed of Jonathan's whereabouts and activities. For the moment he could not intervene. That moment would come, he knew.

He now was convinced that Jonathan had ceded full possession of himself to some evil spirit. He was half-convinced that he himself was affected by all this, but he did not understand exactly how. Not until the disastrous marriage ceremony by the sea was he to have the opportunity of helping Jonathan and of finding out exactly what had happened to himself.

In mid-February, David heard quite by accident of the marriage ceremony Jonathan was going to perform at Dutchman's Point. The bride's father, a prominent broker, was an old acquaintance of David. He immediately telephoned the father and arranged to have lunch with him at his home in Manchester. David was received at first with great warmth as an old friend. But the conversation turned sour, as the reason for his visit became clear: David wanted the bride's father either to postpone the marriage or to engage another clergyman.

Father Jonathan was a good priest, sniffed Hilda's father. Then, unpleasantly, he went on to grumble about the clergy in general, saying that at least Jonathan got the younger generation to say their prayers and to believe in God and take care of the environment— something "men of the cloth" did not ordinarily do. David argued, hinting at his basic fears and suspicions about Jonathan. But it was of no avail. The world was changing, he was told. What was all this sinister talk of evil and of the Devil? Father David did not believe, or did he, in all that nonsense anymore? David's only answer was an expression of his deep apprehension for Jonathan and for his friend's daughter.

Then, if he was so afraid, the broker concluded as he rose from the table, why didn't Father David come himself? He was thereby invited. He would see, the broker added, his daughter would be all right. For once Hilda was going to be gloriously happy. She wanted things this way. She was to be married only once.

"I'll be there," answered David quietly. "Don't worry. But you will have to answer for the result."

The broker stopped and looked at David, thought for a few seconds, then his face clouded over with anger. His words cut into David deeply. "Father David, I am a simple man as far as religion and religious matters go. Whatever happens in that area is the fault of all you clergy. You know"—he broke off, scrutinizing David's face and figure—"sometimes I have a feeling that *you* people are the really lost ones. We lay people have some sort of protection. We were never in charge of religion, y'know." They parted.

MISTER NATCH AND THE SALEM CHORUS

The exorcism of Father Jonathan began in the first week of April and ended only in the second week of May. Totally unforeseen by David, the exorcism of Jonathan proved to be relatively easy. It was David himself who was in jeopardy. His sanity, his religious belief, and his bodily life were in maximum danger. But thanks to David's sufferings, we can form a better idea of the mechanics of possession—at least of one type of possession: how it starts, how it progresses, and where, in the final analysis, the free choice of the possessed comes into play.

While the exorcism of Jonathan was recorded on tape, for the details of David's four-week marathon struggle with himself we have to rely on the diary he kept so punctiliously during that time, together with what he told others of his experience, and my own conversations with him.

When David and Jonathan left the marriage party on Massepiq beach, David drove directly to the seminary, where Jonathan and he stayed until the beginning of the exorcism.

As they drove, Jonathan had one persistent question for David: what was the importance of starting before the sun was high in the sky?

David was frank: he did not know exactly; he might never know; but, with only his instincts to go on, David was certain that the light of the noonday sun had somehow become for Jonathan a vehicle for an evil influence. "For you, Jonathan, it has become contaminated," David said tersely.

Jonathan wept at the implication of David's words. The light and warmth of the sun itself, the most beautiful things in Jonathan's world, had become evil for him. Still, following David's instructions, Jonathan kept the blinds drawn in his room at the seminary. He went outside to take fresh air only in the evening and at night. He avoided the high noonday sun.

The pre-exorcism preparations to which Father David had become accustomed in his work as an exorcist in the diocese were completed by the end of March. Some of these steps—medical checkup, examination by psychologists, family background—had been taken during Jonathan's spectacular seizure the previous autumn. With cursory additions, the preparations were completed. It remained to choose a place, fix a day, and appoint assistants.

David had an inner conviction that there would be little physical violence but much mental stress and a deep strain on his own spirit. He therefore asked a young psychiatrist friend and a middle-aged medical doctor to be his assistants. He had the services of his young priest assistant, Father Thomas, who was to succeed him in June as diocesan exorcist.

The choice of the place of exorcism presented a problem. David favored the seminary oratory or a room in a remote wing of the seminary. Jonathan pleaded for the exorcism to take place in his mother's house, where he had been born and reared. All his associations, his beginnings, and his high hopes dwelt in that house that his father had designed and built himself. Besides, it stood in its own plot of land and enjoyed a privacy unavailable at the seminary.

The bishop, ever calm, decided for them. "Whatever must come out, had better come out privately and discreetly. I don't want half my young seminarians getting nervous and running off half-cocked," he said to David. He added something which David had not expected from this worldly man whose chief claim to fame was his financial wizardry: "No superstition, mind you, Father David"—this with an arching of the eyebrows—"but his father built the house and raised his family there. He also has an interest in the whole matter. His ties are to it, surely."

David reflected on the bishop's last remark; it bore out what he had surmised in other possession cases: there was an intimate connection between definite locales and the exorcism of evil spirits.

They all agreed that Jonathan should remain at the seminary under surveillance by David and his young assistant priest until the eve of April 1, the day chosen for the exorcism. As that day approached, Jonathan became more and more listless, ate little, and relied more heavily on sleeping pills in order to secure a good night's rest.

At 10:00 P.M. on March 31, David drove him to his mother's house. They were joined there that night by the assistants—a precaution David took, again by instinct. At 4:00 A.M. the following morning, awakened by some noise, they found Jonathan fully dressed and searching in the drawers of the kitchen closet. Whether he was looking for a knife to use on himself or others, or whether—as he said—he was preparing some food, David could never be sure. Anyway, since all were awake, David asked Jonathan's mother to make some breakfast. By 6:00 A.M. they were ready to begin.

The arrangements were simple. The room had been cleared of furniture. Its terrazzo floor was bare of any carpet or rug. The window shutters were closed. Jonathan preferred to take a kneeling position, face sunk in his hands, at the small table on which David had placed his crucifix, the holy-water flask, the two candles, and the ritual book. The tape recorder was placed by the window. David wore cassock, surplice, and stole. He made no solemn entry. Standing at the opposite side of the table to Jonathan, his assistants gathered around them both, he got down right away to the business in hand. He recited the opening prayer, put down his book, looked straight at Jonathan, and spoke.

"Jonathan, before we go any further, I want to ask that you, in front of these witnesses, state quite clearly that you are here of your own accord, and that you wish me in the name of Jesus and with the authority of his Church to exorcise whatever evil spirits may possess you or hold any part of you, body and soul, in captivity. Answer me." David looked at Jonathan's bowed head. He could not see his face, only that golden hair, little strips of his forehead between the long, artistic fingers, and Jonathan's graceful hands cupping his face.

"Jonathan, please answer us," he said after a silence. David held his breath in growing suspense.

"I consent to be here"—Jonathan's voice was deep and melodious— "wishing that whatever evil or error is present be exorcised." David breathed easily again. But his uneasiness returned almost immediately, as Jonathan added: "Evil is subtle. Injustice is ancient. All wrongs must be righted. This is true Exorcism."

"We are talking, Jonathan, precisely and only of Satan, the Prince of Darkness, the Angel of Light," David hastened to say with severity. He noticed that Jonathan stirred a little, as if listening intently. "We are proposing to discover that presence and to expel it by the power of Jesus. Do you consent?"

"I consent."

A pause. Then when David was about to put his next question, Jonathan started again. "Poor Jesus! Poor, poor Jesus! Served so badly. Described so poorly. Disfigured so brashly. Poor Jesus! Poor, poor Jesus!"

David stopped abruptly. Jonathan's voice was still bell-like and silvery. David decided to take another tack.

"Now, Jonathan, by the power invested in me by the Church of Jesus, and in the name of Jesus, I wish to put you a second question. Have you knowingly, consciously, within your living memory, ever conceded anything to, or agreed, or even trifled with the Evil One?"

Jonathan's voice came back, musical and calm. "To do that to Jesus would be a betrayal of myself, of my flock, of Jesus' goodness, of the world, of life itself, of our eternal peace . . ."

"Jonathan, I want an answer, an unequivocal answer to my question. This is important."

"On the contrary, Jesus has come to me, and I have become his priest. Praise Jesus! Praise the Lord of our world!"

David had to be satisfied with this answer, so he went on to the next stage.

"Then, Jonathan, we will repeat, first, the Credo, and then your baptismal vows." David hoped in this way to avoid the necessity of going through the formal ritual of Exorcism. After all, he reasoned, if Jonathan could answer thus far satisfactorily, then the possession might just be a partial thing.

David took up the first phrases of the Credo. "I believe in God, the Father Almighty, Creator of Heaven and Earth." There he paused, waiting for Jonathan. But Jonathan had seemingly started before he had ended the phrases, and all that David could hear were the words "the Earth." He started the next phrase, "And in Jesus Christ," but broke off because Jonathan was still talking on.

"Two or three billion years ago, the Earth. Each one of us 50 trillion cells. 150 million in Caesar's day. 3,600 million in our day. 200 million tons of men, women, and children. Two trillion tons of animal life . . ."

"Jonathan, let's get on with it . . ."

"All so that Jesus can emerge. Oh, beautiful Omega! Praise Jesus! Praise the Lord of this world with which we are all, all 200 million tons of us, are one."

David stopped and looked hard at Jonathan. He still had his face sunk in his hands and was still talking.

"Oh, what they've done to it. Jews and Christians. These Judeo-Christians." Jonathan's voice now sank to a whisper of disgust. "The pontiff of creation—that's what they made every man and woman." Jonathan's shoulders shook; he was sobbing.

Again as before, David felt a strangely welcoming agreement in himself for each statement of Jonathan's. Some hidden part of him he had not known was saying again with insistence, "Yes! Yes!"

Jonathan's voice took on a speed and haste of assertion. "And what started as a pioneering weed, a trial species with toads and cock robins, zooming upward to the Jesus Point, suddenly turned and made the planet its playground, the stage of its jig-acting, its domain." The voice sank again to a whispered prayer. "Poor Jesus! Poor world! Praise the Lord of the World for Light! Poor Jesus!"

The surge of agreement in David started to sour. What was it Father G. had said? David's memory started to spin and turn. Panic seized him. He rummaged desperately through his recollections like a man plowing through a pile of old papers in search of a sorely needed document. He searched back to the beginning, back to the first instructions bustly Father G. had ever given him. What was it?

Jonathan's voice broke in on him.

"Father David, you are not with me. Please be with me!" It was insistent. David glanced again at the graceful hands covering the face and intertwined with the golden hair. Jonathan looked like an angel of God clad in light, doing penance on his knees for the sins of men. David wanted to say to him: "Yes! Jonathan, don't fear! I am with you! Yes!" The words rose to his lips like a drink offered. But a quick wave of uneasiness hit him again; and again that question came back like a boomerang: What did Father G. warn him against? What had he said? What was it? Jonathan's voice broke in again.

"Father G. is past and gone." David was shocked by Jonathan's reading of his own inmost thoughts. "Back to the womb of all of us. Let the dead bury the dead, Father David. You and I. We live. Let us walk in the light, while we have it."

Jonathan talked on now, intermingling Scripture with his words. David turned away as if warding off some influence coming at him from Jonathan; and his mind reeled as he tried to regain his lost ground. He looked up at the ceiling. He felt at bay: there was only Jonathan and himself, and between them a strange ether, an invisible corridor of communication. And, all the while, his memory was still groping and working overtime, looking for a firm hold for his mind and will. Ah! At last! That's what Father G. had said: "The Angel of Light." *That's* what he wanted to remember. "The Angel of Light." And Father G. had warned him, too: "Your great danger, David, is that you think too much. Too much of the old cerebellum in you. Listen to your heart. The Lord speaks to your heart."

A strong feeling of relief passed over David. A space was being opened up inside him—free, untrammeled, easy, roomy, fresh, private —untouched by that coiling dark pathway of communication between him and Jonathan.

Then a sharp word—his own name pronounced like the snapping of a horsewhip—hit his ears.

"David! David!" It was Jonathan. This time the voice had an admonitory note, the tone used by a master or a superior. The roles were curiously reversed.

David heard his young assistant priest whispering in his ear: "David, he's shaking. Do you think he's all right? The doctor is afraid . . ." David motioned to him, and looked at Jonathan again closely. Jonathan's face was still hidden in his hands, but he seemed to David and the assistants to be racked with sobs and sorrow.

David decided to try another approach. He had to get a toehold. Somehow he had to get Jonathan to resist the evil spirit possessing him; he had to force that spirit out into the open. And he had to keep control of himself in order to do that.

In retrospect, given David's nature, his action was almost inevitable. And given the reality of his situation as distinct from that of Jonathan, what followed was both inevitable and necessary.

He drew near Jonathan. Commiseration and compassion were uppermost in his mind. He put a hand lightly on Jonathan's shoulder and spoke.

"Jonathan, my friend. Don't give in to sorrow. I will never leave off or abandon my efforts. I will not desert you now until . . ."

"I know you won't . . ." Jonathan's voice seemed to be forced out between the violent contraction of his chest and throat. "I know you won't because"—Jonathan paused and drew a deep breath—"*my brother, you can't*. You can't." It was a dreadful rasp, a curious hiss that reached like a hand inside David's mind. David started to withdraw his hand; and as he did, he felt strange impulses in his mind: a fierce persuasion beat at him that he and Jonathan were the only sane people in that room. The others, his young colleague, the doctor, the psychiatrist, were mannequins, plastic models of reality, picaresque heroes in a cosmic joke. Only Jonathan and himself. Only Jonathan and David.

"You've got it, David!" whispered Jonathan. A rasp. A hiss.

Who was in control?

"Got what?" David hardly had the words out of his mouth when he felt some understanding beyond words, some common current of thought, as if David and Jonathan were sharing a common brain or some higher intuitive faculty that dispensed with the need for word of mouth. "Got what?" David said it over and over again. It was a sort of cry, a protest against deception. For in those moments it all became clear to him. He knew for the first time: he himself was being slowly pervaded by the same spirit of evil which held Jonathan; and he understood Jonathan knew that also.

Jonathan lifted his face suddenly and looked at David. His right hand, with the crooked index finger, came down tightly on David's hand as it rested on his own shoulder. David was like a man who saw a ghost: suddenly pale, shrunken, staring eyes, tight-lipped, short of breath, sweating profusely. For the face he saw on Jonathan was wreathed and twisted, not by sorrow or tears of pain, but in smiles and merriment. He had not been racked with sobs but with suppressed laughter. And that laughter now broke from his lips with a gust of relief. He shouted into David's face.

"You're the same as me, David! Father David!" David's young assistant, Thomas, drew near to David. The doctor and the psychiatrist fell back, overcome by surprise, looking incredulously from David to Jonathan and back to David. David shrugged off the offer of help from Father Thomas.

"You have adopted the Lord of Light, like I have, you old fool!" shrieked Jonathan between his cackling laughter. He loosened his grip on David's hand and rose to his feet. "Physician, cure yourself!"

Jonathan roared in amusement. His laughter filled the little room; he doubled over in merriment, slapping his knee, tears running down his face. "Ha-ha! David, you're a joke. *You're* a soul-fellow of *mine*. You don't believe one goddamn lousy thing of that childish hocus-pocus." Each word hit David like a physical blow. "*Hoc est corpus meum!* You're as liberated as I am, man. You belong to the New Being and the New Time."

Suddenly Jonathan quieted down. "And *you* were trying to exorcise *me?*" The contempt that replaced the laughter was enormous. He leaned forward, thrusting his face close to David's. In a slow, deliberate tone, emphasizing every word: "Get out of here, you puny weakling! Get out of here with these scarecrows you brought with you. Go bind up your wounds. Go find if your sugary Jesus will cure you. *G-e-t o-u-t!*" The last two words were two slowly delivered, heavily loaded syllables of contempt and dismissal.

David was now like a man trying to stand up after a heavy physical blow. "Come, Father David," the younger priest said quietly but urgently, as he took in the look of superiority and command in Jonathan's face. "Let's go, David," said the doctor.

David turned for an instant and looked at Jonathan. The others saw no fear on David's face, only puzzlement and pain. Their look followed David's. There stood Jonathan watching their retreat. His whole appearance had changed. His head was uplifted. He was standing tall and erect. His golden hair fell around his shoulders like a halo catching the winking light of the candles. His blue eyes were shining with hazy light. His right hand was raised in such a way that his stiffened index finger was laid across his throat. His left hand hung by his side.

"Go in darkness, you fool!" Jonathan screamed in a high falsetto. His right hand descended in a vicious gesture and swept the candlesticks off the table onto the floor. The candles went out and the room was in semidarkness. The young priest had the door open. All four men moved out quickly. "In darkness! Fools!" Jonathan's voice pursued them. As they emerged, they suddenly realized that the temperature of the day was already hot; inside, in the room, they had been cold.

David literally stumbled into the lighted hallway and leaned against the wall. Beside the hatrack, Jonathan's mother was sitting in a straight-backed ornamental chair. Her hands held a rosary on her lap. Her head, eyes closed, was bowed. After a few moments, she raised her head and, without looking around at David, she spoke in a quiet voice full of resigned sorrow.

"He's right. My son. The devil's slave. He is right, Father David. You need cleansing. God help you." Then, as if she sensed some apprehension in David and the others for her sanity or her faith, she added: "I am his mother. No harm can come to me." It was an instinctual thing she said, but David was certain she was correct.

David stumbled past her. Nobody looked at her. His companions eased David into a car and drove him to the seminary. Once in his room, he sat wearily with the young priest for about half an hour.

"What are we going to do, Father David?" Thomas finally asked. David made no reply. He was now wholly occupied with himself and with the black reality he had discovered inside himself. He looked at the young priest and felt strangely out of place. What had he in common with that fresh face, the black cassock, the white round collar, and—above all—that look in the young priest's eyes? What was that look, anyway? He screwed up his eyes staring at Thomas. What was that look? Had he ever had it himself? Was it all a joke? A mere charade or piece of imposed childishness? Young priests must believe —like young children. Then they grow up—as children do. And then they stop having that look. Stop "believing"?

"You are surrounded by quotation marks, Thomas," he said stupidly to the younger priest. Then he lapsed into silence still staring at his colleague. What in the hell was believing anyway? That inane look! What was that look! As if all was sugar and spice and goo and kindness and pie-in-the-sky-when-you-die and infantile trust. Why was that look so open and wide-eyed?

"Stop looking like a fool!" David shot the words at Thomas. Then he realized what he had done. "Sorry, Thomas," he mumbled lamely, seeing the young face pale. David began to cry in silence.

"Father David," Thomas drew in a breath. "I have no experience. But you need a rest. Let me phone your family." David nodded helplessly.

In the early afternoon David was driven up to Coos County, back to his home on the farm. His parents were delighted to see him. They now lived alone except for one sleep-in help and a gardener who stayed at the farm.

That night David went to bed in the room he had occupied during his childhood and youth. But some time after midnight he woke up covered with perspiration and shaking like a leaf. He did not know why, but a deep sense of foreboding filled his mind. He got up, went down to the kitchen, and heated some milk. As he returned to his room, he stopped at the door of Old Edward's room. He stood there for a moment, sipping the milk and thinking in a vague, undirected way. As he describes it now, his mind was still clearing, like a jumbled TV picture slowly coming into focus. Then, with nothing particular in mind, but only by some blind impulse, he opened the door of the room, reached for the light switch, and stepped inside.

The room was much the same as it had been the evening of Edward's death, except for one change: a large photograph of Edward, taken a few months before he had passed away, hung over the mantelpiece. It looked down at David. He sat for about an hour in that room. Then, under the same blind impulse, still unhurriedly, he went to his own room, transferred his bedclothes and personal effects to Edward's room, and then went to sleep there.

David stayed almost four weeks on the farm. In the beginning, he went out every day for long walks and to do some manual work on the farm. Sometimes he passed by the copse at the west end of the house, but never entered it. He would stand a while ruminating and then go on his way. He looked up some old friends, and spent a good part of the evenings with his parents.

Toward the end of the first week, this loose and varied schedule changed. He began to spend most of the day and night in his room, coming out for his meals, rarely going outside the house. Then about the third week, he did not emerge at all except to use the bathroom.

He did not open the shutters in his room. He ate sparingly, and toward the end lived on milk and biscuits and some dried fruit which his mother left on a tray outside the door of his room.

From the beginning of his stay he had warned his parents not to be alarmed by his living habits. On his first day there, he had gone to see Father Joseph, the local priest, whom he had taught in the seminary. During the last ten days of David's stay at the farm, that priest was the only human being who visited and spoke with David.

David kept a minutely detailed diary during those four weeks; and, except for certain moments when he lost control of himself (of those moments he has no clear recollection), there is a more or less continuous chronology of events—the inner experience David went through and the external phenomena that marked this crucial period.

During all this time, down in Manchester, Jonathan lived at home with his mother.

Comparison of how David and Jonathan spent specific days and hours during those weeks has been difficult to achieve, but there is clear indication that certain states through which David passed coincided—sometimes to the hour—with strange moments and behavior in Jonathan's life. Our chief intent, however, is to trace David's experience, for, in the technical language of theology, Father David M. was deprived of all conscious belief. His religious faith was tested in an assault which nearly succeeded in robbing him of it all. Mentally and emotionally, he found himself in the state of one without any religious belief whatever. To this extent, David, who still felt that his vocation as priest was valid, had handed over his mind and emotions to some form of possession.

There would have been no struggle, much less any agony, if David's *will* had not remained stubbornly attached to his religious beliefs. Inch by inch, figuratively speaking, he had to fight for survival of his faith against a spirit to which he himself had granted entry and which now made a bid to take him over completely. Consciously he had been admitting ideas and persuasions for a long time. He had not realized until now that all such motivating ideas and persuasions, for all their guise of "objectivity," had a moral dimension and a relation to spirit—good and evil. He had failed all along to realize that nothing is morally neutral. With these ideas, persuasions, and deficiencies as a most suitable vehicle, there had entered him some spirit, alien to him, but now claiming full control over him.

During those four weeks on the Coos farm, David's entire life as a believer flashed by him continually and ever more intensely like photographs being flipped with the thumb—childhood, schooldays, seminary training, ordination, doctoral studies, anthropology trips, lectures, what he had written in articles and books, the conversations he had held, constantly changing panels. When he reached the end, they began all over again.

Cameos. Little scenes. Faces long forgotten. Words and sentences echoing back in half-complete fashion. Vivid memories. Each one with an individual conclusion. The day he told Sister Antonio in the convent school that Jesus could not possibly fit into the communion wafer. David was eight years old. Sister had patted his head: "David, be a good boy. We know what is right." They had given him no choice and no answer. *No choice. No choice*, rang the silent echo.

His interview with the bishop for acceptance into the seminary: "If you become a priest, you are called to a perfection of spirit not granted to the majority of Christians." Spirit is not elitist. *Not elitist. Not elitist. Not elitist,* went the echo.

The echoes rang through the hall of years in David's brain, as the "photographs" continued to flash before him.

He remembered the moment he became convinced that there were no reliable records about Jesus written during Jesus' own lifetime. In the four Gospels, the Acts of the Apostles, and the letters of Paul, there was only what men and women believed and thought they knew 30, 40, 60 years after Jesus' death. Even if they believed they knew, how could David be sure that they knew? He was thinking and believing only what *they* thought and believed. "I have no records. It sounds like delusion." *Delusion. Delusion. Delusion.* The word was a hammer blow in David's whorl of memories.

Then another flash of memory, another change, another bit of evil. Eleven years before, David had gone on a tour through the places where Jesus had lived and died. Immediately afterward, he had visited Rome and spent long days viewing its monuments, basilicas, and treasures. He followed the ceremonies in St. Peter's Basilica. As he started home for America, one question dominated everything for him: What possible relationship could there be between Jesus' obscure life on that stark, poverty-stricken, barren land, and the panoply and glory of papal Rome? Perhaps he understood only now, but he had come to a covert conclusion on that home journey: there was *no real* relationship. Now his memory kept on repeating with little bursts of pain: *no relationship, no relationship, no relationship.*

Four years before, he had opened up an ancient tomb in northeast-ern Turkey. Inside, he and the other archeologists had found a buried chieftain surrounded by the bones of men and animals slaughtered for his funeral. The bones, the weapons, the utensils, the dust, and the pathos of it all had gripped him. These had been men like himself. They had had no knowledge of Jesus. How could they be judged for not knowing anything about Jesus and Christianity? Surely what David had thought of Jesus was too small a concept? Surely the truth was greater than any dogma? Than any concept of Jesus as man or as God, or any form that Jesus took? It had to be so. Otherwise, there was no sense in anything. *Greater than Jesus. Greater than Jesus. Greater than Jesus.* Another jarring echo ringing in his memory.

There gradually emerged a fatal thread that stitched together all the echoing resentments, all the complaints of reason, all the arrogance of logic stripped to its own marrow. And the fabric of faith slipped away unnoticed as this new cloth draped his mind and soul. The thread was David's acceptance of Teilhard de Chardin's theories. Accepting them, he could no longer tolerate the break between the material nature of the world, on the one hand, and Jesus as savior, on the other hand. Materiality and divinity were one; the material world together with man's consciousness and will, both emerging from sheer material-ity as automatically as a hen from an egg; and Jesus' divinity emerging from his human being as naturally as an oak tree from an acorn, as inevitably as water flowing downward.

Jesus—so suddenly integral to the universe, so intimate with its being, so totally physical—was *different* from what religious dogma had said he was, *greater* than Christian belief had ever before understood. Jesus, each man, each woman, all were brothers to the boulders, sisters of the stars, "co-beings" with all animals and plants. All understanding became easy. It all came down to the atom; and it all came up from the atom as well. Everything fell into place.

So much for Teilhard, David thought bitterly.

With an anguish he could not assuage, David realized the conse-quences of all this only now in the lonely struggle and painful vigil for his soul. Any real reverence and awe had evaporated from his religious mentality. For the world around him he had only a sense of joyous kinship—mingled with a certain foreboding. For Jesus, only a satisfying feeling of triumph, just as for any ancient and beloved hero. For the Mass, an indulgent feeling akin to what he experienced when observing commemorative services on any July Fourth. The Crucifixion and the death of Jesus were glorious events in the past, ancient demonstrations of heroic love, not an ever-present source of personal forgiveness and not an unshakable hope for any future.

Isolated with his thoughts and memories, David's question for himself was not where or how things had gone wrong, but how to retrieve his strength in faith. As the years passed continually by his view like so many panels from right to left, David seemed to be close up to them, scrutinizing each detail.

As the days passed, those panels in the panorama moved faster and faster, on and on, repeating over and over. He could still read the details. Each phrase sounded and receded as its corresponding panel came and went. *No choice. Not elitist. Delusion. No relationship. Greater than Jesus. Brothers to the boulders.*

Sometime after midnight at the beginning of the third week at the Coos farm, David seemed suddenly to be drawing away from his close-up scrutiny of the changing panels, or they were withdrawing from him, receding into some background darkness he had not noticed before. He realized he had not been looking at panels passing horizontally in front of him from right to left. He had been close to a revolving sphere that was now drawing away from him. Distancing itself from him and still revolving, it depicted all the phases of his life continuously and without interruption around the smooth convex surface of that brightly lit ball.

From its dreamy depths came the sounds of all his yesteryears— words, voices, languages, music, crying, laughing. The sphere had a mesmeric quality of a carousel giving off a creamy light. David seemed to be looking at himself out there.

Yet a tiny voice kept whispering within him: *Why me? Why am I attacked? Why me? Where is Jesus? What is Jesus?* And all around that revolving sphere lay the unfathomable velvet of a night he had never known.

Staring at the sphere, he knew that in some mysterious way he was staring at the self he had become. Of the room around him, the feel of the chair in which he sat, the rub of his clothes against his skin, of such things finally he was not even indirectly conscious.

Now, without either pause or abruptness, the light from that revolving sphere started to grow dim. More and more of the blackness around it started to patch its panels with shadows, crow's-feet of obscurity, little running lines of invisibility. The self he had been and known was being volatilized into blackness. David felt panic, but seemed to be incapable of doing anything about what was happening to him.

Then he had the feeling that he was no longer looking out or up or at anything, but that he now was out there hanging in that blackness. Feeding his helplessness and panic was the conviction that he was the cause of this black void and that he needed it. Otherwise, it seemed to him, he would drop into nothingness.

Then finally, all he had ever been or known of himself had disappeared. The self to which he was now reduced hung by an invisible thread—but only as long as he could maintain that blackness. David's panic was marinated in a tide of sullenness rising in him, sullenness at being deprived of light, of salvation, of grace, of beauty, of motives for holiness, of knowledge about physical symmetry, and all perception of God's eternity. His reaction to this sullenness: *Why me?*

He was waiting, expecting, almost listening. Hours. Days. His waiting became so intense, so oppressive that he gradually realized he was not waiting of his own volition. The waiting was being evoked from him by someone or something outside him. Yet each time he tried to figure out or imagine who or what was evoking the waiting, his very effort at imagining clouded everything over. The only thing he could do was wait, be made to wait, to expect.

And there set in on him a sadness he could not dispel. He no longer felt any confidence in himself or in anything he knew. For all seemed to be reduced to a situation without circumstances, a pattern without a background, a framework sodden with emptiness through which rushed gusts of an alien influence he could neither repel nor control. He was helpless. And eventually he would fall asleep, awakening only with the light of day streaming in through the bay window.

In the morning he would know it was all real: he was isolated from all he had ever made his own and from all he had ever been. And he had to wait. But, obscurely and earnestly, he realized that whatever it was he awaited, could come to him only under these conditions.

A conversation David had with Father Joseph at the end of the third week reveals the crux of David's struggle and his state of mind toward the last phase of his four-week test. It was Father Joseph's third visit. Each time, he had questioned David about the experience he was undergoing, and each time he himself had left the house overwhelmed by a sorrow and inner pain which he found intolerable. And David had warned him: "Don't delve very deeply, Father. You can only get hurt.

And come to see me in the mornings. In the afternoon I doze a little. Evenings and nights are too much for anybody but me."

This time, stepping into David's room from the sunlit corridor outside, Father Joseph took a moment to get used to the semidarkness. Little lines of sunlight ran around the edges of the shutters. In the far corner beside the fireplace, he saw David sitting at a small table, hunched over a page of writing. A single candle stood on the table; it was all the light David allowed himself.

David stood up and pointed Joseph to an armchair when the priest entered. "Have a seat, Father." Their eyes did not meet while he spoke.

David had not shaved for a couple of days. He was gaunt and hollow-cheeked. There was very little color in his face. But it was the immobility of his features that first struck his visitor. His cheeks, forehead, nose, chin, and neck seemed to be frozen into motionless-ness, as if too much inner determination and too much constant resistance had resulted in a total hardening of his appearance, a setting of his face into an expressionless shape.

His eyes particularly held Father Joseph. They seemed to have grown larger, the lids, heavier, the whites, whiter, the pupils, darker than they had been. Obviously David had been crying a good deal. But at this moment his eyes were clear, steady in gaze, remote in look.

There was no hint of a smile or of any pleasant emotion, but neither was there any unpleasantness. Nor fear. Nor pain. Nor were David's eyes blank. They had an expression; but that expression was totally unknown to Joseph. He had never seen it before in anybody's eyes. And he was at a loss to explain it or describe it. He was looking at the eyes of someone who had seen things of which he could have no inkling.

He knew better than to indulge in pleasantries, even to ask David how he was. They both sat there in silence, both understanding what was in the other's mind.

From outside, some isolated sounds penetrated faintly into the room, a truck passing on the road, the twittering of some birds, a dog barking on a distant farm.

"I don't think the real attack has come yet, Father Joe," David said slowly to his visitor, in whose mind this was, in fact, the uppermost question. Then he added as if to answer a query: "Yes, I will know, because the others will come at the same time."

They both waited. David's visitor knew from previous conversations who "the others" were. David was convinced that his release from this trial could only come through the spirits of Salem Old Edward had mentioned on his deathbed. But somehow or other Old Edward was now associated in David's mind with those spirits.

Then David said: "It's been bad but bearable up to this." Father Joseph shot a discreet look at David: his eyes were hooded as he gazed down at the table. Joseph looked away in an embarrassment he himself could not understand. David's voice was deep, very deep, and every word came out as if a special effort was needed to form it.

"No," David went on, answering another unspoken query of Joseph's. "There is nothing you can do. Must fight it alone. Pray. That's all. Pray. A lot. Pray for me."

There was another long silence. By now, Joseph knew that the silence between them was chockful of a conversation he could not pin down. He could not make out how it progressed or what it concerned exactly. Joseph was a simple man without any subtle ideas and with no complexities in spirit. His heart and instincts had not been smothered in any pseudointellectualism. He did realize that it was a conversation so subtle and intimate that it flew high above all words, in fact did not need words. It passed between them in another medium. But Joseph warily refused even to visualize that medium. He felt that too near an acquaintance with it would mean he would never be able to talk with words again. Words were beginning to be crude, vulgar lumps of sound, insensitive, uncouth, meaningless. David and Joseph were both walking at that moment beyond the thin edge dividing language from meaning, and meaning was now a cloud enveloping them both.

Father Joseph waited until he felt from David that he should leave. Then he started to rise unhurriedly. David said: "Say a Mass for them. They need prayers. I failed them. Now I need them, their help, and their forgiveness." Joseph looked at him questioningly, then stopped the words rushing to his lips. Joseph now believed that David had already been "visited."

For the next week, his fourth at the farm, David's days and the greater portion of his nights were spent on the chair by the bay window. For the last day or so before the final struggle, a curious silence had fallen over him. It was not ominous or fear-filling. But it was so profound and so devoid of any movement in his thoughts, emotions, and memories that the doubt and uncertainty it provoked in him took on proportions of agonizing anticipation.

Yet no amount of anticipation quite conveyed the anguished reality of his "visitors" and their "visit."

The first hint of their presence came about eleven o'clock one night. All that day a storm had raged around the farm. The storm had prevented Father Joseph from making his promised weekly visit. David had spent the time contemplating the sheeting rain and the lightning flashes from his window. Then, except for a distant rumble of thunder and an occasional, sudden, whipping shower, the storm was spent.

David sensed the cloak of exhaustion that always fell quietly on the countryside after it had been thrashed and seared and smothered by wind, lightning, thunder, and rain. Usually the land shook off that cloak quickly and resumed its habitual night stance as a repository of energies hatching, breathing, coiling, exercising, pulsating, self-renewing, waiting for the sun and the light of the new day.

He waited for the inevitable rustling and quickening in the fields outside the house. But tonight the silence of exhaustion seemed to prolong itself. A commanding hand had stopped the course of nature in order to make way for special visitors. And, in David's consciousness, all these changes resided as mere overtones to his mood.

The most acute and self-aware point in his being was still a pulse of expectancy, of waiting that grew deeper and deeper with the prolonged silence over the land. Once more David seemed to hang over that pitch-black void. Waiting seemed once more to be his very essence, the only reason for his continued existence. "As long as I can wait . . ." was his mood. Waiting, straining, to hear, to see.

After perhaps an hour, he knew that somewhere near him there was a curious sound.

At first, when he heard it, his attention did not pick it up. It was so faint, it might have been the sound and feel of the blood pumping in his own ears. But after a few seconds, he began to distinguish it. His body stiffened as the sound grew ever so slightly louder.

He could not identify the sound. Within him, yet in some way connected with the faint sound, little wisps of memory touched his consciousness briefly, tantalizing him as they skipped by, leaving him all the tenser. He seemed to remember. Little splinks, jagged fragments of shattered mirrors reflecting some shadow life; but he could not make out exactly what was being recalled to him.

He realized that the act of trying to remember was itself a blockage to remembering, the act of thinking a hindrance to knowing. At one point, the sound died away completely. He was suddenly alone. And he found himself falling back on the chair brusquely. He had been half out of it, apparently, in his craning forward to listen. His palms and forehead were wet. And his yearning to know seemed infinitely sad.

Then the sound started again. David realized now it was coming from no particular direction. Not from outside the house. Not from inside it. Nor could he say it was coming from all directions at once. He felt foolishly that in some way or other it was a permanent sound that had always been there around him. He always had heard it. But he had never listened to it, or ever allowed himself even to acknowledge that he heard it.

He turned his head right and left. He twisted around, listening to the interior of the room. And with a sudden violence he understood why the sound seemed to come from no direction. For the first time in his life, he knew what it was to hear a sound registering in his brain and mind without any of the normal exterior conditions of hearing— no sound waves, no exterior source of sound, no function of his eardrums. Beyond all doubts or caviling, he knew that it was real sound which could not be heard with the external ear.

The physical strangeness of that new hearing had a mysterious warmth of reality. It was more real than any other sound he could ever hear in the physical world. It broke the silence of the night and his vigil more penetratingly than if a gunshot had exploded outside the window. Intensely pleasurable, because so secret. Deeply relieving, because it dismissed the silence around him in a fashion so intimate to him alone. Absorbing, because it came from no place, yet filled all his inner hearing. But cowing, because in some transcendent way it had no tenderness.

That sound was a whole revelation. He now understood that there was a knowledge of material things and a way of having that knowledge—in this case, of sounds—which did not come through his senses. His fear and distrust battled with this realization whenever a stray sound—the cry of a bird in the night, the hooting of an owl—struck his hearing in the normal way. These new, fearful, wallowing sounds seemed to belong to the very *substance* of audible things and his hearing of them to be absolutely true hearing. The external sounds of the night—even the occasional shuffle of his own feet on the floor—seemed to belong to a fleeting world, artificial, not real at all, but constructed merely by external stimuli and by his own physical reactions.

The babel of internal sounds was growing, and the "artificial" world of his normal life appeared to be like a flimsy trellis with wide gaps or a wall made of widely separated wires. A crude, blustering, overwhelming new reality was rushing in through the holes.

With that, David began to understand vaguely what possession meant, for that inrushing babel was in control of him. He could not eliminate it, repel it, examine and analyze it, decide he liked it or disliked it. It allowed him no reflection or rejection, did not elicit acceptance, caused neither pleasure nor pain, disgust nor delight. It was neutral. Because neutral, it was baleful. And it began to shade his mind and will with its own neutrality of taste and judgment more wasting than an Arctic wind. Whatever beauty, harmony, and meaning had been associated in his memory with sound now began to wither. He felt that withering keenly. He knew its dreadful implications.

"My God! Jesus!" he suddenly screamed to himself without sound. "My God! If all my senses—sight, hearing, smell, taste, touch—are invaded like that, I'd be possessed. I'd be possessed. Jesus! I'd be possessed."

He tried to say "Jesus" out loud, to cry out some prayer such as the Hail Mary or the Our Father, some prayer he knew and had said a couple of thousand times every year for the past 35 or 40 years. But he heard no sound at all from his own lips. He was sure that he had pronounced the words. But possession of his hearing was too far gone.

The babel grew louder and louder by infinitesimal but relentless degrees. The sound itself was without rhythm, David remembers. It was a combination of thousands of little sounds, literally a babel of sounds. It grew louder—approached him in that sense. The many little sounds started to harmonize into two or three particular syllables he could not rightly distinguish. The sounds grew greater, but they coalesced at such a slow pace and with what seemed such interminably long pauses between changes, that a new oppression began to cramp his mind and body. It was his craning, waiting, expecting, his anticipation—all stirred into pain by the hard stick of fear inside him. Yet, within him, some strong, indomitable muscle of soul held firm.

As the coalescing little voices took shape and rhythm, David began to hear the beat of those syllables louder and more distinctly. As the beating rhythm took body, he found his body swaying in unison, his feet beating on the floor, his hand beating on his knee, his head and shoulders jerking forward and backward. He still could not make out the syllables, but the rhythmic beating was animating every part of his body. His own lips started to pick up a syllable now and then. The voices grew louder still. Thousands of them. And more thousands. And more.

Falteringly but with greater accuracy his lips searched out the sounds and fell into unison with the voices that were grating out those syllables louder and louder and louder. His tension grew. His physical movements went faster and faster. The sound of the voices was a roar in his inner hearing now. His own voice picked up the syllables.

Mister Natch . . . Mister Natch . . . Mister Natch . . . Mister Natch . . .

A whole army of voices was marching through his brain and soul, shouting, grating, hitting, screeching that last syllable, *Natch! Natch! Natch! Natch!,* until David felt he was going to turn into a palpitating, jerking string of taut muscles and mad sound.

As the noise reached a crescendo, David had practically let go, surrendered, was waiting for disintegration through sound. Then a new and utterly different note echoed through the din. He stopped slipping, surrendering. Some inner part of him that had not been tainted now came alive.

The new sound was clear, somewhat like a bell, but he knew no metal produced that sound; he knew its notes would not die when the hour sounded and passed. It was a sound that sang rather than rang. It echoed with a promise of permanence, sustained, continuous. It was a living sound. And while it had the haunting beauty of tonal silver speaking musically and without words through purest air, it also came sheathed in that liquidity and warmth whose message is love achieved.

As David's heart sprang up toward the new song, he began to abhor all the more that loutish chant, *Mister Natch! Mister Natch! Mister Natch!* But still he could not free himself from its violent, seductive force. And so there formed a void, an abyss, an unbridgeable chasm whose walls were made of sound, whose floor was purest pain. One part of his mind became a bed of shaking, blustering depression; and his will recoiled from it in spasms of disgust. Another part of his mind was transfused with calm and secure freedom full of repose, immune to any fleck of darkness. *"Between us and thee there is a great gulf fixed . . . they who would pass over it, cannot."* Bits of fright shot like electricity around ragtag phrases trailing in David's memory.

And sound, always sound. Thumping, roaring, cantankerous, raucous, reeling round him like coils that deafened him and smothered him. And then, fresh and far, far above in some region of sunlight and upland calm out of any possible reach, but reaching him nonetheless, there was that other note, opposite, intimate, welling with unimaginable sweetness that wet his face with tears of yearning.

At a certain point, all this immersion in sounding opposites and echoing contradictions became both diversified and intensified. The conflict for possession of his hearing was extended to his other senses and to his inner pooling of senses. As the conflict increased and seeped through him, the fonts of fear and desire, of repugnance and attraction welled up until all his senses echoed his agony.

He fell on his knees, his forehead pressed against the cold glass of the window, his hands locked in prayer, his eyes wide open and staring out at the night but unseeing of other eyes that watched from outside. For the next few interminable minutes, the hurricane contention between good and evil always twisting violently through our human landscape was funneled and focused on that kneeling figure of David, and the conflict seized him totally.

Suddenly, at one moment, he was floating on an inland lake of unruffled waters within delightful valleys carpeted in green woods and peaceful lawns of wild flowers. Ahead lay an eastern sky, its clear blue face bronzed by a rising sun. Then just as suddenly, he was tossing frenetically on a mountain river rushing through a high gorge into which no sunlight reached. Nothing seemed to keep him from drowning or being impaled and crushed on shark-toothed rocks and ugly-headed crags. His body was carried through cascades and rapids overhung and hemmed in by gigantic battlements of sheer cliffs rent with narrow chasms and inhanging precipices. Throughout this violence, he was pursued by the clomping of Mister Natch and wooed by the lilting notes of that other music from far above.

Then again, without warning, all the confusing contrasts increased in speed and variety. He was jammed into a quick-change theater alternating between horror and relief, beauty and beastliness, life and death. There was no sense, neither rhyme nor reason to it all. Now he saw delicate-limbed, silk-clad bodies dancing on a green platform and starching rhythms on the winds. Then, quick as a flash, he was scrutinizing eviscerated corpses, open bellies with the guts plopping and slobbering out on thighs and knees, bodies slit from chin to chine, severed breasts, gobs of eyes and fingers and hair, carpets of excrement. Now it was bunches of heavy, ripe fruit draped between trees or entwined in Spanish moss on a great levee. Then, in the kaleidoscope of insanity that was David's world in those excruciating moments, it was heavy canisters of urine pierced with holes, spraying the gaping eyes and mouths of cadavers, thousands of cadavers, men, women, children, fetuses, thrown higgledy-piggledy over a stony plain.

As the bewildering, horrifying sets of images tumbled in front of his eyes, he felt his control ebbing. He was only sure of one thing: two forces were contending for possession of him, and he could not avoid the flooding of his senses. He could not rid them either of the filth or the beauty. All his life he had been able to control himself. Now control was gone. The invasion continued.

The confusion reached his taste and sense of smell; it invaded every sense and every nuance of his being that was fed by his senses. Bitter and sweet, acrid and flowing, cesspool and perfume, sting and caress, animal and human, edible and inedible, vomit and delicacy, rough and smooth, subtle and pointed, shocking and wafting, dizzying and calming, aching and pleasuring—the contrasts jangled every taste bud and nerve in his mouth, throat, nose, and belly.

He reached the point of near-hysteria when his sense of touch was attacked: every centimeter of his skin was being scraped with rough scales and stroked with velvet, burned by hot points and pained by icicles, then relaxed and massaged by gentle warmth and frictionless surfaces.

The storm in his senses grew more and more intense according as each of the contradictory sensations was pooled within him to make a jigsaw mosaic of nonsense, confusion, aimlessness, helplessness.

Yet, even with all control lost, somehow his mind and will sought an answer to the ultimate question: Why can't I resist? What must I do to repel this? What motivation can I use to expel it all? What do I do? He realized clearly enough that his time was not up, that all was not lost yet; that somewhere in him something must be healthy and active still. For all the while he clung to one thing: the more intense the distortion became and the tighter the grip exercised on him, the more the sheer horror and pain paralyzed any initiative in him—the more beautiful and winning became that song from above.

Its lovely sound was still at immeasurable distances and unreachable heights. In some way he could not understand, however, it was near him. He began to fight for the strength to hear it, to listen. It was not monochrome or single-toned. It was a chant of many voices; it harmonized some ineffable joy with sweeping clusters of chords and congregations of soaring grace notes. Adagio, it was grave but happy.

Resounding, it had a coolness clinging to it. At once it had all the traits of love—its gentle teasing, its collusion and connivance, its favoritism; and beating within it, there was a steady organ-like pulsation that ran deeper than the heart of the universe and as high as the eternal placidness men have always ascribed to unchanging divinity.

At one surprising moment in all the din and the pain, David's heart leaped. It was his only moment of relief and peace, and it came just before the climax of his struggle. It was not so much a beguiling lull that sometimes fools the priest in more ordinary exorcisms. It was a song he somehow knew, sung by voices he somehow knew. And although he could not recollect the song or who was singing it, he knew he was not alone. "Jesus! I'm not alone," he heard himself muttering. "I'm not alone!"

He began to distinguish several voices in that gentle song. He knew them! He knew them! He could not recognize them, but he knew them. They were friends. Where? When? Who were they? He had known them for years, he realized. But who were they? And as the new feeling penetrated to his inner senses and clashed with his loneliness, a wild seesawing emotion started to filter further and further into his mind and will and imagination. He found himself babbling incoherent phrases which were at first unintelligible even to himself. The phrases seemed to come from some inner faculty he had always used but never acknowledged, some source of knowledge that he had neglected for all his years as an adult and a professional intellectual.

"My Salem chorus . . . my loved ones . . ." The phrases were squeezed out of him by some force and strength of his own, his very own. "My friends . . . Edward's friends. . . . Come nearer. . . . Forgive me . . ."

A tiny eddy of understanding began to form in him as he tapped the memory of Old Edward's last days and of the visit to Salem long years ago. It was just in time. For in that moment there began what proved to be the last phase of David's trial.

Moments of terror gripped David immediately: suddenly he felt everything, everything had been wrenched from his grasp and he could not find in himself any conscious reason to reject the clamorous and oppressive influence of Mister Natch. His mind again seemed to be a mere receptacle. His will—the will he had always relied on consciously for his discipline in study and his practical decisions— seemed to be at bay again and unable to carry him to victory.

Terror deepened as his mind became more and more confused, and his will was overcome and strapped down and immobilized by contradictory and poisonously neutralizing motives. What poured into his mind and filled his spirit was like venom.

A pell-mell mob of reasons squealed and screamed within him. Mister Natch pulsed and rasped horribly: *Hoc est corpus meum . . . Hocus-pocus Jesus is, a crucified donkey. . . . Good and truth is man's highest goal. . . . How delightful and human to try the most unhuman. . . . Jesus, Mary, and . . . Satan, devils can fuck, fuck, fuck. . . . I give you my heart and my . . . God will not allow evil. . . . Good is as banal as bad, have both. . . . I desire the salvation of the Cross . . . and I hope to taste the liberty of blasphemy. . . . I love . . . I hate . . . I believe . . . I disbelieve. . . . He created Jesus out of slime . . . and said this my beloved son in whom I am well pleased.* David's will was numbed with pain and exhaustion. All this while, his senses were attacked and confused with the same jangling conflict, until in a land of indescribable idiocy and confusion his touch, his smell, his hearing all echoed: *The good is too good to be true. . . . The evil is too evil not to be true. . . . What is true?*

Now, no solution, no escape, no alternative to the dilemma, no determining factor, no deciding weight in the balance seemed possible. Lost. All lost. All that David had studied, every highway and byway of intellectual reasoning, psychological subtlety, theological proof, philosophical logic, historical evidence—all these became like so many objects, not parts of him, only mere possessions and trash he had accumulated, now thrown into flames that advanced across the threshold of his very being. Everything he threw at those flames was seized, melted, dissipated, mere fuel, unable to resist the burning.

Blackness had almost fully beclouded his mind when David became aware that one thing still remained. Something that defied the blackness and the clouding. Something that rose in him strongly, independently every time that strange, insistent song dominated the clamor wrapping him around. At first, he was merely aware of the sound. Then he began to marvel at its strength, and not at its loudness, for he could not always hear it, but at its persistence in the middle of his pain and encroaching despair. He tried to reflect on it and on the strength that rose in him like a responding chord, but immediately he lost all awareness of it. And, immediately again, the struggle set in, and his attention turned. And no sooner did he hear the song again than that strange, autonomous strength within him rose up.

All at once he knew what that strength was. It was his will. His autonomous will. He himself as a freely-choosing being.

With a sidelong glance of his mind, he dismissed once and for all that fabric of mental illusions about psychological motivations, behavioral stimulations, rationales, mentalistic hedges, situational ethics, social loyalties, and communal shibboleths. All was dross and already eaten up and disintegrated in the flames of this experience which might still consume him.

Only his will remained. Only his freedom of spirit to choose held firm. Only the agony of free choice remained.

"My Salem chorus!" he heard himself say. "My friends! Pray for me. Ask Jesus for me. Pray for me. I have to choose."

Now a specific and peculiar agony beset David. He had never known it before. Indeed, afterwards he wondered for a long time how many real choices he had made freely in his life before that night. For it was that agony of choosing freely—totally freely—that was now his. Just for the sake of choosing. Without any outside stimuli. Without any background in memory. Without any push from acquired tastes and persuasions. Without any reason or cause or motive deciding his choice. Without any gravamen from a desire to live or to die—for at this moment he was indifferent to both. He was, in a sense, like the donkey medieval philosophers had fantasized as helpless, immobilized, and destined to starve because it stood equidistant from two equivalent bales of hay and could not decide which one to approach and eat. Totally free choice.

Mister Natch's clomping rhythm now became the grotesque accompaniment of an evil and sickening burlesque of distortion. A satyr face and body loomed in David's imagination—so real that he saw it with his eyes. Naked. Obscenely sprawled. Bulbous. The nose pointing in one askew direction. Two eyes squinting in opposite directions. Mouth grinning, foaming, crooked. Throat gurgling insane chuckles. Heavy female breasts blotched with warts, hanging nipples, blood-red, and pointing like twin penises. Legs apart, streaked with blood and sperm. One toe doubled back into the crotch scratching and rubbing frenetically. Twisted, irregular fingers with broken nails pulling at lumps of hair and gesturing crudely. Clots of caked excrement around the buttocks.

David caught the odor of cowstalls and open-air privies. He remembered the devil figures of the Greeks and the Asmat. He felt the oldest pull recorded in the history of the human heart. He felt it as an ancient seed of evil he had received from all who went before him, not as a physical gift of terrible import but as a consequence of his being born of their line and, in a sense, accumulating all the evil they had transmitted. Not evil acts. Nor evil impulses. Neither guilts nor shame. Nothing positive. Rather an absence amounting to a fatal flaw. A deathly lack. A capacity for self-hatred, for suicide, not because he could not live forever but because he could so live if only . . . That tantalizing "if only" of mortality which aspires infinitely without being infinite itself. The *fomes peccati* of the Latins. The *yetzer ha-ra* of the Hebrews. "Ye can be as gods knowing good and evil," the Serpent had said in the Bible myth—not adding "but capable only of evil, if left to yourselves."

He had to choose. The freedom to accept or reject. A proposed step into a darkness. The song from on high was silent. The clamor of Mister Natch was stilled. All seemed waiting on his next step. His own. Only his.

Even to be neutral was a decision. For to be neutral now was to take refuge in cynicism; to say, "I don't want to know;" to refuse an appeal for trust; to be alone; just to be.

For a split second it seemed he should turn back and call for the consolation of evil—at least he would be under a tangible control and possessed by that which corresponded to one of his deepest urges. But it was only for a second, because from beyond that crag of decision he heard—or thought he heard—a great cry coming across an infinite distance, not in protest, not in hysteria, not in despair; rather a cry from a soul driven to the outermost point of endurance by pain and disgrace and abandonment. He heard that cry take several forms: "Abba, Father!" "Mother, behold!" "Lord, Remember me!" "In this sign . . ."

It was all David needed to push him, even pursued by his fears, past that crag. He began to think words again, to open his lips, mouthing them soundlessly.

Then panic rose. What if it were all delusion, mocking delusion? The panic became pandemonium in his brain. But now it was matched and outstripped by his violent wish to speak, to get those words out in living sound. Somehow, if it took his last strength, if it cost him his life, he had to pronounce them audibly. His intentions would not be humanly real until he did . . . unless he did.

In his agony, still on his knees and still facing the window of his room, David remained so absorbed in this last effort that he still did not notice the figure standing outside the window. Father Joseph had waited at home for the storm to abate, and then set out for the farm. The only light in the place had been from David's window. Now he stood outside trying to guess what was happening to his friend inside. "Help him. Mother of Jesus. In the name of Jesus, ask for help for him, please." He could see David's lips working silently and his wide, sightless eyes staring into the night.

Joseph was about to tap on the window or wake up the others in the house when he heard David cry out loud, at first in a staccato fashion, then firmly and connectedly and vibrantly: "I choose . . . I will . . . I believe. . . . Help my unbelief . . . Jesus! . . . I believe I believe I believe." Joseph stood stock-still and listened. He could only see David's face and hear his words. He could not enter his consciousness, where the twin chants had once again sounded to the very depth of his soul.

But it was different for David now. He had chosen, and the result was instantaneous. He found, not destruction and helplessness and childish weakness, and not the black slavery of mind and will that Mister Natch had taunted would be the fruits of belief. Instead, a great and breathtaking dimension full of relief and distance and height and depth flooded his mind and will and imagination.

As if the darkness and agony behind him had been but a little transitory test, the horizons of life and existence were miraculously clear now. The air was suffused with serene sunlight and great, calm spaces of blue.

Every scale, measurement, and extension of his life was clothed in the grace and comeliness of a freedom he had always feared losing but had never been sure he possessed. Every slope he had climbed as a young boy—his first attempts at thinking, at feeling, at judging morally, at self-expression—were now covered in beds of high flowers scented, like violets and harebells and columbine. Every cranny and niche where his feet had caught and he had tripped and stumbled during his early intellectualism at the university were now filled with springing green grass.

And his greatest wonder was his new sky, his fresh horizon. Over the years his human sky had become a cast-iron grating—he had been able to send an odd plea winging through the little holes. But his horizon itself had become a tall, unscalable mesh of steel; it was misted with unknowing and agnosticism: with the "We cannot know exactly" of the pseudointellectual, the "Let's keep an open mind" that opens every argument against belief.

Now, suddenly, with his decision made, David's sky was a dustless depth of expanding space. His horizon was an open vastness receding, receding, receding, ever receding, without obstacle or limit or speck or narrowness. He saw himself immeasurably high up, free of trammels, on a zenith of desire and volition, clear of all backward-looking, unhampered by cloying regrets or by wisping mice of memory gnawing at his untried sexuality and his unexpected whims.

David was in full view of all he ever signified as a human being and all that being human ever signified for him, at the ancient heart of man's millennial weakness and on the peak of man's gratuitously given power to be with God, to be of God, and to live forever.

The many figures that had peopled his past he now saw within the eternal light—Neanderthal, *Cro-Magnon*, *Sinanthropos*, Homo sapiens, food gatherers, food producers, Stone Age men, Bronze Agers, Iron Agers, Jew, Crusader, Muslim, Renaissance Pope, Russian Patriarch, Greek priest, Catholic cardinal, Asiatic Buddha, African devil, Satan, Darwin, Freud, Mao, Lenin, the poor of Sekelia, the running and burning figures in the streets of Hiroshima, the dying babies of Bombay, the houses in California's Bel Air, the lecture halls of the Sorbonne, the villas of Miami Beach, the mines of West Virginia, the wafer in his own hands at Mass, the lifeless face of Jonathan. . . .

He was just about to fall into prayer when, for an instant, he heard the two chants again. He was jerked out of his visioning back to the reality of the chair, the bay window, and the night. The heavenly chant was now no more than a single prolonged note on a lute, persistent, limpid, clear, beautiful. Mister Natch's grating chant had been diluted and shattered.

By some mysterious proxy, David felt the pangs of an agony he did not regret. He was, he knew, assisting at the inescapable woe of some living beings whom he did not know, whom he had to hate, but whose fate was catastrophic disaster unmitigated by any poignancy or any pity. Despite the flooding peace and light washing over his spirit, he found himself following the desperate retreat of his wounded adversaries.

The once-muscular, breathing cries of Mister Natch had now narrowed to a thin, piping wail shot through with trills of terror, arpeggios of agony running feverishly and irregularly through every note of protest. That lingering wail seemed to spiral up, twisting and writhing and curling, an insect shaking poisonous antennae while it scuttled backward desperately for home cover in the sewer, a snake whose body was a solid, pulsating pain, stabbing its head upward as it moved away from the fluid lava of that other resounding note—what David always described afterward as his "Salem chorus."

Then he began to feel great distances again. Mister Natch's clamor dwindled, always pursued by that chant of Heaven. As it all grew fainter, David stood up, listening intently. The two chants were withdrawing from him. He flung open the double windows and looked out past Joseph's shoulder, his gaze traveling to the garden and, beyond, to the countryside, the mountains, the horizon. As the sounds withdrew, sucked, as it were, into uncharted spaces among the stars overhead, he searched the sky. The storm center had slipped away to the Eastern seaboard to be spent over the Atlantic. It was cold, probably freezing. Up among the stars he tried to follow the trajectory of those sounds. But the last faint echoes died. All was quiet. He listened, gazing silently upward. There was no sound.

A slow smile of recognition appeared around his eyes and at the corners of his mouth, as he heard the rustling energies of the earth recovering themselves after the storm.

His glance rested finally on Father Joseph, and he motioned him to step inside. The moon was already riding high, bright-faced, a warm, yellow hue to its light. Its very silence was golden and gentle and confident. He and Joseph were about to turn away from the window into the room when a mockingbird started to sing down in the copse where Old Edward used to stroll smoking his pipe in the evenings after dinner. That song came to David as a message from a world of grace, a hint of life without ending; not as Jonathan and as he, David, had taken such sounds of nature; not as intimations of molecules endlessly regrouping, but of endless life for each person, and of love without a shadow.

David sank into his chair and listened. Joseph stood motionless, afraid to disturb him. He looked away from David out at the sky and the trees. All night long until the moon sank and the early lights of the sun streaked from the east, first blue and gray, then red, the two men stayed there, while only the mockingbird's song broke the silence. The song seemed to take on the unruffled calm of infinity. It filled their ears and minds. It poured into every corner and cranny of the room where they were. It was surprising, full of unexpected flights and long, graceful sustainments that teetered on to the edge of melody, then swung away just in time to take up new scales. It was not triumphant. It was celebration of calm, proclamation of continuity, assertion of living's value, confirmation of beauty for beauty's sake, assurance of a morrow as well as blessing on all yesterdays. It came as annunciation, and filled their night silence with grace.

Toward the dawn Joseph heard a low whisper and glanced at David. He was reciting the Ave Maria in the Greek of Paul and Luke and John: *"Chaire Miryam, kecharitomene,"* and repeating that long, leaping compliment the Angel Gabriel paid the Virgin: *"Kecharitomene! Kecharitomene! Kecharitomene!* . . . Full of Grace! Full of Grace! Full of Grace!" Slow tears ran down David's cheeks.

There was no point, Joseph knew, in disturbing him now. The peace of silence and that song were all he needed and what he deserved, all the balm he wanted.

They waited until day broke full and the mockingbird had trilled to silence in a quick descent. They saw it take off from the trees and soar up, singing again as it went until it was a mere speck in the lightening color of the morning sky, alternately sailing and fluttering, until it faded from sight into silence.

David stirred and moistened his lips. He did not look at Father Joseph, but just said: "Let's make some coffee, Father Joe. Then let's get over to Jonathan, before it's too late." Father Joseph did not stir. He was waiting for David's glance and some word. David turned and smiled at the other man: "I know now, Joe. I now know." He paused and looked out the window again. "It is the same spirit. The same method. The same slavery."

A MOTHER'S SONG

Joseph glanced at David's face as he drove. It was firm and expressionless, save for a certain granite-like set to the jawline. His cheeks were hollow, but the growth of his beard filled his face out. The eyes were steady. David seemed driven by some powerful inner force Joseph felt much more than he understood. It made him a little afraid. He sensed vaguely a touch of ruthlessness, a downright and decisive thrust. He looked away from David; and, without warning, he found himself laughing quietly with a surprising surge of ironic humor.

"What's the joke, Joe?" It was good to see David's mouth soften.

Father Joseph had found himself saying spontaneously, "God help the poor Devil," when he saw the determined look on David's face. David grinned and threw an admiring look at his companion. "God bless you, Father Joe. You're never in any danger. You never took yourself seriously enough." Then they both laughed.

They reached Jonathan's house just after sundown that same day. David decided against waiting to round up assistants. He knew he would be in control of this case; he knew he had already bested the "Mister Natch" that had taken Jonathan so much farther into possession than David himself had been.

When they drew up at the house, the front door was open. Jonathan's mother, Sybil, stood in the doorway, a shawl around her shoulders. She was not smiling, but not sad, just quietly matter-of-fact.

"You were expected, Father David," she said, as the two men entered. "They told me you were coming." Then, in answer to the query in David's eyes, she explained that until early that morning, until about three o'clock, Jonathan had been all right; that is, he had remained unchanged. "But," she continued, "when you were liberated, he suddenly got very bad."

Joseph was stunned; he could not believe he had heard her say to David, "when you were liberated." But David's eyes were filled with understanding as she went on. "I'm not worried about my son's body. It's his soul."

For some seconds David stood looking at her. Joseph knew he was excluded from an intimate understanding between these two people. But he knew too that the price of being included was too dreadful.

On the hall table beside them two candles were already lit. Side by side with them were crucifix, ritual book already open, holy-water flask, and stole.

"It shouldn't be too late yet," David spoke.

"It shouldn't be," she rejoined. Then grimacing gently: "It's just I have not long to go myself. And if he must go too, I want us all to be together."

David nodded his head slowly while he stared at the door beyond her. His mood was part wariness, part musing. Then he returned her gaze, saying: "You will be, Mother. Have no fear. You will all be together. The worst is over."

He slipped the stole around his shoulders, took the ritual book and holy-water flask in hand. Joseph held the candlesticks. David looked at the open pages of the ritual. Jonathan's mother had opened it at the page where the main prayer started. Stepping past her, he turned the doorknob and entered Jonathan's room.

It was shuttered and dark. An unnaturally acrid and fetid odor hit his nostrils. Jonathan was sitting on the floor in the far corner, his feet doubled up beneath him. The light from the corridor fell across his face. David read the terror in his eyes, but it was a frozen terror. And David knew immediately: Jonathan would do nothing more, would struggle no more.

Jonathan's mouth was open. But neither tongue nor teeth were visible. Joseph placed the candles on the small night table by the bed. As the light fell on Jonathan, they noticed a curving line of fresh water drops running from wall to wall. His mother had shaken holy water recently in a semicircle pinning her son into the corner. One hand lay by Jonathan's side, but the other, the one with the crooked forefinger, lay on his chest in an eerie gesture. He was deathly still; but his eyes were glued on David's face and followed him as he moved closer.

As David stood over him, Jonathan's eyes were large, bloodshot whites with little half-moons of black irises glinting up at David.

Joseph expected David to start immediately, but David said nothing. He stood there. Silence.

Jonathan's crooked forefinger stirred from his chest in a slight motion toward David. David looked, still and silent. The forefinger wavered in thin air, then fell back stiffly. It was a gesture of helplessness. Jonathan's mouth opened and closed; he was trying to say something.

Still David did not budge or say anything.

Jonathan moved his head from side to side, his eyes still fixed on David, as if he was trying to pry himself loose from some ropes of influence binding him to David. A sudden and visible tremor ran through his body, and he turned his face and body away from David to the wall. He was shaking all over. They could barely hear the words which came muffled and thick from his mouth.

"Speak to me, Brother . . ."

"No brother, Satan! No brother!" David's voice was like a heavy knife. Joseph winced. David was silent again.

"We too have to possess our habitation, Father . . ." the voice began.

"Your habitation is forever in outer darkness. And your father is the Father of Lies." The trenchant sneer in David's voice again hit even

Joseph where it hurt. David, he understood, hated and loathed more than Joseph ever dreamed a man could hate and loathe.

"Even the Anointed One gave us a place with the swine."

"As a sign of your filth," David spat the words out, "and as an indication of your being buried alive in torments."

"Listen! . . . Listen!" the voice went on with a deathly note of desperation. It was almost a wail. "Listen!"

"You will listen and you will obey!" David was not shouting. But every word exploded from within him as a living missile. "You will all obey! You will go forth! You will relinquish all possession of this creature! You will do this in the name of God who created him and you, and of Jesus of Nazareth who saved him! You will depart and get back to the uncleanness and agony you chose. You will do it now. In the name of Jesus. Now. Go. Depart. In the name of Jesus."

Then David's voice changed. He was speaking to Jonathan from a reserve of tenderness and affection clothed in strength that moved Joseph as deeply as he had been shocked just a moment previously.

"Jonathan! Jonathan! I know you hear me. And hearing me, you hear the words of Jesus." Jonathan's body started to rack and tremble. He began to stretch out face down on the floor until only his fingertips touched the corner in which he had been slumped. David and Joseph moved back a pace.

"I know," David continued, "what you have been through. I know where you failed. I know how you were possessed by this unclean spirit. Jesus has paid for all your sins, as he did for mine. But now you have to pay. Believe me, I know. I know that only you can finally consent. With your will, Jonathan. With your will. But you must consent to suffer the punishment. Do you consent, Jonathan? Do you consent? Consent! Jonathan! Consent! For the love of Jesus, consent with your whole will!"

Then to Joseph: "Sprinkle some holy water!" Joseph obeyed. David opened the ritual book and started to recite the official prayers.

From Jonathan's mouth there came a howl lasting longer than any normal breath. David kept reading steadily, while he held up the crucifix in front of him. According as he progressed in the prayers, the howl increased, interspersed with dreadful sobs and groans.

But then they heard a thin voice singing. It came from the corridor outside. Jonathan's mother was chanting a hymn to the Virgin—the ancient Gregorian chant of the *Salve Regina*. As the medieval Latin syllables reached them in her little voice, Jonathan's howling and tremors began bit by bit to diminish. David stopped reading the prayers; he closed his book and listened.

The timbre of the mother's voice was quavering, reedlike. Yet, for David and for Joseph, it reached past their conscious recollections, past all the censor bonds of their adult life, back to the raw hours and days and months and years when once upon a time they were vulnerable to the misery of human unhappiness and when the love they enjoyed from home and family was their only and quite sufficient safeguard against all wounds.

Jonathan's mother was quite literally putting her soul into that sung prayer. Her mother's heart was crying to another mother. And, as far as Joseph could see, only these two mothers could appreciate what was now at stake. He had never been a highly emotional man; but memories crowded up in front of him, and he was gently stung by nostalgia. Joseph's enjoyment of esthetic pleasures had always been limited by an unsubtle mind and lack of personal culture. To his own mother he had never spoken as an adult; she died before he matured.

Until this moment, the woman to whom Jonathan's mother was praying had been merely a brightly lit and inaccessible star in his religious firmament: a Galilean Jewess who, without personal merit, without having thought one thought or said one word or performed one action, had been privileged with a grace no other human would ever, will ever, receive—to be totally pleasing to God's purest holiness from the very first instant of her personal existence. That had been the sum of Mary for Father Joseph. This had been all her dignity. She had never plucked the flowers of evil. She had been preserved. One of God's favorites.

Now, listening with David to that chant, he sensed with a speed that made understanding almost violent what being a mother and what being a child meant. He grasped the mysterious *convivium*, the mutual sharing and togetherness in human living of child and mother, their presence one to the other. And it dawned on him that that presence had no parallel elsewhere on the entire landscape of human living— neither lover to beloved, nor friend to friend, nor citizen to country, nor man to God.

Now this one mother was singing in prayer to another mother with a faith and a confidence that no man could summon. He understood: as mothers who had lived within a filigree work of heartbeat to heartbeat, breath to breath, movement to movement, sleep to sleep, wakefulness to wakefulness, they both had been placed, not at the periphery, but at the luminous center of a child's delicate beginnings in psychophysical life; and both had seen a child pass across the threshold of birth, quickening to consciousness, to recognition, to mentalism, to volition, to meaning.

Jonathan's mother finished the *Salve Regina*. For a moment there was silence. Then she improvised a last, spoken prayer. David and Jonathan heard her say: "You were his mother. You saw him die. You saw him live again. You understand. You could have died of pain on either occasion. Help me now."

Joseph felt helpless against the tears that came to his eyes.

He was aroused by David's voice speaking quietly. In the corner David was kneeling beside Jonathan. Jonathan had sat up and was leaning, not crouching now, with his back to the wall. Both hands were in David's.

Joseph turned away to leave the room. He had understood nothing, he felt. Anyway, it was confession time.

Jonathan had the bleached and windswept look of one whose face has been torn by pain and weeping, the angelic calm and luminosity— almost joy—that Joseph had most often seen on the faces of the dying when, after rebellion and despair, they finally accepted the inevitable and turned fully to belief and hope.

It was an enviable peace.

The Virgin
and the Girl-Fixer

Suddenly the whole scene changed in that Exorcism room, like an eerie and expert theater experience where, in a few seconds, the main actors change costumes and roles and the scenery is switched on invisible wheels, back to front, upside down, inside out, producing a kaleidoscope of change that makes everyone blink in disbelief.

At one moment, Father Gerald, the exorcist, was bending over the possessed, Richard/Rita,° who had sunk his teeth in his own instep. In the next instant, the glaze in Richard/Rita's eyes broke, melting into a lurid gleam of mockery. Greenish. The teeth loosened their grip on the instep. The mouth opened, baring gums and throat, the tongue protruded, quivering on a stream of gray foam bubbles. The whole face was furrowed in irregular lines, as Richard/Rita broke into peals of laughter. Great buffeting gusts of mocking, jeering, Schadenfreude laughter. Laughter pouring from a belly of amused scorn and contemptuous hate.

In a fraction of a second Gerald understood. The Girl-Fixer, invisible to his eyes, was on him, two claws clutching at his middle. His assistants heard the raucous laughter. They held their ears. But Gerald's agony they could not know. All they saw were Gerald's

° Richard O. is a transsexual. In talking about his life before his operation, I refer to him as Richard O. or simply as Richard. Afterwards, until his exorcism is completed, he is referred to as Richard/Rita. In conversation, Father Gerald frequently referred to him as R/R. With Richard O.'s permission, I refer to him throughout this narrative with the masculine pronouns—he, his, him. Today he calls himself simply Richard O.

sudden, violent spasms backward and forward "as if his middle was caught in a vise"; then the screeching shredding of his cassock and clothes, leaving him naked from chest to ankles. After that, all details escaped them in the violent jerkings and writhings of his body.

Gerald felt one claw was now totally sunk in his rectum. Another claw held his genitals, stretching his scrotum away from his penis, jerking at him brutally. Both claws were stiff, cutting like the jagged edge of a tin can, driving deeper and deeper, impaling him. He reeled away from the couch where Richard/Rita lay laughing, laughing, laughing, kicking the air and thumping the couch with clenched fists in deafening bursts of merriment.

Gerald staggered zigzag across the room, bent like a jackknife, involuntary screams gushing from his throat. One claw rocked back and forth within him. Slivers of agony jabbed and pierced through his buttocks and belly and groin, as flesh and veins and mucous membrane and skin tore and ripped irregularly.

A fetid smell wafted up to his nostrils and from behind his head. The voice of the Girl-Fixer beat at his eardrums unmercifully: "You're my sow. I'm on you. Your boar. My snout is giving you the best blow-job in the Kingdom. Shoot, sow! Spread your legs, sow! Your boar is mounting your flesh, opening your little untouched hairs. My prick is taking your virginity. You're no girl. But I'm still the fixer of every box!"

Gerald staggered in spasms, stumbling over his feet, doubled up, flaying the air helplessly, leaving a thin trail of semen, blood, excrement, and screams, until he bumped heavily into the wall, and fell to the floor in a twisted bundle. Blood sprang from a thin, vertical split that opened from the middle of his forehead up into his hair.

Richard/Rita froze into the blazing look again.

The attack had lasted about three seconds. It was over before the others recovered themselves. Suddenly, Gerald's screams and Richard/Rita's laughter stilled, there was a moment without sound in the room, like the farthest edge of whispers. The raw silence after raucous, earsplitting noise.

Then, a flurry of voices and activity. The doctor and the police captain lifted Gerald onto the stretcher that had ironically been brought for Richard/Rita. The four men quickly bound Richard/Rita down tightly to the iron frame of the couch. No one looked at those eyes. All felt the blazing glance on them, intent, triumphant, smug.

"Like tying down a hot, steamy carcass," one of them recalled afterwards.

Richard/Rita's two brothers, Bert and Jasper, eyes swollen red with tears, faces dirtied yellow with panic, carried the stretcher out. As the assistants left the house, they felt the stark contrast between the scene they had just witnessed and the outside world. In the garden by the pond the thrushes were warbling in the first wave of the dawn chorus Richard/Rita had loved so much and which had drawn him to live here in the first place. The sun was shining.

Inside, Gerald's priest assistant, Father John, still wearing his immaculate cassock, settled down in an easy chair to watch and pray. He was wordless. Just to be sure, he held the crucifix in one hand and the holy-water flask in the other.

A year earlier, in the ordered life of the seminary, he had known nothing of all this. Had not even suspected its existence. Evil had been a definition on the white page of a theology manual. And the Devil, well, that had been really not more than a mysterious name for a gentleman thought of in terms of horns, a green face, hooves, and a forked tail. Now John had the bleached, drained look which only youth carries when strain and weariness veil its freshness, and it has neither age lines to show nor makeup to lose, only paled illusions to shield it. It was 6:20 A.M.

There would now be a delay of four and a half weeks before Gerald could resume and successfully terminate the exorcism of Richard/Rita. The violent outcome of the first part of the exorcism would provoke many difficulties for Gerald. His own bishop entertained doubts about Gerald's competency. The psychiatrists involved in Richard/Rita's case decided that Gerald, a layman to psychology, was meddling dangerously with Richard/Rita's mental health. Gerald's own health was a continuing problem. And, as experience taught, even a partial failure to complete an exorcism meant that eventual completion of it would be doubly difficult.

Yet—if at all possible—Gerald had to complete the exorcism of Richard/Rita. For two main reasons. If Gerald were not personally to do so, there would be no guarantee that he himself would be immune from at least harassment—if not worse—by the evil spirit that possessed Richard/Rita. As it happened, Gerald did not survive very long after his successful termination of the exorcism. Apart from that, there was now a definite possibility that an attempt at exorcism by another person would fail.

GERALD

Gerald's housekeeper, Hannah, showed me through the house into the garden and called out to the thin figure in shirt and jeans tending the flower beds at the far end of the garden. As I crossed the lawn, he waved to me: "Hi! Come over and chat. I want to finish this job before sunset." It was about 5:30 P.M. The sun was beginning to cool, but its light was still gilding everything about me in warm yellow.

"Out here among my tulips," said Father Gerald to me with a wave of the trowel in his left hand, "I have great beauty. And peace, of course." Still bending over his flowers, as he patted the earth: "Done much gardening, Malachi, in your time?" I said I had done a little. I asked if I might take notes of our conversation. He laughed lightly in assent. From the start, Father Gerald established an atmosphere of ease: I had been expected; I should take a welcome for granted.

The last thing I had expected to find Gerald doing was tulip gardening. Sitting weakly in a deep armchair reading, perhaps. Or hobbling painfully on a stick to meet me with a wan smile. But enjoying life and tranquillity with obvious measures of physical well-being and quite evident inner happiness—this was almost a shock to me.

There were three tulip beds. He was working the middle one. Beyond them, a row of yellow azaleas. Then the ground sloped down to rolling prairie fields and distant mountains. Somewhere in the sky a small airplane droned.

His casualness was contagious. I asked: "What exactly do you like about your tulips, Gerald?" I was standing over him to one side.

Without looking up, he went on working, answering me slowly and deliberately. "No claims. You see. They don't clamor at you. They just are there. Beautifully. Just *are*." The slight emphasis on that last word had a faint French roll to it. "As you apparently know"—this last with a boyish grin, teasing himself wryly more than he was teasing me—"I have had some dealings with beauty. And the beast. After that, you know beauty when you meet it." He paused, glancing up at the twin mountain peaks away to the far left. But the sun was in my eyes and his features were blurred to me. Then, finishing his thought: "And the beast."

After a minute or two, Gerald straightened up with an unhurried gentleness, facing me for the first time, his arms by his sides, his back

THE VIRGIN AND THE GIRL-FIXER 177

to the sun. Now, four months after he had completed the exorcism of Richard/Rita, in retirement on the edge of a Midwestern town, Gerald, according to medical reports, had about five or six more months to live. At the age of forty-eight he had incurable heart disease and had already survived two strokes.

The man looking at me was slightly taller than myself. Thin-shouldered, blond, gray-eyed, he stood in an askew fashion, as if the center of his torso had been twisted out of shape—a memento not of the strokes, but of the Girl-Fixer; an ungentle reminder of his exorcism of Richard/Rita. A scar ran vertically up his forehead into his hairline. What struck me particularly was his face shining like a beacon—a light all over it, without any visible source. Then there was a dark, oblong patch on his forehead between the eyes. Like a nevus. Mutual friends, referring me to him, had told me about it. "Gerald's Jesus patch" they had called it jokingly but affectionately. The new scar ran through the "patch."

Gerald, they had said, never looks into you, just at you. Not until now did I realize what they meant. Like when you look at a city on a map in order to find out where it is. It was your context that mattered to Gerald, where you were at. Only, I did not know then what he saw as context.

"I know very little about you, except that I am supposed to trust you. Your name—Malachi Martin. Where you live—New York. You were a Jesuit once. Some books to your credit. You wanted to see me about Richard/Rita." His tone was level and low. After a few moments and still looking at my eyes: "Nothing much else, beyond that you appear to have peace in you, but"—with a quick glance all over my face—"you strike me as not having paid all your dues." He must have noticed some involuntary reaction in me, some unvoiced protest. "No. Not that. Those dues we hardly ever pay. I meant: you seem to have tasted beauty's sweetness, but not its awesomeness."

He stopped and looked down at the tulips. "I garden regularly. It relaxes. Tulips—well, I love their colors, I suppose." Another pause. The boyish grin again. "Let's take some tulips in to Hannah for the dinner table."

He bent down again. There had been no tension between us, only briefly on my part, when he scrutinized me for the first time. And now the tension had disappeared. He had satisfied himself about some puzzle in me.

"I do want to talk about Richard/Rita," I said as he set to work again. "But my chief interest bears on you." He worked on in silence for a few moments. An early-evening breeze bent the tulips. The sunlight had dimmed to a very light gray-blue.

"You realize," he said matter-of-factly as if to put to rest any tension I might still have, "you won't get away with it this time. Not scot-free, anyway. I mean, if ever you paid your dues, you'll pay them now—if you go ahead with your project."

"I have thought about all that."

"This is no mere fun and games, Malachi. You're treading on their turf. Dangerously. From their point of view. If I can believe my friends, that is." I began to notice his staccato style of speaking. "But I suppose. You've calculated all that. Eh? Still set on taking the risk. Risk there is. Anyway. You have your own protection. That much I can see."

"I spent two days with Richard/Rita, Gerald."

"All going well?" We both were avoiding the sharp-toothed pronouns, he, she, his, her, and the like.

"As far as I can judge. Of course . . ." Since his exorcism, Richard/Rita had lived in an in-between land of his mind. There was disquieting indefiniteness about him.

"Of course. I understand. But Richard/Rita is at least clean."

"What would you say was the principal benefit to you from the whole matter?"

"Before it all happened, I never knew what love was. Or what masculine and feminine meant. Really did not. Besides, I got rid of some deep pride in myself."

It was now getting chilly. I was happy to stroll with Gerald into the house for dinner. We talked continuously. And, as we did, it became clear to me yet again that, while true cases of Exorcism take their toll, they are not simple horror tales for frightening readers and movie-goers. For all that evening we were delving deeper not into horror, but into the frame of love that makes it possible to expel horror. And the case of Richard/Rita was important beyond many another, exactly because it centered on our ability to identify love, and on the dire risk of confusing that love with what we can only see as its physical or even chemical components.

It became clear that for Father Gerald the importance centered on the same point. Richard/Rita had carried the confusion to ghastly extremes. But for those who could come to know and understand his case, there is a lesson to be learned. I was trying to understand through

Gerald and through his entire experience, so bizarre and violent, what that gentle lesson was.

"Gerald, I want to get back later perhaps to what you meant by 'clean'—you used the term when speaking of Richard/Rita before dinner. But just now, something else is on my mind." We were sitting in his den after dinner. "Having read the transcript of the exorcism and talked extensively with Richard/Rita, my questions to you center around sexuality and love. For instance, why were you nicknamed the 'Virgin' in the seminary?" I had learned this from Gerald's friends.

"I was the only one who didn't know the nickname for half my seminary days. As to their reason for it, it seems I gave the impression of not knowing anything about sex."

"Did you?"

"Not really. I had seen diagrams and pictures, that sort of stuff. I could distinguish a passionate kiss from a friendly or affectionate one in the movies. But sex as such remained a hidden thing for me."

"But didn't you have the normal feelings about twelve or thirteen or fourteen?"

"I don't know what you mean by 'normal.' I never had one of those nocturnal ejaculations. Never yet had one. When I started to grow hair on various places, it sort of wasn't there one day, and the next day it was."

"Did you ever masturbate?"

"Never. Not that I wanted to. I didn't. Erections around the age of puberty and later just were taken by me as *happening* to me. It sounds funny"—he grinned boyishly—"but not as something about which I had to do something. Embarrassing. But then my father took me for a walk and gave me his set speech on sex which he gave to all my four brothers. It always began with the affirmation: 'Look, Gerry, you have a penis. And it is used for two things neither of which it does very well: urinating and copulating.' All of us knew the speech by heart. Then he explained clinically what copulation was."

I steered the conversation to the time just before Gerald had entered the seminary: had he gone out with girls or dated them or done anything more complicated than that? Apparently he used to take the sisters of his school friends to see a movie now and then, usually in a group. He went to some dances, but never really enjoyed them. He avoided them whenever he could. He was embarrassed by girls and by women in general.

He was on his feet now. "Let's take a turn in the garden. It will help oil the wheels." We went outside. It was already night. A few clouds lazed across the stars. There was no moon. The garden was partially lit by the lights from the house. As we walked down toward the tulip beds we entered greater darkness. A few lights could be seen winking on the distant mountainside. There was very little sound.

"Ever kiss a girl?"

"No. Not passionately. Never." He had been looking away while talking. Now he glanced quizzically at me. "Why all the questions about my sexual life?"

"This is my way—perhaps roundabout, but anyhow—this is my way of finding out what you now understand about love and masculinity and femininity, and what you learned in the exorcism on this score."

We stood for a short while taking in the calm of the night and the distant lights. Then I began again.

"Let me put it like this, Gerald. I take it you entered adult life—even your life as a priest—with very flimsy notions of what sex was all about, and . . ."

"There you go again," he interrupted good-humoredly. We traveled a few paces in silence. "I suppose basically I was like that once—minus the experience. I mean: of course, I realized about eighteen or nineteen that there was a very powerful thing called sex. But"—he stopped and looked out over the tulip beds—"it was always something I *knew* about. In my mind. With concepts. In myself, I felt there was this mighty urge. Never gave it any leeway. Once a girl tried to kiss me on the lips. I was frightened by the—uh the—" He fumbled for the right word but couldn't find it. "Look. Something told me if I let it go inside in me, it would rule me." Then triumphantly and raising his voice: "The rawness! That's it. The kiss felt raw."

"And dirty for you?"

"No. Lovely raw. But too lovely. Kind of tumultuously lovely. Only I couldn't handle that tumult, I knew."

We turned around to stroll back toward the house. "Well, anyway, Gerald, what difference did the exorcism make to all this?"

"I suppose the best way to say it is the simple way. R/R thought for years that gender and sex were the same thing, for all practical purposes. So did I, come to think of it. Don't know about you." We were coming up to the house, and the light fell on his face. "You may remember from the transcript. The crux of the Girl-Fixer's resistance lay there. ["Girl-Fixer" was the given name of the evil spirit expelled from Richard/Rita.] And it took all that talk and pain to let me see it."

He stood facing the windows, his face and eyes bright and clear. "In a nutshell, Malachi. As I now understand it since the exorcism, when two people—a man and a woman—love each other, are making love, I now understand they are reproducing God's love and God's life. Sound's banal. And it sounds trite. Even sounds evasive and vague and feathery. But that's it. Either that, or here you have two more or less highly developed animals copulating—rutting, whatever you want to call it—and the ending is just sweet sweat, a few illusions, perhaps, and then a let's-get-back-to-normal-existence sort of thing. Do-or-die. Now-or-never. Go bust in the effort. Anything you like. Could even learn from kangaroos, if that were the way with it." He turned his head in a comical way and said: "Ever see two kangaroos courting and copulating? I did. In a documentary. Extraordinary. Extraordinary." He shook his head.

"Well, apart from any practical significance that might have for you now, Gerald, you being celibate and all that . . ."

"And with a few more months to live," he said gently but not testily, as if to make quite clear he took into account the deadline of his life.

"Okay. Apart from that, maybe we'll get back to that subject. But explain something to me. Isn't there an in-between stage? I mean: men and women aren't just animals. But neither are they performing an act of worship of God. Or are they? Is that what you're saying?"

"Aaaah! The good-and-natural-act business." He was mimicking someone I did not know, probably some professor of his seminary days. "Well." This last word was said with sardonic emphasis. "As I now understand us men and women, we go through this world finding our way through facts and facts and more facts. Mountains of facts. But no matter what we do or get to know, all the time we are *experiencing* spirit. God's spirit."

He looked across to the lights of the nearby town. "And sometimes it's an experience in thoughts we think. Or it comes in words we hear. More often, it's an experience by intuition. A direct 'looking-at.' Some of those perceptions come like messages sent you. You hear children laughing, or see a beautiful valley in the midday sun. But you're mainly passive. At other times, you're doing something. And that's better still. Like when you have compassion for someone, or forgive someone."

We were down again at the tulip beds. He stopped at the middle one, where he had been working earlier, and looked at the silent flowers. They gleamed with wisps of color in the distant reflection of light from the house. "But in love and lovemaking, it's the highest. *Both* are acting. *Both* taking. *Both* giving. Nobody's passive."

At this point I made an objection, saying I had no concept of how men and women reproduce God's love and God's life when they love each other. We might say that, perhaps, in a remote and metaphorical way. But, then, the tulips do the same. And the kangaroos. All these, including men and women, may not know they're reproducing God's life and God's love, metaphorically. But they do. Or don't they? This was my question.

He turned away from me and faced the mountain range. His voice came in short murmurs, as if he were reading cue cards visible only to him. "You remember the Girl-Fixer, and my struggle with it. You remember?" The crux of that struggle between Gerald and the evil spirit possessing Richard/Rita had concerned the meaning of love and of loving. "Well," he continued, "on the plateau of love—and I don't mean the climax of an act of love only, but the plateau of love itself—man and woman are both caught up in a *dynamic* of love. No past. No standing still. No anticipation. No then, now, and next. Just the black velvet across which all stars flash. No oblivion. All . . ."

"But, Gerald, God—where's God in all this? You started off talking about God, as if the lovers were locked into an intuitive sharing of God's life."

He wheeled around and said almost fiercely: "That's God! That's what God is like." He turned away again, as if looking for inspiration. "God's no static and immutable quantum, as we understand those words. That's the God in books. But—an eternal dynamic, always becoming, without having begun, without going to an end. Becoming without changing. No then. No now. No next." As he turned and started to walk back toward the house, I fell into step with him.

"But there are two in our case. Man and woman."

"Ah," he said, tossing his head backward in a slight gesture, "that's the condition we're in. And that's the price."

"The price?"

"Yes, the price. In order to have that participation in God's being, the two must reproduce God's oneness. Must love. Truly love. You can't fake it."

"But what part—if you can speak like that—of God does a man reproduce and what part does a woman reproduce?"

"None. By himself and by herself. Or in himself or in herself. None. Nothing that is physical. Only in love and loving."

THE VIRGIN AND THE GIRL-FIXER   183

"Well, in love and in loving, what do they reproduce?" We stopped halfway up the garden. Gerald was looking at me steadily, as if searching for something. After a moment, he drew in a deep breath and said softly: "As far as I know, God is beautiful, is beauty itself. Beauty in being. Being that is beauty. And God's will is in full possession of that beauty, that being. In human love, woman loving is that being's echo; and man desiring is that will's parallel. In their love, will is locked with being. They simply reproduce, know, participate in God's life and love, in God's self some way or other. Otherwise, let's go back to those kangaroos—or chimpanzees."

"Well, even granting all that," I said to him as we started to walk again, "tell me, what does masculine and feminine mean for you now, in the light of all that?"

"Remember Richard/Rita's crux?" He looked at me, knowing I did. This had been the center of the Pretense in the exorcism. Richard/Rita had presumed the ultimate source of *masculinity* and *femininity* was the same as that of *sexuality*—the body, the chemistry of the body.

"And none of Richard/Rita's most extreme efforts, even the operation, worked for him. He wasn't basically androgynous. No one is, for that matter. We're basically and immutably masculine or feminine. Nature may goof and give us the wrong genitals for our gender. No matter. Apart from a mutant form of that kind, our sexual apparatus corresponds to what we are—feminine or masculine. Androgyny is baloney."

I laughed at the rhyme and the slang. But I had a real difficulty. According to Gerald the feminine—femininity—corresponded to God's being; the masculine or masculinity, to God's will. The essence of God, in our human way of thinking, would be feminine in that case. "If you are correct, Gerald, God, to speak in human terms, is feminine rather than masculine."

"Of course. More powerful. Creative. In her own being, the ultimate theater—not the object—of human longing."

"What about the He's and the Him's and the His's of the Bible? And Israel like a woman God loves and woos? And all that?"

"Just a good dosage of Semitic chauvinism. Plus a lot of ignorance. And a good deal more of all men's chauvinism down the ages. Men have been in charge from the beginning. Even in Buddhism. Just because the Buddha was a man."

"So, feminine is something of the spirit essentially?"

"Only of the spirit."

"And masculine also?"

"Right. A bird doesn't fly because it has wings. It has wings because it flies. A man isn't masculine because he has a penis and scrotum, nor a woman feminine because she has vagina and womb and estrogen or whatever. They have all that—if they have it—*because* she's feminine and he's masculine. Even if they lack some or all of those things, they are still masculine and feminine."

We were back on the patio. Gerald was about to open the door, and I should have left it at that. It was already late. I had to travel back to the town and catch a bus to the airport. Gerald, under doctor's orders, should have been in bed over an hour ago. But chiefly, if I had not gone on talking and probing, I would not have had, as a consequence of my probing, to bear an almost intolerable pain on Gerald's account. I went on unknowingly: "Gerald, tell me one more thing before I leave you in peace. With all that we have said in mind, do you now regret that you never fell in love or that you never made love and never will make love with a woman?"

As always when you make a mistake, you begin to sense it vaguely and go on in desperation trying to remedy the situation.

"I know you don't regret your priesthood. I know your vow of celibacy is dear to you. But, all that aside for one moment, have you regrets?" Gerald let go of the door handle gently. His head bowed as he dropped his eyes. I could no longer catch his expression. The sudden silence between us was not merely an absence of words. It was the abrupt severance of all communication. I felt perspiration on my forehead.

He stood for a moment in the patio light, looking thin, askew, frail, as if a great weight had been laid on him. I noticed age lines and a gauntness that had escaped me earlier. His face was immobile, but the "Jesus patch" was now of a deeper color. Then he stepped slowly onto the grass, limping, and started to walk with short steps down toward the tulips. I followed and started to say something, but he silenced me with a small, slow gesture of his right hand. A couple of yards from the flower beds he slowed to a stop. I did not dare look at him, and at first I heard no sound from him. But I knew he was crying. Then, as the minutes passed, I realized that this was not a sobbing or a voiced crying. He was not shaking, but very quiet and still. His tears were flowing steadily, ground out of him by some deep sorrow long ago accepted and whose pain he knew intimately. Merely, on this occasion, I had evoked that pain and its sorrow beyond his control. I knew he had to finish it in his own way. Nothing could console him and stop those tears. Seneca said once: "When a man cries, either he cries on his own mother's shoulder, or he cries alone." Gerald was alone.

It lasted several minutes. Then putting both hands to his eyes and wiping them, he said simply: "I know you understand the meaning of these." His voice was strangely deep and very unlike the tones he had used all evening. Then it had come from someone alive and vibrant in his own way, walking and talking near me. Now it came from very far away; deep, grave, solemn, he was speaking clearly to me from another terrain where he alone had walked, where his fate had been decided, and where the very self of him had never ceased to be ever since. It was an exorcist speaking from the lonely world he must always inhabit, alone with his grisly knowledge, his bruised memories, and his blind trust locked desperately on to all-powerful love for a final cleansing.

"Don't be sorry, Malachi. No reproaches. It's just that no one should have to put up with this in another. These are tears to be shed in solitude." He straightened up and cleared his throat. I could see him take in the whole horizon, turning his head slowly and meditatively from side to side. "Somewhere in my world," he said out loud, but as if speaking to himself, "somewhere, at some time during the years I have spent in it, there must have been or even now must be someone, some woman with whom love would have been possible. I shall never see her eyes or hear her voice or feel the touch of her fingers. I could have tasted God's eternity and ecstasy with her. And I could have seen God's comeliness on her hair and on her breasts. Somewhere. Someone. But I never shall. Not now. Not ever. I shall never share in her mystery of God's self-contained glory.

"And you know well, I am not crying because of missed opportunity or frustration. So help me." He wiped his eyes again. "In one way, I don't know why I am crying. And, at the same time, I do know very well. Once you finger the innards of a situation such as R/R was in, I think the terrible fragility of human love becomes more beautiful and you are frightened for its safety. Poor R/R and his delicate dreams! He really, genuinely yearned to be feminine and to love as only woman can."

He turned and faced toward the house. His eyes were still wet and glistening, but washed bright: "Is that why lovers sometimes cry tears at their happiest moments?" Apparently, at that moment, the tears started to flow again, because he looked away quickly toward the mountains.

"Many a woman and many a man must have had R/R's same beautiful dream," he said through the pain, "saw it within finger's touch, reached for it, and found it blighted before they held it." A pause. "I don't know why I cry for them. Feeling for them, perhaps. For only Jesus can mend the fracture of their spirit."

I waited until he seemed to have stopped crying. There was one last question I wanted to ask him, about Jesus. But he spoke before I did: "Of course, I have regrets. I would be a liar if I said otherwise. The regrets I have are for the intuitions I never had. Any man or woman I've ever known who really loved, all told me that in really loving, the physical was a couch or bed for a flight of intuitions. He no longer felt himself merely in her or near her. She no longer felt herself merely around him or near him. It went beyond that into—what's this one woman said?—uh—an 'allness' she said. Or, as one man said to me, 'full togetherness.' He meant: with himself, with his wife, with God, with earth, with life."

I asked Gerald if, mingled in his knowledge and his partial regrets, he thought of the loss of children he might have had. He replied that his having or not having children was something else again. I pursued the point, however, suggesting that perhaps one lament of deep pathos and suffering for him in Richard/Rita's case was Richard/Rita's total inability to have children. No matter how much love Richard/Rita dreamed of and achieved, it could never be a life-giving love. His would always be a crippled dream.

Gerald reminded me of what Richard/Rita kept screaming at the end of the exorcism as he thrashed back and forth. He had screamed again and again: "Life and love! Love and life! Life and love!" until they covered his mouth with masking tape. "Now," concluded Gerald, "like Richard/Rita, I will have to wait until I cross over to the other side, in order to find life from love and love from life. At present, I am time's eunuch for life and love in eternity." With the last sentence the timbre of his voice had subtly changed.

He now sounded more or less like the Gerald who had entertained me earlier that evening. We started walking back to the house. As we passed out through the hall and front door, he quoted Jesus: " 'In the Kingdom of Heaven, they neither give their daughters in marriage nor are given in marriage.' No marriage there," he commented musingly. "No need for it."

"Gerald, about Jesus."

He broke in on me. "He was—is—God. No woman, no human lovemaking was needed to enrich him."

"Can *we* make love then, *do* we make love, because we are merely human?"

"Only because we *are* human. Once possessed of God and possessed by God, there's no point in making love. You have all that human love can give you and much more. Love itself."

Nobody who had seen Gerald starting off life as a young priest would have guessed he would end as an exorcist condemned to an early death. Born in Parma, Ohio, reared in Dijon, France, until he was fourteen years old, educated from that time in Cleveland, ordained priest in 1948, Gerald was sent as an assistant to an outlying parish of Chicago.

There and in other parishes Gerald served as an assistant for 23 uneventful years. During that time he acquired a reputation for solid common sense. He was unflappable even in the most trying circumstances. Sometimes he was criticized for being a little too unworldly— "Not very worldly-wise," a colleague would remark now and then. But, whenever a crisis arose, Gerald's judgments and decisions generally proved to be the right ones.

One day he was called by the pastor of a neighboring parish and asked to go there for a consultation. When he arrived at the priest's house, he was told the story of a young man, Richard O., an employee of an insurance company, who had recently come to live in the neighborhood. He was not Roman Catholic, but his two brothers and some close friends of his had gone spontaneously to the old priest for help and counsel. Their brother and friend, Richard, had been deteriorating for some time now. They had tried doctors and psychologists. Then Richard had been persuaded to visit a Lutheran minister. After that, a rabbi had prayed over him. But the deterioration still continued.

Richard's brothers were quite frank when they talked to the two priests in the parlor of the rectory. They gave a brief sketch of Richard/Rita's life up to that moment. "Father, we are not Catholics. We don't believe in the Catholic Church, or in any church, for that matter. But we will do anything, anything at all, go to any length, in order to help our brother." The old priest excused himself and Gerald for a moment. They went outside.

The pastor had several questions for Gerald. Did he think Richard O. was a case of possession? Gerald did not know; he had never come across such a case. Shouldn't they alert the bishop? Gerald had already chatted with "young Billy" (the bishop's nickname among his priests). There was no official diocesan exorcist. The bishop knew nothing about it, and he wanted to know less. "Let's take it step by step from the top downward," counseled Gerald cheerfully.

They returned to the parlor and asked the two brothers for Richard O.'s medical and psychological reports. They could have them immediately, Gerald was assured. Gerald asked if Richard knew of the brothers' visit to see the pastor and himself. Bert said he did not think so.

"He may," Gerald rejoined. And then he went on to explain that, if Richard were really possessed by an evil spirit, he could easily know much more than his brothers told him.

This conversation took place three days after Christmas. The reports arrived early in the New Year. With the permission of his own pastor, Gerald went to live temporarily in the rectory of his old friend in order to be near Richard O. At the beginning of February, having digested the reports and spoken to the doctors and psychologists, he accompanied Richard's two brothers on a first visit to Richard.

Richard/Rita received them quite pleasantly in his house. That day he seemed inordinately happy. He spoke to them about himself and made no bones about his condition. He said that sometimes, as at that moment, he saw things clearly and knew he needed some kind of help. At other times, from what people told him, he went all funny. It was a constant change in him. And it was too painful and abrupt and unpredictable for him to carry on like that much longer. "Help me if you can," he added. "Even if later I tell you to go to Hell, help me. I'll sign any documents necessary."

Willingly, Richard/Rita said in answer to Gerald's proposal, he would go to Chicago and undergo tests by doctors and psychologists of Gerald's choosing. The following day they went to Chicago together. By some happy circumstance the visit there and the tests conducted by the psychologists and doctors went off without incident. Richard/ Rita had no lapse into his sudden fits.

While they were in Chicago, Gerald and the old priest went to see the only exorcist they could track down within reaching distance. He was a Dominican friar, an ex-missionary, who lived in retirement in a Chicago suburb. He smiled grimly as they told him their story.

"Better you than me, boys," he said quietly. "Let me put you through the rite of Exorcism and give you a few tips of my own for yourself and the assistants. I learned a thing or two in Korea. It wasn't all wasted."

The old man inculcated the first principles of Exorcism. He warned Gerald not to try to take the place of Jesus. It was only by the name and power of Jesus, he emphasized, that any evil spirit could be exorcised. He schooled him in the various traps that awaited the unwary: the dangers of any logical argument with the possessing spirit; the need of strong, silent assistants; and the customary procedure of an exorcism.

Gerald had to return several times to Chicago with Richard/Rita after the first occasion. He went by himself to see some theologians in order to get a more accurate knowledge of what went on during an exorcism. Richard/Rita himself had to make several trips in connection with his office work. All in all, it was the beginning of March before everything was in readiness. Gerald felt that he had taken all possible precautions. Intrigued as all the medical and psychiatric examiners were with Richard/Rita's history and transsexual operation, they had satisfied themselves that Richard/Rita was medically and psychologically as normal as any other person, and that he was not indulging in any strange fun and games in order to attract attention. This had been suggested by one of the psychologists. The rite of Exorcism, Gerald decided, would do no harm.

For the actual exorcism, he had chosen five assistants. Richard/Rita's two brothers, Bert and Jasper, had volunteered for the job. The old pastor had secured the services of the local police captain and of an English teacher from the parish school. Richard's landlord, Michael S., a Greek-American, a good friend of the old pastor, had been told of the exorcism and spontaneously offered himself. Gerald chose as his own priest assistant a young man recently posted to his parish, a Father John.

Only once or twice in the last month before the exorcism was Gerald's courage shaken. At one moment, the old Dominican friar took him aside as he and the pastor were leaving him after one of their visits. He asked Gerald if he was a virgin. He was, replied Gerald, but what difference could that make? The Dominican answered him rather offhandedly, trying to play down the import of his question. It made no difference, he said. It was just that Gerald would have more to suffer. At least, that is what he thought.

Questioned closely by Gerald as to why he thought so, the Dominican looked at him for a moment; then he said in a still voice: "You haven't paid your dues. You don't really know what's in you. But"—he wandered over to the door and opened it—"They do. Now"—motioning to where the old pastor was waiting for Gerald— "your friend is waiting. Go in peace. And don't be afraid. This is your lot." As Gerald and his old friend drove back home, they chatted about the whole matter. It was clear to him, the pastor said, that when one spent years in a certain type of job—the pastor in his parish, the old friar in his missionary work—you got a special sense. You can't share it with anyone. You don't want to, really. And what it tells you isn't always pleasant. Sometimes you see dark, abiding presences where others see nothing but light. "It's all very funny," the pastor remarked to Gerald, who had fallen silent and thoughtful. "Don't try to understand. You can't get old before your time. It would tear the heart out of you."

The nearer the mid-March date of the exorcism came, the more unreal it all seemed to the participants, especially to Gerald. This was chiefly because of Richard/Rita. There was in those last days no sign of deterioration in him, no fits. All was calm and normal. He even received them all in his house the night before the appointed day and served them a dinner he had cooked himself. Afterward, he helped them arrange the room where the exorcism would be done and chatted amicably with them before they left. Gerald had brought the paraphernalia of Exorcism with him—crucifix, stole, surplice, ritual book, holy-water flask. On the suggestion of the old Dominican, a stretcher had been borrowed from a local clinic; they might need it for Richard/Rita.

All were to assemble at 8:00 A.M. the following morning. For Gerald there were some swift seconds with an awry note. He was the last down the pathway out to the road where he had parked his car. As he turned back to close the latch on the gate, he saw Richard/Rita silhouetted in the main doorway of his little house. Gerald could not at that distance read the look in Richard/Rita's eyes, but Richard/Rita's hands caught his attention.

When the pastor and Gerald had left him at the door, Gerald remembered clearly, Richard/Rita's right hand, with open palm toward them, had been raised slightly in a goodbye gesture. The left had been resting on the doorknob. But now, as he looked back at Richard/Rita, the right hand was splayed out like a claw pointing toward him. The left, palm turned up, fingers slightly curled, was held stiffly. Gerald felt a shudder in his spine.

"Come on, Gerald! Someone walking on your grave, I suppose?" It was the old pastor pulling his leg good-humoredly. Richard/Rita waved to them again and went inside.

RICHARD/RITA

The story of Richard O. is only in part, but nonetheless importantly, the story of a transsexual. He was born physically a male, but with an ineradicable desire to be a woman. In his childhood his ideas and wishes were nebulous. In adulthood he firmly believed that each one of us can be male or female, masculine or feminine; that each one has an almost equal dosage of maleness and femaleness, of masculinity and femininity, before culture and civilization and social environment, as the persuasion goes, make little boys little boys and little girls little girls. He finally underwent the transsexualization operation—successfully, in medical terms. He then took the name Rita.

Richard had a very clear and very early understanding of the difference between femininity and masculinity, and he was attracted by the seeming mystery of the feminine and repelled by the inadequacy of being restricted only to the masculine. From the age of sixteen on, Richard's aim was to let the feminine in him emerge, so that he could supplement his masculine inadequacy with the self-sufficient mystery of femininity.

From sixteen to twenty-five he actively sought, in full confidence and trust, to think, feel, and act "androgynously"; he was persuaded that he could have the union of feminine and masculine in himself. But the result was a great aloneness (not, at that stage, loneliness) with none of that desired union. At twenty-five he sought in marriage the same union. It did not work; he found neither the unity nor the union of love; and the androgynous persuasion in him withered.

From his divorce at age twenty-nine, through his transsexualizing operation at age thirty-one, up to his exorcism at age thirty-three, he developed into a "watcher on the sidelines," jealous of the supremacy of the feminine, fascinated by the essential function of the masculine.

The mystery of femininity became something to unshroud; in Richard's case his unshrouding of it amounted to blasphemy and a type of physicomoral degradation which haunts him today. The vitality of the masculine became a weapon for him; he saw it as a means of death.

By the end of the summer 1971, he had voluntarily become possessed by an evil spirit which responded to the name of "Girl-Fixer." This possession had started many years previously. His violent revolt against possession ended finally in his undergoing the Exorcism rite performed by Father Gerald. But, until after his exorcism, Richard saw his problem as one of chemical substance, of brain modification, or of cultural adaptation, never as a dilemma of his spirit.

The exorcism was successful. He was freed. But Richard/Rita ended up, as he is today, in an unenviable position: neither male nor female; not a sexual neuter, but, nevertheless, in a no-man's-land between masculine and feminine.

Not all the details of his life are pertinent for understanding what happened to him. We need only a relatively few scenes and details of childhood and early teenage. It is the triple stage he passed through as an adult which illustrates to some degree his condition at the time of exorcism.

Richard/Rita presents in vivid outline the classical puzzle of all possessed people who, though possessed (always to some extent with their consent), still at some point revolt against that very possession. And why should Richard/Rita, and not any of the other transsexuals known to many of us in ordinary life, have been thus possessed in the first place?

Richard/Rita was born Richard O. in Detroit, Michigan, the third in a family of six children (three boys, three girls). The family lived in a semidetached two-story frame house which stood in a suburban area, predominantly white and upper-income bracket. His mother was Lutheran, his father, Jewish; the children were baptized as Lutherans; but religion did not play a prominent role in the family life. His mother's Lutheranism was as unimportant to her as Jewishness was unimportant to his father. It was a family in easy financial circumstances, governed with a light hand, and no more or no less self-consciously united than any other on the street.

Richard's father worked a regular nine-to-five day in an insurance office, spent most of his free time with the boys. He was a boating and open-air enthusiast, and went fishing and shooting in Canada during summer vacations. First, the two elder boys, Bert and Jasper, and then, when he passed his ninth year, Richard participated in these vacations.

An ideal held more or less unconsciously by each of the boys was to be like their father—strong, athletic, outdoor. To be a man. Richard's first memories of this ideal include a day in December when he was in the park with his father walking Flinny, the family dog. He was throwing a ball for the dog to retrieve. As the dog leaped, twisted, caught the ball, and returned running to them, his father remarked that that was how Richard must be—taut, ready to jump and run and catch. The movements of the dog's body became a rhythm of ideal supremacy and independent strength for Richard: leaping, thrusting, and striving as a well-knit frame in an armor of self-reliance and resilience that absorbed bumps, knocks, cold, heat, swift changes in direction, and sudden bursts of energy. "Look how Flinny throws himself into it all!" he remembers his father's cry of admiration and encouragement.

The discordant note in this recollection arises in Richard's memory of what happened when they returned home. When he saw his mother and his sisters, he felt a struggle in himself; and without understanding why, he was comparing their movements and the sound of their voices with those of his father and of Flinny. But the incident passed as a shadow.

The three boys were tall and dark in coloring. The girls were small, narrow-waisted, and blonde, like their mother. A family trait shared by all six children with their mother was the uneven earlobe: the right earlobe was noticeably smaller than the left one.

The girls gravitated, in younger years, to their mother, who never lost a certain apparent dourness, even in her smile and affection. But she had, as well, a hilarious sense of humor sprinkled with irony.

Each child was sent to kindergarten, then public school, and afterward to college. In their world there was no hint of the social developments which were to mark the 1960s and 1970s. Coast-to-coast television was just on the drawing boards. Female liberation was unborn. Later trends such as unisex and bisexuality were hidden. Homosexuality was still in the closet. Sexual permissiveness and the wholesale dilution of the family as a unit were unknown. The young had not yet been seized by the radicalizing passions of 20 years later. They had not yet started that quick and hazardous trek from infancy into immediate adulthood without any childhood and youth in the traditional sense of those words. Little boys were still little boys, and little girls were still little girls. Nobody had voiced any doubt about that.

It was Richard himself who felt the first doubts. The first time a change made itself felt in him always remained clear in his memory. One afternoon in the late 1940s, when Richard O. was almost nine years old, he had the first remote intimations of another world utterly different from the one to which he was accustomed.

Until his summer vacation that year on a small farm belonging to his mother's brother, some 40 miles outside St. Joseph, Missouri, Richard had never known a day not spent in the asphalt streets, among the city buildings, on the cement pavements, accompanied by the continuous hum of traffic, in Detroit, Michigan. He had never seen geese, turkeys, or chickens. Black walnuts, hickory trees, hazelnuts, sweet corn, pumpkins, rabbits, alfalfa hay, timothy, wild ducks, all the common-place elements of a farm were novelties that crowded his mind and sensations for the first time. It was, above all, the immensities of the place that seemed to awe him—the clear sky, the Missouri River, the unblocked view of huge stretches of land.

The incident took place three days before he returned to Detroit. It was about five o'clock in the afternoon. He had spent most of the day on the tractor with his uncle sowing soybeans. Now there remained one more field to be done. It was a long field with a sloping hump running at an angle across its middle. On one of the field's long sides there was a small pond. On the other side there was the thinning edge of a wood which stretched back for about half a mile. It was Richard's turn to rest. He lay down among the trees at the edge of the wood and watched as his uncle drove the tractor in long swatches over the central hump from one end of the field to the other.

These were the last hours of what had been a bright and cloudless day. Across the field and beyond the pond to the west, Richard's eyes could see the sun setting slowly over the Kansas bluffs. His eyes followed lazily the light of the sun already beginning to slant over the bluffs, down across the 20 or so miles of fields and woods that bordered the Missouri, then across the river and back to the black-brown stretch of the field. He listened to the meadowlarks singing on the edge of the pond. High up in the sky, balancing against the wind from the southwest, a bird hovered. Two sounds, both with their own peculiar rhythm, filled his ears. The noise of the tractor, at first mechanical and clashing, became a lovely thing for him. It rose as his uncle passed by where he lay, then sank again as the tractor climbed the hump, went out of sight on the other side. Then it started to rise again as the tractor climbed the far side of the hump, came into view, and rolled down past him and on to the far right, where it turned and came back to cut another long furrow.

The other sound was the light evening wind in the elms and maples around him. At first he did not notice it. Then it thrust itself on his consciousness as a rising and falling series of lightly breathed notes. When he lay on his side and looked up, he could see nothing but the gently moving foliage of the trees and the blue sky as a dappled pavement beyond them.

Almost with no break in his own sensations, he became peculiarly aware of his own body as it lay on the moss and ferns at the edge of the wood. The smell of wild honeysuckle and late May apple flowers mingled with the sharp freshness of some elm leaves he had been twisting and shredding in his hands. He became aware that insects, innumerable to judge from the noise, were droning and buzzing somewhere above his head among the leaves and branches. Everything seemed warm and living; and his body and feelings now appeared to him as part of, not separate from, some throbbing whole, mysterious with its own hidden voices and its shrouded secrets.

He twisted flat on his back, looking up at the waving leaves, translucent with sunshine, and watching the birds flitting from branch to branch, chattering and fighting and picking. He could hear faintly in the distance an occasional bobwhite calling out its two notes. A squirrel ran into his view now and then as it scurried from tree trunk to branch. All his muscles and sinews were relaxed. There was no tension. He was sharing through body and mind in some unperturbed softness and wholeness, but not an immobile or silent wholeness. All and everything was moving, doing, becoming. And, as he now remembers it, instinctively he listened to the wind in the trees as a voice, as voices, as a message of this great, whole softness. The rising and falling ring of the tractor became a background music. He felt unaccountable tears in his eyes and an ache that gave him peculiar pleasure somewhere deep in him.

Years later and in much more critical circumstances, he would admit to himself that those sounds and sensations, particularly the wind, had been the vehicle of some news, some information. It seemed, in retrospect, as if he had been told something and later remembered the secret meaning of the message, but could not recall the words used or the tone and identity of the messenger.

The tractor finally drew up beside him, his uncle climbed down, and they both walked slowly back to the house.

Richard had two more days on the farm before returning home to Detroit. He spent them wandering in the vegetable garden, lying in the woods, or sitting on the edge of the pond. He was trying to recapture that magic moment of the previous evening. But he found only silence. He was, as he put it later, encased again in the hard shell of his body.

His uncle and aunt took his behavior as a sign of unhappiness because he would be leaving soon for Detroit. And when he cried as they turned out of the driveway onto the main road which led them to St. Joseph and his train, they took his sadness as a compliment to them: their nephew wanted to stay. The vacation had been a success. "I will come back. I will come back," Richard remembers saying to nobody in particular. "Please, let me come back."

On his return home, his suntan, the acquired strength of his arms, his healthy complexion, his new and detailed knowledge of farm and country delighted his family. His father was proud: "Now, Richard, you're becoming a real man!"

But it was his mother and sisters who caught Richard's attention. When they talked or laughed or moved, he had feelings indefinably similar to those moments on the edge of the wood. Sisters and mother seemed to carry some detailed mystery, some wholeness, to be supple and malleable. His father and brothers—quick in their movements, deliberate in gestures, assured in their walk, purposeful in whatever they did—seemed to Richard to be wrapped in hard shells. They repelled him. And, at the same time, he felt ashamed at being repelled by what should be his ideal. The voices of his father and brothers had no overtones for him, no wisps of meaning, no subtle resonances.

Although he could not analyze all this at that time, he felt it. Of course, he could not mention it or discuss it with anyone there. All he could do, he did. As if speaking to the wind and the trees and the colors and the birds of the farm, he thought (perhaps *felt* is the better expression): "I don't want to leave you. I want to be as you." At that age and for quite some time afterward, he did not know exactly who that "you" was.

Daily life at home and at school closed in around him. In athletics he was as good as the next boy. He always got good grades. After his twelfth year, he became an avid reader. At home and in school he was known as a normal boy, more studious than outdoor, not overly gentle, not exceptionally shy, not in any way a "sissy" or a weakling, one who easily joined in groups and teams, and exceptionally affectionate and warm as an individual.

Nothing ever obliterated his memory of the farm incident, but he never returned to St. Joseph. Subsequent vacations were spent with his father and brothers in Canada. And it was only toward the end of his seventeenth year that another incident occurred which again effected a profound change in Richard.

He had joined a group of his own classmates who, under the supervision of an ex-forest ranger named Captain Nicholas, were to spend three weeks camping out in Colorado. The purpose of the vacation was to learn some of the arts of survival in the wilderness. Their schedule was a full and very active one. When it was over, they would know something about mountain climbing, swimming, life saving, gathering food, making fires, cooking, trapping, scaling trees, first aid, and seemingly anything else that Captain Nicholas could manage to teach them in those few weeks. When the vacation was finished, the eight had been invited to spend a last evening in the ranch house belonging to Captain Nicholas and his family.

As part of survival training, each boy was to spend one night alone at some distance from the base camp. When Richard's turn for a night "out there alone" came around, he was instructed to spend it in a small clearing on a hillside overlooking a lake about a mile from the camp. He was given a whistle and told to signal in case he needed help. According to camp rules, the other boys and the forest ranger left him at nightfall.

As their footsteps and shouts died away, Richard turned around to gather some brushwood for his fire. He was facing the lake about 150 feet above its surface. It was ringed around with mountains covered with forests. The moon had already appeared full-faced over the rim of the mountainside and cast a sheen of light on the water below and on the silhouettes of the trees around him. The smell of resin was an abiding atmosphere in which he felt as a welcomed stranger. He was aware of very little sound except for the wind shaking the pine trees and skimming the water's surface with light ripples. The air was still warm, with a little chill just creeping into it.

He stood for a moment to take his bearings so he would not get lost as he gathered his firewood. But the hush all around him seemed in a sudden instant to have opened. An invisible veil fell aside, and he was no longer a separate and distinct being from it all.

His first reaction was fear and he groped for his whistle. The rule was: any sense of fear or apprehension must be signaled to the base camp by one long and one short whistle. No stigma was attached to this. It was part of the training program to recognize and respect such feelings.

That first reaction, however, was almost immediately lost in a deeper sensation. Richard will swear today it was the same as if the night with its light, its weaving voice in the pine trees, its smells, and its seeming stillness was remonstrating with him and saying: "I am only secret. Not threat. I don't hurt. I reveal. Do not repel me."

He dropped the whistle from his mouth and sat down on the slope, overwhelmed with one idea that kept drumming quietly at him in words that sounded like his own: "I have yielded. I am going against my training. But I want . . . I have yielded . . . against my training . . ." About this time he felt surrounded by shapes and presences which had lain hidden or dormant up to this point. He was sure they were there, although he could not see them. Fear was gone. Only perplexity remained. The wind in the pines and the light on the water were part and parcel of those presences. But there was something else he could not recognize, could only accept or struggle to reject. Something spoke in the wind and shone in the light. All together, these mysterious things wove a web around his perplexity, washing it in a strange grace and, at the same time, softening some part inside him, some part of him that was supposed to be hard and insoluble, but that now was becoming soft, supple, diffuse, flowing into some mystery. He remembers murmuring again and again: "I have yielded . . . I want to . . . against my training . . ."

Then, even in the darkness, he began to notice details: the variant colors of rocks around him, different kinds of ruffles on the water, various shades to the trees, successive notes in the wind. And, in flashes of memory, was back in the past: on the edge of the woods in St. Joseph, listening to his sisters and his mother chatter and talk, watching his father dancing with his mother at a family celebration the previous winter, holding the hand of a high-school girlfriend as they walked home from the cinema.

And, as that deep core of him melted, he heard his father's voice in a frequent phrase used to his sons, "Chin up, young man!" dying away into repulsive jumble, "We men must be strong. Chin up chin up young man chin man strong chin up man . . ."

He felt his body shudder as if shaking off scales or armor. It did not go limp or cling to the ground. Rather, it was now a supple continuation of ground, light, the voice of the wind, the silver of the moon, the silence. His body seemed to hold the possibility of all natural things at once. He knew it was incredible. There was one last, clutching moment when something in him warned with a sharp voice.

But, after an instant's inner pause, he appeared to himself to let go, willingly to accept, and to do so in almost poetic language: "I don't know you. I want what you are. I want to be in that mystery. I don't want a man's hardness and strength. I want your wholeness." He actually spoke the words. They tumbled out half-whispered, incredulous—for his brain kept telling him he was alone at night on the mountainside. But something more powerful, not in his brain, kept enticing him. He responded: "I want to be a woman . . . yes . . . man woman." He did not know the sense of what he was saying, but he kept saying it. And everything that night responded to him in turn—infallibly, it seemed to him—and said: "You will be. You can be. You will be. Secret. Strong. Mystery. Open. You will be. You can be. Woman. Man. Soft. Hard. All. You will be. You can be."

He lost track of time. He lit no fire. He did not budge from where he sat. The moon rose and set. The wind waxed and waned. There were occasional cries from night owls, and once or twice the scream of a bird surprised by some night killer. Richard's memory recorded all this indirectly. Filling those hours was something else: the voice or the sensation of a voice which soared and sank in a melody of notes.

Richard now underlines two things in his memory of that song. It had no particular rhythm, no detectable beat. It seemed to be fully and completely, but only, melody. More significantly, it told him nothing new or shocking or awesomely strange—he seemed to himself to have had all its notes already recorded in him; but now they were evoked as echoes to the melody. And, as they resonated, they delineated a quality or condition in which he always was but had never realized, much less ever expressed it in his taste, walk, glance, in the corners of his words where meaning's shadow hid, or even in his perception of the world around him.

But no longer now was knowledge a thrust outward to grasp an objective, to obtain an exact pinpointing with the lens of logic—"fixing the cross-hairs on it," as his shooting-enthusiast father used to put it. In that melodized condition, all objectives were received within a delicate maze of sensibilities, emotions, reactions, intuitions. And, over all, a sense of sacrament, of pact with what made water and earth and air simultaneously strong and tender, soft and unyielding, masculine and feminine. For this sense of the possibilities of all natural things at once, in one condition, was an inner persuasion now. And he felt a light-footed, almost unstable touching on all things, with strength that was gentle, with firmness but no pride, with definitive choice but no violence.

On and on that melody went throughout the night, until at sunrise his classmates and Captain Nicholas found him sitting on the slope, fresh-faced, smiling, a little dreamy, but fully awake.

Only Captain Nicholas noticed the change in Richard: the peculiar haze at the back of his eyes and the way he turned his head to greet them as they approached him. After the first bantering, as they were all clambering down the slope toward the camp for breakfast, the captain drew abreast of Richard and said: "You okay, kid?" When Richard turned his head to the ranger, the haze Captain Nicholas had caught in his eyes before was gone, just as if Richard had pulled veils down closing off his inner state. His answer was normal: "I had a ball. Did I do okay?"

A week later the vacation was over. The entire party left the mountains in the late afternoon, climbed down the slopes, and walked to the forest ranger's wayside post where they had left their station wagon. After an hour's ride, they arrived at the ranch house, where Captain Nicholas' wife and daughter, Moira, greeted them. They were all tired; and after dinner all went to bed.

Richard, however, did not sleep very much. From the moment he met Moira, he had a renewal of his recent experience on the mountainside.

Fresh from that experience and still full of the pact he had made with the air and the water and the earth—the ecstasy of it all was quite vividly present to him for weeks after—Moira seemed to Richard to be a walking, breathing embodiment of a secret figure he carried in his memory. She seemed an answer to his prayer uttered on the mountainside, and the model he had felt promised him in the shadow of that slope. He saw the unconscious gravity of her head, the light strength of her figure as the light strength of that figure he had felt beside him on the mountainside that memorable night; the gentle swaying of her walk as an expression of its freedom. And all the details of her appearance and person were a revelation of what he desired to have most: the husky tones of her voice together with the natural grace of her hand movements, the sense of privileged look her eyes carried, at least for him, and the soft bed of feeling that he knew cushioned her laughter and made it utterly different from the loud laughter of his companions.

Some of the other boys had noticed his fascinated look on the evening of their arrival at the ranch, and he became the immediate butt of their banter. "Richard wants to make her! Richard has the hots! Richard wants to lay her!" He took it all in good part, even when one of them seriously offered to "fix him up" with Moira.

Moira herself recalls being quite aware of the joke during that evening. At first, she had the usual reactions, half-amused, half-embarrassed. And she probably would never have been of any help to Richard if she had not taken the initiative. It was in the morning before their departure. Richard came down early to find Moira preparing for breakfast.

From the beginning Moira quickly sensed that this was not just another young man flirting with her. Nor did he act shyly. Beyond a cheerful "Hi, good-mornin'," he said little in the beginning, but started automatically to help her in the breakfast preparations. But she had a strange conviction that she and he had an unconscious agreement or bond. The feeling was disturbing at first; then it became a surprising pleasure.

As they worked she asked if he had any sisters.

"Three." His expression was blank, neither pleasured nor disdainful.

They busied themselves setting the table. He glanced at her once or twice. Then: "The trip was fantastic. Ever been out there?" She shook her head, waiting for the usual litany of events, feats of male endurance and strength. But Richard continued: "I found what I want to be out there."

She asked if he wanted to be a forest ranger. "No! No!" Richard answered. He had found out, he explained, what sort of person he wanted to be. He looked up at her, his eyes shining. Moira braced herself for some protestation of eternal love and irresistible attraction. But Richard, eyes still shining, said only: "On the level, Moira, I want to be like you."

Moira's first impulse was to burst out laughing, make a wisecrack, and carry on. But something stirred within her cautioning her. She turned away quickly to the stove, disturbed, a little frightened. He worked on, talking all the while.

He said he knew he sounded funny, but he meant what he was saying; it was hard to explain, but he wanted to tell her. She tried to interrupt, but his voice cut across hers hard, almost in reproach. She looked around at him. His eyes were filled with tears. He still had the shining look, but a strange expression of an apologetic grimace touched his mouth fleetingly. "Sorry. Didn't mean to shout."

"You weren't shouting. I just opened my big mouth." She followed his glance out the wide floor-to-ceiling windows of the kitchen. The mountains covered with forests crouched out there, their distance foreshortened in the morning haze; they looked as if the boy and girl in the kitchen could touch them with outstretched hands.

"Whatever it was, Richard, it was very beautiful," she said to break the tension of the silence. "I hope you get what you want. It must be very beautiful."

"You know, then. You know." He was excited and boyish, still looking out. "I will get it. For sure, now."

Moira had no clear idea of what he was thinking. Since her early teenage she had been used to boys of various types for which she had her own names—the "brawns (athletes, outdoor types), the "softies" (nice but weak), the "teddy bears" (effeminate), the "profs" (studious, serious). They all talked about themselves and nearly always in terms of achievement in school, in business, in sport, or with other girls. She was sure now that Richard fitted into none of her categories. The caution about him she had felt earlier in the conversation had given away now to a sensation of fragility in him matching her own. She felt that he knew—even if he did not possess the instinct for—that detailed intimacy so characteristically feminine and the real bond between all women as compared to and distinct from men.

Richard talked on happily while they finished the breakfast preparations. He spoke of feelings and tastes, of touching trees, leaves, grass, flowers, of the smell in the air, of the wind, of the silence, and of his desire to be as "inside" himself as she was and as independent as his father was. It was a staccato speech, punctuated with pauses, over forks and spoons and glasses, running on pleasantly and softly. Just before the first pair of legs bounded down the stairs, he paused; and she, looking him straight in the eye, said: "Richard, shouldn't you ask someone . . . ?"

"No one of them will understand. You know that," he answered immediately but not abruptly. "Don't worry. I have plenty of advice. From the right ones. When they're finished, I'll know how to feel things, to be really boy and girl. All in one."

Moira remembers protesting with all the earnestness she could convey and trying to tell Richard that his "plan" sounded like the hardest and maddest thing in the world.

"No!" Once again his tone had changed to a rough note. She caught a glint at the back of his eyes which recalled her dim memory of an Alsatian baring his teeth and growling at her long ago when she was three. Now she was afraid. He told her abrasively: "Only a few can get it." He was smiling, but she did not like the smile. "That's the name of the game," he remarked some moments later.

Moira thought that he was going to continue talking. But at that moment the kitchen was invaded by seven other young men, loud, laughing, joking, looking for breakfast, and loosening the spell of a situation that had become uncomfortable and eerie for her. Moira saw the veils closing over Richard's eyes. He became once more the easy, good-natured, smiling companion she had seen entering the house the day before.

Back home in Detroit a few days later, and into the school year, Richard continued to live in the memories of his vacation. Without knowing it, he was probing deep into one of the most mysterious elements of human personality: gender. In retrospect we can see how the peculiarities of his personal makeup were responsible in some degree for his later development. They do not, however, explain in any way the onset of possession.

After one more year in high school, Richard went on to college. During his first year there, both his older brothers got married. His three sisters had already left home and were married. Although he spent a lot of time comparing himself to them, Richard never really knew them. He never engaged in any deep conversations with his sisters, and he did not get any clear feeling for their points of view where they differed from his.

He majored in mathematics, taking English literature and French as extra credits. He corresponded regularly with Moira in Colorado, and with time a deep friendship sprang up between them. Sometimes he spent vacations with her and her family; sometimes Moira came to Detroit and spent time with Richard's family. Moira was studying English literature and journalism at the University of Denver. She intended to enter the field of publishing.

Toward the end of his second year, he had a conversation with his father, who was taken aback to find his son spouting what seemed to him to be very advanced and unorthodox ideas about sexuality. Richard had read all of D. H. Lawrence, Virginia Woolf's *Orlando*,

George Sand's *Indiana,* and a host of other books his father had never heard of. He could quote anthropologists and social scientists in support of his views about matriarchy and woman's superior power and status.

His father consulted the rabbi of the local synagogue. And, during the following Easter vacation, Richard and his father went to see the rabbi. The rabbi found Richard quite sensible and his views reasonable. He pointed out to Richard and his father that the original Hebrew in the Bible does not say God created Eve, the first woman, from a *rib* of Adam. The word used at this place in the Bible means "one of two matching panels." He further pointed out that this Bible account is essentially androgynous. "So man and woman are equal halves of the same entity," concluded the rabbi, "but woman is most like God because she has the womb of creation in her." It was all very confusing for Richard's father. But Richard found in it a fresh impetus for his dreams of femaleness.

Toward the end of his last year in college, Richard spoke to his father about a job in the insurance office. He had no particular desire to specialize in any subject. Medicine and law did not interest him. What Richard was really looking for was a situation in which he could achieve his dream.

In early June 1961, at the age of twenty-one, Richard took up daily work at his father's insurance office. He proved a very willing apprentice. He was conscientious, took instructions, worked long hours, willingly gave up weekends to work on difficult claims, and studied law at night. His father was very proud of his decision and his performance. His mother loved having one son still at home.

In his free time Richard continued reading. He spent long hours walking by himself. Since he was out of college and no longer forced to take part in group activities, he began to elaborate his ideal.

He had one constantly recurring dream day and night. Once and for all, he fancied, everybody knew he was woman and man all in one. It was public knowledge, he dreamed, and accepted joyfully and admiringly by everyone. He wore either male or female clothes, according to the ebb and flow of his sexuality. His skin was either smooth or hard, his voice metallic and masculine or husky and deep, his hair long or short, his mind logical and rationalizing or intuitive and feeling, his breasts round and full with marked nipples or flat and formless, his genitals male or female. But he was chiefly female and feminine—with a very marked peculiarity.

In his dream he had, as a man, attracted a beautiful woman who possessed his own female face and body. She was he in female form. When they made love together, he was not merely a male entering a female. He was a female taking a male into her secret mystery. He not only had the male sense of arrival and expansion. He had the female sense of falling through the velvet veils of that mystery where wreaths of creation and shaping forms of arcane worlds wove around him with soft murmurs of love.

Sometimes in his dreams, all this took place at home in Detroit, sometimes at the lakeside in the Colorado mountains, sometimes in exotic lands. But most often the entire scene was played out in a small house surrounded by trees and standing on the edge of water. Wherever he traveled for the company, Richard began to keep his eyes open: perhaps, he would find a house similar to the one in his dreams.

His relationship with Moira now became something more than close friendship. Moira, in Richard's eyes, was still the woman of his Colorado experience and he felt she could be part of his continuing dream of perfect man-woman love. And Moira was in love with Richard. It seemed perfect—on the outside. Gradually it became a mutual assumption that they were engaged and that they would eventually get married. In Moira's mind this would take place when Richard got a promotion in his company. In Richard's mind it could only take place when he found his dream house.

In mid-1963, Richard's company sent him to Tanglewood in eastern Illinois as a temporary substitute for a sick member of the local office. In Tanglewood, Richard found several advantages. His new boss liked him very much. It was a far cry from the urban ills of midtown Detroit. His new post was in effect a promotion. The Tanglewood office was just beginning to expand, and Richard could be in on the ground floor of the company's ambitious programs.

Chiefly, however, Richard found what he knew was the nearest approach to the house of his dreams. It was called Lake House: single-storied, standing on three acres of land, with sliding glass panels in the back giving on to a large pond. The original owners, back in the late nineteenth century, had covered the three acres with trees, chestnut, sycamore, pine, elm, birch, oak. On his first visit to inspect it, Richard heard the wind in the trees by the water's edge. He knew this was his house. And it was for lease.

By that autumn, he had moved into Lake House. With the

recommendation of his new boss, he obtained a permanent transfer to Tanglewood. Then he wrote triumphantly to Moira asking her to marry him. She answered immediately by telegram.

They were married in Tanglewood on June 21, 1964. They decided not to go away for their honeymoon, but to spend it at home in Lake House. By their own choice, also, they arrived there alone in the evening of that day. All seemed perfect. The weather had a gentle balm to it all day; the sun was warm, but a light wind sang in the trees keeping everything cool and clean. "Our house is clean, not pots-and-pans clean," said Moira misquoting F. Scott Fitzgerald, "but wind-swept clean!"

In all the years of their friendship and engagement, they had never gone beyond a very occasional kiss of passion. Again, as with many other aspects of their relationship, each had assumed that the other wished it that way. Their first evening and night together as married people was something Richard had lived again and again in his dreams. It proved a total disaster, however, and not because they both were virgins, but on account of Richard's strange behavior and Moira's reactions.

They had taken hours in going to bed, strolling down by the water and through the trees, chatting on the porch, and gazing quietly at the night all around them.

Eventually they were side by side. Moira's mind and body, by that time, were totally attuned to Richard's movements, the warmth of his body, the smell of it, the urgency he felt. She glanced at his face, her eyes full of invitation. Richard was lying on his back, his face turned toward the open glass panels. He seemed to be listening to the night sounds outside around the pond—the wind in the trees, the ruffling of the water, the owls hooting.

Then he turned his head toward her: "Now, darling," he said, strangely quiet, "now Lake House is full of them. I am all of me tonight."

Moira did not understand. She didn't care. He was already kissing and caressing her, entering her. And, eyes closed, her hands all over him, she started for the first time to feel the urging climb of ecstasy in loving.

Then she heard his voice—this time with a note of stridency—saying: "Open your eyes! Look at me!"

The sight of his face froze every muscle in Moira's body. It was like a flat, featureless surface without a line. There was no expression on it.

His mouth was closed. His eyes were open, but, unblinking and still, they were mere sightless hollows glazed over with a dead patina.

"You're not seeing me, Richard," she said weakly.

But his body had become enormously heavy; she could breathe only with difficulty. She felt a sudden shooting contraction in her belly and groin. A sweat of pain broke out all over her body like a thin film. "Richard!" she tried to call out.

Richard was not with her. From the moment he turned back from the window, he had seen no one but his female self. When he entered Moira, a storm was on him over which he had no control. It was carrying him, petrified by increasing longing and intensifying loathing at one and the same time, at a speed which ruled out any resistance on his part. Longing and loathing were becoming so intertwined that the more repulsion he felt, the more readily he gave in to longing. But this only brought on increased loathing, so that longing and loathing became one. And both were coming from inside himself. He was their source. The higher he went on that first level of ecstasy, the lower he went on that second level of disgust.

All Richard could see was that beautiful face of his female self flung back in an effort to match his passion. At the same time he began to feel her hands on him as claws scraping his back and buttocks, first lightly, then with increasing pressure and tearing his skin. When she opened her eyes, their deep blue was swimming with feeling. Then they narrowed and glinted with a beige glow that reminded him of pigs' eyes, but his fascination with all this only swelled.

"You're not seeing me, Richard!" he heard his female self saying. "Look at me! Look at me!"

He groped with his body for her inner mystery, trying to explore every curve and cranny of her vagina. And, as he did, he felt in himself the rocking motion of something hard and angular. He heard the voice: "Let me take you, secret and all, mystery and all, Richard"—he could not know if it was his own voice or another's—"I'm your fucker . . . your fucker. Let me!" The voice died away again to a heavy, labored breathing that rose and fell with increasing gusts. It seemed to be acquiring a voiced character, a sound produced in a spittle-filled throat, wheezing, grunting, blowing, inhaling.

Now his longing and loathing were reaching a climax. There was no ejaculation. Rather he swelled and grew bigger and swelled with desire until he felt his middle opening up; and, with a loathing that held him hypnotized, he knew that an alien body was pouring fluid through him, hot, sticky, scorching. Loving and disgust became one. He started to thrash and flail.

By this time, Moira was screaming with fear as his terrible weight pressed down on her. She began to choke on the scream. Suddenly, he was off her. Her voice trailed away.

Richard was over by the far wall, a letter opener in his hand. He was standing with his back to her, tearing and gouging at the wall with wide sweeps of his hand, scraping paper and plaster on to the floor, while he hammered the wall with a clenched fist. A muffled groan rising and falling was all she heard from him.

His back, buttocks, and legs were a field of criss-crossing welts, scrapes, and lesions oozing with little pinpoints of blood at various places.

By now, Moira was afraid for her life. Without hesitation, she was out of bed and running through the door. She grabbed her coat and the car keys, flung the hall door open, and made for the car. "Moira!" she heard him shout brokenly. "Come back! Moira, don't go. Help me! Come back!" But by then she was halfway down the drive. She found her parents asleep in their hotel room. She never returned to Lake House or to Richard. Two years later she obtained a divorce from him.

Richard's dream was shattered. But there was something else in its place. He knew now that he had something new in him, something alive, something alien to him, but now his familiar and cohabitant.

He spent the two weeks of what would have been his honeymoon inside Lake House, rarely eating, refusing all callers, never answering the telephone. Gradually he returned to normal life. He was back at work in the office on the appointed day.

Outside office hours and activity, unless he was traveling, Richard stayed at Lake House. He never received visitors. Even when his family came to see him, they stayed in one of Tanglewood's hotels. Lake House was his refuge and his castle. On weekends he lay in bed in the morning waiting for sunrise. Regularly, as the first streaks of gray light appeared, the birds started to sing in the trees. First one here and there, then another one or two, then two or three together, until the house and garden were filled with the dawn chorus of thrushes, finches, robins, wrens, starlings.

At night and at any time possible he listened to the wind singing in the trees. It still brought tears to his eyes. And always he strained to remember the voice behind the wind and to capture its message and the identity of the messenger. His outlook was still filled with the mystery and power of femaleness. And, he was sure, the wind spoke of this and the birds sang of it.

Richard was now in the second stage of his development. His old idea of an androgynous self had melted. On his trips for the company business, he spent time regularly with prostitutes, and occasionally had relations with female clients and office personnel. He repelled any homosexual advances.

He admitted to himself after a while that in all these sexual encounters it was not a genuinely male sexual desire that impelled him. It was rather a jealous curiosity about the female and the feminine. He was always watching on the sidelines. No woman ever came back to him a second time. And more than one prostitute remarked as she left him: "You're freaky."

He once invited a woman to Lake House because he wished to have relations with her while listening to the wind. Everything went well for a while, but something frightened her, and she fled from him as precipitately as Moira had.

It was frustrating for him. He could only speculate about the female ecstasy and experience. He noticed that some women, in having intercourse, moaned in a dying fashion, turning their heads as if to avoid blows or to catch a mouthful of air. And he wondered what sort of lovely death that could be under the knife of female pleasure and secret power, and what sort of enshrined mystery a woman possessed that enabled her to live and die all over again the next time. For that was how he thought of it.

But, in the meantime, his own identity—sexual and otherwise—underwent an eclipse. For three years he never listened to or looked at another human being. He merely heard and saw them. He lost, therefore, any grasp on his own identity. He had no clear perception of who he was, what he was about, where he was going, where he came from. The pattern of his identity was in disarray: an essential piece had been withdrawn invisibly but with shocking results. All the earlier personal lines, geometrically clear and personally pleasing, had melted into a criss-crossed haze. The fine tones and delicate shades of taste and distaste, like and dislike, attraction and repulsion lost stability and definition. All were now clouds and swirls of the unknown and the unpredictable. The various gears of his inner mechanism in mind, will, memory, brain, heart, gut feelings were working at cross-purposes.

He stood helplessly hip deep in the running streams of impulses

where before a sharp instinct or a brilliant perception had teamed
with a never-failing voice in his heart. The self he originally proposed
to free and ennoble had become indeterminate; it was colored by any
element injected into him. He was a cracked bell jangling to the blow
of any hammer. He was a bag of emptiness blowing and puffing on
insubstantial air. Living now in an inner uncertainty of selfhood that
nothing could dispel, he had become the reality of his former
nightmare: a nonperson for himself. What he had cherished as a dream
of happiness had become in reality an empty void.

And this was not all. He found out on one particular occasion that
already within him there were impulses he could no longer govern,
and that these impulses seemed to arise from his original ambition to
enjoy both masculine and feminine qualities. On that occasion he
recognized the big change in himself. It was around the middle of
December 1968. He was on the road for his company. The weather
was very bad: snow, sleet, strong winds, gale warnings. On his last
evening in the city he was visiting, he was walking home from a late
meeting with a client. It was around midnight. No one was out at that
hour in such wintry weather. Richard walked because the wind, his
wind, was blowing with a high-pitched sound—almost a warning, but
still enticing.

The way to his hotel led him past rows of detached houses. About
half a mile from the hotel, he heard a moaning sound from some
bushes and trees that stood in a deserted area between two houses. He
stopped and looked around. There was no one in sight. Most of the
nearby houses were dark, their owners probably asleep or absent.
Richard followed the direction of the moaning. Behind the bushes he
came across a spread-eagled form. It was a young black girl. She had
been raped and stabbed. She was practically naked; her clothes had
been torn off her. Between her legs and at her shoulder blood stained
the snow in small, dark patches.

Richard was fascinated. He watched her for a while. Then he lifted
his head and listened to the wind, feeling its fingers brushing and
striking his face. He crept forward, keeping his head down against the
wind, then stopped and watched her more closely. The girl was still
moaning; her head twitched now and then.

Richard remembers very little else. He recalls tearing off his own
clothes feverishly (he was afraid she might die before he finished what
he wished to do). He talks almost tearfully now of feeling an
irresistible desire to have relations with her then and there. He recalls

the wind whistling music in his ears and then, marvelously, changing that music to words. He remembers catching the last glance of the girl who stared at him for one instant before her eyes went completely dead. He felt her body shudder.

Then apparently he stood up in a frenzy of triumph—he had achieved the ultimate watch on woman, he felt. He was seized by a great giddiness as the wind whipped around him. And now, for the first time, he sensed clearly that all his thinking and willing and feeling and imagining led like so many strings back to some central point in him where they lay in the hand of another, who controlled them and him. He felt the security of being controlled and the promise of success: "You shall be as woman!"

Afterward, when he reflected coolly on the incident, he realized that even in her death throes that woman had shown him the power of the feminine; his sexual relations with her had been a revelation for him. He knew that a decision had been made for him. He did not, as yet, guess from where that decision had come. But he did know what he had to do.

In the new year Richard went to New York. In previous years he had read extensively about transsexuals and the new transsexualizing operation. He now put himself under the care and supervision of a doctor who assured him that within 16 to 20 months, if all went well with the tests and preparations, he could have the operation, remove all trace of his male inadequacy—this was how Richard looked at his genitals—and acquire the organs of a woman. In late 1970, after passing successfully through the psychiatric examinations, and the necessary changes in the chemistry of his body having been produced by repeated treatments, Richard underwent surgery and emerged successfully from his convalescence in a new state of almost delirious happiness. He returned to Lake House. His mother and father came to see him, as did his brothers and sisters. They had become reconciled to his new status as well as to his newly adopted name of Rita. His boss at the insurance office was persuaded by his father that Richard could do the same work even better than before. So two months later, Richard was back to a normal life of daily work. As Rita.

The tempo of Richard/Rita's inner existence now changed. He found his outlook running in two main streams. One was the expected femaleness resulting from the operation. He found greater delight in little details—of cloth, of a story, of colors, of people's voices, in architecture. No longer did he look for large, sweeping lines in the world around him, nor did he feel inclined to argue logically or to engage in verbal polemics. He felt himself more vulnerable, more susceptible to praise and flattery, on the watch for compliments from men. He had a varied sexual life: he did not discriminate between old and young, ugly and beautiful. It was enough for him that he was desired and that they all found in him something that mystified them while holding them.

The other stream in his outlook was pockmarked with some stinging deficiencies that distressed him continually. When he had intercourse, for instance, he felt a great deadness in himself: there was no after-feeling of warmth and togetherness and perpetuity. And often this lack was accompanied by an inner bitterness that drove him into rages. It became an obsession with him "to make love and feel life" in himself after he had done so, and to hear his partner express himself in similar terms. But nothing he did ever produced a ray of hope in this direction, until he met Paul.

Paul, a Chicagoan, a former minister who had turned to banking and brokerage and become a millionaire in the process, was a very impressive character. Tall, good-looking, with salt-and-pepper hair, suave, well dressed, educated, a very good conversationalist, Paul had a brilliant smile. He and Richard/Rita liked each other from the first moment they met at a cocktail party. Richard eventually told Paul his life history. He was surprised by Paul's matter-of-fact reaction. What amazed Richard/Rita more than that was Paul's understanding of his difficulty in having intercourse and in its aftermath.

"I think something can be done about all that, Rita," he said. "But you will have to consummate a carefully arranged marriage."

"Marriage? But marriage is impossible—at least very difficult," answered Richard.

"Not the marriage I have in mind. You just need the right partner under the right circumstances. You don't realize it, but you have been preparing for quite a while for this marriage. Leave it all to me."

Richard/Rita did not understand what Paul meant, until he participated in the Black Mass on June 21, 1971.

The invitation he received from Paul was ostensibly for a midnight party. It was a sultry night without a patch of wind. When Richard/Rita arrived around 10:00 P.M., he was struck by the lavish surroundings. The house, dating from the previous century, stood in its own grounds. About 80 guests were drinking and eating a cold buffet around an open-air pool illuminated by tall, thick candles. Another 40 guests were dancing inside in the ballroom. The air was full of chattering, laughter, music, and celebrations. Paul immediately introduced Richard/Rita to a table at which two young women and their escorts sat. Merriment pervaded the group. Everybody was excited and happy.

From his position, Richard/Rita could see both ends of the pool. At each end there was a long table covered with food, drinks, ice buckets, and flowers. Behind each table, a long, wall-high, embroidered red curtain hung from a pole. A butler in black evening clothes stood motionless by each curtain.

Richard/Rita felt surprisingly at home. He joined in the laughter and talk around the table, and cheered as some of the more mellowed guests shoved each other fully clothed into the water.

At 12:45 P.M., Richard/Rita suddenly noticed a hush. Nobody was speaking any longer. The stereo music had gone silent. Without his realizing it, about three-quarters of the guests had departed. The two couples who had been at his table had excused themselves shortly before, saying that they wanted to dance.

The guests who remained had fallen silent. They stood in two groups at either end of the pool, facing each other across the water. Then, Richard/Rita noticed his tall host signaling to the two butlers. With a solemn movement, they pulled aside the curtains.

When the curtains parted, Richard/Rita could see a low altar table at either end of the pool. Above each altar there hung an ornament in the shape of an inverted triangle. At its center there was an inverted crucifix, the head of the crucified resting on the angle of the apex of the triangle. From the interior of the house he now heard the low peals of an organ. And someone was burning incense there, so that the fumes drifted out lazily and lay across the air like slowly twisting blue serpents. Then the guests started to undress in an unconcerned fashion, each one dropping his or her clothes where they stood.

As if on signal, both groups turned and started to come around the sides of the pool toward Richard/Rita. He started to get up when Paul's hand fell on his shoulder gently but firmly: "Wait, Rita." The naked guests filed around him and stood stock-still. Nobody had yet spoken a word. Then Paul took Richard/Rita's arm so that he stood up. Twenty pairs of arms stretched out from all sides; and unhurriedly, calmly, they undressed Richard/Rita. His host, Paul, was nowhere to be seen at that moment.

Then one guest, a young blond man in his late twenties, came forward. Around his neck he wore a narrow black stole. There was a ruby ring on the index finger of his left hand.

"Rita," he said evenly to Richard/Rita, "I am Father Samson, willing minister of our Lord Satan. Come! Let us adore."

His voice, the hands and fingers of the guests, the low organ music, the sultry night, the light feeling in his body, the languid odor of the incense, all this fell into a pattern of softness which Richard/Rita felt all around him. He turned as gravely as the others and walked in procession around the pool, past the tall candlesticks, until they reached one of the altars.

Now he had no further difficulty in understanding what they required of him. He waited passively and quietly.

They easily lifted Richard/Rita and placed him on his back flat on the altar. Father Samson then appeared carrying a chalice. Someone placed a small folded cloth on Richard/Rita's pubic hair. Samson stood the chalice on the cloth. Then Richard/Rita heard three voices chanting the opening words of the old Latin Mass: *"In nomine Patris et Filii et Spiritus Sancti,"* to which they added the extra name: *"et domini nostri Satanas."* Richard/Rita now understood. He felt a strange exultation.

Father Samson had begun reading from a black-bound book held by another naked guest, a woman of about thirty-five. He gestured gravely as he proceeded. The others had grouped themselves around in two concentric circles: the inner circle, all males, had placed, each one, the left hand on some part of Richard/Rita's body. Those in the outer circle, all females, had placed their hands on the hips of the males.

Just before the consecration, a woman pricked a vein in Richard/Rita's arm, letting some drops of his blood fall and mix with the wine in the chalice. Once Father Samson had uttered the words of the consecration ("This is my body . . ."), the guests paired off, lay down on the floor, each man lying between the legs of a woman. Father Samson parted Richard/Rita's legs, mounted the altar, entered Richard/Rita fully, took the chalice, sipped it, held it to Richard/Rita's lips so that he could sip it, and handed it to the nearest pair. While this pair was sipping the chalice, Father Samson started rhythmically to push and pull in Richard/Rita, saying as a refrain: "Say-tan! . . . Say-tan! . . . Say-tan!," lengthening the first syllable as he drew partially out of Richard/Rita and hitting the second syllable with hard emphasis as he drove into Richard/Rita. As each pair handed on the chalice, they started to copulate following the rhythm of Father Samson, until all—men, women, and Father Samson—were chanting and copulating in unison. Richard/Rita was the only silent one.

He lay, eyes closed, while Father Samson chanted on him. For the first time Richard/Rita felt a strange tingling starting at his buttocks, up through his spine, up the nape of his neck, around his skull, down into his shoulderblades, past his middle and abdomen, in around his vagina and down through his groin and calves, to the tips of his toes. For all the world it felt as if an electrifying fluid was being poured into him from Samson. Richard/Rita opened his eyes to look at Samson, but the light was too dim, and the blue trails of the incense were weaving through his vision.

Richard/Rita could hear heavy breathing, but he could see no face, only the outline of a head. He murmured: "Father Samson . . . Lord Satan . . . Father Samson . . . Lord"—but he was interrupted by a harsh, grating sound of single words coming to him through the heavy breathing. "Girl-Fixer! . . . Girl-Fixer! . . . Girl-Fixer!" Richard/Rita no longer heard the chant of "Say-tan!" Now all seemed to be joining in "Girl-Fixer! . . . Girl-Fixer! . . . Girl-Fixer!" Father Samson's index finger was now deep in Richard/Rita's rectum, massaging, scooping, probing, pulling, pushing. Richard/Rita felt his own semen being loosened and flowing; and, inside him, he had a sharp sensation of very hot, sticky oil squirting around the wall of his vagina as he heaved and shook. "Have me! Girl-Fixer! . . . Father Satan . . . have me . . . smell me . . . fuck me . . . through . . . through . . ." Richard/Rita's voice rose steeply into a loud scream. The organ notes thundered, filling the air. As each pair of the guests reached orgasm, they screamed and groaned in a jumble of half-words: "Sayt . . . fuck . . . take . . . Sayt . . . have . . . smell . . . cunt . . . prick . . ."

The scene subsided slowly. As the waves of pain, pleasure, and exultation ebbed in Richard/Rita, he knew that he now had a shadow—or, at least, that is how he described it. It was not glued to his body, nor did it fall on the ground beside him wherever he went. It was like a twin spirit or soul of his own soul or spirit. And it possessed his own thoughts, memories, imaginations, desires, words.

Richard/Rita again opened his eyes. Father Samson was gone. Paul, his host, unsmiling, grave, helped him off the altar and motioned him to stand, legs well apart. One by one each of the guests came forward on their knees. Bending the head and pronouncing the long word "Say-tan!," they clamped their lips over his vagina and sucked. Then they backed away out of the pool area.

When the last guest was gone, Paul handed Richard/Rita his clothes, helped him to dress, led him around the house to the front, where a limousine waited with its engine ticking. The chauffeur opened the door for Richard/Rita. "You belong now, Rita. Serve him well" was Paul's parting phrase.

As he lay in bed later, Richard/Rita could sense his shadow near him and with him. He felt secure. When sleep came, it was dreamless and deep.

The aftermath was terrible. He now found that all his sexual activity—whether in fantasy or in fact—had become of the same texture as that repulsive level on which he had moved the night of his wedding to Moira. And it reduced all pleasantness, pleasure, beauty, joy, ecstasy, to sexual terms which today he characterizes as "animality." It made him feel and think and live like an animal in heat, an animal which by a freak accident had been provided with a self-conscious mind and memory, but which would shortly lose those faculties and revert to being just animal.

Richard/Rita is the only ex-possessed person I have known who still has a clear memory of what precise differences the culmination of possession made to his inner self—mind, memory, will, emotions, imagination.

The entry point of continued possession, its bastion, was his imagination. In listening to him, one has to remember Richard's specific problem: gender and sexuality were one and the same for him. Once possession was completed, it seemed to him that he had an invisible but tangibly felt shadow, a twin of himself but yet distinct from him, and that from that point onward self-control and direction in him were exercised by that twin.

He points to the fluid or electrifying effect he received from Father Samson at the Black Mass. For it now appeared to Richard/Rita that in his conscious hours all his thoughts and willing and remembering and sensations (and, therefore, all he said and did in the view or hearing of others) came in a very different way. Now continuously his imagination—rather than his memory or his senses or his reasoning mind—received "imprints" or "messages": images, pictures, diagrams. There was also some other force or influence he could not accurately name. But because it specifically, directly, and exclusively concerned his sexuality, he calls it the S-factor.

Once his imagination received one of those "messages" or "imprints," then the whole internal mechanism of thinking, willing, remembering, and feeling with his five senses came into play. The control thus exercised on him was absolute. If he smelt an odor, if he desired something, if he remembered anything, if he thought or reasoned, it was all made possible by a prior "imprint." And consequently any words he spoke or actions he performed were made possible only by that source.

The exercise of his sexuality—his desire and its consummation—was under the strictest control. The desire came without warning: it did not arise due to any exterior stimulus.

To cap it all, there were other moments: hours of high possession when the control exercised over him acquired an intensity which blotted all else out. In "normal" time of possession, he was still self-aware, i.e., he saw and felt himself under the inescapable influence of those "imprints," but it was he himself who thought, remembered, imagined, spoke, walked, acted. At the "high moments" of possession, it seemed to him that *he* no longer did any of those things. The very insides of his soul or spirit seemed to be drenched in another's being.

He himself felt reduced to a tiny pinpoint of identity, to be imprisoned in the most solitary of solitudes, while every fiber and sinew of his life was permeated with an alien tyranny, a brute authority.

And, as he is able to relate it now, only in that microscopic reduction of himself did he spontaneously revolt. There he had no memory of the past—only a memory that there had been a memory. Nor had he any anticipation of the future—only a consciousness that anticipation was impossible. Neither praying nor cursing, neither praise nor blasphemy was possible there. It was an undivided and infinitely sad present, an awareness of oneself surrounded by utter blackness and nothingness. The very self of Richard/Rita always refused (although it could do nothing about expelling) that constant shadow.

Richard/Rita is emphatic on one point: the strict separation and distinction between the detectable and measurable area of his thoughts, emotions, memories, external actions, sensations, etc., on the one hand; and, on the other, the self he never ceased to be. All through his enigmatic experiences, that detectable and measurable area varied and changed under the influx of differing intensities, as masculine and feminine, male and female traits ebbed and flowed in him. Psychologists would, justifiably in their terms, describe it as rather extensive changes of personality. But the self—whether reduced to the pinpoint of possessed slavery or free within the general control of the central point in his imagination—that self never ceased to be the same.

Asked about the suffering specific to possession, Richard/Rita says that the genuine pain of possession does not come from any physical distortion, deterioration, or ravages—these most of the time provide the possessed with a savagely twisted pleasure and thrill. But it lies instead in what he calls the "mirror of existence" of the possessed.

The unpossessed, the normal person, is aware of the self he is only when it is reflected in another person or in things other than himself. And, without ever realizing it, when we perceive ourselves reflected in someone else or in objects other than ourselves, we instinctively compare that reflection of the self with an ideal measure we have formed but which we usually leave unspoken, even unthought. It is, however, ever present to us when we make comparisons of ourselves. This is the third, the hidden third, necessary for all comparison between two things. To be self-aware is to be able to compare our selves with the reflection *and* with the ideal measure.

The possessed has no such awareness. For in the state of possession, the self-consciousness and self-awareness of the possessed becomes absolute solitude. There is no hidden third, no ideal. Metaphorically speaking, in possession a mirror is held up in which the self of the possessed sees only itself in itself in itself in itself and so on in an infinitely receding number of self-containing, self-mirroring images, with no end in sight. And this awareness is, by definition, complete and unending solitude.

For those near Richard/Rita—his office colleagues, his immediate family, the few friends he had made in the immediate neighborhood of Tanglewood, there was a marked change in him dating from June 1971 onward. Their memories of this change are unanimous and date from about the time of the Black Mass—of which they knew nothing, of course.

Richard/Rita now always wore male clothing; but ordinary people, who did not know his story, could not make out exactly whether it was a man or a woman they were meeting in Richard. Then there was the smell, not unpleasant, just pervasive. It has been described by some as "musky," by others as "faded perfume" such as you get when you open an old chest of drawers, by others still as "a clean animal smell." It pervaded Lake House, his room at the insurance offices, his car, his clothes, even his handwritten letters. People always found it distinctive; some found it repulsive. It varied in strength.

Finally there were his peculiar fits. His normally deep-blue eyes would take on a greenish hue. Some hidden glow or luminescence emphasized the down of his face, neck, arms, hands, and legs, so that he looked sort of furry; but when you looked closely, you saw only skin. He spoke very little, mainly single words and at an extremely slow pace, accompanied by a combination of chuckles, grunts, snorts, twisting of his eyebrows, and mouth grimaces that contorted his lips around his teeth. Yet it was the indescribably roughened tone or timbre of his voice that disturbed people the most during his fits.

At first sporadic through the summer of 1971, these fits increased in frequency, so that by late October they were of daily occurrence. There was then a peculiar fear-causing element in any conversation with Richard/Rita—and his job was 80 percent of a talking nature. When anyone spoke to him, their words seemed to fall into a deep, deep hole and to be lost. They felt he hadn't heard or that, if he had, there was no communication between them. Then, as they were giving up or trying again by repeating what they had said, he spoke either in single words or in a series of disconnected words. They made sense and, most of the time, gave an answer. But they seemed to come from far in the distance, from the bottomless depth of that hole into which their words had fallen. Impersonal, uncommunicative of any personality, unwarm, at that stage Richard/Rita reminded some people of the humanly unresponsive effect a tape recording gave them.

People quickly learned that his responses and conversation always made sense. Indeed, they were highly intelligent and relevant. His business judgment was better than ever before. But always the freakish atmosphere communicated by the tone of his voice disturbed them. This, together with an almost overnight suspicion in his colleagues that "wherever Richard/Rita is, there is always trouble," finally brought his dismissal from work and caused him to lose his friends one by one.

The "trouble" was eerie. At first, it affected mainly his life at the insurance office. But gradually it affected anyone who contacted him even fleetingly—the delivery boys from the grocer, druggist, and dry cleaners, his cleaning woman, the laundry woman, his gardener. Once it got to a policeman who gave him a traffic ticket. And eventually it affected each member of his family who visited him. The "trouble" was strictly reminiscent of what happened at the Tower of Babel in the Bible story. Men and women who had known each other for years and had worked together intimately for substantial periods of time suddenly started to misunderstand each other and to wrangle and quarrel. To some onlookers of such "trouble," it seemed as if what one person said was heard backwards by another person; i.e., with exactly the contrary meaning that the speaker intended. The "trouble" affected only those talking and dealing with each other. But once any onlooker got between the disputants—entered their "atmosphere," so to speak—he or she was also affected by the "trouble"; and there was an additional source of babel and confusion and wrangling.

Incidents of this kind took place always and only where Richard/Rita was present physically. He seemed to be highly amused at the whole thing, but he himself never got caught by the "trouble."

The "trouble" also affected those writing or typing in his presence: they wrote or typed the opposite of what they meant, or it turned out to be complete nonsense. And all incidents of the "trouble" cumulatively pointed too strongly in Richard/Rita's direction to be explained in complete disconnection from him.

When there was no fit of any kind and no "trouble," Richard/Rita's accustomed sweetness of character and affability came to the fore. The change at those moments was almost shocking.

It was some time before Richard/Rita realized why he had lost friends, why he found people turning away from him, and why he became unpopular in his office.

In the last days of October he was fired. His brother, Bert, came in to see him. Then Bert went and talked with his immediate boss. From what Bert learned from him and from others in Tanglewood, joined to his own impressions, he concluded that his brother needed psychiatric care. But Richard/Rita's behavior then became a hide-and-go-seek game. Whenever he visited the psychiatrist, he was absolutely normal; and the psychiatrist could find nothing wrong or sick about him, no matter what diagnostic means he used. Indeed, the psychiatrist concluded that Richard/Rita's dismissal from the office was based on the boss's repulsion of Richard/Rita as a transsexual; and he advised Richard/Rita to sue for damages and reinstatement in his job.

But matters took another turn when Bert and Jasper came and stayed with him for a long weekend. Richard/Rita had several fits.

And the "trouble" was again very evident. Now, in his calm moments, Richard/Rita talked to them frankly and pathetically. He had begun to know in a dim and fragmentary way something of the drastic changes in him.

His brothers stayed on at his house, determined to get to the bottom of it all. Richard willingly underwent a complete physical checkup. The results were negative. Further psychiatric examinations were equally fruitless.

Bert and Jasper together with Richard/Rita decided to ask the local Lutheran pastor for some advice. He diagnosed Richard/Rita as a soul who had neglected God and prayer. When the pastor's counseling was of no avail, they called on the local rabbi. This man, a very saintly person, consented to read some prayers in Richard/Rita's presence. He also read some texts of the Talmud and explained them to the three brothers.

The following days, there was no change in Richard/Rita's general condition. They then decided to call on the local Roman Catholic pastor. The three of them walked over to see Father Byrnes, who already knew Richard/Rita by name and sight. He listened to them, but threw cold water on any expectations of concrete help. It wasn't because they were non-Catholics, he explained apologetically, and he sounded sincere to them. But he didn't know what to do. Sure, he would include Richard/Rita in his prayers. But, they shouldn't forget, so had the others. And what good had all that done? It didn't seem enough, Father Byrnes concluded. Bert took Father Byrnes aside and pleaded with him: his brother was ill in some peculiar way. Doctors and psychiatrists had given up on him. Didn't Father Byrnes know some Catholic priest who might help?

"Call me tomorrow, after midday," Father Byrnes answered. He had just remembered Father Gerald and his great common sense.

THE GIRL-FIXER

The morning of the exorcism Richard/Rita rose early, bathed, washed his hair, carefully sprayed himself with deodorant, and applied his favorite perfume to neck, breasts, wrists, and behind his ears. He put on a pair of dark blue slacks, a red turtleneck sweater, and loose sandals. His long black hair was brushed and combed in a simple manner. He wore no makeup or jewelry.

When he was dressed, he went out and fed the ducks in the pond, walked around for a while, then returned in time to greet Gerald's assistants at the door.

Partly because his two brothers were assistants, it was almost like a group of intimate friends gathering for a reunion or for the celebration of a very private event. Richard/Rita collaborated laughingly and pleasantly, making coffee, arranging the room for the rite of Exorcism, and in general was very apologetic and apparently appreciative of the "inconvenience being given," as he said repeatedly. For the exorcism, Richard/Rita's bedroom had been chosen by Gerald after some discussion, and mainly because it seemed to be the place Richard/Rita wanted most to avoid.

When all was ready, Richard/Rita sat down with the assistants and waited, sometimes chatting, sometimes praying with them, until Gerald's car was heard in the driveway. Bert went out, reported to Gerald, then came back and told Richard/Rita to sit or lie down on the couch. But Richard/Rita insisted on waiting for Gerald.

Gerald entered the bedroom with Father John. Both wore their ceremonial robes. All, including Richard/Rita, knelt down as they recited a prayer to the Holy Spirit. Then, with Richard/Rita still kneeling, the assistants arranged themselves around Gerald. He opened the exorcism with a prayer from the official ritual.

Richard/Rita interrupted gently and boyishly. "Father Gerald, don't you think we could hurry all this up? What I really need now is a blessing and everybody's prayers and good-will wishes."

He stood up and shot a radiant, embarrassed smile of charm and gratitude at each one present. Bert's heart was torn at the sight of his baby brother. Most of them felt embarrassed, much as if—it was Jasper, Richard/Rita's older brother, who made the remark later—as if they had come to arrest someone for murder and found the supposed murderer and his victim making love instead. Richard/Rita looked very feminine that morning.

Gerald too was taken aback. His mind raced. Had he made a mistake? Either they had made fools of themselves and of Richard/Rita, or they were victims of a deeper deceit than he had anticipated. But there was no time for reflection or pause. He had to make a decision. The police captain and the teacher were looking at him as if to say: "Let's get out of here, Father. Let's leave well enough alone." But Gerald knew he had to make certain.

"Fine, Rita," he said, surprised at his own acting, but smiling nonchalantly. "Let's do just that. Here, John, give me the holy-water flask. Jasper! Take my prayer book and put it in my briefcase. Bert, please make more coffee. Someone go and telephone the rectory and tell them I shall be back for lunch. Rita, hand me the crucifix from the table beside you, and let's get on with the blessing."

Afterward, when discussing the events of that morning, all agreed that the moment Gerald finished his request to Richard/Rita some sharp change took place in the room. It was a qualitative change, as effective and as abrupt as a complete, instantaneous change in the perfume of the air or in the room temperature. Some of them, not guessing Gerald's ulterior motive, had started automatically to do what he had asked them before he made his request to Richard/Rita. But the mysterious change in the room as Gerald spoke to Richard/Rita brought them all up sharply. "Like red lights all around me," said one. "Like a warning bell," commented another. "An eerie feeling in the nape of my neck," was the teacher's description.

"We knew that suddenly another presence had become palpable to us. We knew it was bad, bad, bad," declared Bert afterwards.

They all turned around and looked at Gerald and Richard/Rita. Gerald was standing almost on tiptoe, his request had been so barbed with intent and its impact on Richard/Rita so tangible for him. Richard/Rita had sat down on the couch, a picture of puzzlement. His forehead was a field of furrows. His eyebrows were almost touching in quizzical expression. His mouth was tightly closed, the lower lip clamped over the upper one. All color had drained from his cheeks. They couldn't see his eyes. He was looking at his lap, where both his hands closed and opened, from fist to open palm, then from open palm to fist, continually, jerkingly, and slowly. Gerald held his own hand up for silence and attention.

"Rita," he said softly, "hand me the crucifix." Tears started to glitter on Richard/Rita's eyelashes and then ran silently down his face.

"I want to be left alone. Please"—the voice was feminine and husky and agonizing. Another burst of tears. He sobbed. "It's all too much—I know none of you understand what has happened to me. Moira does—ask her. But this is all a charade—I need only to be left alone." More sobbing.

Gerald looked at Bert. Bert shrugged as if to say: Your decision! Gerald opened his ritual: "In the name of the Father, and of the Son, and of the Holy Spirit, we are here today to pray and ask that in the name of Jesus Christ, the Lord of Heaven and Earth, whatever evil spirit may have entered and possessed this creature of Almighty God's, Rita O., will obey . . ."

The rest was drowned in Richard/Rita's sobbing. He had turned gently as if wounded or struck, and lay down on the couch, his back to Gerald. They all listened to Richard/Rita, not hearing any more the words Gerald was reading. They could only hear that sobbing, crying voice, wailing and groaning with uncontrollable sorrow, his whole body shaking with each sob, every sound of his voice filtering through his throat and mouth as a terrible reproach to all present.

". . . and that whatever ill-effects the evil spirit has caused in Rita," Gerald wound up, "may be cleansed and purified by the Grace of the Lord, Jesus." Gerald concluded the first prayer.

At this mention of the name of Jesus, Richard/Rita stiffened and turned flat on his back. His face was not a picture of tears and sorrow as they all had expected, but a writhing mass of hate, fear, and disgust.

"Take your Jesus and his filthy crucifix and his stinking holy water and his withered priest and get out of my house." Both his arms were stretched out at this point, the palms toward Gerald, warding off his stare. "Take 'em out of here. I want to be alone."

Gerald saw Bert starting to go forward. "Bert!" he said sharply, "stay where you are—just one moment." Bert stopped.

"Bert, save me from this lousy Catholic priest and his hocus-pocus. Bert! Bert! Help me!" Bert started forward again. This time, John, the younger priest, touched Bert on the arm: "Give Gerald one more moment, Bert," he whispered, "just one more moment. We've got to be sure."

"Bert!" continued Richard/Rita sobbingly, "I was supremely happy until he started at me. It's all a mistake. I'm a woman, Bert. I'm a woman. Like your Marcia [Bert's wife]. Like Moira. Like Mummy. Like Julie [Bert's secretary]. See!"—and Richard/Rita tore down the zipper of his slacks and opened the top button: "See! I've got pubic hair and a cunt just like Marcia. Look, Bert! Come and feel it! It's hot and wet. I can hold you, Bert, I can hold you now better than Julie. Remember we used to masturbate together in bed as kids? Now you can enter me. Help me, Bert. I'll be yours if you do!"

Bert fell back ashen-faced. Gerald reached forward, took the crucifix, held it up in front of Richard/Rita.

"Rita, all will be well. We will leave you alone. Only now you have to do what you did a few days ago in the rectory." When Richard/Rita had come with Bert and Jasper to see him, he had laid his right hand on a crucifix Gerald always kept on his desk and said: "By this, I swear, Father Gerald: I want to be whole and entire and right with God." All the time this ability of Richard/Rita to touch the crucifix had given great encouragement to Gerald. It meant that the possession of Richard/Rita was an incomplete process as yet. Except in its advanced stages, possession varies in its effects and characteristics.

But now Richard/Rita lay down on the couch, legs spread, hands resting on his groin. They waited. His chest rose and fell as if he were sleeping. Outside, the weather had turned dark. The wind was rising, shaking the trees around the house with an irregular whining sound.

Then Richard/Rita's mouth opened and after what seemed minutes they heard him speak, but with another voice. It was throaty, rasping, slow, indistinguishable as to sex—it could have been female or male. It was like the voice of some very elderly people—a hint of falsetto, a trace of bass, but weary and ponderous, requiring effort.

"I know you're supposed to be a virgin, Father Gerald. What would you know of woman—or of man, for that matter?"

Gerald decided to break in. "Tell us who you are."

Richard/Rita was silent a moment; then he spoke as if in a joke. "Who I am? Why, Rita, of course. Who else? Stupid!"

"If you are Rita whom we know, sit up, and take this crucifix."

"Rita doesn't want to. Nah!"

"Why then are you sulking, Rita? Why not sit up and talk like an ordinary human being with us?"

"Because . . . because . . . because I am not ordinary. Listen!" Richard/Rita's head turned toward the shuttered windows. His eyes fluttered as if looking at a passing scene. His head turned back. "I am not ordinary."

Gerald had his ritual book opened again and was about to start the next part of the exorcism when a new thought suddenly occurred to him: if he *was* merely speaking to Richard/Rita, wouldn't he be missing the point of the exorcism? And couldn't Richard/Rita, or whatever evil spirit possessed him at that moment, carry off a magnificent deception—pretend, in fact, to cooperate? No! He had to break down the facade, if facade there was. Gerald was groping blindly to the truth of Father Conor's analysis without having had the benefit of Conor's instruction. Cold experience was his hard teacher that day.

He closed the book slowly, grasped the crucifix between his palms, and started to question Richard/Rita. Now the exchange between them settled down to a rather calm question-and-answer exchange. And it lasted that whole day. At one stage Rita fell silent. After fruitless attempts to get answers from him, Gerald went outside, washed, took some food, and returned. The day was already advanced. The doctor had monitored Richard/Rita's breathing and pulse. All was normal. As Gerald returned, they all began to feel the biting cold in the room. James attended to the radiator, even went down to the boiler in the cellar. The cold still persisted.

Gerald started again to question Richard/Rita. This time Richard/Rita started to answer. Gerald probed, provoked, queried, objected, interrupted, set traps, and tried in every way to break down the resistance he felt in Richard/Rita. But whatever he did, Richard/Rita turned it aside with long, rambling answers, descriptions of sexual acts, analysis of the male and female, small insults and jeers, an occasional snide remark. So it went through the night and the small hours of the morning.

We will never know now, but that procedure might have lasted indefinitely until common sense and the limits of endurance indicated to all that the exorcism was a failure—or, alternatively, that Richard/Rita had never been possessed, but was just very abnormal in quite an ordinary sense of the word. After many hours, however, Gerald began to sense that at times he almost touched something, then it would escape his grasp. At times, also, the others in the room would have a strong sense of something alien, pressing on them. Then it would lighten and disappear. All were becoming fidgety. All were tired.

The end of their waiting came unexpectedly with one blanket statement of Gerald's in answer to a protest of Richard/Rita.

"But any ordinary woman wants to be held and cherished by her man," Gerald was saying, "and, after that, to lead him where he could not otherwise go. Hand in hand. And in truth. And in love. Not in power or in superiority. They walk in God's smile. They reproduce his beauty." Gerald was touching the very chord that had obsessed Richard/Rita since his operation.

Richard/Rita stiffened. "Why the hell don't you leave me alone? You and your God! Who needs his smile or his beauty?"

Gerald was alerted by a new note in Richard/Rita's voice. He could not recognize it, but he knew it as a new note. And he had an idea.

"Why? Because I know you are not Rita. I know you are not Richard. I know that Rita—Richard—loves God, his smile and his beauty. But you—whatever or whoever you are—why don't you come out from your lies and your deceptions and face us?"

All hell—as the police captain said later—broke loose. Richard/Rita doubled up, his head resting on his feet, his body pumping spasmodically. The assistants held him and tried to straighten him out. They could not move him; he was as heavy as pig iron. The couch shook and trembled. The wallpaper above the bed peeled off, starting in one corner, as if invisible fingers had yanked it violently. The shutters shook and rattled. Richard/Rita started to break wind and scream at the same time. Everybody there began to feel a peculiar pressure of threat and fear. They started to perspire. Nothing had prepared them for this feeling of incalculable danger.

"Let everybody hold! Stay calm!" It was Gerald warning them. He was now aware that he had touched the essential core of their problem. But he was still in the dark. He drew near the couch and bent over Richard/Rita, who was quite still; but his body was doubled up as before, his head resting on his feet.

"Rita," he said in a clear, loud voice. "I tell you: we will keep on struggling for you. So, you, you keep on fighting and resisting."

Richard/Rita jerked and shook for a few seconds, then his teeth sank into the instep of one foot.

Gerald straightened up. He changed his tone to a sharp, inquisitorial, and imperious note: "You, Evil Spirit, you will obey our commands."

Again, the rasping voice: "You do not know what you're getting into, priest. You cannot pay the price. It's not your virginity merely that you'll lose. And not merely your life. You'll lose it all—"

"As Jesus, Our Lord, bore sufferings, so I am willing to bear what it costs to expel you and send you back to where you came from."

This was Gerald's first error. Without realizing it, and in what looked like heroism, he had fallen into an old trap. They were now on a personal plane: he versus the evil spirit. No exorcist can function in a personal way, in his own right, offering his strength or his will alone to counter and challenge the possessing spirit. He never should try to function in place of Jesus, but merely speak and act in concert with him as his representative.

For Gerald the cost of that mistake was high. He had never dreamed that physical punishment could be so intense. It was a full three weeks before he could get up and hobble around his room in great pain; that violent attack on him would eventually prove lethal for Gerald. But these were not his deepest sufferings. In those few seconds of storm when he was hurled across the room and slammed against the wall, it was a sense of violation that shook and tore him.

Only then did he realize that, up to that moment, indeed all his life, he had enjoyed an immunity. An inner bastion of his very self, the core of his person, had never been touched. Sorrow had never reached it. Regret had never pained it. Nor had any twinge of weakness or guilt ever ached there.

The strength of that private self had been its immunity. His professional celibacy and physical virginity had been merely outward expressions of the ultimately carefree condition of spirit in which he had always existed. In a sense, sin or wrongdoing had never touched him there, not because he had so decided, but because the choice had never presented itself.

But, in a twist of egotism, that immune part of him had been the source of his pride as it was of his independence. And friends who marveled at his constancy as a priest and ascribed it to a genuine sort of holiness could never have known—no more than Gerald himself— that Gerald's ultimate strength was tainted with a great weakness: the self-reliance of pride. The physical pain and injury that afflicted his body during and after the attack was as much a symbol as it was tangible expression of an inescapable weakness and fragility to which he was heir merely by being human.

He recovered sufficiently from the attack, but he never again had that old sense of immunity. Instead, there was born in him a heightened feeling of helplessness. And, for the first time in his life, he acknowledged his total dependence on God. And his outlook was now permeated with that poignant sense which Christians traditionally had described by a much misunderstood word: *humility*. It was a grateful realization that love, not simply a great love, but love itself, had chosen him and loved him for no other reason but love. "Only love could love me" had been a saying of an ancient English saint, Juliana of Norwich.

In the meanwhile, Gerald had to make a decision: to proceed with the exorcism or declare it officially over. Richard/Rita was now in an abnormal stage even for him. He needed round-the-clock surveillance. Usually he lay on the couch awake or asleep, or he stood by the window apparently looking and listening. He was docile to any suggestions of his brothers, but no one else could influence him. He ate sparingly, had to be washed like a baby, lapsed periodically into a strange, babbling incoherence, and could not bear any mention of Gerald, of religion, or of Exorcism. Nor would he allow any religious object near him or in his house. He always seemed to know when any such object was brought in. His cleaning woman, for instance, used to wear a medal around her neck; she had to leave it at home. If his brothers had spoken to Gerald, Richard/Rita would know it when they entered his presence. A scene would ensue, never violent, always heart-rending and full of pleas to them that they save him from further bother.

Gerald's health, meanwhile, was precarious and his friends became worried. The doctor told him that he had developed a damaged heart, and his physical lacerations had been very severe. The doctors had patched him up to the best of their ability.

Besides his physical sufferings, Gerald was the subject of an odd change in his sensations. He could not, for very long, see or touch any material object without this change taking place. As he told me later: "I seemed to be looking through it and around it—not beyond it. For in some peculiar sense it was no longer there. Instead, with some sight other than that of my eyes, I was held by the perception of a condition or dimension or state for which I have no words. It—that condition—seemed to be the real world. The material object—table, chair, wall, food, whatever it was—seemed utterly unreal, to be nothing in fact. And even my own body was for me an imagined shell permeated with and held up by that other condition."

The effect of all this was very disturbing, especially when he met others. What *they* saw was a thin, pale-faced man crooked in his stance, leaning on a cane, who seemed to be looking at them with the impersonal scrutiny of a stargazer or a map reader. He was still kind, affable, even jocular, and always good-humored. In conversation, he seemed to be very interested in people, not so much in themselves, as in what they signified or where they stood spiritually. This was a novel attitude for Gerald. What *Gerald* himself now found was that every man and woman he met underwent the same "conditioning" in his eyes as material objects. But, differently from objects, once the underlying and invisible condition of a person became clear to him, he sensed a new element.

He found it hard to express in one word or one phrase this new element. When he went to great lengths to describe it, he ended up—with constant assertions that he was only using images and metaphors—talking about "light," "blackness," "presence," "absence," "a web of yesses." His description of someone might be: "He's been saying, 'No, no,' all his life." Or: "She has never really said, 'Yes,' to the 'presence.' " Or: "They're in a very black context." Practically speaking, he found, this new way of looking at people placed him at a distance from everyone, no matter how well he knew them or liked them. Any knowledge of them through his mind and any attachment to them by his will was only possible in this new dimension.

The pastor of his rectory went so far as to consult one of the psychiatrists whom Gerald had originally consulted about Richard/Rita. When Gerald left the hospital and was convalescing at the rectory, Dr. Hammond together with a colleague turned up at the rectory to see him one afternoon. He had run a complete check on Gerald's background, he told Gerald, from his childhood to that moment in time. He and his colleagues were convinced that Gerald himself had been severely traumatized, and—more seriously—that, because Gerald could not really understand sexuality and its complexities, he had unwittingly evoked an alienated condition in Richard/Rita. In their opinion, and for the sake of their professional integrity as well as Gerald's own sake, they would ask Gerald to place himself voluntarily under their controlled observation at the clinic. Richard/Rita, they thought, would respond to normal therapy.

For different reasons, the pastor was equally adamant in this point of view. Rumors of the exorcism's strange result had filtered to the bishop of the diocese. And he sent word to the pastor that he expected him to arrange everything so that there would be no more trouble and no fresh rash of rumors and scandal. One report had it that Richard/Rita had raped Gerald. And this was not the ugliest of the rumors floating around the parish.

Gerald, at first very angry with the psychiatrists, finally began to see it their way. Or at least that was what he said. He added, however, that they should not oppose his finishing the exorcism. If he could only do this, he assured them, then he would be satisfied.

The final decision, of course, rested with Richard/Rita's family and with Bert in particular. Bert was convinced that Richard/Rita's condition was the work of the devil, and that Gerald or another Catholic priest should be allowed to complete the exorcism.

It was all very trying for Gerald. He felt "like a museum specimen or a medical case," as he remarked to the pastor. Besides, something in him told him that Richard/Rita could not go on and survive as he was, nor could he himself leave the exorcism unfinished as it was.

"I have no death wish, Doctor," he said to the senior psychiatrist. "But neither have I any illusions about myself or about you. I cannot have long to live—even my own doctors agree on that. You have no religious beliefs whatsoever, on your own admission. Unless we strike a compromise, we will go on talking while Richard/Rita vegetates and I die. So let's make a deal."

The deal was made. With conditions. Dr. Hammond was to be present at the exorcism. If he and the doctor, independently of Gerald, decided the resumed Exorcism ritual should be aborted at any particular point, Gerald would abort it. The exorcism would not be allowed to go beyond two days at maximum. On the other hand, Gerald would be in complete control as the exorcism proceeded. Dr. Hammond would behave exactly as one of Gerald's assistants. There were one or two other conditions, mainly to help the professional assessment and examination by the psychiatrist. But Gerald was satisfied. He had gained an opportunity to finish the exorcism.

It was clear to Gerald now that only when he had attempted to uncover and separate the evil spirit's identity from Richard/Rita's, only then had he been attacked. He would take up at that very point where the process had left off and proceed with great caution, not drawing attention to himself in any way and endeavoring to rely on the power of the official ritual and the symbolism of his function.

Early one morning, then, four and a half weeks after the violent interruption of the exorcism, Dr. Hammond drove Gerald down to Lake House to resume the exorcism of Richard/Rita. The assistants were there already, together with Father John. It was a somber day. A strong wind again bent the trees around the house. It started raining shortly after they arrived and continued all day and into the evening.

Lake House itself was still and quiet. Richard/Rita was lying on the couch quietly dozing when Gerald arrived. Then, as if on signal, he doubled up and sank his teeth into his instep, opened his eyes and fixed them silently on the door through which Gerald and John would enter. Bert and Jasper, both carrying signs of the last few weeks in drawn looks and low voices, stood with the police captain and the teacher. Nobody spoke very much. As Gerald entered, Richard/Rita's eyes blazed with a fresh light. He moaned hungrily as a dog would for more food. His hands were opening and closing. Gerald gathered up his strength as he took his place beside the couch. He had carefully prepared his opening statement. But before he could speak, Richard/Rita beat him to it. Loosening the teeth hold on his instep, and still glaring at Gerald, he said: "Gerald, darling, why all the trouble? Look what you have brought on yourself. You needn't bear all this pain. You have no need to pay such a price." It was the same trap. This time Gerald was ready.

"The price—whatever price is necessary—has already been paid. You will obey the authority of Jesus and of his Church. Announce your name."

Even as Gerald spoke, the pain ran quickly through new lanes in his flesh and bones. The lower part of his body, from his navel to his toes, grew rigid. The assistants saw the veins bulging on his forehead. He was fighting for control, struggling not to lose consciousness, straining to hear. Waiting and straining. Richard/Rita sank back flat on the couch in a deflated fashion, eyes closed, arms and hands thrown across his chest.

After a dull pause, when he had almost given up hope of evoking obedience from the spirit, Gerald began to hear something that resembled a voice but that was totally unintelligible to him. At first, he thought that a group of people had arrived unannounced on the front lawn of Lake House and were congregating close to the front windows. But when he concentrated on that direction, the sound seemed to be coming from Richard/Rita, then again from the back of the house. He distinctly heard several voices talking at the same time, breaking off, starting, laughing, occasionally grunting, even yelling in a mock fashion. They seemed to be both male and female, but the female voices seemed to dominate. Then the chatter died away as if they had all moved away from the house.

Gerald stared at Richard/Rita: he was silent and motionless. Gerald was about to speak when the voices started again. This time they were in the room, but tantalizing him: when he concentrated on Richard/Rita, they seemed to come from behind him; when he turned around, they seemed to come from Richard/Rita. He began to feel as if fragments of voices were free-floating and moving around the room. The assistants had not been prepared for eerie happenings such as this because Gerald did not have enough experience or knowledge of Exorcism to give them very detailed warnings. The strain they were undergoing showed in their constant perspiration and trembling.

Dr. Hammond's reaction would have been comical under any other circumstances but these. As Father John told it afterwards, the psychiatrist started off with a professional expression of "business as usual"—grave, expressionless, watchful eyes, steadily taking notes. After a few minutes, his note-taking stopped, the expression on his face changed from the bland professional to incredulity, then a touch of impatience (as if he were being subjected to a practical joke), and finally the slightly ashen look of a man catching up for the first time with something unintelligible and alien to his opinion, threatening to his sanity and self-control.

Gerald's puzzlement and dismay increased, because now he thought he could distinguish single words and phrases of one voice in particular; but every time, other words and phrases broke in and cluttered his hearing. It all ended up as abstract gibberish.

Then the various strands of female voices seemed to quicken in pace and to start blending into one pitch and timbre, as if, syllable by syllable, all were catching up on a lead voice. And the male voices began to slow down in attack and amplitude, until they became a series of squeaks and sonorities more or less parallel but never coinciding. The two levels, male and female, began to mingle and sound as one in various syllables, but there were always overtones and annoying echoes muddying his efforts to understand. Gerald decided to intervene.

"Whatever or whoever you are, you are commanded in the name of Jesus to state your name, to answer our questions."

With that, the volume of noise started to increase and with it an uncontrollable dismay and fear in Gerald. He felt himself the target of some leviathan voice croaking from bloated lungs, cavernous throat and mouth, a voice of curses, abuse, blasphemy, in which his secret sins, ill will, obscenities all echoed and rolled and issued as a malignant challenge.

Young Father John found the sounds in the room almost unbearably disturbing. He sprinkled holy water around Gerald and then around the couch. The noise rose to a fresh crescendo, then started to fall away. Richard/Rita, all this while, remained stretched out flat on his back.

As the babel died away in a mumbling and choking sound, Gerald received the first onslaught of the Clash. Nobody had prepared him for it, and nobody had told him what to do. The old Dominican friar in

Chicago had merely said that at some point "the old fella" would have to come out as himself. He warned Gerald to take care at that point—"It's worse than I can ever hope to tell you." It was.

Gerald's greatest quality—stubbornness—now became the source of his torture. For he could not, would not let go. He had locked his will into that of the evil spirit. Even if in some exorcists the Clash starts in the mind, the imagination, or in a powerful intuitive sense of theirs, it finally comes home in full force to the will. From the start it was in Gerald's will that the struggle took place.

Up to that moment he had felt his will pushing against a steel wall of resistance and attack. Now the wall seemed to melt and flow all around, while his will plunged into the molten heart of liquid heat that scorched and sizzled and frittered away every thew and sinew of his will, searing through every trace of padding and protection a human will employs—hopefulness, anticipation, remembrance of pleasure, satisfaction in fidelity, conscious ability to change or not to change, surety, persuasion that one is doing the right thing.

It was not a darkness of mind, but a nudity of will. It was the place of deepest poignancy and sharpest sorrowing that any human being can reach while in a mortal condition. Dante had described it as the pathos of the soul which is not condemned to Hell (and knows that), but has no means of knowing if Heaven exists and yet must persevere in hope that apparent hopelessness is a prelude to happiness and reward.

Then the Clash materialized in his physical self. One by one, his hearing, his sight, his senses of touch, smell, and taste were affected. His vision became blurred—almost the same as when one videotape is played over another; both are clear enough to be seen, neither is clear enough to eliminate doubt. In his eardrums there began the sort of ache produced by a sudden burst of a jackhammer; and the ache continued. Whatever he touched gave him the funny shiver through the small of his back and spine he used to get when somebody rubbed a pane of glass with a dry thumb. His mouth tasted as if he had been chewing sour milk and flour. And a wild odor he could not define lodged in his nostrils. Not of rottenness or putrefaction or sewage, but a sharp odor that his sense of smell could not take without a stinging recoil seizing his sinuses and the back of his mouth and throat in revulsion.

His assistants saw Gerald as he began to jackknife over. Two held him, one on either side; but, faithful to his instructions, they did not attempt to lead him out of the room. "Can you make it, Father?" asked Dr. Hammond. Gerald's only answer was to jerk his head in a quick gesture.

The uncanny pressure was climaxing inside in his will and outside in his body. He felt the recently healed wounds in his back and belly loosening and flowing, the scabs giving way, and a salty sting in the opening flesh. He felt the wetness of his own blood and sweat. And Gerald knew he now had to make a supreme effort.

"Your name! You who torment this creature of God. In the name of Jesus, and because of his power, your name! Now! Your name!"

He heard the last rumbling traces of that attacking voice fading away. Richard/Rita stirred as if prodded with a sharp knife, writhing his head, neck, and back. He groaned. Then all in the room heard a little gravelly whisper, not faltering, just deliberate and slow.

"Girl-Fixer. The Girl-Fixer. Girl-Fixer. We fix 'em. All sorts of girls. Young, old, married, unmarried, lesbians, neuters, girls who want to be fixed. Those who want to be fixed like girls. Anyone. We fix 'em. Oeeeeeeeeeeeh!" It was a larynx-shaking yelp. "We fix 'em right!"

Gerald's weight on the arm of his assistants grew heavy. The pressure on him was increasing again. But he knew the name now. Girl-Fixer. He had broken through the deadly charade and he knew with every instinct that he must pursue hard before his advantage could slip away.

"You *will* tell us: how many of you are there? Who are you? What do you do? Why do you hold this creature of God in slavery? You *will* tell us. Speak!"

Gerald would have gone on repeating the same commands, but the younger priest made a small gesture reminding him he was falling into a repetitive pattern. They both waited. Gerald was still fighting the poison inside him. All his pain was with him.

"Take you, for example, Priest!" The contempt and hate in the tone was chilling. "We fixed you, didn't we? Just feel, kiddo. Or just try to do something with your end, fore or aft. Oh, yes! We fixed you. Oeeeeeeeeeeeh!"

Gerald steadied himself and tried to wet his lips; his mouth was dry and furry. His sight was getting blurred again. He had to keep at it. The teacher lifted a cup of water to his lips. He had to keep at it. He moistened his tongue and started again.

"Tell us, in the name of Jesus . . ."

He was interrupted by a low groan from Richard/Rita. Its agony

paralyzed everyone; joined to the volume of pain and suffering in his
own body, it struck Gerald dumb. Each of the others was affected by
that groan: each one's imagination and memory went out of control.
The police captain was back in the Korean prison camp where he had
languished for two years; his buddy was groaning his life away in pain,
as a grinning interrogator scraped the flesh off his ribs. The teacher
was back in Surrey, England, in 1941, beside a German plane that had
crashlanded, bursting into flames; the trapped German pilot was
screaming, *"Mutti! Mutti!"* as he burned inside the plane. Richard's
brothers were standing beside a shuddering, dying wolf they had shot
over ten years ago during a hunting trip in Canada with their father;
the wolf was groaning defiance and coughing up blood and staring at
them. The doctor was back on a house call of the previous winter
when he had watched a father, bending over the still-warm body of his
dead three-month-old baby son, choke in hoarse, dry sobs. Everyone
felt guilty, as of murder or willful torture. Someone or something was
suffering untold pain and blaming them all.

Only John, the younger priest, had no horror image or dreadful
memory. He tried to finish Gerald's command. And it was a painful
mistake.

"Answer," he said loudly, his voice cracking with nervousness. "In
the name of Jesus, answer our questions . . ."

"Don't, John," Gerald interrupted thickly. But it was too late. The
damage was done. The groaning stopped. Richard/Rita rolled over on
his back, then sat up. There was a sudden, dreadful lull. The others
were jerked back to the present. They tensed, ready to jump and hold
Richard/Rita down. But all Richard/Rita did was to open one eye. It
appeared luminous, slitted, evilly joyous, focusing on John.

"Ah! The lily-white cur!" Each word came out like paste squeezed
slowly from a tube. Everyone present and listening waited on every
syllable. "We'll fix you. In time." Gerald was filled with pity for John:
now *he* was in for it.

"You'll lose some of your hair. And you'll sit in a confessional and
secretly wonder why they do the things they confess to you. And the
wonder will change to curiosity. And the curiosity to desire. You won't
admit it, but you will end with desire. To murder. To steal. To fuck.
Whatever they tell you. And you'll feel the prick in you and you'll
fudge on the monies. And you'll tilt the bottle. Then you'll let her hot
hands soothe your fever"—the sarcasm was biting—"and when you
get up, she'll drive you to the sea for your health and you'll have a

quickie in the back of the car—all for the love of your sugar-coated Jesus. And she'll need more and more of your love of God. And more. And more. And more. And"—the voice was now at a screaming crescendo—"you'll take several wives of several men, just to console them. You'll be a whoremaster on the altar, you lily-white cur. And you'll be afraid to confess it." Richard/Rita started to screech and howl with laughter, rolling around the couch. "Maybe"—he stopped laughing and fixed John again with the one eye speculatively— "maybe, you'll come even into *my* box."

The captain laid two strong hands on Richard/Rita's shoulders, restraining him firmly but gently. He was suddenly quiet. Then he turned the one eye on the captain and wrinkled his nose in mock disgust: "He'll screw your wife. Yours! She wants him already. A nice clean young man no woman ever had."

"Frank, hold it," Gerald said hurriedly to the captain. He squeezed John's hand to reassure the young priest. He was now standing erect by himself. He reassured them all with a glance. Then slowly and in a solemn tone of voice to Richard/Rita: "Your name is Girl-Fixer. You will answer our questions." Painstakingly he listed them: "How many of you are there? Who are you? What do you do? Why do you hold this person whom Jesus saved?"

Each question acted like a hammer blow on Richard/Rita. With each one Richard/Rita sank back further on the couch. He seemed to shrink and diminish as if being flattened. A look of trapped horror spread over his face like a film.

Gerald continued: "I ask these questions in the name of Jesus. You will answer."

Richard/Rita's body relaxed and went limp; he lay on his back, eyes closed. The captain loosened his hold finally and stood back. Gerald motioned to the assistants; they moved away from the bed. Richard/ Rita's two brothers looked at each other for a brief instant. They recollected later: their horror was almost equaled by their curiosity. What malign and dark forces had seized their brother? Why? Could he be freed of them? Would they give up?

The pressure on Gerald was lightening inch by inch, he felt. He could feel little pockets of relief throughout his body. His vision started to clear up again. His ears stopped aching. He was no longer bleeding. He still had the inexorable gnawing around his middle, but now it was a dully insistent pain, steady, unwavering, predictable.

For a few minutes Richard/Rita's mouth opened and shut alternately. They could see his tongue moving inside, his cheeks tautening and loosening, his Adam's apple jerking up and down. He seemed to be forming words soundlessly.

Then they began to hear him, at first faintly as a distant whisper, then in half words, then broken phrases, finally in whole sentences punctuated by trailing pauses and delivered in that gravelly tone which not even his brothers recognized as that of the Richard they had known all their lives. Dr. Hammond, too, had recovered his composure, and was once more engaged in clinical observation of what was happening.

"How many of you are there?" Gerald repeated. Then he leaned forward listening intently. Bit by bit, he began to pick up the middle of words, the beginnings of phrases.

". . . numbers . . . no bodies, fool . . . can you can't . . . numerality . . . spr—— . . . negative math . . . count only in power . . . unbroken will each and eve—— . . . stick together . . . gargantuan push on little pygmies . . . no one solitary . . , off on their own . . . nothing . . . any one of us alone is nothing, has nothing . . . among us, a single spirit is merely a few fibers—will, mind—strung out on a measly being forever headed to an eternal absence, an endless vacuum . . . a belly on two legs stumbling aimlessly across the dry bed of confirmed hopelessness . . . that's each one alone . . . impossible . . . nothing, a real nothing . . . hating, loathing, loving unlove and unloving . . . together around a human or hating the High Enemy . . . oaaaaaaaaaah . . . the push and shove and dent we make, the Kingdom, the Kingdom, there High Enemy never rules, dense, indistinguishable, one mass, one will, one complete beast, one brilliance pouring from the Daring One to all the others. So that humans back into the corner . . . take darkness as their lot, disease and pain and death and darkness . . . on all sides scratched, bitter, stung, deadened, maddened by the crawling members of the Kingdom, the Kingdom . . ."

"Have you all various names?" Gerald interjected. "Are you all equal? What are your identities?"

The voice coming from Richard/Rita had sunk to a stage whisper.

"Brilliant! Brilliant!" the psychologist breathed wonderingly to Gerald. "Just the question to be asked!"

"Must you go further on this line, Father?" Bert asked Gerald, watching his brother in dismay.

"Kindly wait, my dear man." Dr. Hammond's eyes were bulging

with interest, his face flushed with anger at the interruption. "This may be a landmark case of multiple personality."

Gerald looked sideways at the psychiatrist. It was a look more of pity than surprise. But there was no time for more.

". . . round and fat and red and black and male and female and what they do or smell like or walk like or do like, pygmy humans . . . names, what names? . . . a breath of little lungs . . . it's what we do, we are . . . millions if you count the wills, the minds, infinite if you weigh the hatings, the living hatings . . . one above the other, no one is all, all are under one, some so near the Daring One they have intelligence only the High Enemy can match, some so low they are turds, the shards, the lumps beneath his heel, the dust between his toes . . . and loving it all, all the degradation . . . anything to disfigure beauty."

A fit of crackling, cackling laughter seemed to grip Richard/Rita. Whatever or whoever was amused, it was a frightening look Richard/Rita now wore: his mouth drawn back, all his teeth bared, his cheeks lined from the stretching of the lips, chin bobbing up and down, nostrils flaring and distended—and the ugly horror of that amusement. This was no belly laugh or dry, subtle joke, no reaction to fine wit or deep humor. Just a triumphal screeching sound undulating out on felt waves of satisfaction for hate, of acquiescence in unhappiness, of refusal to envisage any existence but that of living in death, of mercilessness, of perpetual banality exalted into a way of existence.

Gerald spoke again. "What do you do, you of the Kingdom? Girl-Fixer? All of you? What do you do?"

Richard/Rita was now covered with perspiration. His clothes and the top of the couch were sodden. The temperature of the room had become stifling in the last hour. A stale odor hung in the air. Each one present had a throbbing headache. Bert and Jasper had begun again to support Gerald on either side. Both the brothers looked like men wounded and bled dry of any feeling. They had been numbed by compassion for their brother and by fear for his well-being. Father John was saying his rosary beads. The teacher and the police captain stood on either side of the couch. Listening to Richard/Rita's rambling talk, they seemed to have shrunk to shadows of their former selves, their burly forms drooping and listless.

The only one still spry, coldly thoughtful, active, still moving around and in apparent control of himself, was the psychiatrist. In spite of his apparent stress, there was a gleam in his eyes, picked up by his steel-rimmed spectacles, that bespoke the professional behaving predictably in the teeth of invaluable experience. Dear God, Gerald prayed silently, let him be spared the price of any further stupidity he may yet commit.

Dr. Hammond, however, concentrated on Richard/Rita's reply as his body stiffened on the couch. The police captain and the teacher held Richard/Rita down. Jasper left Gerald's side and placed his hands on Richard/Rita's ankles. They could all "feel" the resistance coming.

"Why should we reply? The High . . ."

"Because Jesus commands you. And his cross protects us. And you were defeated by his sacrifice. And you *will* obey. Answer."

Again Richard/Rita went limp. The groaning started and lasted a minute or two. James could feel his brother's whole body vibrating as if electric waves were being shot through it in quick, successive spurts.

"We . . . we . . . leave us to the Kingdom. You hear! Rita is one of us now. Forever. You cannot have Rita."

"Rita is baptized. And saved. And forgiven. You do not anymore have the freedom of Rita's body and Rita's soul," Gerald shot with a savagery he never had felt before. "You will tell us what you do, how you fix. Answer. In the name of Jesus."

For a few minutes, Gerald had the impression that the confused babel of voices was starting again, but it came to nothing. In that tiny, limping, unknown voice, Richard/Rita spoke again. It was the weird and unaccustomed voice that made him a stranger to his brothers.

"Oh, it starts with the box and ends with the box. So long as we make them think the box is all, we fix them. We can make a whore of the grandest—all legal, all secure, if once . . . if once they think the box is woman, woman a box . . . the greatest insult to the High Enemy, because woman is likest to the High Enemy. A man is a thing. A woman is being. We fix them so they think . . . it's nothing but a big, fat dick in a sea of hormones, and smellings and screams, and all the shouting and jabbing and pulling and jerking. Tie them to the dickybird tight in his cage. Tie them to that. Don't let them see beyond. And she will make the man in her image. Tie him too . . ." Richard/Rita broke off, turning on the couch and gasping as if for air. "You! Priest! We've fixed you for . . ."

"No, Girl-Fixer. Jesus has defeated you. In his name you will answer: why do you hold this creature, Rita, in slavery? Why?"

Gerald in his inexperience was following a dangerous yet apparently elementary line of reasoning. It seemed logical to him to insist on finding out why or how Richard/Rita had come to be possessed. But there was always the danger that his own mental curiosity would conquer his better judgment. He might, in that case, advance so far as to tamper with the innards of evil and get injured beyond repair.

As it turned out before the end of the exorcism, it was not Gerald who suffered the consequences of such tampering.

"We do as we are bidden by the Daring One. Rita was our prey, our soul. Rita chose to be a box, to be a box, to be a box, to be a box. Even when the High One spoke, he chose to be a box, to be a box, to be a box."

Gerald, by some inner sense, felt that one single, personal strand of evil and resistance had faded or was fading from the scene; it felt as if a lesser intelligence was now coping with his questions.

Richard/Rita began to struggle and gasp again. Gerald reflected for a moment. What next? Should he keep silent and let all things quiet down? Should he press forward and extract more information? He remembered the old Dominican saying with a shake of the head: "If you get a chance to squeeze them dry of words, do so. If you can, press them to tell what exactly happened. But don't get into a give-and-take of a normal argument. They will always beat you. And a beating can be more than you can take."

Gerald looked again at Richard/Rita; his body was thrashing back and forth jerkily; the assistants were looking at Gerald for some direction. He decided to ask one more question.

"Evil Spirit, in the name of Jesus, announce the trap in which you caught Richard/Rita. I ask this by the authority of the Church and in the name of Jesus."

Richard/Rita's horrible voice answered: "We start with self-growth, self-discovery. We tell 'em, we told Rita: First, you must be yourself, find yourself, know who you are. They stick their noses in their own navels and say: I like my own smell! Then, that woman alone, woman alone, is the thing to be. She has it all within her, but man has it all hanging out."

The assistants had moved away from the couch and stood in almost unbelieving fright near Gerald. Bert no longer supported Gerald, but leaned on the night table.

"To be a woman is to be completely independent, we tell them. No guilt. Not masculine. Not feminine. Complete in herself. Cunt and clit in one. Androgynous. Free of guilt feelings, of all responsibility to a man. Biologicaaaaaaaaaaal!" Richard/Rita's voice stretched out, caressing the last syllable. At a sign from Gerald, the assistants moved back and laid hands on Richard/Rita. A pause. Then: "To be freed from any need of other. Let them think that they are past ambition of ecstasy on a prick, but totally sensual because they can laugh at love and all its makings; that they are developing their own self-contained skills; that her own intimacy with herself is the whole world, without the intrusion of the male; that she is full of internal spaces in herself, infinite spaces, infinite enough to contain all she could ever wish to have or be; that she can be tranquil, full of personalities, many-sided, all of man, without his tomfoolery, all of woman without the alley-cat carry-on."

Richard/Rita stopped. Only the four pairs of hands restrained him from getting up. His legs and arms wrestled for a few moments, then ceased. He groaned again and began to mutter inaudibly.

"Speak, Girl-Fixer! Speak! Let us hear your voice clearly!"

"Then . . . then . . . the same old trap. The same old trap we've taken many in—we still catch them in. That they fuck as necessarily as birds sing, as water flows, as the fire burns. Merely to show how independent they are. How superior they are. That if they don't breathe for fucking, live for fucking, sing in fucking, they can't breathe, cry, sing, love, or do anything. Be liberated. That's what they begin to say. Man, woman, or goat, little boy, or if it comes to that, little girl. And then, when Rita got there—Oeeeeeeeeeeeh!" It was a yelp of triumph as before.

Gerald was in command. There was not even a vestige of the Pretense now. But Richard/Rita was still caught in the teeth of this wild, evil thing and was virtually flung about on the couch as the Girl-Fixer cackled on.

"And, after that . . . one penis. Then another penis. Then a third. A fourth. A fifty-fourth. A forest of 'em. Sharp stakes. All the same. Oeeeee! And then the hate at being loved so. And the disgust at hating. And the hating of so loving. And the loving of hate. And the lying in wait for the penis. And the laughter at its nonsense. And the slavery. Many of us are the rump of the Daring One. Every Rita is a piece of his shit . . ."

It was enough. Gerald broke in brusquely. There was only one question more. "At what point in time did Rita give over possession to you? When was it consummated?"

"In the snow. In the wind. We knew then we could find a place in him. Bend him to our will. But he had invited years before . . ."

Gerald decided that all he wanted to know had been told. The evil spirit had been sufficiently subdued and humiliated. Now it could be expelled.

"Lord God of Heaven, in the name of Jesus Christ, your only begotten son, and in the name of your Holy Spirit, we pray that you will grant us our prayer and free this your servant, Richard, from the toils of slavery and the foul possession of this evil spirit." Gerald had been looking up at the ceiling during this prayer. Now he looked down at Richard/Rita, held up the crucifix, and prepared to begin the final exorcising prayer.

Dr. Hammond broke in, whispering urgently in his ear: "Father, don't let it stop here. Let me put a few professionally oriented questions."

In spite of his dislike of psychiatrists and his general annoyance with this one, Gerald remained afraid for him. He whirled around painfully, urgently pleading in a cracked voice: "For the love of Jesus, Dr. Hammond, for your own sake, keep your mouth shut. Stay out of this. You don't know what you . . ."

But it was too late. Dr. Hammond had gone over beside Richard/Rita. He sat down on the edge of the couch and began to speak calmly, persuasively.

"Now, Rita, we have nearly finished. This is almost at its close. You will be calm. There's nothing to be fearful of. Answer my questions. And after that, you will wake up."

Richard/Rita stopped turning and twisting. He lay utterly still. His face relaxed. The expression around his lips softened. Dr. Hammond, rather tense in the beginning, now began to relax. It was a mistake on Gerald's part to allow the psychiatrist to do this. No experienced exorcist would have permitted such blatant and dangerous interference. It was dangerous not only because the whole exorcism might break down and be completely lost, but it could be possibly fatal for the person so unwary as to reach out in ignorance and touch summary evil. So it proved in one sense for Dr. Hammond.

A sudden, dull silence fell in the wake of his opening words to Richard/Rita. After all the pain and noise and groaning and strain, that silence was surprisingly alien to them all. One by one, each head lifted. Hammond's professional air—his blue business suit, his spectacles, his knowing tone, his very confidence in moving to Richard/Rita's couch and sitting down to speak, overruling Gerald's warnings by his behavior—all this made them think, as the policeman recalled, "After all, this may be more normal than I thought."

But what Gerald sensed was not the lifting of an evil presence, but a shift. Dr. Hammond had fallen into the same trap as Gerald had done four and a half weeks before, and with infinitely poorer defenses than even Gerald had had. Only Gerald and the teacher grew tense with the fear of understanding.

But suddenly, almost in unison and as if their unwinding had been something you could see and hear, they all stopped unwinding. You could almost see and hear the sudden cessation of flooding relief. In that silence they were listening. A change was taking place. They all sensed now what Gerald and the teacher had sensed. A change in something or somewhere near them or connected with them, with that room, with Gerald, and with Richard/Rita.

Finally even the psychiatrist stopped, his professional calm ruptured. He had the half-annoyed, half-hurt look of someone interrupted in the middle of a sentence. He looked quickly at Gerald and the others, alarm spreading across his features. For the first time in his professional life, Dr. Hammond was face to face with something he knew was far beyond his reach to categorize as a verifiable known or unknown. What he was then beginning to perceive, he felt, he had always known but never acknowledged, even in the deepest moments of the eight years of analysis through which he had successfully passed.

But his scientific mind was his only ready defense, and he kept up the protest in his mind: Verify! Get the facts! Test them! But he knew. There was no verifiable fact. There was a reality made transparent to him. Before this moment, he would have labeled this a product of the irrational. But it now appeared to be real beyond all reason. And he had always known it.

Slowly they all began to hear sound. It was, at the beginning, like the sound of a crowd or mob—feet pounding faintly, voices shouting, screaming, yelling, jeering, talking, distant whistling and grunting. They could not fix from what direction it came. The teacher glanced out the windows at the pond. The trees were moving gently in the wind; a few ducks paddled around in the water; the evening was still bright. Then the noise sounded nearer, just as confused as ever, but now with one overall mood or note: mourning for an ineluctable sorrow. Listening to that sound on the tape recording of the exorcism, and as it grows louder and louder, one begins to get the conviction of listening to the tortured murmurs and helpless protests of a mob in agony, keening and wailing for deeps of regret, screaming and groaning for the ache of punishment and unremitting penalty, yelling impotently in condemnation, vibrating as a whole beast of suffering, as some protean heart thumping in the mud and squalor that history never recorded and human mercy had never penetrated.

Over and above all the voices but constantly weaving in and out among them, there was the full scream of a woman orchestrating all the other noises and voices around itself as their theme. It came in great rising and falling curves, louder and fainter, still louder and then fainter, regular, upbeat, jarring, resounding with a passion of pain and lost hope.

Gerald noticed that everyone in the room seemed to be bending, lowering his height as if afraid of something moving in the upper part of the room. Nothing was visible up there.

Dr. Hammond sat as if unable to move from the edge of the couch. Richard/Rita's lips turned blue, his eyes open and staring vacantly. The attending doctor moved to his side to take his pulse and found his body very cold, the pulse steady but weak.

"Father, this cannot go on much longer," Father John managed to shout to Gerald. "He's taken enough already."

"Not very much more! Not very long, now!" Gerald shouted back. But the remainder of what he wanted to say went unsaid. It was the psychiatrist who now claimed his attention. Dr. Hammond had slipped off the couch and stood in an askew way looking halfway around over his shoulder at Richard/Rita, his eyes narrowed with apprehension, his notebook fallen and forgotten. No one, the psychiatrist included, could shake his mind loose from the web of pain and regret pervading the atmosphere.

The noise and the din of sobbing and mourning rose finally to an undulating pitch. Richard/Rita's face suffused with color; red patches and streaks discolored his arms and neck. Even his eyes deepened in color. He was trying to speak.

Gerald was alerted: something was coming, and he felt he must make his final challenge very fast.

"In the name of Jesus, you are commanded to leave this creature of God. You will go out of Rita and leave him whole and entire . . ."

Richard/Rita's sudden scream split their eardrums. "We go, Priest. We go." It was a million turbulent voices as one, full of eternal ache and pain. "We go in hate. And no one will change our hate. And we will wait for you. When you come to die, we'll be there. We go.

But"—Gerald heard the sharp injection of hate hissing through the sorrow—"we take him." Richard/Rita's hands suddenly swept up in a wide arc toward Dr. Hammond. It was a quick but clumsy movement.

Hammond jumped backward. And Richard/Rita fell off the couch to the floor as the assistants jumped forward and held him down.

"We already have his soul. We claim him. He is ours. And you cannot do anything about that. We already have him. He is ours. We needn't fight for him."

Richard/Rita was wheezing like someone being asphyxiated, eyes bulging, neck muscles standing out, his long hair falling back, his chest heaving, as he half-rose in his effort. "You can't get him back. He is ours. He does our work. He doesn't need a box. He puts everybody else into it."

All calm was gone from Dr. Hammond; his face was a picture of black fear.

"Here . . . we can't stay here any longer." It was still the voice from Richard/Rita, and it was full of inflexible pain and bitterness. "There is too much to suffer here. Where will we . . ." The voice trailed off.

Richard/Rita kicked and scratched at the straining assistants. Then he started to scream until at last he fainted, and above and around them the last syllables of his words trailed off into the din of voices. They spiraled up to a thin, high note, then sank to a thumping resonance like the bellowing of a gored bull. Slowly they faded into the distance. Those many tortuous voices, those myriad footfalls with decreasing rhythm and ever fainter sound all began to withdraw farther and farther from their presence, like a funeral procession plodding its way inch by inch, swaying and twisting, out of the city of man, swallowed by the great, unknown wilderness of the surrounding night. That single beating scream of the woman still rang dolefully but more and more faintly above the dying echoes of the withdrawing multitude, until finally there was only a little swatch of sound rising and sinking, rising and sinking, and in the end never rising again out of the silence.

As the sound had receded, Richard/Rita's struggling had progressively ceased. The tension holding everyone had lessened and lessened until they realized one by one, as they lifted their heads, moved uneasily, then looked at each other's faces, that they were standing alone with each other in a small bedroom, that there was a curious silence, and that their world was still right-side up. It was over. All was well.

Gerald glanced at the psychiatrist. He was leaning back against the wall, spectacles in one hand, while he cried unreservedly into his other hand. "Bert, see to him, will you?" Gerald said gently.

"Leave me. Leave me be," muttered Dr. Hammond, in between his tears. Then he drew a deep breath: "I'm all right. Leave me be." He walked slowly to the door, pulled it open, then half-turned and looked back at Richard/Rita and at Gerald. He had the look of someone unjustly hurt; and his eyes held a puzzlement and appeal. Then, without a word, he turned and went out. He would have conversations with Gerald later. But now he had no words. And he was tired beyond belief.

After about 20 minutes, they lifted Richard/Rita on to the couch. He was coming to. He motioned with his hand to Gerald. He was obviously very weak but quite self-possessed and aware. Gerald saw the smile in his eyes and faintly at the corners of his mouth.

"Father, I have not felt so restful and so light in ten years. I . . ."

"No need to say much now, Rita," said Gerald.

"But, Father Gerald, I . . . I am happy for the first time for a long time."

"We'll talk about it later," Gerald said, smiling through his pain; he was bleeding again and his pelvis was riven with an aching soreness. He straightened up as much as he could, and turned to go.

"Father Gerald!" Richard/Rita struggled up and leaned on one elbow. He was looking out the window. "I am . . . I . . . please . . . call me Richard. Richard I was born. Richard I will die." He glanced up at Gerald. "The rest of it"—his gaze traveled down over his body—"for the rest of it, let's rely on God and—and Jesus." He paused and looked away as if remembering or trying to remember something. Then, looking again at Gerald, "Father, they told me . . . or I heard them say—I don't know which—there isn't much time . . . you know . . ." He broke off lamely.

"I know, Richard," Gerald said trying to smile, but feeling the lead weight inside him. Somewhere deep in his belly a gray slug was eating his vitals. And somewhere in his heart, a lump of coldness had taken up residence. "I know. I have known for quite a while. I know. It's all right. It was my own choice."

Outside on the driveway, Dr. Hammond was sitting in the driver's seat of his car waiting. The engine was already started.

"Going to be a very wet night, Father Gerald," he said. Despite the strain, there was a note of cordiality and respect Gerald had not noticed before. "Let me drop you on my way to the office. I must get my report on tape tonight before I forget anything. They can type it up tomorrow."

Gerald slid in painfully beside him and waved goodbye to Jasper, who had been helping him.

"Tell me, Dr. Hammond," he said chattily as they swung out on to the main road, "do you believe in the Devil?"

Uncle Ponto and
the Mushroom-Souper

"Uncle Ponto!" Jamsie screamed in fury as he reached for the door of his apartment. "Uncle Ponto! This time, I'll do it. By Jesus, I'll do it. You'll see! I'll do it." He banged the door after him. As he scrambled down the steps into the street and fumbled with the car key, he muttered angrily: "That does it—permanently, eh? That does it. I'll fix you, you little bastard."

Jamsie was shaking all over his tall, raw-boned frame. He was gripped by a sense of frustration that put him almost out of control of himself. His reddish hair and high complexion had always been startling for people. But now his cadaverous face was flushed with passion, his eyes were blazing. His appearance must have been frightening.

In a few moments he was at the wheel. Fumbling and cursing, he got the car started, made a quick, jerky U-turn, and was immediately off gathering speed as he headed away from San Francisco.

Jamsie was seething with an accumulated rage so great that he continued to shake. He had put up with Uncle Ponto's annoyances for over six years. Finally he had had enough. Even though Ponto had left him alone a lot of the time, and even though he had been able to sleep in peace in his own apartment at night until fairly recently, and even though he had at times even relished the eerie company of Ponto and got a kick out of their encounters, nevertheless, on this early Saturday morning, he had had enough. Ponto wanted to move in completely and permanently and immediately, to take him over, him and his entire life. And something had broken inside Jamsie. He had to finish the whole thing now.

"You won't bother me any more. You'll get off my ass. You'll . . ."

Jamsie's voice trailed off. A glance in the rearview mirror was enough: Uncle Ponto was on the back seat, that same uncouth smirk on his face that always enraged Jamsie.

"I told you before," Jamsie shouted violently into the mirror, "that is a dirty smile. A pig's smile! A foul, swinish smile!" Then in a sudden excess of anger and frustration: "Hell! Hell! Hell!" He paused to negotiate a corner. "Hell again! Now you've asked for it, Ponto. This is it."

He lapsed into silence, breathing heavily, and drove on. Now and again he shot a furtive glance into the rearview mirror to reassure himself that Ponto was still there. Jamsie could see the squarish head ending in what was almost a point, the narrow forehead with the tiny zigzag eyebrows slanting upward, the large, bulbous eyes with the whites so reddened that you could hardly distinguish them from the deeply pink irises. And Ponto's nose and mouth and chin—what there was of chin—had always reminded Jamsie of a long, thin pencil stuck in a very ungainly Idaho potato.

Ponto's face looked as if it had been put together in the dark by several people working at cross-purposes, with each part coming from a different face. No one part really matched another part. Even his face color, a brownish-black, clashed with his sparse blond hair, which sat like a cheap toupee on top of that peculiar pointed head.

He would have been comic-looking—and Jamsie sometimes had a good laugh at his facial characteristics—were it not for the normal expression on Ponto's face. For it was in no way the comic face of a circus clown, in which irregularity and human feeling combined to give a sense of pathos. Ponto's was a caricature of a human face. Where the clown's face read: "Laugh! But know that I mirror the helplessness of us all," Ponto's face read: "Don't laugh! But do despair, because I mirror the real absurdity of you all." And what really prevented Jamsie from any constant amusement about Ponto's face was the thick transformation through which it could pass. At times it did not look human at all. It was something else for which Jamsie had no name—neither animal nor human nor even a nightmare face born in bad dreams or shown in the Chamber of Horrors.

"All I'm asking for, all I ever asked for," Jamsie remembers Uncle Ponto saying softly sometime later, as they drove onto Highway 101, "is that you let me come and live with you. I won't be in the way. You need a friend like me."

Jamsie snorted with rage; his steering became erratic for a moment.

"You see," Ponto continued in his primest tones. "You see! You shouldn't have got so upset. You're not as good a driver as your father, Ara, was."

"Leave my father out of this," Jamsie grated.

Ponto's voice was something else again. Never loud, even when Ponto was screaming, it had a painful effect most of the time. It left ringing echoes inside Jamsie's hearing, so that any kind of extended conversation with Ponto ended up in jabbing earaches.

As a matter of fact, Ponto had only started to bother him long after his father's gradual degeneration from self-supporting artisan to New York hack driver to part-time pimp to dope peddler. Yes, and long after his mother's taking to prostitution on New York streets as a last, desperate means of livelihood.

Leave them out of this, Jamsie thought silently. What lay between himself and Uncle Ponto was entirely personal.

In brief, Jamsie had had enough of Uncle Ponto's harassment. Two years of sudden appearances morning, noon, and night, and of uninvited interventions that had wrecked his personal life, all this had finally become too much. In the beginning Jamsie had even welcomed Ponto's unpredictable antics. They had provided some relief to his boredom. At times he had been amused, stimulated, even bettered and helped in various practical difficulties. And, after years of creeping horror prior to Ponto's first appearance, years of being pursued by strange, intangible threats, Ponto was at least a visible butt for Jamsie's general anger at life and at people—and at himself. But that had been merely the beginning.

It might have continued like that if Ponto had not changed his tack. But, after a while, Jamsie had found that Uncle Ponto was pressuring him. From being an occasional visitor and companion, Ponto had started to assume the role and privileges of a familiar, a close associate, an intimate friend. It was only then that Jamsie had received the full blast of Ponto's twisted personality. And it had been too much for Jamsie.

They were coming up to San Jose. Ponto had started to speak again. But Jamsie had been taken in by Ponto's put-ons before. He clamped his lips tight, resolved to give Ponto the old silent treatment. It had occasionally worked in the past.

Jamsie had heard it all before: what Ponto thought of his father and mother; how he, Jamsie, should stay away from women and liquor ("Women are death," Ponto dinned into him; "booze makes you easygoing"); who really was Jamsie's friend in this life—Ponto himself, or people like Lila Wood, Jamsie's onetime girlfriend, and Lila's friend, Father Mark. On Ponto rambled.

Jamsie had just passed San Jose and entered Highway 52, and was heading eastward to Hollister. Ponto's tone took on a note of suspicion.

"You told me you didn't like San Benito County, Jamsie!" A pause. "Jamsie!"

Jamsie kept his eyes glued to the road.

Ponto changed his tone. Now he was wheedling. "Just say, 'Yes,' Jamsie." Ponto was almost plaintive. "Just say, 'Yes.' You've no idea . . . I don't want to go back . . . All those homes up there . . ." Jamsie glanced up at the houses dotting the hillsides. "There's no welcome for me up there in spite of their boozing and bitching and despair."

With no reaction or answering word from Jamsie, Ponto fell silent. Jamsie stared ahead. Another long silence.

Sometime later, as Jamsie turned south on Highway 25 into the San Benito River Valley, a sardonic smile crept involuntarily across his mouth. I'll show you, he was thinking. You little sonavabitch. This will rid me of you, get it all over with, once and for all.

Uncle Ponto was agog again. He was becoming frantic.

"Jamsie, you're opaque to me now. Stop THAT! You hear me! Stop THAT! I'm getting bad vibes, very bad vibes. All darkness and fog."

The memory of Lila's friend, Father Mark, came back to Jamsie again. "Mushroom-Souper," that's what Ponto had derisively nick-named Father Mark. On the one evening Jamsie had visited with the priest, Mark had treated him to mushroom soup made from his own recipe. Afterward, Jamsie had talked with him into the small hours of the morning, telling him of his early life, of Ponto's harassment, and of his own deep despair and continual rage against life. Mark seemed to understand much more than he was able to explain to Jamsie. But several times during that conversation, Jamsie had found himself incapable of going along with what Mark proposed: to get rid of Uncle Ponto. Always, at that point, Jamsie felt an unaccountable fear. If Ponto no longer existed in his life, what would happen? It was just as if Ponto represented some security or as if in some way or other he had given his word to Ponto.

He glanced at Ponto in the rearview mirror. Ponto was leering contentedly. The sight of that gash Ponto passed off as a smile roused Jamsie's anger again. He could not restrain himself.

"You're the son of the Father of Lies!" he shouted poisonously at Ponto. "That's what Mark said Jesus called him . . ."

Jamsie's ears were split by a high-pitched scream from Ponto. "DON'T!" Ponto shouted. "Don't mention that person's name in my presence. Don't mention THAT!" Ponto's queer face was contorted in utter misery.

There was silence for a while. Jamsie glanced at either side. How happy he had been here in this countryside with his father for a few days of a childhood visit years before. Eastward stood the Diablo Range—an ironic touch to the situation, Jamsie thought. To the west ran the Gabilan Range. Ahead lay the Pinnacles National Monument. They should arrive within an hour at the park.

Got to get it over with, Jamsie began saying to himself over and over again. But, as the memories of his childhood happiness passed before his mind, he began to wonder. Got to free myself, he found himself thinking. Got to rid myself of this "familiar," got to free. But Ponto started to chatter again and interrupted his thoughts.

Every time he started to think, really to think, Ponto would interrupt. That, he realized, was what capped his resolution to end it all: this perpetual muzzling of his thoughts and feelings. When Ponto talked in his strange way, his words seemed to drown all of Jamsie's thinking. He could not think or feel.

Jamsie pressed down on the accelerator. He had to get to the Pinnacles.

Then, without warning, pain blocked his memories and dulled all thought. He felt the pressure inside his chest. He had experienced it before when trying to resist Ponto. It began at his rib cage just beneath his skin; and, as it had during the last few weeks, it started to contract inward toward the center of his body. It seemed to be pulling at his brain trying to force it down his spinal column.

All Jamsie could think of was the counterstratagems Mark had tried to teach him that evening.

"Jesus," he muttered under his breath.

Then he began to spell the word out letter by letter. "J-E-S-U-S, J-E-S-U-S, J-E-S-U-S." About 20 times. Next he spelt the name out by running down the alphabet from A to J, from A to E, from A to S, from A to U, from A to S. Then he started all over again.

He did not do this as a prayer. He had been taught it by Father Mark as a means of blocking Ponto's influence.

The internal pressure started to lessen. He could breathe again.

"Jamsie," came the horrified squawk of Uncle Ponto. "You know I don't like that. I don't like that at all. You know very well. I can't stand that. Stop it this minute, or I can't go on. You will lose me, you hear. You will lose me."

Jamsie started laughing, first of all quietly in his throat, then uncontrollably out loud.

"My friends and relatives won't like this at all," squeaked Ponto, voice high-pitched, elbows beating against his sides, hands wringing in the air. Jamsie laughed and laughed. This was what he used to call Ponto's "duck fit."

At least *that* worked, he thought. He did not know why that name disturbed Ponto. But Jamsie laughed from sheer relief nearly all of the next 32 miles. He had a pain from laughing. He was profoundly relieved to have got the best of Ponto for now, at least.

At times he stopped laughing when his thoughts became grim. Then, catching sight of Uncle Ponto's pointy little skull, heavy lids, and chinless face covered with that fretfulness of Ponto's "duck fit," he would start laughing again.

At the gate of Pinnacles National Monument the ranger took his money. Jamsie parked the car beside the Visitor's Monument, bought a map and a flashlight, and set off across the chaparral of Pygmy Forest. He knew where he wanted to go. And he was almost jubilant. But immediately Uncle Ponto was by his side. Jamsie now paid no attention to him. Something in the air exhilarated him. He felt freer than he had for a long time. He started to walk quickly. "Reservoir, here I come!" he hummed to the tune of "California, Here I Come!"

Ponto started to wheedle him again. "Jamsie, sit down a moment. Smell the hollyleaf cherry, the manzanita, these wild flowers. Sit down and rest a while. You were told to watch your heart. You're my investment. You're home for me. You're not going to walk all nine miles up and down, are you? Please! Jamsie! Please stop and talk it over with me. Please!"

Jamsie kept on. As he started to climb up to Bear Gulch Caves, he opened the map.

"It's no use, Jamsie," said Ponto. "I tell you, it's no use."

Jamsie turned his back on Ponto, searching the map for his way to the reservoir. But Ponto was up to his tricks again. Every time Jamsie's eyes and finger came near that name on the map, the name shifted. It shifted and sidestepped and dodged him, zigzagging across the map.

Jamsie began to get angry and then fearful. He slammed the map onto a flat rock and plunged his finger at "Reservoir." But it was too late. "Reservoir" slipped off the map and shot up into the sky over his shoulder.

Jamsie sprang up, cursing and hurling profanities at the blue sky where the word "Reservoir" danced and flowed around like a pennant towed by an invisible airplane. He swayed as he squinted up. Suddenly, "Reservoir, here I come" danced around in the sky. Then a whole skyful of dancing words spelled out letter by letter—and backwards: S-U-S-E-J, E-I-S-M-A-J, S-U-S-E-J, E-I-S-M-A-J.

Jamsie stamped on the ground. He was violently angry again. "To Hell with you and your tricks, you filthy brute. To Hell with you and your tricks . . ."

But he only heard the echo of his own shout and knew he was alone. He looked up. All was quiet. The sky was clear and blue. There was no trace of Uncle Ponto. The dancing letters were no more. He *was* alone.

He grabbed the map and stumbled on. Now his mind was made up.

After another half mile, Jamsie entered Bear Gulch Caves. He had been here about 20 years before with his father, and his memory started to serve him.

Halfway up through the narrow corridor of the cave, he began to hear more than his own footsteps. At first, it was the splashing of unseen cascades and the gurgling of underground streams. But quickly he began to realize a voice was becoming audible. It was Ponto's, of course.

"Jamsie, you know I will have to give an accounting for all this foolishness. I am responsible."

The voice came from above. Jamsie pointed the flashlight to the roof. Long ago some huge blocks of rock had fallen across a narrow fissure in the canyon wall and stuck there, closing it from the light of day and forming a roof. Ponto was dangling in between two of those rocks, his eyes glittering with malice. "Oh! I'm here all right."

"What the . . ." Jamsie was about to erupt; then all the fight drained out of him. He suddenly felt weak and helpless. In a sort of desperation, he started to run and stumble through pools of water and over rocks, wetting his feet and scraping his shins and ankles. Behind him, always near, came Ponto's mocking voice: "This can only end badly, Jamsie, if you keep on like this. You have to come back to me in the long run, you know. You can't do without me now. Not now!"

That "Not now" pursued Jamsie in a thousand echoes. It increased his panic and his need for flight.

Then he saw glimmers of daylight ahead of him. He scurried on, pursued by Ponto's voice echoing from every cranny. Finally he clambered up the last few rock steps cut out of the cave walls, and into the sunlight. Ponto's voice seemed to die away into the darkness he had just left. He was out of breath, perspiring from every pore, and shaking. He had bruised his elbows, knees, and ankles. His hair had fallen over his eyes.

But the sight now before him was a sudden distraction from his panic: the reservoir, calm, blue, unruffled, glasslike, without the merest ripple. And reflected in its face were the brown and gray and black spires and pinnacles of the surrounding land, undisturbed images intertwined with the greens and ashen-whites of the vegetation. It was a perfectly still mirror world in which the only movement came from the few clusters of utterly white clouds reflected from the sky. There was no sound whatever from the great things around him. Distance was telescoped. Time paused for him.

Then, in a little inner explosion of a new panic, Jamsie noticed the Shadow over to his right. A tall finger of brown-gray crag jutted out of the cliff wall over there. The Shadow stood beneath it and out of the glare of the sunlight.

Over on his left Ponto's exasperated voice called out from the cave mouth: "Well, if you have to do it, get on with it. Get it over with! Go on, Jamsie! An ideal place for it!"

Jamsie glanced over at the Shadow. In the darkness beneath the crag he thought he saw a movement, like someone sighing with relief that the desired end was near.

Ponto's voice struck at him again: "Go on, fool! Jump! They tell me it's okay now. Jump!"

As Ponto's voice died away, the Shadow moved beneath the crag ever so slightly. It might have been bending forward a little in order to follow more closely what Jamsie was about to do. Its outline, still dim, became more visible in its general details.

What Jamsie now found strange was his own lack of rage and fear. For the first time in three years, he felt neither. Instead, he felt that relief and easement of body and mind somehow akin to what you experience when you fill your lungs with air, after having held your breath to the point of suffocation. Why am I calm now? was the question he put himself.

He turned his head and gazed at the Shadow, as if he knew the answer to that question lay in its direction. That question and others were agonizing. His eyes calmly bored into the darkness surrounding the shape.

In the few moments before the Shadow slipped back into obscurity, Jamsie had enough time. The face, the head, the way it stood, all the details began to fall into place for his memory. The Shadow was tall, abnormally tall. And bulky. The body was covered in black folds. He could see the two arms raised at the elbows, the palms of the hands turned out toward him, the fingers clenching and unclenching. The head was lifted up, thrown back, as it were, in a fixed haughtiness, a resisting pride. Dimly he could make out eyes, nose, mouth.

The shape of that face riveted Jamsie's attention. It had all the details of a human face. Yet it was not human. It was something else. Where had he seen it? That face had been with him all his conscious life, even in his childhood and during his teens. And from the first day he had taken a job. Sure, it was Ponto's face. There was something of his father's face there, too, the face Ara had late at night when he was on a "job." And others he had once seen but had now forgotten. Many others.

It all took a few quick moments. As the Shadow receded noiselessly into the darkness beneath the crag, Jamsie became conscious of another element in himself. It was a tiny voice of instinct, a primal part of him still alive and vibrant. He knew he had seen the father of all man's real enemies. The Father of Lies and the ultimate adversary of all salvation, of any beauty, of each truth throughout the cosmos of God's working.

Beneath the crag there was suddenly only darkness. Jamsie's eyes fell away from the Shadow's hiding place. His thoughts came back to the reservoir.

He looked at the smiling calm of the waters and up to the North Chalone peak. He remembered what his father had said to him when they had looked at it together years before: someday he would climb all 3,305 feet of it. Waters and peak were clean—wholesome in some way Jamsie could not explain but did feel intensely. He could not, he thought to himself now, he could not soil them with his own dead and bloated body floating face down, its back to the peak, its juices polluting the water. Just the thought now made him feel uncouth, almost sacrilegious.

He looked away quickly from the clear surface of the reservoir. He stood stock-still. His mind was blank, his eyes, unseeing. He no longer desired to end it all here. But he could not think either of returning to the increasing torture of life with Ponto. "I have no desires at all," he thought helplessly. Then, as though pointing out to himself something he could not quite grasp, he repeated again and again: "I'm in shock. I'm in shock."

Ponto broke in peevishly: "You can do nothing, desire nothing, are nothing—except a human wreck about to kill yourself." Then viciously: "You"—a long drawn-out pause—"are finished"—again the cruel pause—"dead already, but you don't know it." A short pause. Then, like a pistol shot: "Jump!"

Jamsie did not budge, did not even shake or move. He was certain that Ponto lied. He knew that his will was not helpless, although he did not know what to do. He knew now that preserved in him was a deep desire stronger than any other. He felt tears coming to his eyes; and he knew those tears were forced from him by that deep, deep desire.

Alarm entered Ponto's voice again. "Jamsie! Be a man. Get it over with!"

Jamsie looked over his shoulder at the Shadow's hiding place. It had not gone. It seemed to have lost its undulating ease and draped complacency, to have gone rigid in some way he could not fathom.

Then Ponto started to chant in his eunuch's voice: "Jump-uh! Jump-uh! Jump-uh! Jump-uh!"

The words with their rhythmic extra beat hit Jamsie painfully as hailstones lashing his ears. He sought some escape, some gimmick to block those quick, stinging blows.

"Jump-uh! Jump-uh! Jump-uh!" went Ponto's voice in a high, spiraling tone, speaking quicker and quicker.

Jamsie's thoughts started to go awry. The torment of that voice was becoming too much. He remembered Father Mark and his instructions. The trick, that was it! The trick! He began desperately spelling out the name of Jesus again and again: J-E-S-U-S. J-E-S-U-S. J-E-S-U-S. Then he ran all the letters together like an incantation— J-E-S-U-S-J-E-S-U-S-J-E-S-U-S.

But now, he found, those letters and their piecemeal pronunciation meant more to him than a gimmick. The pain of Ponto's chanting diminished. Jamsie's tears flowed more sweetly, more as a relief than a gesture of suffering.

The tears blurred everything as he threw one more glance at the sky and the water, then heard himself break the silence of all nature, shouting, "Father Mark! Father Mark!" He shouted the name over and over. The echoes came back at him from all sides, from above and below, *Father, Father, Father . . . Mark, Mark, Mark,* and died away over the rocks and pinnacles.

He stepped back a little, then a little more, then some more, away from the edge of the reservoir. He turned back, looking toward the cave mouth and then at the Shadow. He realized he would have to pass by them both if he returned to the Monument Gate by Bear Gulch Caves.

The echoes died away. The Shadow beneath the crag had dwindled into itself and was almost indistinguishable again from the darkness beneath the crag. There was no sound from Ponto.

In the silence, Jamsie turned around and stumbled off down by the Moses Spring Trail, hugging the walls of the canyon. He was alone all the way down. The two hours of respite were welcome. When he arrived in full view of the parking lot, he was still saying two names, Jesus and Mark, over and over again to himself.

The ranger looked up from the magazine he was reading. "Need any help, buddy? You look beat."

"The phone. May I use the phone?"

Within a few minutes Jamsie was talking with Father Mark. "Stay where you are, Jamsie," Father Mark told him. "Don't drive back, whatever you do. Wait for me."

That evening Jamsie returned with Mark to San Francisco. They spoke little on the way. As they approached the rectory, Mark sensed a new unrest in Jamsie.

"What is it? What's wrong?"

"Ponto. He hasn't said a word. He hasn't appeared. I wonder if . . ."

"Don't. Just don't." Mark spoke firmly. Then he added drily, "Your old Uncle Ponto couldn't sit in *this* car."

Jamsie nodded. But he remained uneasy.

As they entered the rectory, Jamsie was not sure if for one moment he had not seen Ponto inside the gateway. The shadows cast by the street lamps were playing against the gate pillars and seemed to be a rustling cover for some rigid forms towering above him, leaning forward in an askew fashion, watching his every move, waiting for some moment of their choosing.

JAMSIE Z.

The case of Jamsie Z. presents us with an almost open-and-shut example of what used to be called "familiarization" or possession by a "familiar spirit" in the classical terminology of diabolic possession. I say "almost" because, in Jamsie Z.'s case, "familiarization" was never completed. Jamsie resisted, was exorcised, and the intending "familiar spirit" was driven out of his life.

"Familiarization" is a type of possession in which the possessed is not normally subject to the conditions of physical violence, repugnant smells and behavior, social aberrations, and personal degeneracy that characterize other forms of possession.

The possessing spirit in "familiarization" is seeking to "come and live with" the subject. If accepted, the spirit becomes the constant and continuously present companion of the possessed. The two "persons," the familiar and the possessed, remain separate and distinct. The possessed is aware of his familiar. In fact, no movement of body, no pain or pleasure, and no thought or memory occur that is not shared with the familiar. All privacy of the subject is gone; his very thoughts are known; and he knows continually that they are known by his familiar. The subject himself can even benefit from whatever pre-science and insight his familiar enjoys.

Although there was a definite connection between certain events and traits of his childhood and the experience that culminated in his exorcism, it was only after the age of thirty that he was openly approached by a "familiar" spirit and proffered "familiarization." From the age of thirty-four onwards he was subjected to multiple forms of persuasion by the spirit calling itself Uncle Ponto. But Jamsie's case does illustrate many of the traits of "familiarization" and the inherent dangers for those who give even a token consent to "familiarization."

Jamsie was born in Ossining, New York. His father, Ara, was of Armenian descent; his mother, Lydia, was of Greek descent. Both were third-generation Americans. Ara was a carpenter by trade, and played the clarinet in his spare time in order to earn extra money. Lydia belonged to a Boston family whose large fortune had been made in ship chandlering and on the stock market.

Lydia saw Ara for the first time at a small evening concert in Glen Ridge, New York. Improbable as it seemed to her family, she fell in love with Ara then and there. And Ara with her. On Lydia's eighteenth birthday they were married, over the violent objections of her family. Even the threat of being disowned and cut off entirely from the family fortune could not stop Lydia.

Jamsie was born one year later, in 1923. The family lived in Ossining for another five years. But by 1929 Ara and Lydia had decided to move to New York. He was not making enough money in Ossining. Lydia's mother and father were pestering Lydia to desert Ara and to return to the family with her son. New York, Ara and Lydia thought, would provide more work for Ara and a greater anonymity for the three of them. Ara had a letter of recommendation to a taxicab-fleet owner. He and Lydia had high hopes of success in the city.

In October 1929 the family moved to New York, taking with them some blankets, kitchen utensils, Ara's clarinet, and an old family icon of the Virgin that Ara's father had left him in his will. They first lived in a three-room walk-up in Penn Street. After a year they moved to a two-room apartment at Lexington Avenue and 25th Street. There they lived until Ara died in 1939.

Lydia, once more living in a big metropolis, wrote out a memento of their arrival in large black letters and hung it beside the old icon on their living-room wall: "Today, our first day in New York, George Whitney bid 204 for U. S. Steel." It hung there beside the icon for years; and these two objects were the center of Jamsie's earliest recollections.

But the golden age of New York which had begun at the end of the Civil War was just coming to its close, although few guessed its imminent collapse. New York's strength and prestige as the source of funds and leadership for the nation had been established in that 64-year period: great New York fortunes were made; famous New York homes were built by a Brokaw, a Dodge, a Carnegie, a Stuyvesant, a Whitney, a Vanderbilt, a Frick, a Harkness, the city's big financial district was created to sell the country all kinds of services. After World War I, most of New York's energies were turned toward Europe. But the old leadership was gone, and New York's manufacturing declined. As one writer put it, the financial soul of New York "worked itself up into a lather of paper profits and then collapsed." Ara and Lydia arrived just in time for that collapse.

Nevertheless, their first seven years in New York were relatively happy ones. Ara did not immediately use his recommendation to the taxicab-fleet owner. Instead, he worked as a handyman and carpenter, first around his own neighborhood, and then venturing down around Washington Square and up as far as Yorkville. Lydia at first stayed at home with their young child. Then, as Jamsie started parochial school, Lydia took a daytime job in an Armenian laundry.

In the opinion of the present writer, the New York which Jamsie knew from his earliest years had something rather intangible but definite to do with his later experience of attempted "familiarization." Between 1820 and 1930, over 38 million people had immigrated to the United States, and a good one-sixth of these had stayed in New York. The doormat for those "ragged remnants" was the Lower East Side.

New York was then a city of nearly seven million, with 25 foreign languages in daily use and 200 foreign-language newspapers and magazines to satisfy the needs of this heterogeneous population. "No one can become an American except by God's grace," wrote I. A. R. Wylie in the early 1930s. And, for the long-standing Yankee Protestant Establishment, New York, which was in the first third of the twentieth century five-sevenths Italian, Jewish, German, Irish, Hungarian, Armenian, Greek, Russian, Syrian, and otherwise foreign, was not American. The felt differences between the Establishment and the newly arrived was more than ethnic. The Establishment had adopted none of the ancient gods of the New World; they had imported their Christianity, which had no roots in pre-Columbian history. The millions of immigrants came from lands where their religion (mainly Christianity, with Jewish and Muslim minorities) had its roots deep in ancient pre-Christian cults. European and Middle Eastern pagan instincts were never rooted out; they were adopted, sublimated, purified, transmuted. In that mildewed baggage of morals, ritual practices, folk mores, social and familial traditions, the new Americans surely transported the seeds and traces of ancient, far-off powers and spirits which once had held sway over the Old World.

Jamsie's childhood until he was nine passed without any serious disruption. Home life was orderly and secure. Mornings and evenings he ate with his parents. Most evenings, Ara would take out the clarinet and play for his wife and child. Every night, as a small child, Jamsie knelt with his mother in front of the ikon and said the night prayers she had taught him, while he looked into the wide eyes of the Virgin.

His father took him to ball games and boxing matches. Some Sundays they went roller-skating down Wall Street; at other times to the zoo, or for nickel rides on the Staten Island ferry; and two or three times a year he took Jamsie for a swim in a hotel pool. In the summer months there were all-day outings to Coney Island.

The three of them left New York only once. It was a week's vacation in San Francisco made possible by a gift of money from Lydia's parents. Jamsie never forgot the outings on that trip with his father, and their evening meals at Fisherman's Wharf, and the day's visit they made to Pinnacles National Monument.

As Jamsie grew up, he gradually moved around the East Side and got to know and like its ethnic mix, its smells, sounds, and sights. In the early morning he picked his way to school past windows stuffed with bedding and fire escapes where people were still sleeping. As he wandered home, his ears were filled with the medley of dialects used by pushcart peddlers and shopkeepers—Tuscan, Serbian, Yiddish, Ruthenian, Sicilian, Croatian, Cretan, Macedonian.

Jamsie was in his tenth year when his parents began to notice a strange trouble that seized him from time to time. Sometimes, among the clutter of plaster saints, brass pots, secondhand garments, Balkan stogies, mezuzahs, and other bric-a-brac that filled the shop windows, Jamsie caught sight of what he called a "funny-lookin' face" or "a face with a funny look." Then he was seized with a violent fright and literally fled home in a blind panic. He used to arrive white-faced and trembling at Lydia's side. She always knew what had happened—or so Jamsie thought—and she was able to calm him down and still his fears.

As he grew older, the "funny face" incidents became rarer, but they never totally disappeared. As a child, he was never able to describe that "face" to his parents. They, wisely, never insisted on details. But from what they could understand, it seemed the child's terror was caused, not by any particular ugliness in the "face," but chiefly because of the curious conviction Jamsie had that the "face" knew him personally. "It looks at me and it knows me. It does!" he used to sob to his mother.

Gradually Jamsie worked out a sort of home geography for himself. He made many friends among the Hungarians living between 82nd and 73rd Streets. His father had distant relatives living there; and once a month or so, Jamsie visited them and was fed on goose-liver paste, stuffed cabbage, and chicken paprika. He skipped the neighborhood of the Bohunks (Czechs and Slovaks), who lived just below the Hungarians.

For it was lower down on Lexington Avenue, between 30th and 22nd Streets among the Armenians, and with the Greeks in the West 30s and 40s that he felt at home. He spoke a little of both languages. His boyhood friends were there, and he was never frightened when with Greeks and Armenians. He never saw his "funny face" among them.

In the late spring of 1937, when Jamsie was fourteen years old, Ara made an important decision that ended forever the happy days of Jamsie's childhood. Ara was not earning enough money as a handyman-carpenter, so he utilized that old but carefully guarded recommendation to a taxicab-fleet owner. Very shortly afterwards, he became one of approximately 25,000 licensed hacks in the city. He drove a two-year-old Y-model Checker for Burmalee System, Inc. Jamsie was very proud at first of his father's cab with its silver roof and the black-and-white checker band running around the middle of its yellow body.

Ara worked a 12-hour shift, driving approximately 50 miles a day to service 12 to 15 calls. On a good day he might bring home $3.00 from the meter and $1.25 in tips. It was no good. The constant sitting at the wheel, the endless war with the New York policemen, who were out to eliminate cruising cabs, the weariness at the end of each grueling day, the small earnings brought in by this labor, all produced a change in Ara which alienated him from Lydia and frightened Jamsie.

He no longer played the clarinet for them in the evenings; he locked his "old stick," as he called it, in a drawer of the living-room bureau. There were no more family outings. Instead of the occasional game of pinochle and hearts with some friends, he stayed out late drinking with other cabbies. He developed ulcers, spent two weeks in the hospital with kidney trouble in November 1938, and had a back condition before the end of the year.

For a while, only his language grew coarser for Jamsie—"palooka" (a cheap fare), "high booker" (a big fare), "rips" (fares over $2), and so on were his father's new expressions. But matters got worse. At the beginning, Jamsie and Lydia took turns keeping Ara company as he cruised long hours in his cab. When Lydia found out that Ara had fallen into the easy money of occasional pimping, steering out-of-town clients to hotels and parlor houses for a percentage of the "take," she forbade Jamsie to go with Ara at night. But Jamsie, by now a boy of very strong will, disobeyed.

Now and then, as he sat beside Ara in the cab, Jamsie was struck by some trait in his father's face. Once, while he sat in the cab late at night and his father was chatting on the curb with a pimp and two of his girls, Jamsie thought he saw that trait on all four faces as they laughed together as at some joke.

The "look" did not frighten him, but it repelled him. At the same time he was fascinated by it. As time went on, he deliberately looked for it. He found, however, that he only noticed it when he did not look for it. It was as elusive as ever; he could not pin it down.

At times that "look" acquired a terrible intensity. Two related incidents that happened in 1938 stand out in Jamsie's memory.

With his father and some friends he had gone to see the Brooklyn Dodgers play. It was at a moment toward the end of the game when all the fans were on their feet cheering Cincinnati's Johnny Vander Meer, who was making baseball history by pitching his second successive no-hit, no-run game. Shouting and cheering like everyone else, Jamsie looked around at the excited crowds. And from deep in the middle of the faces there leaped out at him that "funny-lookin' face." It was looking at him. It knew him, he thought. He froze into silence and looked away in panic. Then he glanced back at the spot where he had seen it, but it was gone. All he could see were the fans shouting and gesticulating.

Exactly one week later Jamsie was sitting with Ara in the cab late one night listening to the Louis-Schmelling fight. As the fight reached its climax, Ara's face became more and more contorted. In the last few moments leading up to Joe Louis' victory, Jamsie saw on his father's face a very intense look which was quickly developing into that "funny look." There was, again, something unhuman about it; and he could not catch sight of any trait which he had always associated with his father's beloved face. With each of Louis' blows to Schmelling, and as the voice of the announcer got higher and more excited, the "look" became more apparent on Ara's face. With the gong and Louis' victory, the tension broke. The strange look passed quickly, and Ara became normal and composed again. But Jamsie could not forget the incident.

As time passed, his fear of the "look" began to lessen, but his curiosity was greater. What was that "look"? And how was it that he had seen it at the ball game and then again on his own father's face, blotting out the kindness and love Jamsie had known there all his life up to that point? And what connection was there between all that and the "look" or "funny-lookin' face" he used to see as a child?

Around this time the family reached a low in its fortunes and well-being. Ara was developing a serious drinking problem, and the more he drank, the less money he brought home. Lydia, at first frantic about their needs, finally became morose and gathered into herself. Her young son was beginning to grow up. She began to feel alienated from him and Ara.

Jamsie had already been hired as a pageboy by NBC. He left school to take the position, partly in order to bring in more money to his home, partly with the intention of pursuing a career in radio. In the early days of radio, NBC hired young men as pageboys for a two-year apprenticeship, then graduated them to guides, and afterward trained them in some branch of the flourishing radio business.

Things went from bad to worse for the family. There was no longer enough food in the house. Lydia was always in arrears with the rent. And, unknown to Jamsie but with Ara's consent, Lydia made her decision. Jamsie found out about it late one night in March when he returned from work at about 11:00 P.M.

At home, to his surprise, he found his mother dressed in her best clothes. Her face was heavily made up. She was sitting in the living room gazing silently out the window into the night. When he came in, she did not turn around or say a word to him. But he knew she had something to tell him. As he waited, his eye was drawn to the old icon hanging on the wall behind Lydia. She had draped a black cloth over it. He looked from the ikon to his mother and back again several times before he understood that she was going to become one of the prostitutes he had seen his father introducing to clients.

Lydia stood up then, as if she had heard him thinking. She knew he had realized what was happening. "I'll be late, Jamsie. Don't wait up for me." He said nothing.

When she had gone, he sat down and remained there thinking for about two hours. He knew without a doubt what his mother had in mind. It was written all over her. But there was something else he now knew: although he was alone as far as his mother and father were concerned, he had the strangest feeling that he was in someone else's company. Finally he looked around the living room slowly and then through the window at the city.

When he went to bed, he still felt deserted by his parents, but he was nursing some secret which he did not yet understand.

Lydia became one of about 5,000 prostitutes in New York City. After a few weeks of lone-wolfing, she got herself put on the calling list of a parlor house in the West 40s. Jamsie got to know her routine. She slept during the day, rising about 5:00 P.M. If by 10:00 P.M. there were no calls for her from her madam, she went out for the evening. She worked Fifth and Madison Avenues between 43rd and 56th Streets. She would stop at the better bars, do some over obvious window-shopping, always on the lookout for clients. Sometimes she would give one of her clients a call. She worked this way until dawn. Then she returned home to sleep.

After a couple of months she became a member of Polly Adler's parlor house on Central Park West. By that time, too, she had established her own list of personal clients whom she called regularly. When Polly Adler got into trouble with the authorities, Lydia simply transferred her loyalties to another madam in the West 50s.

As Jamsie got up each morning and looked in at his mother before he left, he found that over the months the expression on her face was changing. Instead of the look he had always seen there, he might see various traits of that "funny-lookin' face" of his childhood terrors. But now there was no terror. Rather, he began to feel a strange kinship with the look.

With the passage of time, Lydia noticed the difference in Jamsie's reaction to her, and they established a new respect for each other.

Ara, in the meantime, still driving for Burmalee System, Inc., had tried to move in as a steerer for crap games in the 49th Street and Broadway area. But the territory was already controlled, and the incumbents let him know in no uncertain terms that there was no room for him. Then he went deep into the numbers racket and illegal horse betting. In those times, about one million illegal bets were placed each day in New York. There was money to be made. As a numbers agent, he got ten percent of the take on each bet handed over to the collector. In time he himself became a collector, delivering bets to the central "policy" bank.

Finally Ara found a source of easy money in drug traffic. There were between 20,000 and 25,000 heroin addicts in New York of the 1930s; and opium dens flourished on Mott and Pell Streets, as well as in Harlem, Times Square, and San Juan Hill. Diluted heroin was sold at

$16 to $20 an ounce. A "toy," or small tin box of opium, sold for about $10 on the street. Reefers fetched 50¢ each, or two for 25¢ in Harlem.

In the beginning Ara merely bought reefers in Harlem which he sold at a profit downtown. Then he became a runner, transporting the little packets strapped beneath his armpits. There were times during these months when Ara—and less frequently Lydia—were so changed in their faces and so "funny-looking" to Jamsie's eyes that some of his old fears returned momentarily.

Ara had begun to build up a clientele and make some money in the traffic of narcotics when he seemed suddenly to go to pieces. He became gaunt and thin. His moods were unbearable in their rages and black depressions.

One evening, a rainy Friday late in December 1939, Ara arrived home drenched to the skin. He had been up for three days and three nights. His teeth were chattering. He drank more than usual. He coughed up blood during the night. The next morning, Lydia had not come home, and Ara was in a high fever. All the strain of seven years suddenly broke him.

Jamsie called old Dr. Schumbard finally. He said Ara was dying of tuberculosis. Ara refused to go into the hospital. There was nothing Jamsie could do.

The next few days were a nightmare. Lydia did not come for the entire weekend. Ara's fever could not be reduced. He was frequently delirious and drank when he was not. Jamsie finally went out and scoured all his mother's haunts until he found her. Together, they watched over Ara, waiting for the end.

While he was sitting one evening by himself at Ara's bedside after Lydia had gone out for a while, Jamsie had the feeling again of someone being near him. It was not unpleasant and not at all frightening. He recalls that his feeling was more or less pleasurable, as if a friend or confidant had come to be with him when he had no one else. The sensation did not last all the time, and it varied in intensity.

About eight days after he had collapsed, Ara suddenly sat up in bed one morning and started to scream at the top of his voice: "I want my old stick! You hear! All of you! My old stick. Just a few more hot licks! I want my old stick!" His face was bathed in that "look."

Jamsie and Lydia tried to hold him down, but Ara fought them off. He scrambled out of bed in his bloodstained nightshirt, hobbled into the living room, unlocked the drawer where he had hidden his clarinet. He took it out of its case and screwed on the mouthpiece.

"Just a few more hot licks before we kick the bucket, heh!" gibbered Ara, spittle drooling from the corners of his mouth. The silver stops of the clarinet twinkled in the sunlight.

"Me old stick!" Jamsie heard him mumble.

Ara blew a few uncertain notes, tried some scales, went into a few bars of the upper register, then low down, all the time gaining fullness of tone and sureness.

As Jamsie and his mother watched, Ara began to adlib some blues. He tottered and stumbled unsteadily around the room, scraping over the worn carpet, bumping into furniture. He paused for a moment in front of Lydia's handwritten memento and cackled at it derisively. Then, playing again, he stumbled away and then back, until he stood looking at the old icon still covered with the black cloth. His face got serious. There was silence for a second. Jamsie remembers hôlding his mother's hand in anguish as they both watched Ara.

Then Ara played the first bars of an old Armenian hymn to the Virgin. He started to sway back and forth. Lydia and Jamsie both moved quickly to help him, but they were too late. Trailing off in the middle of his song, he doubled over, coughed violently, and fell forward, clawing the air for support. His hand caught the black drape over the icon, and it came away as he fell.

When they reached him, he was on his back, the black drape clutched in one hand, the clarinet in the other. Above him, the icon glimmered in the morning light with its old gold, blue, and brown colors. For the first time in many years, Jamsie looked at the tranquil eyes of the Virgin.

Then he looked at his father's face, and a weight was lifted off him. In death the "look" had gone. Ara's features had returned to something resembling what they had been ten years before. Jamsie never forgot that change at his father's death. He still could not understand the "look," but he was glad for Ara that it had gone. Ara was buried in Brooklyn's Greenwood to sleep with the other 400,000 people already there.

The following week Lydia told her son he was on his own. Except for two visits, Jamsie was not to be with her again until her death in 1959. As he walked up Broadway that day of parting with his mother, all he heard were Lydia's words: "You're on your own now."

The old el had been torn down; and they were starting the 6th Avenue subway. Jamsie stood for a long time watching the workmen. A flood of resentment took hold of him. They were spending $65 million on that subway, he had read in the newspaper. But his own father was dead, his mother was an aging prostitute, and he had been helpless to change any of that. It all made no sense.

A curious new feeling was building up in him. Without moving, without seeing anything different or hearing an ethereal voice, he felt as if an alternative to his misery of loneliness was being offered him. It was accompanied by fear. But he experienced also the same strange sense of companionship as on the night he first knew his mother would be a prostitute. He was alone, but he was not really alone. He felt the loss of his father very deeply. He had deep misgivings for his mother's well-being. Yet both of them slipped into the background of his mind. In the forefront was this new, unsettling, but rather welcome feeling of being wanted, of not being really alone.

In that moment, for the first time, he was certain that there was, indeed, some presence, someone or something present to him, and that to accept it meant renouncing any genuine love for his father and mother as he had known them in childhood and early youth.

In 1940 Jamsie was promoted to guide at NBC. Then, on the invitation of a very close friend of his father, he went to live and study in Oklahoma City. The friend provided him with enough money to follow courses in journalism and broadcasting; he did part-time work to supplement his income.

The years in Oklahoma City were tranquil ones for Jamsie. There was no recurrence of the "funny look." He rarely had a sense of the strange presence, and he formed some solid friendships.

He moved back to New York in 1946, at the age of twenty-three, and started to build a career in radio. Outside work, he lived a quiet life. He spent most of his time either at home listening to records and reading, or wandering the streets of midtown and lower Manhattan.

He always hoped he would find his mother. Nobody in her old haunts seemed to know where she was or what had happened to her. Eventually word reached him from an old family friend that she was living in Flushing. He had one long visit with her there.

Lydia was much deteriorated. There was still a deep feeling between them; but both felt and tacitly decided that, except for some serious personal crisis, they should see each other rarely. Meeting was too painful.

At the same time, Jamsie was also engaged in a search of a very different kind. Once he set foot in New York again, he caught glimpses of that "look"—in the subway, from the middle of crowds, aloft among the neon signs, in movie houses, and sometimes late at night, before he went to bed and when he stood looking out the window at the lights of Manhattan.

And he now felt something else that was new and, in its own way, reassuring: a violent and unconquerable persuasion that he had always known what "it" was, who "it" was. His old fright was transformed into an insatiable urge to remember. If he could only remember what "it" was.

Sometimes, in off-moments, he seemed to be on the verge of realizing what or who "it" was, of recalling the place and the time when he had been told about it. He could not shake the idea that he had been told about it.

But his efforts always ended in frustration. Just as names and places were about to rush into his mind and to his lips, something would happen inside him, and he would lose his grip on them. His frustration at this continual defeat began to produce a rage in him.

Jamsie had one last meeting with Lydia. She had moved from Flushing to lower Broadway. During those few hours he spent with her, all his rage and frustration was dissipated. Lydia, by now living on church welfare, spoke to him slowly and quietly about his father and about his own future. This was the last experience of human tenderness Jamsie was to have for many years. Later he left word of his whereabouts with the local precinct and the church authorities who helped Lydia, promising to keep them posted of any change in his address. He kept that promise.

It was during this period of Jamsie's life that his colleagues at the radio station began to notice that he talked to himself; even more oddly, he occasionally flew into solitary rages. Of course, the moment Jamsie realized other people were watching, he became a very amiable and smiling man, to compensate for any unpleasant impression he might have given. Yet, time and time again, he could be seen walking alone on the streets or in the corridors of the radio station, or standing in the washroom, his eyes wide and staring, his nostrils flaring, and his lips drawn back over his teeth as if in some deep, internal, all-absorbing effort.

After two years in New York, Jamsie was transferred to Cleveland. Here he had his first paralyzing dose of what became commonplace in his life a few years later.

One evening he was walking down Euclid Avenue on his way home.

All day his mind had been opening and closing on the endless puzzle: when and where had he been told about "it," about that "look"? Since his arrival in Cleveland, all appearances of the "look" had ceased. But this only seemed to increase his curiosity and his need to know the answer. Tonight, it seemed to him, he was very near to recalling exactly.

As he walked on, memories and words began to gather up out of a deep darkness of recollection and slowly to take shape. He was almost craning forward as he peered within himself with profound intensity to catch them. He began to feel excited, as he felt a growing realization that this was the moment.

Suddenly, just as he was about to see those images and say those words, the words and pictures—as he describes it—seemed to form themselves into a long, quickly moving stream and "floated like lightning" out of the top of his head and up into the sky. It had all escaped him!

He jumped up and down on the pavement in frustration, looking up at the night sky with tears in his eyes. Then, when he saw nothing up there but clouds, he turned away and went dejectedly toward the small restaurant where he normally took his supper.

At the door of the restaurant he stopped in astonishment. It was too much! There, at the back of the dining room, among the crowded tables and chatting people, he saw a face with that "look." He pushed his way past waiters and packed tables. But when he reached the place where the "face" had been, he found two staid people, an aging man and woman, eating their dinner in stony silence. They looked at him briefly and disinterestedly, then went on eating.

From that moment, Jamsie was convinced that somebody or something was playing hide-and-seek with him. But he could not figure out how it was all done or why. It became frequent in his daily life for words and memories to behave like the floating lightning and to "dive" out of his skull. Sometimes he saw them silhouetted against the sky before they disappeared far, far up into the clouds; sometimes they went so fast he could not catch sight of them at all.

In successive years and at various stations where he worked (Detroit, 1951; New Orleans, 1953; Kansas City, 1955; Los Angeles, 1956), the story was always the same. He tried once to explain it all to a psychiatrist in Los Angeles, but he found the sessions with him unproductive and infuriating.

He had one friendship with a woman in Kansas City that might have become serious. But one evening, only a few weeks after they had begun dating, Jamsie treated her to such an uncontrolled exhibition of rage, frustration, and jealousy that she broke up with him then and there.

Just about a year after his transfer to Los Angeles, he had his first face-to-face meeting with the source of his trouble. He lived in Alhambra at the time, and drove each day to the radio station.

One evening, as he drove home in the dusk, he again sensed that curious presence for the fourth time in his life. The car radio was playing a medley of songs. Suddenly, as "California, Here I Come!" was being sung, the words seemed to plaster themselves all around the sky in front of him. He had already had a lot of crazy things like this in his life, and, while he could not ignore it, he could cope with it. As "California, Here I Come!" continued to plaster itself around him, Jamsie switched off the radio.

Then something caught his eye in the rearview mirror. It was a face.

As with so many of the strange things that kept happening to him, Jamsie felt neither fright nor surprise. He seemed to himself to have expected it, to have known it was there all along. The eyes of that face were looking at him and he knew—without knowing how—that he knew their owner.

There were no more words floating or plastered around him now. Jamsie slowed down, waiting all the time in silence. But there was no sound and no movement from the back seat.

He glanced again in the mirror: the large, bulbous eyes were still looking at him. He could not believe they were really red. Must be the reflection of the street lights, he thought. The face had a nose, ears, mouth, cheeks, a funny chin much too narrow for the rest of the face, a kind of high-domed forehead ending in a somewhat pointed head. The skin was dark as if from long exposure to sunlight. He could not make out if it was white or brown or black-skinned.

But something more than the vividness of that face puzzled him—the absence of something. The face was certainly alive—the eyes glinted with meaning, even laughingly. The head moved silently now and then. But something was lacking, something he expected in a face, but which this face did not show.

As he turned slowly into the driveway to his garage, he heard a voice, chiding and familiar, in tones he would expect a eunuch to have: "Oh! For Pete's sake, Jamsie! Stop acting the fool. We've been together for years. Don't tell me you don't know me."

Jamsie realized that this too was somehow or other true: they had been together for a long time. Everything, even this, had the same curious familiarity about it.

As the car came to a standstill in the garage, he heard the voice again: "Well, so long, Jamsie! See you tomorrow. Wait for your Uncle Ponto!"

As Jamsie entered the house, he thought he smelled a strange odor. At the time he connected it in no way with Uncle Ponto. It was a momentary thing, and he forgot about it immediately.

This happened on a Monday evening. He could not sleep that night. And, although he did not know it then, Ponto's visits would multiply quickly until, for six years, he would be dealing with Uncle Ponto almost on a daily basis.

The following Sunday Jamsie was driving the short distance to Pasadena when out the window to his right he saw Ponto craning his head down from the roof of the car looking in at him upside down through the window. Ponto was moving his left hand as though pitching a ball, and with each gesture he seemed to throw a word, a phrase, or a whole sentence into the sky where it remained for a while and then danced away over the horizon.

"WELCOME TO JAMSIE MY FRIEND!" ran one message. "GREATEST BLOW-OUT FOR THE MIND!" was another. "PONTO! JAMSIE! PALS! REJOICE! PASADENA HERE WE COME!"

And so it went. Accordingly as Ponto threw each message into the sky, he turned back and grinned at Jamsie. When Jamsie swerved dangerously because of the distraction, Ponto shook his finger in mock reproof and flung a "LET ME DRIVE YOU!" sign across the sky. Then he disappeared.

This was the flamboyant beginning of Uncle Ponto's attendance on Jamsie: Uncle Ponto, the spirit that was to harass him for years, finally press his claims to be Jamsie's "familiar," and twice drive him to the edge of suicide.

Gradually Jamsie got to know Ponto's general appearance. But he never saw him whole from head to foot at any one time. Ponto's face, the back of his head, his hands, his feet, his eyes, all were parts of Ponto he saw from time to time. To Jamsie's eye, somehow accustomed before the fact to all these bizarre happenings, Ponto was not misshapen, yet Jamsie knew that Ponto was hardly shaped like a normal human being. And then there was that funny lack in Ponto's face. Something *was* lacking.

His head was too large and too pointed, the eyelids, too heavy, the nose and mouth always contorted by an expression Jamsie could not identify with any emotion or attitude known to him. The skin was too light to be black, too dark to be white, too reddish to be sallow, too yellow to be sunburned. His hands were more like mechanical claws. His body—seen in parts—seemed to have the flexibility of a cat and to be thinner than his enormous, pointed head. His legs were bandy and disproportionate—one knee seemed higher than the other. Ponto's feet were splayed, like a duck's, and all the toes were of even length and the same size.

Jamsie was sure Ponto was not human. Beyond that, he was sure of nothing except that Ponto was real—as real as any object or person around him. What Ponto did was real and concrete. So, for Jamsie, he had to be real. At the same time, Jamsie again and again found himself wondering why he was not frightened by Ponto. And occasionally he did ask himself if Ponto was a spirit or a being from another planet. But in the beginning each appearance of Ponto merely fired his curiosity.

After a while Jamsie realized that he could anticipate an appearance of Ponto by the queer smell he had noticed the first night; and, when Ponto disappeared, the smell lingered on afterward for about an hour. It was not a bad smell, as of sewage or rotting food. It was just a very strong smell; it had a trace of musk in it, but laced with a certain pungency. Jamsie could only describe it as the way "red would smell, if you could smell red."

The smell always gave Jamsie a feeling of being alone with something overwhelming. In other words, the effect of the smell was not primarily in his nose but in Jamsie's mind. It did not repel, did not attract, did not disgust, did not fascinate. It made him feel very small and insignificant. And this bothered Jamsie more than all the other odd things.

As far as he could calculate, Ponto's overall height was about $4\frac{1}{2}$ feet. Yet whenever Ponto appeared to him, he seemed to be the mirror image of something gargantuan hovering nearby, and in some confusing way the smell was tied closely to that sense of nearness of overwhelming size. If Jamsie felt any personal threat at that stage, it had to do with the effects of that smell.

At the end of his "visits," and just before he disappeared, Ponto took to giving Jamsie a questioning look out of the corner of his eye, as if to say: Aren't you going to ask me about myself? Jamsie, naturally stubborn, resolved not to ask, not even to notice this gesture of Ponto—if he could bring that off.

Ponto kept on appearing at the oddest places. Since his first, chiding words to Jamsie, and except for the words he flung, floated, and plastered all over Jamsie's horizon, Ponto never said anything in these early visits. He appeared in the back of the car, sitting on the radiator in the living room, inside the elevator in the upper corner, swinging from one of the overpasses as Jamsie traveled on the freeway, in restaurants, on top of the cash registers, at Jamsie's desk in the studio, on top of the engineer's table in full view of Jamsie as he sat in the sound-room broadcasting.

Ponto pushed swinging doors in the opposite direction to Jamsie. He placed money on the counter of the delicatessen to pay for Jamsie's groceries, ripped the dry cleaner's plastic bags, turned on faucets, turned off the ignition of his car, switched on the headlights, and in a thousand ways kept a regular—though, for the first few months of 1958, not a frequent—reminder of his presence in front of Jamsie.

During the early months of 1958 Ponto never interfered with Jamsie's work, he rarely appeared in his apartment, and he never bothered him at night. In fact, Jamsie found he could sleep all night undisturbed. He had a feeling Ponto was somewhere near watching him—or perhaps watching over him; he did not know which. After a while, the bizarre antics began wearing on Jamsie and whittling his patience and control very thin. Jamsie became convinced that he had seen Ponto somewhere else or had known somebody very like Ponto in previous years, though surely he would not have forgotten so odd a figure as that little fellow!

Finally Jamsie's patience wore out, and his curiosity—certainly understandable in the fantastic circumstances—led him to his greatest mistake with Ponto. He yielded to an impulse one day and asked Ponto what he wanted. Ponto at that precise moment was swinging from the lamp in Jamsie's office.

"Oh, just to be with you, Jamsie! I thought you'd never ask! Actually I want to be your friend. Did you ever know anyone as faithful and as attendant on you as I am?"

Then he swung away into nothingness.

Jamsie's innocent question opened floodgates. He now became the object of a continual barrage from Ponto that went on week after week. There would be no letup for years.

Ponto would start talking the moment Jamsie left his apartment to drive to work. Most of his conversation was harmless and inane, sometimes unintentionally funny, more often ludicrous, and quite often with a twist to his remarks that caused Jamsie some inner disgust.

For a long time Jamsie kept himself under control; but he lost his temper with Ponto for the first time when he sprinkled one of his conversations with jibes about Lydia and crude remarks about the female hyena. Jamsie fell into a frothing rage with Ponto, telling him in a series of profanities to leave his mother out of the conversation and to get out of his sight and hearing.

"Okay, Jamsie. Okay!" Ponto said resignedly. "Okay. Have it your way. But we belong to each other." He disappeared.

The experience left Jamsie shaking with rage. But, after a couple of hours, restored to the normal world of his work, and being reasonable, he began to ask himself seriously if he were not imagining it all. He was sitting at his microphone waiting for a commercial to end and the signal from his engineer to take up his broadcast.

As if to answer his inner thoughts, Ponto appeared and began plastering short words on the notice board the engineer used to pass silent messages to Jamsie when he was on the air. "FORGIVEN!" it read. "BACK SOON! CARRY ON, PAL!" In spite of himself, Jamsie saw the twisted humor of it all, although he doubted that Ponto was bright enough to be funny. Ponto was doing what came natural to him. Jamsie found himself grinning at the engineer, who, taken by surprise by this show of geniality on Jamsie's part, grinned back at him sheepishly.

Ponto's conversations, except for some of the bits and scraps reported here and dictated to me by Jamsie, escape Jamsie's memory now. They were nearly always inconsequential and only sometimes annoying to the point of making Jamsie fall into a fit of anger. But, because he answered Ponto sometimes or made comments on Ponto's behavior—all this under his breath—the people at the station accepted the fact that Jamsie Z. "talks to himself a lot" and, as one put it, "is a little looney on certain points—but aren't we all?"

In spite of everything, things went well for Jamsie's career. In fact, Jamsie's reporting was good and his ratings were high.

In August 1959, news arrived that Lydia had died in her sleep.

Jamsie returned to New York for a couple of days to wind up her affairs. Lydia had made a will by which Jamsie, the sole heir, received two possessions: the old icon and Lydia's handwritten memento of George Whitney's bid of 204 for U. S. Steel. Jamsie brought them both back to Los Angeles and placed them in a closet where Ponto had the habit of making himself comfortable. Ponto objected to the icon very strongly, but Jamsie was adamant.

"Okay, pal. Okay. Okay," Ponto said. "But some day we'll get rid of that useless garbage. Won't we, pal?"

In the fall of 1960, Jamsie was offered and accepted a very good radio spot in San Francisco. He moved up from Los Angeles, and after he had settled into his new apartment, Jamsie arranged to drive over and meet his new station manager.

"Jamsie, the hour of decision is approaching." Ponto, of course, had come to San Francisco. He was balancing at the moment on the fire escape outside the apartment house and talking through the window. Jamsie said nothing.

"Jamsie! Promise me! No sex and no booze! You hear? Jamsie! Promise your old Uncle Ponto. Come on, pal, promise!"

Curiously Jamsie had never touched a woman since his days in Cleveland. Somehow, all desire had left him after that first experience of words escaping like lightning from his skull.

"Actually," Ponto tittered ridiculously, "I don't expect much trouble from you along that line. Hee! Hee!"

Jamsie glared at him for a second, then continued with his preparations to go out.

It was in what Ponto said next that Jamsie heard the strange note of urgency that sometimes overloaded Ponto's eunuch's voice.

"Now we all have our place, you hear? And I can't appear as often as I like, and as often as I have in the past. I have my betters, too, y'know. You won't believe it, but I have."

On the way to the radio station, Ponto, riding in the back seat, seemed to be seized with a sort of hysteria. His speech started to come faster and faster and to be deteriorating. Finally he no longer made any sense at all. He prattled on about lasers and roast chicken and whisky and the moon. Jamsie only recollects phrases such as "Jupiter rotates every 9 hours and 55 minutes." "Car necking, masturbation, and good grades." "Hurrah for the Golden Gate but don't go near the water!" "Its cheer creak."

Jamsie drew up at the station, left his car, and started to make his way in. Ponto went along, prattling incoherently all the while. Jamsie rang the bell at the front gate, but no one answered. He wandered to the back. Still Ponto kept talking, his words utterly meaningless. Jamsie tried the back door. It was locked. He was about to return to the front when, without warning, there was silence. Ponto had disappeared. In retrospect, Jamsie is certain that any sudden disappearance of Ponto meant the approach of someone Ponto feared.

"Are you looking for someone?" A balding man in his mid-fifties, tallish, thin, wearing rimless spectacles, had come out from a side door Jamsie had not noticed, and stood looking at him with his head cocked to one side.

"I'm coming to work here," Jamsie answered easily. "I'm looking for the station manager."

"You must be Jamsie Z.," said the man. "I'm the station manager. Beedem's the name. Jay Beedem."

Jamsie shook hands and took in Beedem's features. He thought for a second he might have met Beedem before. He could not quite tie it down.

"Come in and let's get acquainted."

As they sat across from one another in Beedem's office, Jamsie scrutinized his new boss, trying to place him. Beedem meanwhile put Jamsie a few questions and then proceeded to fill him in on his future work at the station. He was a precise man, obviously, and neat almost to a fault—shining bald head, carefully groomed side hair, immaculately clean and tasteful clothes, slightly foppish, good teeth, masculine hands with well-manicured nails. His face was roughly an oval shape not very lined for his age. But his eyes and mouth attracted Jamsie's particular attention.

After about a quarter of an hour of conversation, Jamsie concluded that his boss's eyes were completely closed to him. Jay Beedem laughed, glanced, conveyed meanings, and questioned him with his eyes, but all this seemed to be as revealing as images skipping across a film screen. There is no feeling there, thought Jamsie to himself. No real feeling. At least, I can't see any. Each smile and laugh was only on Beedem's mouth. He did not seem really smiling or laughing.

Jamsie really does not have any fully satisfying answers about Jay Beedem, even today. In retrospect, he will still say that the vague impression he had of having seen Beedem's face before he met him in the flesh came from the traits of that "funny-lookin' face" reflected in Beedem's face. In fact, one important element of the exorcism, recorded on the tape, has to do with the strange face of Beedem and the "look."

Ponto always kept in the background when Beedem was with Jamsie. And whenever Jamsie approached Beedem for a discussion or for help or encouragement, he left Beedem in the same sort of inner torment and turmoil that gripped him during his worst moments with Ponto. The keynote of that turmoil was panic, the panic of someone finding himself trapped or ambushed or betrayed.

While it remains speculation, a very good case can be made for Jay Beedem being one of the perfectly possessed, a person who at some time in his career made one clear, definitive decision to accept possession, who never went back on that decision in any way, and who came under the total control of an evil spirit. It was on this very suspicion that, in the exorcism, Father Mark felt he must try to see if there was some link between Beedem and Ponto that was harmful to Jamsie.

But when Jamsie left Beedem that first day, all the problems he still speculates about today were then in the future. Over the next days and weeks he settled easily into a daily routine. He loved San Francisco. He liked his new post. He got on well with his fellow workers; they respected his abilities and he never let them down professionally. He had pleasant relations with Cloyd, his producer, and with Lila Wood, the chief researcher on Cloyd's staff. With Jay Beedem his relations were correct and formal. But as time went on Beedem made no secret of his growing dislike and contempt for Jamsie's peculiarities.

Their colleagues, who noticed the ill-feeling between the two men, put the whole thing down to a difference in temperament between them: they just did not get on well together. Everyone else easily forgave Jamsie's idiosyncrasies, for he had developed a broadcasting style all his own, "and it was good for business." Jamsie was not slow to recognize that he had Ponto to thank for much of that.

Uncle Ponto would gyrate around him in the studio saying irrelevant things only Jamsie could hear. He would produce statistics, figures, facts, and data which Jamsie would automatically incorporate into his patter of broadcasting, keeping up an incredible stream of banter. It was bright and amusing, a cheery-beery-bee kind of prattle full of various irrelevancies about this, that, and the other, all strung together with "but" and "whereas" and "lest I forget it" and "as the actress said to the bishop" and "let me tell you before you forget you ever heard me talk," until after about three minutes he would throw in a punch line about a product he was advertising or a ball game he was reporting or some bit of national news the station wanted to highlight. This style became his signature, well known and valued, on the air. For the first few months in San Francisco, therefore, Jamsie secretly valued Ponto's presence.

It was only after a protracted period that he saw the first sign of real trouble. On his way home one evening Ponto, on the back seat of the car, said: "Jamsie, let's get married."

Taking this as just a part of Ponto's usual nonsensical prattle—of which there was always quite a lot in those days—Jamsie thought Ponto would prattle on to something else if he kept quiet. But Ponto was serious, and he said so.

"Jamsie! I'm serious. Let's get married."

Goose pimples started on Jamsie's arms and legs. For the first time, Jamsie began to be seriously afraid of Ponto. He drove on in silence, but his mind was full of a new apprehension.

The next day in the station cafeteria Jamsie was joined at the table by Lila Wood, Cloyd's researcher. Ponto was somewhere among the coffee urns, gazing quietly at Jamsie. Lila, like others, had noticed Jamsie's deep depression that day. But, as she says, she also sensed the grain of fear running through him.

Knowing better than to tackle Jamsie head-on, she said lightly as she rose after lunch: "Wanta share a steak tonight with a friend and me?"

It was the first time in a long while that anyone had approached Jamsie so nonchalantly. He had become accustomed to people avoiding him socially. He looked at Lila in disbelief. But Lila knew how to deal with the situation. "Okay," she said as she turned away smiling. "See you at 5:30."

Jamsie stared after her. Her voice, or something in her voice, affected him. As he said afterward, "It was like a short chord of beautiful harmony struck in between the squalling of 200 squabbling cats and ten jackhammers all going at the same time."

But his reverie lasted a short time. Ponto's voice broke in with a new sharpness. "I heard all that. Heard all of it. That smelly young bitch. Do you know her friend? You will. I do! A balding pig. That's him. Isn't man enough to get between her legs even."

For just a few moments Jamsie felt impervious to Ponto's corroding accents, and it was a very great relief. He just smiled at Ponto. Ponto's face twisted in anger; and, with a sort of a leap backward and upward, he disappeared.

Immediately Jamsie felt a solid lump of agony within him. This was something new. It started somewhere around his middle. Then it moved to his spine. One spike of pain hit his coccyx, another pierced his testicles, a third prodded up through his spinal column; and from the nape of his neck it seemed to branch outward in two directions. One stream invaded his lungs. He grew short of breath and felt dizzy. Another stream reached upward into his skull and gripped his brain, as though contracting it. He remained sitting for a few minutes, his chin in his hand, waiting. It passed.

As he stood up, he heard Ponto's voice. "You see, pal! You see! You already belong to me in great part. Watch it tonight!" Ponto was not visible, but the smell was there.

That evening Jamsie went home with Lila. She had just prepared three steaks when her friend rang at the front door. Jamsie opened the door to a stoutish man, completely bald, whose blue eyes looked at him with an expression of good humor.

"I'm Father Mark, Lila's friend. You must be Jamsie. She told me about you. Glad to see you."

As Jamsie found out, Lila had an ulterior motive for the invitation. Before the evening was out, Jamsie was talking freely to Mark. Mark seemed to know all about Ponto's behavior. The only thing he did not know was Ponto's name; and when Jamsie told him, he gave a short little laugh and said: "Good God! I thought I'd heard them all. But—Ponto! God!"

The two men made an appointment to meet the following evening. Mark even promised he would make some of his own special mushroom soup for which he was so well known among his friends.

After that mushroom soup dinner at Mark's rectory, Jamsie told Mark his life story, omitting nothing. Mark listened in silence, puffing a long church warden's pipe that reeked of tar, and interrupting now and again with a question.

It was past midnight when Jamsie finished. Mark put down his pipe, reflected a little while in silence, and looked at Jamsie speculatively. The silence was not uncomfortable for Jamsie. Then Mark spent the next hour telling Jamsie what he thought of the whole matter.

Jamsie, according to Mark, was the object of an evil spirit's attentions. There were hundreds—and, for all Mark knew, perhaps millions and trillions—of different spirits. "You don't number spirits as you number human beings," Mark told him. He explained that in his experience, which was considerable, it appeared that each kind of spirit had its own characteristics and techniques of approaching humans. However, a certain kind of spirit—not a very important one—always sought to become a "familiar" of some human being, man, woman, or child. Rarely—but it did happen—did a "familiar" spirit possess an animal.

What was a "familiar"? Jamsie wanted to know. Mark explained that the key to the "familiarity" which such a spirit sought to obtain lay in this: the person in question consented to a total sharing of his or her consciousness and personal life with the spirit.

Mark gave an example. Normally, when you are walking around, eating, working, washing yourself, talking, you are conscious of yourself as distinct from others. Now supposing you were conscious of yourself and of another self all the time, like Siamese twins but inside your own head and in your consciousness. And supposing that the two, so to speak, shared your consciousness. It's your self-consciousness, your awareness of yourself, and at the same time, it's the consciousness, the awareness of that other self. Both at the same time. No getting away from one another. "Its" thoughts use your mind, but they are not your thoughts, and you know that. "Its" imagination likewise. And "its" will also. And you are aware of all this constantly, for as long as you are conscious of yourself. That was the familiarity Mark was talking about.

Jamsie was aghast. "My God," he says now, "I had already gone down that road, at least part of the way. I didn't know what to do. I was lost!"

Mark answered Jamsie's panic. He was not lost. He had never consented to full possession by the "familiar." He had just been invaded. But he was going to be more and more pressured to accept full "familiarity."

What could happen? Jamsie wanted to know.

"You can be worn down," Mark said quietly. "You can be taken. Like any of us. You're up against a force more powerful than you can ever hope to be yourself."

Then Mark looked Jamsie straight in the eye and asked him directly if he wanted to undergo Exorcism.

Strangely, Jamsie was speechless. Then slowly he asked in great concern: "Would that mean Ponto would never return?"

Mark told Jamsie that, if the exorcism were successful, Ponto would be gone forever. He concentrated his attention on Jamsie's every move and reaction. He was only now beginning to be able to measure how far Ponto had extended his hold on Jamsie.

"Well," he said finally, with a great effort to appear relaxed, "what is it going to be? Do you think we should go as far as that?" He did not want to send Jamsie off half-crazed with fear.

Jamsie was confused. Memories of his loneliness and his having been deserted by his parents crowded his mind. Was this Ponto affair as bad as Mark made it out to be? Couldn't he keep Ponto at a distance anyway, and still enjoy the exotic character of the whole affair? Besides, wouldn't he lose some of that verve as a broadcaster that was now his great asset?

Mark chatted with Jamsie for a while about all this. He poured them both another drink. Jamsie was not ready to accept Exorcism. Mark had to wait for Jamsie.

Very earnestly Mark gave Jamsie some practical advice. The whole point, he said, was to resist invasion. Enjoy—if that was the word, Mark said wryly—Ponto's antics and his stimulation, but resist invasion, Mark insisted. For instance, if Jamsie were to feel a strange grip on his mind, memory, and imagination, and he was not able to resist it, he should adopt a simple trick in order to offset such a "grip": spell the name of Jesus out letter by letter, over and over. It was this stratagem that was to save Jamsie from suicide at the reservoir later on.

When Jamsie asked if he could use any other name, Mark said with a laugh that he could, but that he would find only that name effective. Mark explained the essence of Exorcism—what it meant, and its effects in the possessed. Finally Mark told Jamsie to call him: "Night or day. Wherever I am, wherever you are, whenever it happens to be, I'll come immediately to you. But don't delay, if once you decide I can help with Exorcism."

When Jamsie got home that night, he could not sleep. But Ponto did not appear.

About a month later, when Jamsie went for his yearly medical checkup, the doctor told him that all was well except for his heart. He should be careful of too much excitement. The doctor prescribed some tablets and regulated Jamsie's diet. The doctor asked him if he was worried about anything. Was there anything preying on his mind?

Jamsie was surprised at the sharpness of the doctor. Yes, he admitted, he was very preoccupied with personal matters. The doctor recommended that Jamsie think about consulting a psychologist—just to chat over things, relieve the strain a little. He gave Jamsie the name of a man whom he could personally recommend.

Jamsie thought over the matter for about a week. He could not accept Mark's conclusion that Ponto should be exorcised—not because he did not believe that Ponto was a disembodied spirit, or "anyway partially disembodied," he thought wryly, but because he could not face up to daily life without Ponto's disturbances.

But then he began to wonder why he liked such disturbances. Because Ponto's possession of him had already gone a certain distance? That was what Mark thought. Or because, as he preferred to think, Ponto was the one relief in an otherwise bleak landscape—and, into the bargain, a marvelous stimulus for his work? Or was this precisely the trap Ponto had laid for him? All the lines crisscrossed in confusion. And the confusion only got worse when he began to have all sorts of doubts about Mark's judgment and intentions. These priests were always looking for converts anyway, he thought. Yet Mark sounded so sincere. Perhaps, after all, a talk with a good psychologist would be helpful.

All that week, Ponto did not appear.

It was when he was driving to his first appointment with the psychologist that Jamsie heard Ponto for the first time in eight or nine days.

"The shrink's all right, Jamsie. He's a good man; and you go and do what he says. But if you would only listen to me and do what I want, you would need no shrink." Jamsie went anyway.

The psychologist recommended by his doctor passed Jamsie on to a psychiatrist colleague. Jamsie spent over 18 months in therapy, but the results were terribly disappointing.

The therapist started off by warning Jamsie that his psychological condition was precarious indeed. He needed extended treatment. But after about six months, the therapist reversed his judgment. He said he could not find any genuine psychological imbalance or abnormalcy in Jamsie. All of Jamsie's accounts of Ponto, the therapist said, were concocted holus-bolus by Jamsie, were deliberate inventions. The damned thing was a hoax, and he for one didn't think it was funny. Jamsie finally persuaded the man that this was no hoax, and went on earnestly with therapy for another year. But finally, when it was clear that there was no appreciable change for the better, Jamsie gave up on psychiatry.

During this period of therapy Ponto appeared regularly and with his usual behaviorisms, but he never really distressed Jamsie. In fact, Jamsie was glad to see Ponto. He seemed more real than the therapist and all his analyses. And, as Ponto remarked to Jamsie one day, "You and I, Jamsie, are one, real flesh and blood; but that shrink lives in his head. Now I ask you: Which is the better off?"

Toward the end of Jamsie's treatment with the therapist, Ponto seemed to grow impatient, as if he had a deadline to meet in Jamsie's case. More and more, Jamsie found that Ponto's thoughts, reactions, feelings, memories, intentions were present to his consciousness, even when Ponto was not visible. He began to experience two sets of thoughts and feelings—his own and Ponto's. He always knew which were which, but he literally had no privacy of mind.

Amazingly enough, except for an occasional clash with Jay Beedem, who always treated Jamsie with marked coldness, Jamsie's work continued to be excellent. But by November 1963, internally, inside Jamsie, life was becoming unbearable.

Jamsie remembers clearly that it was from December 1963 that a new desperation began to take hold of him. Ponto did not let up. He kept devising new antics and developed the habit of appearing in Jamsie's apartment at the end of the day and not disappearing till Jamsie went to bed. He chattered on and on, usually urging Jamsie to do something—quit his job, take a trip, hate this person or that—but most often to "let Ponto in."

Jamsie remembers one incident clearly. He had returned home one evening very late. Ponto appeared on his living-room table and spent about an hour juggling words and phrases and colored lumps of sound—or so it seemed to Jamsie—in the air. Then, as Ponto grew more intense, he developed a chant that grated terribly on Jamsie, a sort of "rhythm and grunt." He repeated a word over and over with a little rhythmic grunt after it each time. "Let me in," he would begin. Then over and over and over: "Let-uh! Let-uh! Let-uh! Me-uh! Me-uh! Me-uh! In-uh! In-uh! In-uh!"

The staccato beat was torture to Jamsie. He finally screamed at Ponto to stop.

In the months following, Jamsie was treated to repeat performances along this line, sometimes once a week. Each time, Jamsie would be reduced to shouting and screaming in order to silence Ponto. Neighbors complained regularly about the noise.

Very late one particular evening in December of 1963, after having had his nerves jangled in this way by Ponto for too long, Jamsie could hardly believe it when Ponto was finally quiet for a while. Jamsie soaked up the badly needed tranquillity.

But rather soon he began to hear a new sound. He listened intently. He could hear Ponto's voice clearly, but it seemed to be caught up in a babel of other voices similar to Ponto's.

He could not tell what was being said. There was a lot of laughter and many exclamations. But the whole thing reminded him of how sometimes he used to listen to the radio in his home of the 1930s and get nothing but a rising and falling stream of static together with indistinct and far-off voices.

As Jamsie strained to hear, there was a pause and silence. Then Ponto's mincing voice from the kitchen: "Jamsie, would you mind if some of my associates and family joined us? After all, we are going to get married, aren't we? And soon, eh?"

The babel of voices started again and seemed to be approaching the door of his living room.

Jamsie froze for a second; then, seized by a blind, rushing panic, he stood up and dashed out the door, got into his car, and sped as fast as he could to the Golden Gate Bridge. His mind was numb, but his emotions were in turmoil. He felt cold, unwanted, persecuted, desperate. He could not take any more of it. He wanted out. He stopped in the middle of the bridge.

"It's no use, Jamsie."

Jamsie knew the voice. God! He could have cried. There he was, balanced on the damned guardrail.

"It's no use, my friend. You and I have much to do before your life ends. Why do you think I am to be your familiar? So that you die young? Don't be a fool!"

Jamsie turned away. For the first time he had the feeling of being beaten by Ponto. He made his way slowly back home. There was no hurry. He did not know what to do anyway. He thought aimlessly of Mark. But what the hell, the shrink hadn't helped. What could Mark do for him?

Ponto did not appear again that night, but it was a very brief rest for Jamsie. The nighttime had always been a great source of strength and recuperation for Jamsie; and even though Ponto had been encroaching a little more all the time, there had always remained some hours at night when Jamsie was alone, relatively at peace, and could rest. Ponto had never stayed the entire night without asking Jamsie's consent.

But now Ponto insisted: they had to be intimate. What he meant by that Jamsie was never sure. But it did mean he would spend nights in Jamsie's apartment. And with a significance that escaped Jamsie, Ponto wanted him to consent. They were going to be married, weren't they? They were going to make the whole thing legal, weren't they? Ponto said, grinning in his crooked fashion.

After weeks of badgering, Jamsie was ripe to make a drastic decision. Anything would be better than this torture. Should he finish it all by suicide? Or would it be better to telephone Father Mark? Or should he just give in to Ponto and see how things worked out?

The worst of the badgering sessions with Ponto occurred on February 1. Ponto installed himself in Jamsie's bedroom. Jamsie spent the night stalking up and down his living-room floor, making coffee to stay awake, arguing in a loud voice with Ponto, weeping continuously, smoking and drinking intermittently. He could not get rid of Ponto. And he could not make up his mind. He needed time. It was the pressure on him by Ponto to make a decision that was crushing his spirit.

Finally he decided to make time for thinking and analyzing it all. He would ask for a leave of absence from the station. During the leave he could go over all the events of the last few years, consult with the psychiatrist again, see Father Mark, and get sufficient control of himself to form some decision about a wise course of action.

When he arrived at the station early the following morning and went to see Jay Beedem to request a few days' leave, his difficulties took a new form.

Beedem spoke without lifting his face from the notes he was reading. Beedem had noticed the increasingly peculiar behavior of Jamsie over the last few weeks, he said. Beedem did not think a leave of absence was the solution. Of course, Jamsie had some overdue vacation days coming to him. But Beedem felt that, if Jamsie continued creating a tension among the other station employees, there could be no other alternative but to fire him.

The tone was neither friendly nor unfriendly. Neutral. Very cold. Impersonal.

Jamsie still thought he could get through to Beedem if he could just give him some idea of the dimension of the personal problem that was torturing him. But when he tried, Beedem broke in slowly and emphatically: "If you cannot make right decisions in personal affairs, you cannot be trusted with matters that involve our clients and our listeners."

Then Beedem lifted his head for the first time since Jamsie had entered his office. Jamsie looked for some spark, any inkling of hope for himself. Beedem's eyes were blank. Really blank. No metaphor. They could have been made of colored glass, except that, unlike glass, they did not reflect the office or the objects around them or the light from the windows.

Jamsie knew then that there was no use trying to get through to Beedem. He said something about catching up on the vacation days he had missed. Beedem bent once again over his notes.

As Jamsie closed the door on his way out, he threw a quick look back: Beedem was sitting bolt upright in his chair, eyes fixed on Jamsie, glaring steadily. Beedem was looking through him, Jamsie thought. Was that a look of hate and sneering contempt in Beedem's eyes? Or was it simply the natural reaction of a harried station manager to yet another personal problem of an employee?

Going down the corridor to his office, Jamsie tried to remember some of Mark's after-dinner conversation with him. He seemed to be the only one Jamsie had met who was sure he had a bead on Jamsie's problem and what to do about it. But nothing was clear to Jamsie now. He sat down at his desk. He tried to clear his mind. He wanted to go over everything that had happened to him since he had taken up work at the station. His thoughts were in a maelstrom. He could not think logically. Words such as "good," "evil," "Satan," "Jesus," "Ponto," "marriage," "possession," "free will" twirled and tumbled around inside his head. He could not straighten them out. Then "Beedem" began bobbing up in front of his mind. Beedem? Just like that, with a large question mark. "Jay Beedem? Jay Beedem? Jay Beedem?"

"Jamsie, I've got the schedule for next month worked out." It was his producer, Cloyd.

Jamsie looked up stupidly and muttered: "Jay Beedem?"

"Oh, he's seen it. It's okay. We're all set. Wanna see it?"

Jamsie took the schedule. But he could not concentrate on it now. "I'll call you, Cloyd," was all he could manage.

When he was alone, he tried again. It was no use. He could see

Mark's face, Jay Beedem's face, Ponto's face, his own face, Ara's face, Lydia's face, Cloyd's face. And Jay Beedem's again, with that look of contempt and hate. But they were *all* question marks now.

Slowly Jamsie began to calm down; and he tried to get some questions in order, at least. Was Mark right, and was he being invited to be possessed? Was he possessed already? Was Mark just another priest trying to make a convert out of him? Or maybe somewhere along the line the shrink had been right? Was he paranoid or schizophrenic? Making it all up?

Still restless, his thoughts switched back to Beedem. What was he anyway? Just another stupid, heartless jerk? No, this guy had something else. And he had it in spades. Until today, when Jamsie had happened to glance back, he had never seen Jay Beedem display an emotion. Nothing from inside. He had never even seen him really laugh.

He started to think more about Beedem as a person. What did he know of him? Beedem was a natural salesman. He could speak in 10,000 different tongues and tones, so to say, when he wanted to sell something. He had a vicious wit and could turn without warning on anyone and cut them down mercilessly in public. He often used four-letter words as if they were gilt-edged securities to guarantee the authority and accuracy of what he said. The women at the office shunned him. Some had slept with him once—but no one ever repeated the performance. He was either feared or despised, even when he made people laugh.

Uncle Ponto still never appeared when Beedem was around. Ponto appeared everywhere else, goddammit, Jamsie thought bitterly. Why not whenever he was with Jay Beedem? Why not today, when he could have used a little of that glib coaching?

Some strange edge to Beedem worried Jamsie. He was angry, sure. But that wasn't it. He just couldn't get it together in his head.

Then all of a sudden Jamsie was distracted from his thoughts about Beedem. It had been a long time since he'd worried about it, but now he felt he had to solve the old puzzle of the "look," the "funny-lookin' face." Great! As on that crazy night in Cleveland, he was sure now he was on the verge of discovering what he had "been told about it." For the first time in years he tried desperately to get all his memories together, in order to piece the fragments into a composite robot sketch.

Time and time again, as he sat at his desk, he thought he had it. His knuckles were white as he gripped the arms of his chair in the effort. But each time, the bits fell away from his bidding. He sat hunched up in his chair, laboring at this mental sketch; and slowly, bit by bit, the fragments started finally to fall into place and stay put.

After some time, Cloyd stopped by Jamsie's office again. He found Jamsie in extraordinary efforts of concentration, groaning and muttering to himself. When he could not get Jamsie's attention, he became frightened and ran for help. He found two station engineers, and together all three of them watched Jamsie, wondering what they should do.

Jamsie, meanwhile, was totally absorbed in his effort. He was on the very verge, he felt. But, at once, all the fragments fell apart into a long, jagged line at the end of which were Jay Beedem's unsmiling eyes. Then, again in a lightning flash, the line of fragments seemed to pour out his right ear, make for the window, and disappear up into the blue midday sky. The last trace he saw of it was Jay Beedem's face, for once broken by an ear-to-ear grin, trailing off at the tail end of the retreating line.

Jamsie clapped his hands to his ears. He was shouting, a tangled, throaty gust of protest and rage.

Finally he heard Cloyd's voice coming from a great distance: "Jamsie! Jamsie! Are you okay? Jamsie! Wake up!" He felt three pairs of hands on him, and he looked into the frightened faces of Cloyd and the two engineers.

"What's going on here?" It was Jay Beedem, calm, dispassionate, annoyed, and bored all at once. He stood in the door and motioned with his hand to the others to leave. He told Jamsie almost paternally that he should take the rest of the day off.

Jamsie felt completely beaten. He had not solved anything. He had not understood anything. It was idiotic for things to start flying out of his head again. He had not even gotten a leave of absence. The rest of the day off! Thanks a lot, he thought.

He stood up drooping and bowed, almost in tears. Jay Beedem stood aside. Jamsie stumbled out of the office, down the corridor, and out it into the parking lot to his car. It was Jamsie's last day at the station. He would not see Jay Beedem again. But at that moment Jamsie could not think ahead for five minutes.

The moment he entered his apartment, he knew Ponto was there somewhere. There was that smell . . .

"Now, don't be angry, Jamsie," the voice came from the hall closet.

"I'm going to remain away from you until you call me. Don't be angry. Just give the matter some cool thought." Jamsie brightened slightly. But fatigue took over. He fell on the bed, and in a few minutes was fast asleep.

It was about seven o'clock on Saturday morning when he awoke quietly. He was sure that some sound had awakened him. He listened for a few moments. Then he heard a rustling and scraping sound from the closet where Ponto had been the previous night.

Jamsie grew tense and suspicious. What was Ponto up to now? He tiptoed over, stood listening a moment, then jerked the sliding door of the closet aside. What he saw galvanized him with a disgust and outrage he had never felt before, even in his worst times with Ponto. Ponto was sitting on top of the old icon, picking away at the bits of mosaic that composed the face of the Virgin. Already the eyes were two sightless black holes, and Ponto was working on the mouth.

When Jamsie looked in at him, he stopped in a leisurely fashion, one fingernail curled around a mosaic fragment.

"We won't be needing this garbage, Jamsie, will we, you and I?" He smiled self-assuredly. The smell wafted around Jamsie's nostrils. "After all, I can't spend the night with this thing beside me, now, can I?" Ponto smirked.

Jamsie saw red. All the resentment that had piled up inside him since his early teens—his anger at being frightened, his frustration about that "funny-lookin' face," his disappointment with his father and mother, his final desire to be rid of Ponto and his importunings, his perpetual loneliness—all burst out from his inner self, flooding his mind with a nausea against knowing anything more about life. In that moment his will went rigid with a firm decision that pointed him to dying and death as his only release and hope of rest.

For some seconds he stood swaying from side to side, his head aching. Then he broke into the desperate rage that propelled him like a wild man, swearing and cursing out loud, as he bolted down the front steps to his car.

THE MUSHROOM-SOUPER

There was nothing very unusual about Father Mark A.'s childhood or about his family. Mark is a native New Yorker. His father, still alive, is a Yankee from Maine who settled in New York after World War I. His mother, now dead, was a Kelly from Tennessee. Her family had come over from Ireland to America in the late eighteenth century. She had been educated in Kansas City. When she came to New York to stay a while with relatives, she met her husband. He worked in a large accounting firm.

Mark was the third of five children. His two brothers still live in New York. One of his sisters married a Swiss manufacturer and lives in Zurich. The other sister, a missionary nun, was in the Philippines when World War II broke out. She survived in a Japanese concentration camp, but she was badly weakened and died in Manila after the war was over.

All in all, no one could have guessed that a man of Mark's normal and uneventful background would be the one person who could not only believe, but understand Jamsie's predicament, or that Mark's father's rather prosaic profession as an accountant would be the chance link to complete the chain of circumstances.

As a young man, after a year and a half of college, Mark entered the diocesan seminary. Seven years later, in 1928, along with eight other men, he became a priest. He spent ten years as an assistant in four parishes of the New York diocese. He became known as a hard worker and a very effective priest. He was practical rather than mystical, an activist decades before that was fashionable, and very hard to discourage. Those who knew him then recall him as bouncy, almost jaunty, with clear blue eyes, quick gestures, ready words, sudden flare-ups of temper and equally quick returns of good humor.

Mark himself tells how in those early years life always seemed to him to be made up of "scenarios." Each situation was composed of people and objects. You assessed the people, got to know the objects, and plotted your course of action, your "scenario," for that situation. Mark shunned any wishy-washy ideas about "motivations" or any "mystical realities." To many of his contemporaries he seemed to have a shallow and brittle approach. And, indeed, Mark now admits that in those early years it was as though his inner self was covered with a hard, protective rind that nothing pierced. He was impervious to any emotional appeal; and he was not held up or influenced by the intangibles of a situation.

When Mark was about to be moved to his fourth parish, his ecclesiastical superiors offered him a choice: a parish in the suburbs, or one in the center of midtown Manhattan. Mark chose without hesitation to work in the heart of the city. And for the next two years he experienced a new set of problems, totally different from those he had been confronting in the outlying parishes where he had already served.

At that moment in its history, just prior to World War II, New York was a mecca of sorts, and not merely for those with financial and economic interests. Serviced by 21 tunnels, 20 bridges, 16 ferries, 6 major airlines, New York received 115,000 visitors on an average day and an additional 270,000 out-of-town delegates who came to 500 annual conventions. Through trunkline railways, buslines, airlines, highways, they poured into the city and, as one statistician of that time calculated, on any one given night the hotel bedsheets in use would have covered 840 acres of Central Park.

The visitors could stay in any one of 460 hotels with a total of over 112,000 rooms costing anything from 25¢ in the Bronx to $50 per day at the Ritz. And, with or without the courteous and patient help of the eight young ladies in Macy's City Information Bureau, they found their way to one or another of New York's 9,000 restaurants, where they ordered their heart's desire from Irish stew, Japanese sukiyaki, and Creole gumbo, to Swedish smorgasbord, Budapest salami, and Cephalonian afgalimono.

"Hard-boiled New York is just a three-minute egg" rhapsodized the *Convention and Visitors Bureau* in one of its blurbs. Visitors rapidly discovered the soft center of that marvelous city. But Mark discovered that there was also a smell of human suffering and degradation.

Mark's parish was in the center of the tourist and hotel area. Between chambermaids, bellhops, desk clerks, cashiers, stewards, chefs, waiters and waitresses, and kitchen help, Mark calculated that there were 50,000 to 75,000 men and women whose hours were irregular and long. They went to bed when most church services were starting. Many were holding down two jobs at the same time. There was no way for these men and women to keep religion as part of hotel-life schedules. But it was such a hidden problem—or at least one nobody would normally think of—that it was practically neglected by every church.

What heightened both the plight and the peril of those neglected people in Mark's eyes was the web of organized crime—mainly in drug traffic, prostitution, and the numbers game—into which many were willy-nilly drawn. From simple steering of individual visitors to pimping for one or another of the several madams and their parlor houses; from simple bet collecting to bet agenting; from drug running to drug peddling and distributing; the road in every case was easy to find and too attractive not to try. Even with the Seabury investigation in 1930 and the breakup of the Luciano syndicate by Thomas Dewey some time later, there was no real cessation of this traffic in crime and vice.

Mark's father, as a certified accountant, handled the affairs of some major hotels in New York City. When Mark took up his new post, his father provided him with introductions to some of his friends and clients in the area. It was exactly the opening Mark needed in order to get to know the conditions in the hotels and restaurants, and to talk often and easily with the personnel. His factual mind seized on the salient elements, and his priestly experience and instincts indicated to him what could be done to meet the religious needs of the hotel and restaurant workers.

By the time his next tour of duty came up for consideration two years later, he had his mind more or less made up as to what he wished to do.

In August 1938 he got his chance. He had a long discussion with his superiors. He had a simple proposal to make: to undertake a special mission as chaplain extraordinary to the hotel and restaurant personnel in New York City. As Mark presented the case, it must have sounded like asking to go as missionary to savage lands. The superiors were impressed with his analysis of the situation. They were not difficult to persuade. The decision was made, and Mark went to live in a midtown parish rectory. He was relieved of all duties in that parish. It was to be merely his home base.

His new parish actually lay in every hotel in Manhattan and Brooklyn Heights. He divided this parish into six areas based on a rough grouping of hotels. The Grand Central area was centered on the Commodore and the Biltmore. The Penn Station area had the New Yorker as its center point. Times Square was relatively self-contained. The East Side was dominated by the Waldorf-Astoria. The Central Park group centered around the Plaza and the Sherry Netherlands. Brooklyn Heights centered mainly on the 2,641-room St. George.

But Mark's beat was not exclusively hotels, and it definitely was not all first class. He knew restaurants, nightclubs, swing joints, dives, second-, third-, and no-class hotels. He was as familiar as the "regulars" in the Paradise Cabaret on Broadway and in the Cotton Club on 48th Street (where, as he recalls, "50 Tall Tan Girls" danced to Cab Calloway's music). He knew Billy Rose's Casino de Paree, and was well known at swing joints such as the Onyx, the Famous Door, the Hickory House.

It was not surprising that Mark got to know some of New York's best chefs (and some of the worst!). Partly as a means to help him reach the hearts and minds of some of his "parish," Mark began to take an interest in cooking. One fine day he even found he had a genuine talent for cooking and that he had a real interest in it.

It would not be long before he found that this was not the only part of his new life that would reach inside and become part of him always.

Mark was on a late-night call—ordinary for his new beat—when he had his first close brush with a force that would later become the focus of all his efforts. It was at the bedside of a young prostitute who had been found bleeding and unconscious in a vacant lot near Ninth Avenue and 43rd Street. This and Sugar Hill in Harlem, where the mulattoes plied their trade, were the cheapest and the most dangerous areas in prostitution. Mark never went there except on urgent call.

When he entered the ill-lit room where the girl lay, her mother was there. She indicated the little cot in the semidarkness of one corner. The girl was moaning in pain. In the shadows at the foot of the cot Mark could see the figure of a man wearing a hat and overcoat, hands thrust in his pockets. As Mark approached the cot, the man took out one hand and held it up in an arresting motion. Mark stopped.

"Who is this?" Mark asked the girl's mother in a whisper.

She shook her head. "I don't know, Father. He used to be with her now and then. He came in a few moments ago. I thought he . . ." She trailed off helplessly.

Mark was now close enough to see the girl's eyes in the semidarkness. They were open and fixed on the man at the foot of the cot. The little light thrown by the single bulb in the room picked up the oddest expression in her eyes. Mark's mind flashed in a split-second memory to a pet rabbit he had had as a boy. One day he found the rabbit huddled and shivering staring at the cat that hovered by its cage. The ugly glitter in the cat's eyes—its superiority, its mysterious pull on him, its cruelty and disdain—was hypnotic. The fear that paralyzed the rabbit was dreadful and pathetic.

"She doesn't need you."

The words came from the man standing at the foot of the cot. The accent was normal. The tone was authoritative. There was no hint of hostility, just utter finality.

Mark fumbled for his crucifix and the little bottle of holy water he always carried. He had decided in that instant to give the girl a blessing and to leave it at that. He was not begging for trouble. Perhaps she was not even Catholic.

"That is enough."

The same voice again, but this time the tone held a definite menace. There was an implicit "or else" in those three words.

Mark was puzzled. Perhaps the man did not understand. He turned and faced the dark figure. It seemed to withdraw deeper into the shadows.

"But I'm . . ." Mark began by way of explanation.

But he never finished the sentence. The entire "scenario" as he had seen it up to that moment disappeared. It all became clear to him. The hard rind seemed to have been peeled off of his inner self; and he became wholly sensitive to what lay behind the "scenario" facing him—the girl, the man, the old woman, the dingy room, and the peculiar atmosphere enveloping all three of them. He was instantly aware of multiple relationships stretching taut like invisible cords among all present.

He drew back almost in shock at what he now understood. He knew that somehow the girl was in thrall to that man. And he knew it was far beyond the thralldom of a prostitute to her pimp. Somehow the man could assert his claim with a brutal authority.

The girl's mother touched Mark on the arm. They left the room. Outside, their conversation was brief.

"No, Father," she answered his question. "He's not her pimp." She looked at him with eyes full of despair. "I thought you'd get to her before they arrived."

"They?" echoed Mark with a new sense of shock. The mother nodded her head and stared steadily at him. He made a move to go back in.

"No." She laid a hand gently but firmly on his arm. "No. You're still young. You don't know what you're up against. You can't deal with anything like this. Yet." And then, already moving away from Mark to the door of the apartment, "Save yourself, Father. She's already in their grip."

She opened the door, and then closed it between them before he could ask any more questions.

"You can't deal with it."

He never forgot the woman's words. But it took him some months and many experiences before he began to understand that he was more than once up against cases of possession. Sometimes the situations resembled that of the dying girl, but not always.

At the end of the year Mark went to his superiors again and asked to speak to the official exorcist of the diocese. There was none, he was told, at that particular moment. But, said the official with whom Mark talked, if any cases of possession came up, they would call Mark in. He said this with the jocularity that is so often the sign of total ignorance. After all, the official added, with what Mark had been through, and if Mark's suspicions were true, he already had more experience than anyone else they knew.

The official's tone may have been light, but the result of the conversation was serious. Mark was now official exorcist of his diocese.

With intermittent breaks in his routine and some trips to other parts of the country and to Canada, Mark's ministry in New York lasted for 24 years. During that time he developed his knowledge and skill in dealing with cases of possession (real and counterfeit—he always said that out of every hundred claimants there might be one genuine case). But, more importantly, he became aware of an entire world of the spirit about which he had been taught nothing in the seminary and which seemed to flourish as the dark underside of life in his beloved New York.

Mark still gave the impression of jaunty objectivity. But now there was a deep underlay of awareness and shrewdness. And he was open and sensitive to the slightest trace of diabolism, while highly skeptical of all claims of diabolical "attention."

It was a source of some amazement to his close associates and superiors that he did not go the way of most exorcists. A few years' active ministry in Exorcism, and the majority paled, as it were: they seemed to wither in a variety of ways; some by illness, others by premature aging; others still because they seemed to have lost the will to live.

"Most of us crawl away and die somewhere quietly," Mark said as we talked one evening. I knew he was right.

"Why not you, Mark?"

"Well, you see," Mark began jokingly, "I have this great pal upstairs, and when I start into one of those exorcism businesses, he comes along and holds my hand." But at the end of the sentence Mark's eyes were away over my head and his expression was not in the least jocular. It was luminous and fixed on some object or person I could not identify.

One colleague of Mark's with whom I talked had been a close friend since their seminary days. They had always exchanged confidences. But all that had changed. He told me he had long since realized that Mark's inner life had been invaded by a dimension of which he knew very little and at which he could only guess.

Mark seemed all of a sudden very old and deeply weary to his friend. For most priests, as for most lay people, the world of the exorcist is totally unknown. The toll it takes is incommunicable and can pass unnoticed for years, even by those nearest to the exorcist.

But in those days Mark was still a young man. He lost most of his hair before he was thirty-five, but so did his two brothers. His health remained excellent. He exercised frequently, and rarely seemed to be affected adversely by his job. For two or three weeks after his first brush with an evil spirit, he seemed retired into himself and to be in deep thought. Then he snapped out of it. When he came across his first case of a "familiar" spirit (the subject was a pimp arrested for a multiple murder), he was completely befuddled, as he now admits. "Evil was very hard to trace," he recalls. "And I had two psychiatrists telling me that this was a classical case of multiple personality." In spite of the psychiatrists' opinions (which seemed to be somewhat confused, anyway, Mark recalls) and his own puzzlement about the case, Mark decided to try Exorcism because of four cardinal "symptoms": the physical disturbances accompanying the presence of the pimp, the pimp's physically uncontrollable and violent reaction to the crucifix, to the name of Jesus, and to holy water.

The only type of possession that produced a strange and unwonted tension in Mark was what he came to discern as "the perfectly possessed." His colleagues learned of such cases from Mark only because from time to time they sensed a peculiar tension very unusual in Mark. And occasionally they questioned him, thinking that he had had some accident, or that he was in some danger, or that they might help solve some problem. What they saw in Mark at such times, as they or some of them came to learn, was not a nervous tension, but rather an intense watchfulness and wariness which, his friends felt, was directed even at them. At those times he gave the impression of extreme guardedness. He was tight-lipped, gimlet-eyed, and curt in his conversation. When they finally were able to draw him out, and he gave them some idea of the condition of those who, he found, were perfectly possessed, they were taken aback by his totally negative attitude. This, too, was very unusual in Mark.

To all questions as to why there was no room for mercy or hope in such cases, Mark would try to recount some of his experiences with the perfectly possessed. But most of all he reflected the reality of the experience in a stare of such stark and concentrated realization that no one could pursue the subject further with him.

At the age of sixty Mark asked for a sabbatical. His health was still good, but something was changing in him. The years had piled up inside him an accumulation of disgusts and reticences that finally even he could not ignore.

His preference for a temporary location fell on San Francisco, where he had many friends and acquaintances. By April 1963, he was in residence there. He was given little by way of duties in the parish where he was staying, and spent most of his time in the open air.

But his compassion and his professional interests were aroused when Lila Wood, one of his acquaintances, talked to him at length one day about Jamsie Z., whom she had recently met at the broadcasting studio where she worked, and who not only seemed deeply troubled, but was more or less politely shunned by everybody.

Mark asked Lila many questions, until she had given him a fairly detailed picture of Jamsie's odd behavior. Even from this secondhand description, Mark was pretty certain that in Jamsie he was probably up against a case of a "familiar."

What distressed Mark most in his own first long discussion with Jamsie was his strong impression that, short either of a miracle or of Exorcism, Jamsie Z. was on the high road either to complete possession by his insistent "familiar" or to suicide as the easiest way of ridding himself once and for all of his misery. Mark knew the symptoms. And, more importantly, he had acquired over the years an instinct for the crisis point of "familiar" possession. The instinct was like that developed by painters for color and hue and chromatic intensity. That instinct could not be taught, but could only be learned by experience.

The person harassed by the "familiar's" advances, in the extreme stages of that harassment and just before the final outcome, generally begins to have dim perceptions of some more potent figure or force, as a greater shadow thrown by the lesser "familiar" or that which follows on the "familiar."

After Jamsie Z.'s unmistakable experience at the reservoir, Mark knew several things: there was no doubt in his mind that Ponto was totally real; there was no doubt that he, Mark, would be making a fatal mistake to be put off by the bizarre and often unbelievable predicament of Jamsie, or to dismiss his rages and antics as "psycho" behavior; and there was no doubt that Jamsie had reached the critical point.

The exorcism involving Jamsie Z. and Uncle Ponto lacked much of the violent, scatological, and pornographic elements that accompany other types and cases of possession. The struggle was at a different level, involved a different genre of spirit, and concerned a possession whose intensity was achieved over most of a lifetime.

Mark had come to know by experience that the degree of intelligence and knowledge that generally seems to characterize "familiars" is very low, sometimes approaching the level of half-witted children. "Familiars" seem to have only a small quantum of factual knowledge and very little power of foresight or anticipation. They appear to be bound by cast-iron rules and to be in strict dependence on a "higher" intelligence about which they talk frequently and to which Ponto, for example, had to have recourse at every crisis.

The "familiar" gives the impression of a weak mirror reflection, so to speak, of a greater one. So great seems this dependence of the "familiar" that it never directly engages the exorcist.

This attribute of the "familiar" spirit in particular complicated Mark's efforts. It meant he was working by proxy, or on a secondhand basis. Jamsie was the only one able to hear and see Uncle Ponto, and Jamsie had to verbalize it all for Mark. Ponto could hear and see Mark, but it was only when Ponto's "superior" took over that Mark was dealing directly with the evil spirit.

In excerpting Jamsie Z.'s exorcism, the choice fell primarily on those exchanges that bring out two points: first, the process of Jamsie's possession, and second, the extremely complex relationships implied by this kind of possession—Ponto's relationship as the "familiar" to Jamsie as the possessed, on the one hand, and the relationship of both Jamsie and Ponto to the "superior" spirit, on the other hand.

Mark's past experience of possession by "familiar" spirits had taught him one principal difference between the exorcism of a "familiar" and that of the other kinds of evil spirit. Other types of possessed find themselves almost completely bereft of their freedom. They are saved solely by an influx of grace, channeled through the ministrations of the exorcist. But the victim of the "familiar" spirit is quasi-possessed by the "familiar," until he gives final consent to the "familiar" and to a "sharing" of himself. Even then, the loss of control over one's inner self does not appear so deep that contact with the exorcist is to all intents and purposes impossible for him, as it often is in other types of possession where the evil spirit "hides" behind the identity of the victim and responds *instead* of the victim. In this type of possession, it is almost as though the "superior" spirit "hides" behind the "familiar" instead.

Being relatively free, then, and not out of contact with the exorcist, the victim of the "familiar" *must be active* in his own exorcism. He, in fact, must be the final source of his own liberation by accepting the healing and salvation from God. And, in this sense, the exorcee in such a case is the one who enables the exorcist to complete his work.

Mark spent quite a lot of time explaining to Jamsie this peculiarity of his forthcoming exorcism. Jamsie, like many others, had never reflected on his freedom. Free will was just a vague and abstract term for him. It took Mark a good deal of explaining to get Jamsie to understand that he had to exercise an option. This was the basic option of *free* will. Mark could only indicate to Jamsie *when* he should make a tremendous effort of will. Only Mark would be in a position to know the precise moment at which Jamsie could most effectively make that choice.

A peculiarity of this exorcism had to do with a ploy of Ponto's that had the same mischievous quality about it as many of the antics that had worn Jamsie down so much. The exorcism could be performed only after the sun went down. In fact, it was not always possible to start immediately at sundown; Ponto might not respond or appear for quite a while. And it was not possible to continue the exorcism after sunrise. This was not considered by Mark to be characteristic of this type of possession—just a mark of malice on the part of Uncle Ponto and his "superior." The night held terrors for Jamsie from which he was free during the daytime. That was a plus for Ponto and his "superior."

On the other hand, during daylight hours, Mark had ample time to consult the psychiatrist who had dealt with Jamsie. He also had Jamsie thoroughly checked by a doctor of his own choosing.

The psychiatrist remained in his unwavering conclusion that Jamsie was not suffering from anything like paranoia or schizophrenia. And finally during the exorcism itself Mark found that the Uncle Ponto

Jamsie saw and heard informed him accurately about things which Jamsie could neither have known nor guessed.

Each session of the exorcism took place in a basement room of the rectory where there was virtually no probability of interruption by the outside world. Jamsie sat on a kitchen chair at a table except for the last portion of the exorcism. The assistants were four in number: a younger priest Mark had pressed into his service, two young friends of his who worked in a law firm together, and a local doctor whose judgment Mark felt he could trust.

Jamsie's exorcism lasted over five days.

Mark always began each session with the *Salve Regina*, a prayer to the Virgin, and he ended with the *Anima Christi*, a prayer to Jesus. Only in the last two sessions were there any violent objections channeled through Jamsie to these prayers.

The first three sessions of the exorcism were full of irrelevant discourses by Uncle Ponto (all put into words by Jamsie). Mark bided his time and was certain he could afford to wait. He knew that sooner or later Uncle Ponto would break down and his "superior" would have to intervene.

This is what happened in the fourth session.

UNCLE PONTO

The time was 4:15 A.M., just an hour before sunrise. Mark had started the fourth session a little after midnight. He had pounded Ponto with questions through Jamsie for four hours, but Ponto had dodged them with prattling and nonsense.

At this late moment in the session, Mark saw Jamsie straighten up in the chair and look to one side. To Mark it was obvious: Jamsie was seeing more than Ponto now. This was the first flaw, the first sign of weakness, the first indication Ponto's "superior" might be coming to his aid. Maybe Mark's pounding with questions had not been so wide of the mark after all.

Mark's mind raced back over his most recent questions and hammerings at Uncle Ponto. He could think of only one thing that might have evoked Uncle Ponto's "superior." In answer to a spate of nonsensical remarks on Ponto's part, Mark had said in tones of utter disdain: "We have now come to the end of your intelligence. You have no more defense and no more explanations why this human soul should become 'familiarized' by you. You are repeating yourself. You are a nothing and worse than a nothing compared to the power of Jesus. In *his* name I tell you: you have to go forth and leave this person and go back to the one who sent you. You and he are defeated by Jesus."

"It's the Shadow, Father," Jamsie was staring, almost transfixed. The eyes of the pathetic young prostitute of nearly 30 years before, staring at the man in the shadows at the foot of her bed, seemed to stare for a moment from Jamsie's face, so similar was the look.

Mark went on inexorably. "You are completely at the mercy of Jesus, you and all associated with you. Jamsie, however, is protected. You have no greater one, no one to make up for your stupidity."

He glanced at Jamsie: "What is it, Jamsie? Tell me! Quick!"

Mark was afraid Jamsie would be stilled by fright, or by some power Ponto held over him, or—as had happened in other such cases—that Jamsie would fall unconscious before he could clue Mark in.

"He's talking rubbish, Father," Jamsie answered with difficulty.

Jamsie began to draw short breaths, as if breathing was now difficult for him. Then he started to cringe and draw into himself. His hands went to his neck as if to support his head. His face turned red. The doctor looked at Mark but made no move yet. The two young assistants stirred, ready to jump to Jamsie's aid. Mark quieted them with a gesture, then went on.

"We think Jamsie had better die with the blessing of the Church than live on in such a condition."

"No! No!" It was Jamsie, repeating for Mark what Ponto said, but with great difficulty. "I cannot fail. I must have my home. They will not allow that Person . . ." Jamsie broke off and started to gag and choke.

Mark went on. "We think Jesus, the Lord of all things, is coming to expel you, you puny and filthy being, expel you and send you back defenseless and stupid where you came from. Jesus cannot be opposed."

Mark stopped. Jamsie's eyes had closed. His hands fell to his sides in a helpless gesture. He started to slither from the chair to the floor.

"Quick!" Mark said to the assistants. "Get him on to the cot."

As he slipped off the chair, Jamsie's body lodged between the chair and the table, resting not quite entirely on the floor. His fists were clenched and held tightly to his neck, his head was sunk on his chest, his shoulders hunched, his knees bent, his toes splayed out straight and rigid. He was a twisted mass of hard angles and awkward curves. At first, the assistants and Mark thought Jamsie had merely got jammed at a difficult angle between the chair and the table. But after a moment's effort and examination, they realized that they could not budge his body. It was heavier than anything they could move. They shifted the chair and table away. Jamsie fell heavily to the ground as if drawn by an invisible magnet. Throughout all this his eyes were open and staring sightlessly.

Perspiring and helpless, the assistants looked up at Mark.

He held up the crucifix and in a loud voice said: "I command you, Ponto, I command you in the name of Jesus! Let go of this creature of God. Cease to pin him to the ground. Let go, I command you!"

Jamsie's body suddenly loosened. His head lolled to one side, his eyes turned upward until only the whites showed, his hands unclenched, and his arms rolled to his sides lifelessly.

Quickly the assistants picked him up and laid him on the cot.

"Tie him down," said Mark. Then to the doctor: "Take a look, Tom. Just make sure, will you?"

The doctor checked Jamsie's pulse and looked at Mark forebodingly. "Take it easy, Mark. He's very low. I have no means of knowing how low without more thorough checking. Take it easy."

Mark nodded. He knew he was close to a break in Ponto's resistance. He motioned to them all to stand back. He took the holy-water flask from the young priest and, raising his hand, faced Jamsie as he lay on the cot.

Mark sprinkled holy water on Jamsie in three deliberate gestures— he looked like a man throwing a grenade each time. And each time he pronounced in quick succession the words of his greatest reproach. He was addressing the "superior."

"Lurking Coward. Filthy Traitor. Defeated Rebel. Come out from behind your miserable *secundo*, your toady. Come out. And be shamed once more. Once more be defeated by Jesus. Be thrust into the Pit."

As his assistants saw him at that moment, Mark had completely changed. Up to this point, he had spoken softly, cautiously, every word and expression coming out of him after a weighty pause. Now he seemed suddenly to be a foot taller. At the same time he seemed coiled up. His face was hard; his mouth barely opened as he spoke; and, on the tape, there is a sudden, unexpected sense of onslaught and fierce hatred and contempt in Mark's voice.

In answer to Mark, there came a slow and very weak moaning from Jamsie. It gradually picked up in speed and volume, growing higher in pitch and deeper in resonance. Jamsie's body shook and vibrated beneath the leather straps holding him to the cot.

"Or are you a *secundo* of Jesus also?" Mark continued in the same deadly tone. "A real *secundo* of his triumph? Traitor and Father of Lies, promiser of vain victories? Are you also broken by . . ."

Mark got no further. His gibes had hit home. Through Jamsie's open mouth all present in the room could now hear distant and mincing words, each one peeled out of some acidulous throat, licked by a contemptuous tongue, and thrown in a leisurely and deliberate fashion at their ears like sharp darts of scorn. They all felt that scorn. And they all feared.

"Clot of mud. Little puppy of fucking animals. Talking beast. Praying with one end and excreting with the other. Depending on mercy. Asking for forgiveness . . ."

The contempt was like burning acid to those listening.

". . . smelling like a dunghill. Rotting into a juicy cadaver. Be silent! Retire! Leave this animal to us, the Most Hi-i-i-i-i-i-gh . . ." The one syllable of the last word was strung out in a long note that had a wailing quality of regret. Mark noted it, and took the only way out: attack.

"Declare yourself, in the name of Jesus!" A long pause. Jamsie's face was bloodless, drawn. The young priest was about to say something when that voice spoke again.

"We have never yielded to any power. And we will never . . ."

"Then we will begin the exorcism, the cursing out of you, the expulsion of you and all of you in the name of . . ."

"No-o-o-o-o-!" Again, that long-drawn-out wailing note. The voice had lost its contempt. There was a sudden urgency in it, almost a craven note.

Mark had broken a hole in the attack, he knew, and he jumped in with both feet.

"Your name!" Mark's command came before that long wailing "No" was finished.

"Names are for . . ."

"Your name! By the authority of Jesus' Church, your name, I say!" Mark was not shouting, yet his voice filled every part of the room.

"We are . . ." Again the wailing note, but this time with a growl-like resonance. "We are all of the Kingdom. No man can know the name. We are alllllllll . . ." The "l" echoed and echoed until it finally died away.

"What shall we call you then?" Mark was still insistent. "In Jesus' name, what name will you obey? In Jesus' name, what name will you obey?"

"Multus-a-um. Magus-a-um. Gross-grosser-grossesste. Seventy times. Seventy-seven Legion. All . . ."

"Multus? Shall you obey this name, in the name of . . ."

Mark was interrupted by Jamsie. He was suddenly awake, his eyes wide open and bloodshot, his body pushing against the straps, his legs kicking.

"Sit on his legs," Mark said. The two assistants did so.

"UNCLE PONTO! UNCLE PONTO!" Jamsie was screaming at the top of his voice with a desperation that froze them all. "UNCLE PONTO! DON'T GO. IF YOU GO, WHAT WILL THEY DO TO ME? UNCLE PONTO! UNCLE PONTO!"

Mark drew back and thought quickly.

Jamsie continued blabbering incoherently. Then, in a lower tone, as if wearied by his recent efforts: "Yes . . . thought you were after my . . . no, please . . . don't do that and . . . night . . . radio with Jay Beedem . . ."

Mark was thinking. He turned away. The others could see his face cloaked over in a withdrawn look. For a few seconds he seemed to be elsewhere, to be totally abstracted from the situation. Then he rounded unexpectedly like a whiplash, his voice rising in anger.

"Multus! Multus! Answer us in the name of Jesus. Answer! Answer! By dismissing Ponto! Answer!" Mark waited for a moment. Then he repeated his command.

"Answer! *By dismissing Ponto! Answer!*"

Jamsie's eyes clouded over, his head fell back, his body went limp. Mark had his answer. He knew: to all intents and purposes Ponto was gone; he was now dealing directly with Ponto's "superior." Mark's aim now was clearly to get all the information he could from that "superior," to find out in particular as much as he could about the tangled lines of the attempted possession of Jamsie and thus clear the way for a successful expulsion of the evil spirit. Multus, like all evil spirits, could not stand the light of truth.

The doctor pried open one of Jamsie's eyes, felt his pulse, and nodded slowly, warningly to Mark.

Mark fired out a series of questions.

"When did you start working on Jamsie?"

"He was chosen before he was born."

"When did he know you were after him?"

"He knew long before he knew he knew."

"How did you gain entry to him?"

"He wanted it. Those who might have taught him otherwise, we corrupted. But he chose to be entered. Only one opposed us."

"Who?"

"He never knew him."

"Who?"

"His father's father. He was given that role by . . ." The voice wailed away in the same regretful note of sorrow.

"By whom?" Mark insisted. No answer.

"By whom?" Mark repeated the question, and added: "Or shall I tell you by whom?"

"By that Person who is beyond notice by us. By the Claimer of all adoration. By the one who never received and will never receive our adoration . . ."

"Did you make Jamsie see the 'funny-lookin' face'?"

"No. His protector. We would never frighten him away. We are more powerful than that. It was his protector trying to warn him."

Now the tone had changed. A new truculence had entered it. Mark heard it and whitened. He had presumed too much. The voice continued gratingly. It was as if the owner of that voice saw Mark's discomfiture. A hail of sharp questions rained down on his ears, and his mind started to boggle under the weight of the images they evoked.

"Do you think you have escaped us, Mushroom-Souper? Do you think that one of these filthy whores didn't change you? How many times have you lusted after them? Remember the Harlem house and the seventeen-year-old? Remember when she shoved her pussy at you and you saw the black hair glistening on those tawny thighs? Remember your hard-on? Ha! Ha! Priest! You fucking priest! You little burning cock! Ha! Ha! Your prayers were of no avail then. And your Virgin with her lily-white conception was of no avail. Or did you remember to tie the rosary around it and hold it down? Remember! Remember? Remember your wet dreams? We do. So we do. And you do! Don't you think a bit of you belongs already to us? Prieeeeeeeeeeest!"

Mark was beaten temporarily. He staggered back. And then he saw Jamsie: both eyes open, his mouth split in a wide, full-toothed grin. He was listening and laughing. Mark got the message. Ponto and his "superior" were leaving.

The young priest tapped Mark on the shoulder and pointed to the window. Thin pencils of sunlight were pointing in from the outside. Another bright and hot day had started.

Mark heaved a sigh. Another half hour, he thought, and he would have nailed down the "superior." "Okay. Let's wrap it up for now, until tonight." He had recovered his nonchalance. "We meet at 10:00 P.M. sharp. Get some rest. Tonight's the night."

Then they did what they had done each day before this. Mark recited the *Anima Christi*. Afterward, he went upstairs and said his Mass. The four assistants took turns watching over Jamsie. In an hour or so after that, he woke up with no memory of what had happened the previous night.

On the last night of the exorcism Mark had a plan to precipitate events if Ponto delayed very long in coming. He had a trump card up his sleeve. There was a certain risk in playing that card; and in what he proposed to do he was incurring dangers on himself as well as on Jamsie.

But the alternative was almost as stark and forbidding. Jamsie was getting progressively weaker in his resolution to undergo the rite of Exorcism, to resist, to *survive*. He could collapse completely at any moment. He could, indeed, fall into a comatose state as a prelude to an early death—Mark had known such cases—or he could emerge in a state of complete shock. In either condition, Jamsie would be inaccessible. And Mark himself would be left forever with a nagging doubt about Jamsie's fate. There would be no way of knowing if he had become one of the perfectly possessed, immune to any touch of therapy, isolated from any saving intervention, trussed, mummified, and locked away safely by the evil power that possessed him perfectly. Or if he had gone insane in a strictly psychological sense of the word. In any such condition it would be impossible to know how much he perceived of the other world, or if he could pray and exercise his belief and thus cooperate with God's grace for ultimate salvation.

Mark fervently wished to avoid the dubious and dangerous character of such an ending to the case of Jamsie Z.

Mark's trump card lay in a fact that had emerged during his routine inquiries about Jamsie and his general background.

Jamsie had been baptized at home by his grandmother over the kitchen sink. He had been born in a very weakened condition. The attending doctor had despaired of his survival, and his very pious Armenian grandmother had baptized him, because she feared the priest would be too late. From what Mark could find out, there was a reasonable doubt that Jamsie's baptism had been valid.

Jamsie's grandmother had known very little English and she certainly did not know the words of baptism in English. It was she who had poured water over his baby head. But, it appeared, the Irish midwife who was helping Lydia, Jamsie's mother, in the childbirth, had pronounced the words of Baptism.

If this were so, then the Baptism had indeed been invalid. The same person who pours the water must pronounce the words. Otherwise, no Baptism of that kind is valid. The baby is not baptized, has not become a Christian.

To create even further doubt, the parish priest, who had finally arrived much later, never bothered to correct the doubt and baptize Jamsie provisionally. Such "conditional baptism" is usually conferred in such cases. But, for whatever reason, apparently this had not been done.

Now Mark proposed to baptize Jamsie. Instinctively, as an exorcist, Mark knew that the "rejection" of Evil Spirit implied in Baptism of an adult was something a mere "familiar" could not handle. The "superior" would have to intervene in a new way in order to protect the common interest of "familiar" and "superior" alike.

And then it was Mark's object to attack the peculiar bond between the "superior" spirit and its "familiar" spirit. That much done, Mark would no longer have to deal secondhand; he would have the "superior" in the open—not temporarily as in the previous sessions, but as the "responsible party," so to speak. From then on Mark could handle things as in a more "normal" exorcism.

Having spent, therefore, one hour waiting for Ponto to come, Mark had Jamsie lie down on the cot, where the assistants strapped him securely. He now proceeded with the Baptism, Jamsie answering all the queries which are put to an adult person about to be baptized, reciting the Creed and making other professions of faith.

This went on for a short while in relative calm, until Jamsie broke off in the middle of a sentence. His voice changed, and he said quickly to Mark: "He's coming back. He's in a terrible state."

Uncle Ponto was obviously with Jamsie. Mark's plan had worked that far. He and his assistants listened to one end (Jamsie's) of a bizarre conversation and tried to guess what was said at the other end (Uncle Ponto's).

"I will not have you in my life." Jamsie was looking over to the door of the room. He was silent for a few seconds. Then he spoke in a waspish tone. "What happens on Jupiter and what I could do with much money—a million bucks—is all hogwash. I want to be left . . ."

Now Jamsie was looking at the ceiling, now at the window, now over toward the door again. "That won't help at . . ." His face flushed with anger. "But why should I be afraid to die? Others have had to go."

Mark and the others continued to listen in silence. Evidently Ponto was in a bad state.

Jamsie broke in: "Mark says Jesus said you're a goddamn liar and . . ." Interrupted, Jamsie looked over in the corner and scowled. "I'll talk about what I damn well please, and listen . . ."

Then something happened of an abrupt and quite unexpected nature. Jamsie's eyes grew larger, the whites of the eyes shone. His face seemed to cave in, to lose some substantive strength. He shrank back on the couch, into himself.

Mark was by his side in an instant and laid his hand in Jamsie's. It was a prearranged signal between the two of them. Jamsie had time to press Mark's fingers lightly, then he started weeping and sobbing.

"It's no use." His fingers let go of Mark's hand. "It's no use. I'm finished. He's back. They're all back."

Mark took the crucifix and started immediately. When he did, Jamsie seemed to go to sleep suddenly, his jaw sagging, spittle running down his chin.

"Multus!"

"Mushroom-Souper!" The words were pronounced with a velvet smoothness, but icy cold.

"Multus! Answer us. It is you and no one else?"

"Mushroom-Souper, you ludicrous little pigmy. We have our mark on you. All this hocus-pocus will not keep you or him that belongs . . ."

"Multus! Answer us!" Mark had the spirit where he wanted it. "Jamsie's 'familiar' is Ponto. Why do you say he belongs to you? Who are 'us' then?"

"You smelly ones walk around in bodies of slime and mud and muck. You say one, two, three, four hundred, seven million, a trillion. Ha! Ha-Ha!"

"Multus! Is Uncle Ponto you? Are you Uncle Ponto?"

"We are spirits. There is no one, two, three, four, hundred, seven million, a trillion. We are kinds and species. We are spirits! Powers. Dominations. Centers. Minds. Wills. Forces. Desires."

"Answer in the name of the Church. Answer the questions of Jesus' authority. Are you Uncle Ponto?"

"Yes! Ha! Ha! No! Ha! Ha!" The laughter froze the blood in the listeners' veins. It was a rollicking sneer of contempt, no fun in it, no humor. Then: "Ponto is us without the intelligence of the Claimant."

There was a trap ready to spring on Mark. But Mark knew better than to ask who the Claimant was. Claimant, Master, Prince, Leader—it all came down to one being: the supreme intelligence of evil which had led and which leads all intelligences in revolt against the truth of God. Mark never felt in all his life that he wanted a direct tussle with that personage. Deep instinct of his own limitations held him back from such a step.

Instead, Mark pursued his urgent quest of uncovering the relationship between Uncle Ponto and the Shadow. "But Uncle Ponto uses his own intelligence on his own account."

"Never." The definitiveness of that word hit them all.

"Ponto's intelligence is subordinate to you."

"Always." The answer was a stony blow. Imperious. Curt.

"And Ponto's will?"

"Those who accepted, those who accept the Claimant, have his will. Only his will. Only *the* will. Only *the* will. The will of the Kingdom. The will of the will of the will of the will of the will . . ." The voice faded down from a curt, domineering tone to a sniveling, breathed whisper and died away. Mark detected the sudden influx of fear in it.

The young assistant priest also caught that note of fear, and, in a kind of victory yell, he leaned forward with a sudden ebullience: "Hit them hard, Mark!"

Mark rounded on him, his eyes blazing. "Shut your mouth!"

"That is right!" came the mincing tone. "That is exactly right! But our quarrel is with you, Priest! We have years to deal with this little virgin and to show . . ."

Mark broke in. "You will speak when questioned. Only then. And you will tell us in the name of Jesus," Mark thundered, his annoyance with the young priest's mistake filling his voice and channeled at the spirit, "you will tell us: Jay Beedem, has he consented to your power?"

There was complete silence. Only Jamsie's breathing could be heard. Mark had never met Beedem, but he figured oddly in Jamsie's story, and Mark's nose caught a strange scent there, even from a distance. He needed to know if there was an essential connection Beedem had with Ponto or with his "superior" that affected Jamsie.

"Jay Beedem," insisted Mark. "You will tell us when . . ."

"No." It was summary and definitive. "We will not tell you anything, Priest." Silence again.

"By the authority of the Church and in the name of Jesus, you . . ."

"That Church and that Person have no authority over Jay Beedem. . He is ours. Ours. Ours. Ours. The Kingdom. Ours."

Mark drew a deep breath. This was not new for him, but it always gave him a sinking feeling to find out that someone was protected by summary evil, protected even from the touch of grace. He knew better than to pursue the subject. Once before, about ten years before, he had tried. And the onslaught that ensued had interrupted the exorcism (which someone else had to start all over again and finish), and left Mark literally dumb and deaf for about five weeks. Something vital had almost died in Mark that time. He had challenged Evil Spirit on its own secure ground.

He switched to another tack. "Your funny-looking face: what was the purpose of that?"

"The funny-looking face was not our doing. We do not frighten those we prospect."

"What result was effected by showing Jamsie that face?"

"By it, his protector wished to acquaint him with the face all take on who belong to us . . ."

"Was it this," Mark interrupted almost involuntarily, "that stopped Jamsie at the reservoir? That face?" There was no immediate answer.

Mark got the faintest hint of something strange happening to the others in the room. He glanced quizzically at his young priest; his face was beaded with perspiration. Mark paused.

Then all four assistants flung their hands to their ears, their faces screwed up in expressions of pain.

"Mark, for the love of God, get them to stop that whistling!" the doctor was shouting at the top of his voice. "It will stun us."

He and the other three started to moan in pain; then all four were shouting and screaming, their heads and bodies turning this way and that, backing away from the cot where Mark stood beside Jamsie's inert body.

Mark took a step toward them, but quickly withdrew. He tried again, and again withdrew. Every time he stepped outside a certain invisible circle around the cot, his ears were assailed by the most horrible and deafening hail of high-decibel sound.

As his four assistants writhed and withdrew slowly, they were looking at Mark, imploring help. He made animated gestures to them indicating that they should keep backing away. They did so until finally, within a foot or so of the back wall near the door of the room, all four suddenly stopped writhing in agony. Their faces lost the lines of pain and concentrated effort.

They looked at Mark finally as though across a huge distance filled suddenly with silence and fog. While Mark could see them clearly, he could not hear them at all. On their side, they could only hear Mark and see his lips moving and his hands gesturing in a distorted fashion. It was like looking through frosted glass into a sunlit room; they saw everything, but unclearly.

Rooted to the opposite side of the room with their bodies to the wall, it was through this weird medium that his four assistants saw Mark's final settling of Jamsie's exorcism. It was a shadow play of horrors for them.

They saw Mark's figure turn partially away from them to face Jamsie's body on the cot. They saw Mark lift the crucifix. They saw his lips move and at first heard nothing. Then, as from a great distance and through a low, rumbling noise like a continuous avalanche of pebbles down the side of a mountain, they began to hear his voice.

". . . shall be as we bid, because it is in the name of Jesus that we bid you answer us. Was it the face that stopped Jamsie from suicide?"

Another voice, the one with the mincing words, broke through in a guttural tone, sharp, decisive, cold, inimical. "Are you interested in that funny-lookin' face, Priest? Would you like to see it yourself?"

"Answer our question," was Mark's rebuttal to that invitation to be curious. "Answer it!"

"Yes. Ye-e-e-e-e-e-e-e-e-es." The voice was grating out the sounds grudgingly. "It was that face. We are always present when inferiors are about to make a killing."

"So every time you were present, Jamsie's protector endeavored to let him see that face?" There was no answer to this.

Mark went to another point. "Why did you allow Jamsie to see the . . . the . . . the Shadow?" Mark stumbled over that one, and then regained his composure. There had been moments in his own life when he had been about to make some important decision and, he now realized with a little shiver, there had been some sort of shadow present. He had always put it down to something else. But the wisps of memory disturbed him now. Those moments had been during his bouncy, jaunty days, his "scenario" days, when everything had to have a logical and describable cause, and it was all very simple.

"We did not. Notnotnotnotnotnot." The word was a thump of sorrow and regret and dreadful aching. Mark felt it. He went on, pressing his questions, still holding the crucifix high.

"Why did a common look exist between the Shadow and Uncle Ponto and Jay Beedem and the pimp and many others; why did a common look exist?"

Mark could see a change in Jamsie that his four assistants could not see through the haze that kept them apart. Jamsie was now wide awake, but his eyes were not on Mark. They looked up to his left. Mark was careful to note this, but he kept looking steadily at Jamsie. He repeated his question. He was getting closer.

"Why the common look? Is this another part of your evil stupidity?"

"Beyond our control." The words came with difficulty. "We also . . . must submit . . . in material things, we . . . also bound . . . Person beneath contempt holds . . . holds . . . holds . . . holds . . . ." The voice started to get slurred. "Ho-o-o-o-o-o-o-o-l-l-l-l-l-l-dsdsdsdsdsdsdsdsdsdsds" The voice died away in an angry buzz until there was no more sound.

"Why the common look?" Mark kept staring at Jamsie, looking for any hint or clue in his reactions.

Still pinned to the opposite wall, Mark's assistants were suddenly horror-struck. They shouted and screamed in warning to Mark. He could not hear, but continued to face Jamsie.

At first what they saw seemed vague, a bulky shape, rearing up behind Mark, much like a cat standing crookedly on its hind legs, front paws lifted, claws open and spread-eagled, ears flattened against its head, mouth opened to hiss.

They heard the distorted rumble of Mark's voice as he continued the exorcism. There was nothing they could do but watch and pray.

"What do you place in those human beings so that they get that look?"

And the voice came rasping out in a slow, steady tone: "Obedience to the Kingdom. They give their will. We fill the soul. What's inside peers out willy-nilly . . ."

Jamsie, still strapped down, had raised his head from the bed to stare at the threatening form behind Mark. It was constantly weaving back and forward, turning from left to right as if seeking something. But to Jamsie it was less like a cat and more like a man swathed in heavy, black clothes. Mark, intent on watching Jamsie, did not follow the direction of his gaze.

"You have to come out." Mark began his final pounding at the spirit. "You have to manifest yourself and leave this human being. In the name of Jesus!"

The assistants, all still at bay, could see both faces—Jamsie's and the darksome figure's—contorting at this moment. "And not only you, but your inferior and slave, your Uncle Ponto. Him and all who go with him. Out! I say! Out with all of you."

Mark's assistants were now in utter panic. All they could see was the menace to Mark from behind him. They tried to move forward against the excruciating rain of sound.

"We will never rest until we avenge ourselves on you," the voice was saying, "we will leave this miserable blob of muck dead when we go."

"Life and death are not yours to give or take. They belong to Jesus."

Jamsie started at that moment to scream, wild hysteria in his voice.

Mark's ears were filled with that scream; he held the crucifix and prayed out loud, using only two words: "Jesus! Mercy! Jesus! Mercy! Jesus! Mercy! Jesus! Mercy! Jesus!"

Then his ears were hit by the agonizing screams of the four assistants: they had left their sanctuary-prison against the opposite wall, had penetrated the space between the wall and the cot where Mark stood beside Jamsie, and were once more writhing under the impact of the torture that stabbed at their eardrums.

But even through the din of Jamsie's shouts and his assistants' screams, deepened by his own praying, chanting voice, Mark heard one sound that reassured him and gave him hope.

It was the rattling of the pebble avalanche that had never really ceased, but now became more defined. It was a hubbub of wordless voices and senseless syllables all running together and splitting each other in fragments, interrupting and fractioning and changing each other, an undistinguishable medley of sorrow, regret, foreboding, agony. It persisted in rising and falling waves, then started to build up and up to a crescendo.

Mark took his cue: it was the confusion of defeat and rout. He hurled the words of his power at it all.

"In the name of Jesus! You must depart! Unclean ones! There is no room for you! No dwelling in this human being. For Jesus has commanded: Go! And you go! Go! Go!"

Mark remembers clearly stopping at this point. He did some quick thinking. By now the possessing evil spirit should have been sufficiently weakened and Ponto's grasp on Jamsie sufficiently diluted for Jamsie to make his fatal and all-important choice.

Mark bent down near Jamsie's ear, speaking in a gentle, firm tone. He remembers almost word for word; it was the choice that always came in some way. "Jamsie! Jamsie! Jamsie! Listen to me: Now! You have to choose! You have to make a choice! Either you take a step in trust. You renew your faith. Blindly, mind you, blindly. Or now you yield to Ponto and to all of Ponto's friends. Jamsie! All of them, Jamsie! In the name of Jesus, choose! Now choose, Jamsie!"

In his turn, Jamsie recalls that at this moment he woke up to the confusion around him. Gradually, as in a thinning haze, he began to make out dim figures besides the Shadow behind Mark, and he saw zigzag gestures, the ceiling and the walls of the room; he felt the pressure of the straps across his chest, middle, and legs. His mouth was dry, he remembers, but he was breathing easily.

Farther away from the bed, he could not see anything except as a fuzzy gray-black background—the closest comparison Jamsie can give to describe that blurry background is what he saw when he once tried on the very powerful eyeglasses of a friend who was almost blind. Everything blurred together and seemed to darken.

Closer, he could see the figures of the assistants as they held their ears and struggled with that deafening whistling noise. One was staggering. Two had fallen to the floor. One was standing upright, moving slowly and agonizingly toward him.

Still nearer to him, he could see two or three single figures, together with a multitude of shapes and forms. Ponto was there, but some infinite distance away. Jamsie could not understand this: Ponto was near, yet far. He seemed to be all squeezed together as if his body was boneless and someone had caught it in an invisible clothes wringer narrowing his girth, splaying his limbs, bulging his eyes. And his look was no longer merely importunate and mischievous. For the first time it was nasty, Jamsie felt, nasty, bitter, hating, desperate all at once.

Ponto's agony seemed to be multiplied by a whole river of forms and shapes—torsos without heads, heads without bodies, arms and legs without a trunk, fingers without hands, toes without legs, bellies without a body, genitals floating free, long plaits of gray and yellow hair—all wreathing and snaking fitfully, aimlessly around Ponto in zigzag tracery.

Closest to him of all, except for Mark, Jamsie saw the Shadow. It loomed up above him with a superhuman stature. It was neither black nor gray nor white but an indefinable amalgam of shifting darkling shades, much like the smoke from wet coals—never still or calm, but ruffled and rippling irregularly. Head, shoulders, hands, mouth, eyes, feet were clear enough to be perceived, but not clear enough to be described.

Jamsie heard Mark's voice then, gentle, firm, finalizing.

"Jamsie! Now is the time to choose. Remember! I told you. You! You choose. *You* have to choose. Of your own free will."

Somehow or other, Mark's voice was reaching Jamsie in spite of the din and the distracting gyrations and febrile jumping of all those forms.

"Choose! Choose! Yours is the choice. Now!" Mark's unhesitating syllables clung to Jamsie's memories.

Jamsie could not see Mark's face as Mark bent down to speak in his ear, but the Shadow's features were clear. A kaleidoscope of expressions passed over that face. Jamsie began weakly to remember. Where had he seen this expression? That expression? The next one? The last one? They all seemed different, yet they all seemed to be the same.

Then Jamsie realized that the various changing expressions were repeating themselves over and over again, coming and fading and returning in a carousel set to the din and shouts and screams.

"Choose! Choose!"

It was Mark's voice again. Jamsie turned. He tried to make out Mark's face. He could not. From forehead to chin Mark seemed to be faceless. But he still heard Mark's voice.

Then his memory began to clear. The expressions became more familiar. Yes . . . yes . . . that was his father's, Ara's . . . and that one Uncle Ponto's . . . the pimp's . . . Jay Beedem's . . . Jay Beedem's?"

"Choose! Jamsie! Choose!"

Then, interspersed with the changing faces, Jamsie began to see the other funny-looking faces he had seen in all the years back to his childhood, 1960, 1958, 1957, 1949, 1942, 1941, 1940, 1939, 1938, 1937, 1933. And he began to see that his fright for all these years had been a form of fascination, that even while running away from the "funny-lookin' faces," he had been inviting them, that he had *wanted* to be found by them!

Inside his deepest self another movement started, beyond his willing. The desire to be rid of that fascination. But there was still the agonizing fear and doubt. "If I stopped looking at that carousel," Jamsie today describes his feelings at that point in the exorcism, "I felt I would cease to exist. I would die, die, die sort of thing."

Then his fascinated gaze faltered and flicked away from the carousel of faces for an instant over to Mark's face.

Mark was no longer faceless for Jamsie. He did not have the features Jamsie knew as Mark's. Still, Jamsie knew, they genuinely belonged to Mark. Another puzzlement for Jamsie.

He peered at Mark, staring at the eyes and the nose and mouth. The colors of his face were beginning to glow and shimmer in old gold, in tarnished silver, faded blue and brown and yellow. Jamsie half-feared to find some phase of the "funny-lookin' face" on Mark, but there was none. And he had no fear or fright. Another emotion, other thoughts were coming to Jamsie.

Mark's voice reached him again. "You must choose, Jamsie."

Jamsie glanced again at the Shadow. In all its bulk and in every weaving curve of its changing face and figure there was now a certain cringing. Jamsie read hesitation there, even as he found himself fascinated always by the changes.

Jamsie began to look back and forth from the Shadow back to Mark, then at the Shadow, slowly at first, then quickly. And Mark's insistent "Choose. Make your choice, Jamsie!" came to him again and again.

Suddenly he understood. He *was* free. No one would force him. No one *could*. He was free—to go on immersing himself in the changing horrors of the Shadow, or to look at Mark and make an opposite choice.

He started to gaze steadily at Mark; and in that look he knew he was choosing.

There were no words on his lips. He had no sentence in his brain, no concepts in his mind about that choice. He was choosing, merely because he chose to choose; and, choosing thus, he was freely choosing.

And as the thrust of his choice gathered strength within him, he began to recognize the new lines and shades in Mark's face: all the traits of goodness and joy and freedom and welcome he had ever known in others—Lydia and Ara of years ago, Lila Wood, the old icon at home in New York—all were there as so many frames, as mirrors reflecting an immense beauty and joy and peace and unshakable eternity.

Slowly Mark's features became clear, Mark's solid features, tense and granite-like, his eyes closed, his hand still raised holding the crucifix. The Shadow was receding like smoke from a cigarette being dissipated in the air. And with it all the noise and din was fading away weakly into silence.

Over Mark's face there was a film of fine suffering drawn tight like gauze. Jamsie was stung with compassion. Mark had said to him: "If we get rid of the Enemy, Jamsie, I will be the last to feel the lash of his tail."

Mark had lost sight of Jamsie by then. He was in his own travail, his own agony, his own payment of pain.

It was the young assistant who described the change in Jamsie. There was no more hint of struggle. A great calm filled Jamsie's features. Mark's voice still boomed, even though the noise had died away. Mark was repeating again the two words: "Jesus! Mercy!"

The young priest knew that Jamsie was free at last. He unbuckled the straps that held Jamsie down on the cot.

"Mark!" Jamsie shouted to the exorcist as he rose up from the cot. "Father Mark! I'm free!" Jamsie touched Mark on the arm. "Father Mark!" He took Mark's hand and felt the icy cold of those fingers. He stood a few moments waiting.

Then finally Mark lowered the outstretched arm which held the crucifix. His eyes lost the glassy stare; he blinked and Jamsie saw the look of recognition returning in Mark's eyes. And Mark saw in Jamsie's eyes and on his face an expression of peace and lively hope which had never been there since he had known Jamsie.

The Rooster
and the Tortoise

It was 6:00 A.M. exactly by the clock tower in the Piazza della Liberta of Udine when the party of eight Americans left the hotel in two limousines. Everything in their trip had been planned down to the last detail in timing and ceremonial.

The date was July 23, and already they felt the high summer heat. Within 15 minutes they had made their way through the narrow streets past arcades and porticos, out of the city, and were on the undulating road down through the coastal plain. Now and again, when they crested a hill, they caught glimpses of the Adriatic Sea as a glinting blue band on the horizon. To the far north stood the Alps, white and on guard.

Their destination was the village of Aquileia (population 1,500) some ten miles south toward the sea. For Carl, the leader of the trip, this was to be a homecoming: long ago he had lived, suffered, and triumphed in Aquileia. For Carl's seven companions, it was a pilgrimage to a venerated shrine.

The two men riding with Carl in the first limousine were his friends and associates; the woman, Maria, had been his assistant for four years. The four college students in the second limousine were psychology majors and Carl's student assistants. Besides being a highlight in their studies, the trip was a mystical celebration for them.

In the first limousine, Carl led the conversation in jubilant tones: "We are on the brink of discovering what Christianity was like before the Greeks and Romans distorted it." He was a thick-set man in his late forties, of medium height, with close-cropped, coal-black, curly hair and beard; high rounded cheekbones beneath a high forehead, eyes not merely black, but shining black, like polished agates. He had a Roman nose, long, straight, with a slight hump in the middle. The lips were full and sat over a strong jawline. He was tanned and healthy-looking. He wore a light suit over an open shirt.

As he spoke, he gestured quietly to emphasize his meaning. The ring on his right index finger flashed in the morning sun. It was a wide gold band adorned with a gold image of a tortoise. He toyed with the two emblems of an ancient Roman god, Neptune, a dolphin and a trident, which hung on his neck chain.

Carl was a qualified psychologist, with a prior degree in physics. His studies had led him into parapsychology and research concerning the nonordinary states of human consciousness. Under the impulse of his personal gifts as a psychic, he had been experimenting in astral travel and reincarnation.

After 11 years of intensive work, he was going to Aquileia accompanied by associates and students. For here, as he and the others had learned a few months previously during one of Carl's trances, he had lived some 1,600 years previously during a former existence as a public notary named Petrus. In that trance, which had taken place under controlled laboratory conditions, Carl accurately described not merely ancient Aquileia—its amphitheater, forums, public baths, palaces, quays, cemeteries, triumphal arches, and shops. He had given a detailed account of how the fourth-century citizens of Aquileia had reerected a public statue of Neptune which a religious sect had overturned in the previous century. Some weeks after that seance, news had come independently from Aquileia telling precisely of such a statue and of a Latin inscription backing up Carl's statements.

Carl had also given details of a mosaic floor that was part of a fourth-century Christian chapel. And he added something piquant which fascinated his associates and students: a description of a very ancient ritual that used to be performed by Petrus and his companions at one particular spot on that mosaic floor.

The purpose of their present trip was to reenact that ritual on July 23, the summer festival of the god Neptune.

Now, in the first limousine, Carl was again describing that particular spot and the ritual. The spot was a mosaic medallion depicting a fight between a red rooster and a brown tortoise. Apparently Petrus and his companions—"Christians of the original kind," Carl commented—used to come and stand in single file to the right of the medallion. Then, one by one, they used to step on the Rooster (symbol of the intellectual pride and imperial power-madness which "had corrupted genuine and original Christianity"), then kneel, and looking at the Tortoise (symbol of immortality and eternity), pronounce the Latin formulae: *Ave Dominus Aquae vivae! Ave Dominus immortalis qui Christum fecisti et reduxisti!* (Hail, Lord of Living Water! Hail, Eternal Lord who made Christ and took him back.)

It was this corrective religious aspect of Carl's experiments and researches that had attracted the interest and attention of many—in particular, of the group accompanying him this morning.

Norman was reared a Lutheran, but in his late teens had rebelled against the traditionalism and conservative beliefs of his church. He became convinced that Luther was a wanton rebel and Lutheranism a mere sixteenth-century invention having very little to do with the original teaching of Christ and the first Christians.

Albert, Carl's second associate, was a former Episcopal priest. After three years in 'the ministry, he took up studies in psychology, convinced that his church was no longer speaking the language of modern people and no longer delivering the original message of salvation Christ had preached.

Of the four psychology majors, the group riding in the second limousine, two were Catholic—Donna and Keith; one, Bill, was Jewish. Charlie had been baptized in the Presbyterian Church, but had converted to Judaism two years previously. All four had been educated in the prevalent idea of their time that Western Christianity was a product of Greek philosophy and Roman legalism and organization, and the churches were shams and false representatives of the genuine church of Jesus.

The group's plan for this morning was quite simple. Without any fanfare or fuss, they intended to stand around Carl while he reenacted that ancient ritual over that particular medallion in the ancient floor of the cathedral. They had a tape recorder and movie camera. All Carl's words and gestures were to be recorded on tape and film. Norman, a close and longtime associate of Carl and a fellow psychologist, was to act as monitor: at each stage he would announce into the recorder what was happening during the visit, even as it was being filmed. They half-expected Carl to be able to uncover further evidence of Petrus and his ancient fellow believers. As psychologists, Carl and his companions hoped to obtain some new insights into the parapsychological from the experience.

Four and a half miles south of the Venice-Trieste freeway, they entered Aquileia. Everything was drenched in blinding sunlight. All colors were fused into the brightness of the day. Circumstances were favorable for Carl that morning in Aquileia. All trace of modern life and activity was dormant. On that summer festival of Neptune, the god of the sea, as they made their way slowly toward the cathedral, all living humans were asleep and hidden, as if Neptune had spread his net over them. Even the dogs and chickens were still asleep. A solitary cat licked and preened itself on a rooftop in the shadow of a chimney.

Maria touched Carl's hand, smiling. He responded to her expression of satisfaction with a quick smile, but he said nothing. They were all gazing out at the village streets as they rode toward the square. Houses, taverns, shops became indistinct shapes in the haze of heat and light. For those with eyes to see, this twentieth-century time frame was now transparent. In the boiling quiet they sensed the presence of ancient gods, of lisping shades, and of all those who once walked there in their pride, their sorrow, their loves, and their defeats.

The village was almost incongruously dominated by the huge cathedral and its spired campanile. Aquileia, a 2,000-year-old city, was once the fourth most important Roman city in the world, after Rome itself and Capua and Milan.

Then joined to the Adriatic by six canals, it was the only city outside Rome empowered to strike its own coins. The capital of a strategically and economically vital province, it was famous for its theater and its religious festivals, its celebration of mysteries, and its curative waters. It was the meeting place of Roman emperors, popes, synods; residence of its own patriarch; prized by German and Austrian kings; fought for by Slovenes, Huns, Avars, Greeks, Franks, English, Danes.

Now Aquileia is an obscure little farming community off the beaten track, a forgotten and inconsequential village not shown on general maps, and described by sardonic clerics in Rome as "a cathedral with some streets attached to it."

Carl's party drove directly to the cathedral; they had made arrangements with the guardian. As they got to the door, the student assistants began the "experiment." Donna started the movie camera, and Bill started the tape recorder. All was set. Every one of them was tense and expectant. A certain air of happy quest descended on them.

Their course now was to enter the cathedral, walk down its central nave, turn right at the sanctuary, and descend into the ruins of the fourth-century chapel.

Carl's behavior changed the moment he stepped out of the limousine. He was no longer smiling and relaxed. He had that "look" his associates had come to know so well—his eyes heavy-lidded and almost closed, the head lifted, hands hanging by his sides, and on his face a special glow of absorption and reverence they had come to associate with his "trances." There were hints of ecstasy and happiness at the corners of his mouth. The utter calm of rapture seemed to descend on him: his forehead and cheeks were utterly smooth, free of wrinkles and lines, as if the skin were suddenly made young again or drawn tight by an invisible hand.

But the general expression of his whole face was abstracted and bloodless. There was no hint of a personal expression, no indication of a word about to be pronounced or of a passion about to erupt, neither confidence nor fear, neither welcome nor hope of welcome, neither compassion nor expectation of compassion.

And around the eyes, in a way none of his associates and students could ever explain, there was what they had come to call the "twist"—some crookedness, some wry misshapenness, as if the natural contours of skull, forehead, eyes, and ears had been splayed out of kilter by some superhuman force residing in him temporarily with tremendous and awe-full power. It was ungainly and uncomely but accepted by those around him as inevitable. Carl always referred to it as "my divine suffering." For his theory—or rather his belief—was that during psychic trances a human being with an "open soul," as he used to phrase it, was "taken over," was "possessed" by the superhuman. The merely physical frame of that human being was overwhelmed—suffered, in that sense—by the inrush of silent divinity. The thin wall of reality separating the divine and the human was temporarily breached, and the human was "marinated" in the divine.

Now all waited. Carl had to move and talk. There must be no outside interruption, no external stimulus. The minutes ticked by. They still had not moved from the entrance. Carl's lips moved, but there was no audible sound. Then he shifted his stance, turning slowly in a half-circle, first toward the sea six miles away, then in the direction of Venice in a southwesterly direction. As he turned, he had a questioning expression on his face. He seemed to be waiting.

They heard scraps of words and sentences: ". . . the fourth canal . . . Via Postumia . . . must have the integral number of . . ."

But his voice sank to a whisper and died away completely by the time he was facing in the direction of Venice. On his face, there was now a look of thunder and bitterness. His lips were working furiously as if in heated argument or commentary. But they heard nothing. Again he turned around, to face the cathedral door.

"Now 0800," recorded Norman. "Carl is moving into the cathedral. His right hand is raised in salute, palm turned outward."

Carl's face was calm again. His lips had ceased to move. They entered a great golden-brown sea of silence, sunlight, and color arched over by the stone ribs of a roof that curved and soared away out of sight.

Then Carl headed straight down the 110-foot nave. Sixty-five feet wide, the floor was one whole ocean of mosaics flanked by solid columns on either side; it ended in a semidomed apse where the high altar stood. The sun's rays were pouring in through the nave windows and slanting down upon the expanse with dovetailing shafts of light and shadow. Dust shimmered in paths of light, flecking the air with colors of the mosaics and the surrounding walls, red, yellow, ochre, purple, orange, green.

For three-quarters of the nave the little group walked solemnly and steadily over that magic flooring teeming with designs of garlands, birds, animals, fish, ancient Romans, all glowing with deep tints and sophisticated forms.

Carl made only one detour: when he reached a particular medallion set in the floor, he paused. His lips were moving again: ". . . weakness . . . to prefer death to strength . . . prostituting humility of this weak . . ." Then in staccato repetition under his breath he uttered the old Roman words for Rome's cruel strength: *"Virtus, virtus, virtus, virtus . . ."*

Norman glanced at the medallion. "Carl is circling this mosaic of the Good Shepherd," he recorded.

Carl's own voice tapered off with whispered tones of disgust: ". . . braying   donkey . . . Alexander's   god . . . a   braying donkey . . ."

After this, Carl walked on calmly until he reached a broad mosaic band beyond which they saw a composite picture of the sea. The ancient artists had depicted boats, fishermen, fish of all sizes, sea serpents, dolphins, and a recurrent theme: Jonah, the Old Testament figure, in the mouth of a whale.

Carl's behavior became erratic at this point, and his face again mirrored anger together with confusion and contempt. He drew back with a low hiss of breath, his body almost crouching. Then he bobbed his head from side to side, as if seeking an exit between dangerous thorns.

Norman recorded, his voice stumbling as he followed Carl's changing course. "Carl is moving to the left. Slowly . . . now to the center, now to the right—no, he is moving leftwards again, stepping on a Jonah medallion." Then in an aside to Donna, who was still filming all of Carl's movements, "Move over in front of him, Donna, move up front, please." Donna did so.

Painfully, with sudden stops and cautious steps, Carl made his way up to the steps of the sanctuary. As Donna directed the camera at him, his eyes were wide open and blazing with an anger Donna had never seen in them. "Carl is turning back," Norman continued to record. "He is going toward the tunnel door." This tunnel led down to the fourth-century chapel over which the present cathedral was built in the eleventh century.

Donna was the first to reach the rectangular floor of the ancient chapel. She photographed the arrival of Carl, Norman, and the others. Carl now walked unerringly forward, but bowed his head several times as if acknowledging presences the others could not perceive.

The floor was another elaborate mass of Roman mosaics—pheasants, donkeys, fruits, pastoral figures and scenes, flowers. Carl did not stop until he reached a wide band of orange marble which ran the width of the chapel.

"Carl is standing at the orange band," Norman continued his recording. "Beyond it are many geometric designs."

After about 30 seconds, Carl's behavior changed. His face lit up. His head was lifted high. Both hands were outstretched. He stepped across the orange band and walked straight to a medallion lying just beyond the geometric designs. This was the spot where the ancient ritual was to be enacted. The medallion showed the Tortoise glaring up at the Rooster.

Carl's companions gathered around the medallion. Donna stood opposite Carl, the camera directed straight at him. "Carl's hands are joined, palm on palm, at his chest," Norman whispered into the microphone. "His eyes are closed. This is it."

No sooner had Norman said this than Carl opened his arms to full length on either side of him; he raised his head until his eyes were directed upward behind closed lids. His companions began to hear half words and syllables of that ancient incantation he had come to recite: *". . . aquae viv . . . immortalis . . ."* But he seemed to gag or stutter when he reached the word *"Christum."* He never fully pronounced it. It came out as *"Christ . . . Christ . . . Christ . . ."* (rhyming with "grist"). And as he stuttered over that first syllable, his voice got louder and louder, and his breathing became faster and more labored.

"Here, Bill, take the mike," Norman said quickly, "but hold it so that we can still catch my comments and his words." He had been instructed by Carl that, if there were any unforeseen block or difficulty, he was to take Carl lightly by the hand and guide him in on top of the Rooster.

Carl was still stuttering: *"Christ . . . Christ . . . Christ . . ."* Donna at her camera noticed the white foam gathering at the corners of his mouth. Norman reached out to take Carl's right hand in his. "God!" he exclaimed in a loud whisper, "his hand is like ice."

Carl was now struggling. He had ceased speaking. He was like a man trying to forge ahead and walk against a strong, buffeting wind. His hand trembled in Norman's, and his whole body vibrated in his effort to push onward, to step on to that Rooster in the mosaic medallion. His lips were drawn back over his teeth in the effort. The skin on his face tightened and whitened; and although he no longer spoke, there started in him a low moan like a man expelling his breath in a vast, heaving attempt to push past an obstacle.

Norman felt the icy cold entering his own fingers and hand, deadening all feeling there, loosening his grip on Carl.

The moaning rose in volume, changing to a growling, then increased in volume again until it resembled the shouting of a man through clenched teeth. Norman had let go of Carl's hand by now and was standing back, confused and dazed. The others had drawn back a few steps in apprehension at this unexpected turn of events. Carl was now alone, still facing Donna across that medallion.

At the height of that peculiar muffled shout from Carl, a change seemed to come over him; and the shock was too much for Donna. Suddenly, it seemed, what had been buffeting Carl closed in around him like an invisible cocoon. Some unseen bonds and wrappings tightened around his entire body, squeezing and narrowing him, binding him in a crunched fashion and bending him down lower and lower to the ground. He seemed to diminish in size. The expression of effort and straining rage on his face was replaced by a look of crushed, broken helplessness, almost of infantility. It was the look of one trying to draw into the smallest possible diameter of his own body.

Donna still held the camera in operation, but she whispered in panic: "Somebody help me! Please! Quick!" Nobody budged; they could not take their eyes off Carl. He was whining in an up-and-down fashion, as if pain and struggle had emptied him. It was a protest against agony. All this became too much for Donna. The camera slid from her fingers to the floor. And the last shot taken of Carl shows him bending forward, his hands locked tightly across his chest, his head twisted to one side, eyes closed, his tongue between his teeth, and an expression of resignation, defeat, and repose on his face—the same that many have seen on those who have been garroted or drowned. It was an emptied-out look.

The clattering fall of Donna's camera broke the frozen fascination of the others. Bill and two students finally rushed to help Donna. Norman and the others lifted Carl up. As they did, his body relaxed from its rigid posture and he was carried limp and unconscious out into the open air.

All were perspiring and shaken. Carl's body was cold. They poured some drops of whisky between his lips, and he began to recover. After a while, he breathed normally and opened his eyes.

"Carl," Norman spoke quietly, "Carl, it will be better if we go on to Venice now."

A little over a week later, back in New York, Carl was far from all right. Even after a few days rest in Venice and Milan, and the long flight home, Carl was still in a dazed condition that none of his associates could understand. He was no longer the commanding, self-possessed, and self-confident leader he had been. He ate and slept fitfully, talked very little, canceled all his scheduled appointments.

Carl seemed to be reliving again and again the scene in Aquileia, always in the same way: he muttered and talked, sometimes strode around the house and garden reenacting each step of that disastrous morning. And always, at the crucial moment, he went into the same queer seizure. It was Donna who remarked one day that he seemed to her to be trying to carry the Aquileia incident past that difficult moment at the medallion.

Finally Norman and Albert called Carl's father in Philadelphia. Carl was taken home. A long rest was prescribed by the family doctor.

There was no suspicion in anyone's mind that Carl was possessed or in the process of possession, until one night when only Carl and his father were sleeping alone in the big house. His father was suddenly wakened from sleep. Carl stood by his bedside, crying quietly. He spoke very clearly, although not all he said seemed coherent to his father. He evidently wanted help from a priest. He named him: Father Hartney F., who lived in Newark, New Jersey. And Carl wanted his father to call the priest then and there. It was after midnight, but his father was sufficiently alarmed to call the priest. Father was out, his housekeeper said; she would give the message to him when he returned.

Carl's father had just hung up when there occurred one of many peculiar apparent coincidences that marked the case of Carl V. The telephone rang. The man's voice at the other end was level and pleasant. He announced himself as Father F. Yes, he would like to see Carl; that was why he was calling. No, he was not in New Jersey; he was in Philadelphia. No, he had not been contacted by his housekeeper.

"Mr. V., I must ask you to trust me as a man and as a priest. I have something to say to your son which is for his ears only." His father looked at Carl, then handed him the telephone. Carl appeared to listen, tears flowing, his face drawn. All he said was "Yes" a few times; then a slow "Tomorrow. All right." He hung up and, without looking at his father, turned slowly away and left the room.

Carl spent three weeks in New York with Father F., for a first round of pre-exorcism tests. He was back home by late August. During September and October he commuted frequently from Philadelphia to Newark and New York. At the beginning of November the exorcism began.

CARL V.

Although there are many in the field of parapsychology who deplore the disappearance of Carl V. from their midst, very few are acquainted with the circumstances in which he finally renounced all research and study of this very modern branch of knowledge. Carl was already a brilliant psychologist when he turned to parapsychology. Many who knew him and his gifts predicted that he was the right man in the right place at the right time doing exactly what needed to be done. They could see the premature termination of Carl's career, therefore, only as unfortunate, a loss to the cause of true humanism.

Carl was not only very intelligent. He apparently possessed to an eminent degree some psychic gifts that are highly valued nowadays and the object of much research, such powers as telepathy and telekinesis. He found, in addition, a suitable academic location where he could exercise and study those gifts. Within that ambient he was surrounded by men and women of talent, students of ability and acumen. And, to cap his potential, there were two or three major events in his personal life that placed him in a category all by himself.

There was first a vision he had had as a teenager. There was, too, unexpected support of his general ideas about parapsychology from an unusually reputable quarter with the appearance of Aldous Huxley's book *The Doors of Perception* in 1954. In addition, Carl himself enjoyed altered states of consciousness at various levels for almost ten years (1962–72). As early as 1965 he began to have constant perceptions of the "aura" surrounding objects—the "non-thing aura," as he called it. Finally he achieved his first "exaltation" (his own term) in 1969.

In retrospect, Carl himself now assumes that, while his "exaltation" had a definite psychic character, at its core it was the threshold of diabolic possession.

But in the meanwhile, what gave a particular cachet to Carl's career was the scrutiny of admiring colleagues who were applying their scientific principles precisely to such phenomena as altered states of consciousness, visions, astral travel, telepathy, telekinesis, reincarnation.

What added a new dimension in Carl's case and in his own work was the authentically religious bent of his mind. Carl V. did, indeed, set out to find the truth about religion, Christianity, in particular. And the combination of psychic gifts, the extraordinary progress of what seemed to be his personal powers, and his religious leanings all gave him a peculiarly commanding appeal in the late 1960s and early 1970s. For in the decadence of organized and institutional religion people had begun to switch their active interest to parapsychology as a possible source of religious knowledge and even of wisdom.

Indeed, as far as human judgment can go, we can only surmise that

Carl should have achieved much in his chosen field if his life had not been upset by diabolic possession and the consequent exorcism.

There was little that distinguished Carl either from his two brothers or from his school companions during his early childhood. His family had plenty of money and enjoyed considerable influence in their hometown of Philadelphia. The family was Mainline Protestant and worshiped at the Episcopal church. Carl's growing-up was not particularly difficult. No misfortunes or tragedies hit the family. Neither the Depression nor World War II affected it very adversely. Carl did well in school and at sports. He traveled a good deal with his family, visiting Europe, South America, and Hawaii at various times.

The first manifestations of any extraordinary psychic gifts came slowly, and only gradually did his parents realize that Carl had capacities beyond the ordinary. When Carl was between seven and eight, they began to notice that when, for instance, his father or mother were looking for something—a newspaper, a pen, a glass of water—more often than not Carl would appear almost immediately carrying what they needed.

They put this down to coincidence at first. But then it became so frequent and, at times, so eerie that they set out to determine whether it *was* merely coincidence. After some weeks of close and discreet observation, they concluded that Carl did know in some way or other what they were thinking at times.

They might have brushed even this aside if they had not one day overheard his brothers asking Carl to bend some nails. Obligingly Carl bent and twisted two one-inch nails by "feeling" them with his index finger and thumb.

Carl's father consulted a psychologist. A long series of discussions followed. Carl was brought by his parents to that psychologist, to another psychologist, and to a psychiatrist. The unanimous decision, after some testing, was that the child had incipient psychic gifts of telepathy and telekinesis. They maintained that he should not be made to feel out of the ordinary. His parents should endeavor to get him to recognize his gifts as nonordinary and to restrict their usage.

The difficulty with all this decision making behind Carl's back totally escaped Carl's parents and even the psychologists. For, without realizing fully its implications, Carl knew what they all thought and knew their decision. In a subtle recess of his child's mind he decided to go along with the entire plan. But from that day on there began in him that "aloneness" that marked him in later life.

Carl obeyed his father's suggestion that he bend no more nails, that he no longer tell people what they were thinking, and that he take no more initiative due to any telepathic knowledge he had of their wishes. By his eleventh year, as far as his parents could see, all manifestation of psychic powers seemed to have ceased in his external life.

But, in reality, Carl had now got a command over these powers in himself that no one realized and that he guarded almost as a jealous and lonely secret. Only occasionally did he slip. In a fit of temper he might smash a cup in another room or shout at a companion some boyish insult to match the insult the boy was about to launch.

In spite of this continued connivance on his part, Carl's excellent relationships with his father and mother were genuine. In later years, after his parents divorced, Carl remained closest to his father.

As the eldest child, Carl was looked upon by his two brothers, Joseph and Ray, with something approaching awe. The three of them had an intimacy and openness with each other that lasted beyond childhood. It was within that framework of boyhood intimacy that he told Joseph and Ray of his vision at the age of sixteen.

From their accounts and Carl's recollections, it appears that the vision took place in his father's library one evening as Carl was preparing his homework. He glanced at the clock. Dinner was served punctually at six o'clock each evening. He had, he saw, one minute to go, just enough time to find a particular volume of the *Encyclopaedia Britannica* and open it to the article he needed for his written composition.

After he found the information he was looking for, his consciousness underwent a peculiar change. He was not frightened; instead, the change put him in what he describes as a great hush. He no longer saw the book in his hand or the shelves of books in front of him. He no longer even felt the weight of the volume in his hand. He did not feel the floor beneath his feet. But he did not miss them. They seemed no longer necessary.

He did not perceive all this directly. Only on the periphery of his consciousness was he aware of perceptual changes and of his lack of any need for physical feeling of his surroundings. His attention was riveted on something else, something totally different from, but in a mysterious way intimate to, all his experience up to that moment of his life.

It was, first of all, an atmosphere. There was much light, but, he says, a dark light. Yet, that darkness was so brilliant that no detail escaped him. He was not *looking at* something or *at* a landscape; he was *participating in it*, so clear was every detail shown and conveyed to him. What he saw was dimensionless: no "over there," no "up" or "down" or "large" or "small." Yet it was a place. Objects were in that place, but the place was nowhere. And the objects located in that space were not found by coordinates, or seen by the eye, or felt by the hand. He knew them, as it were, by *participation* in their being. He knew them *completely*. Therefore, he knew what they were and where they were. And even though they had a relationship to him and to each other, it was not a relationship of space and distance and comparative sizes.

Not only was normal spatial dimension in abeyance as nonextended time. It was not that time seemed to be suspended. There was *no* time, *no* duration. He was not looking at the objects for a long or a short time—it could not have been seconds. Neither could it have been an infinity of hours or years. There was no sense of duration. It was timeless. Yet he did clearly, if indirectly, perceive a time. But it was, again, an internal time and seemed to be the total existence of himself and of all those objects without perceptible or receding beginning, and without an ending or an approaching ending.

As for a description of that landscape and the objects "in" it, Carl could only speak vaguely. It was a "land," he said, a "countryside," a "region." It had all you would expect—mountains, sky, fields, crops, trees, rivers. But these lacked what Carl called the "obscurity" of their counterparts in the physical world. And, athough it had no apparent houses or cities, it was "inhabited": it was full of an "inhabiting presence." There was no sound or echo, but the soundlessness was not a silence, and the echolessness was not an absence of movement. It seemed to Carl for the first time he was freed from the oppression of silence and rid of the nostalgia produced in him by echoes.

As he took all this in, or as he was embraced by all this—he could never distinguish exactly which was a truer way of speaking—there was in him a sudden desire. That desire had a purity and a sacred immunity that freed it of any aching and did not imply a want in a way we normally understand. It was a summary appeal, but without request. It was desire as its own confirmation. It was substantial hope as its own trust. Yet it *was* desire. He would describe it at times as a "Show me!" or a "Give me!" or a "Take me!" or a "Lead me!" arising in him. But, he said, none of these expressed the bones and marrow of that desire. And over all his desire and desiring self there was an all-satisfying acceptance and acceptability.

Then the whole focus of his vision changed. It was the highlight of his real wonder. He was listening to a small voice and seeing a face he cannot describe. He heard words and saw expressions he cannot put into language. The dominant trait of the voice and face was expressed by him later in the word "Wait!" He did not know what that "Wait!" meant or what he was to wait for. But the whole idea was intensely and deeply satisfying.

Carl does not know if the vision would have "lasted" and carried him farther or not, for he was suddenly jerked out of it. "You've exactly one minute to finish." It was little Ray. "Hurry up!"

An immense sadness welled up in Carl at that moment, an indescribable sense of loss. He saw the cold books, the long, hard shelves, and his little brother's face. He felt the volume in his hands and the floor beneath his feet. He glanced at the clock. It was one minute to six o'clock.

As he hurried to his table, he had tears in his eyes. But, afterward, he could not make out whether they were tears of pain or thankfulness. He never knew.

Before going to bed, he confided in Joseph and Ray. "Perhaps it was Grandma telling you something," Ray suggested helpfully. Their grandmother had died the previous year. "No," said Joseph, "it was from God. They told us in Sunday school that God sends these things to show you what's going to happen."

Carl often wondered subsequently about this unique event in his life. What was he to wait for? Who or what had been talking to him? What had he been so desirous of at that moment? But, in spite of these questionings, the vision remained in his memory with a sweetness that nothing could dispel. And it made one subtle difference in him which many noticed but few understood. In his own mind it separated him from all others. He was never quite "with" others, never fully together with them. At parties, dinners, meetings, lectures, he would see himself essentially separate from the others and on the sidelines.

He was, indeed, waiting. Only years later did he know what it was he had been told in the vision to expect.

Carl entered Princeton in 1942, got his master's degree in psychology in 1947, his doctorate in 1951, spent six more years studying and doing research. Four of those years saw him in the United States and two in Europe. He returned only in 1957, to take up a permanent teaching post on a Midwest university campus. In those 15 years, from 1942 to 1957, some major changes took place in him.

The first and probably one of the most important was due to the influence of a fellow student, a Tibetan, Olde by name, whom Carl met in 1953. Olde gave Carl a firsthand introduction to "higher prayer," as Olde called it.

Olde had been born in Tibet, reared there until the age of ten, then educated in Switzerland and Germany, and had come to the United States for doctoral studies. He claimed to be a member of an ancient Tibetan religious order, *The Gelugpa* ("The Virtuous"), and that he himself, as his father before him, was one of the *sprulsku* or reincarnating lamas.

Olde's first personal conversation with Carl took place when Carl happened to hear Olde reading a précis of the thesis he was writing. The subject was the relationship between Yamantaka, the god of wisdom, and Yama, the god of Hell. Carl asked in all innocence why statues of Yamantaka always showed the god with 34 arms and 9 heads. Olde's answer, a seeming nonsequitur, struck a strange echo in Carl. It was one answer Carl never forgot:

"The more arms and the more heads Yamantaka is seen with, the more you can see the *other*. And only the *other* is real."

The *other*? The *other*? The *other*? Didn't he know the *other*? What or who was the *other*?

Carl looked at Olde. And he understood quietly without effort: each extra arm, each extra head was meant to make nonsense, literally, of an arm and a head as a real thing. Any *thing*, an arm, a head, a chair, a leaf, any *thing* in itself was unimportant, was significant and real only because of an other, the *other*. Thingness was in itself a negation. It was the non-thing that mattered, because only the non-thing was real. And he seemed to see also that this was why, ever since his vision, he had had a tendency to withdraw, to remain on the sidelines, away from involvement with things, removed from being wholly occupied with their thingness.

In a gentle dawning within him Carl felt a surge of the same sadness that had gripped him when little Ray had burst in on him years before and his vision had been rudely terminated. "It [that moment with Olde] was the most maturing moment of my life up to that point," Carl muses in retrospect today. For, during it, he felt again not only that sadness, but his ancient boyhood desire, felt all the pains of nostalgia as a most acceptable suffering, and at the same time heard again down the corridors of his memory that still, calm, reassuring "Wait" replete with its promise and guarantee of fulfillment.

Carl and Olde saw much of each other. And before long Olde was initiating Carl into "higher prayer." From his own family life and Sunday schooling, Carl had learned the ordinary modes of prayer. It consisted of set prayers, hymns, and the occasional spontaneous self-expression used during grace at meals or when he prayed in private.

Olde overturned all Carl's ideas and habits. Words, he said, and, even more importantly, concepts impede "higher prayer" and all true communication with what Carl as a Christian called "God" and what Olde called the "All." Carl, he said, would have to train himself for "higher prayer."

Day after day, Carl sat beside Olde, while Olde trained him in the basic attitudes of body and "tones" of mind. The conditions of body were simple to grasp. Quietness (early morning before sunrise or late at night when no sound disturbed the campus), elimination of any distraction—a comfortable sitting position, loose clothes on his body, as little light as possible. But all this and the steps still to come were merely preparatory and temporary. Olde explained that, if Carl progressed, he would leap definitively over all physical difficulties to "higher prayer." And he would be able to "pray" while surrounded by 20 jackhammers pounding away in the middle of a bronze-walled room. (This was Olde's image.)

Carl quickly attained the required physical quietude and concentration. The next steps took time—and they ushered Carl to the threshold of parapsychology. As Olde explained it, Carl had to be clear and clean of any "thingness." It was easy for Carl to understand how to void his imagination of images, how to close off his memory so that no memory images passed in front of his mind, and how to eliminate even the most peripheral image consciousness of his body position, of the clothes on his body, of the warmth or the cold of the atmosphere around him, of his own breathing. But for quite a while he balked at the ultimate step. Olde instructed him that at this point he might go around in circles forever and never get any farther at all. Most people, in fact, did just that.

The ultimate step was to eliminate his own conscious realization of—therefore his concepts and images of and feelings about—his very condition at that moment of prayer. For a long time he had no control over his mind to keep himself from realizing he was emptying his mind; and he had no control over his will, with which he kept *desiring* to empty his mind. It all seemed a vicious circle. You disciplined your mind to think no thoughts, your imagination to indulge in no images, your feelings not to feel. And you did this by your will. But then, it appeared to Carl, his mind was full of the idea "I must have no thoughts." His imagination kept seeking images of itself without images. His feelings kept feeling that they had no feelings. Around and around he used to gyrate until he emerged tired and strained and disappointed.

"Don't give up," Olde consoled him. He told him it could be worse and that he was sure Carl would one day find the secret—a mere, a tiny, an almost unnoticeable adjustment. "When you make it, you will know." He repeated these same words again and again to Carl.

But for quite a while Carl made the summary mistake of *trying* to make the "adjustment." He did not and could not know that, if you made that peculiar "adjustment," you simply made it. Not with your mind, not with your will, not with your imagination or memory, but you as a thinking, willing, imagining, remembering self. All your thingness suddenly of itself became a transparency through which the non-thing, the other, clearly appeared. And once through that stage, you entered a shadowless, formless, thingless region of existence where only reality reigned, and your unreality, your thingness had no vogue, no role, except as the counterpart of allness.

The moment Carl achieved that condition of "higher prayer," Olde abruptly terminated their association. "Now, when you want to pray, really to pray," Olde concluded his instructions, "you know how to do so."

It was Carl's last year at Princeton as a doctoral student. He had more leisurely years of study and research in front of him before he took up a university career. He was avid to go on under Olde's direction; and as Olde was staying on as lecturer and researcher at the university, Carl could see no problem.

But Olde would have no more of him. Why? This was Carl's question to Olde as they walked over the campus in the early mornings. Why?

Olde would say very little. He had, he admitted, introduced Carl to the *Vajnayana*, "the thunderbolt," the vehicle of mystic power. But no persuasion on earth would get him to channel Carl further in

Mantrayana, the vehicle of mystic spells. "What I have done is enough," Olde grunted. Then as an afterthought: "What I have done is dangerous enough."

Carl still could not understand. He persisted, asking Olde to explain or, if he could not explain, at least to suggest a direction for him.

Finally one day Olde seemed to have no more answers. Every soul, he said, which turns to the perfection of Allness is like a closed-petaled lotus flower in the beginning of its search. Under the direction of a master or guide, it opens its eight petals slowly. The master merely assists at this opening. When the petals are open, the tiny silver urn of true knowledge is placed in the center of the lotus flower. And when the petals close in again, the whole flower has become a vehicle of that true knowledge.

Looking away from Carl, Olde said gratingly, almost inimically: "The silver urn can never be placed at the center of your flower. The center is already taken by a self-multiplying negation." A pause. "Filth. Materiality. Slime. Death."

Carl was stunned, literally struck dumb for an instant. Olde walked away from him, still without looking at him. He was about five paces away when Carl broke down. He could only manage a choking exclamation: "Olde! My friend! Olde!"

Olde stopped, his back to Carl. He was utterly calm, motionless, wordless. Then Carl heard him say in a low voice and not particularly to him: "Friend is holy." Carl did not understand what he meant.

Then Olde turned slowly around. Carl hardly recognized Olde's features. They were no longer the soft traits of his friend. Olde's forehead was no longer a furrowless expanse as before, and his eyes were blazing with a yellowish light. Harsh lines crisscrossed his mouth and cheeks. He was not angry. He was hostile. That picture of Olde was burned into Carl's memory. Olde said only this to Carl, words Carl could never forget: "You have Yama without Yamantaka. Black without white. Nothingness without something." It was the last time he ever spoke directly to Carl.

As Olde turned away again, Carl had a sudden reversal. He seemed for a few instants to be absorbed in "higher prayer." His surge of frustration and anger gave away to contempt and disgust for Olde. Then as he looked at Olde's retreating back, he was filled with a warning fear of Olde and what Olde stood for. Somehow Olde was the enemy. Somehow he, Carl, made up a "we" and "us" with someone else, and Olde could not belong to it.

"Enemy!" he suddenly heard himself shouting after Olde.

Olde stopped, half-turned, and peered over his shoulder at Carl. His face was back to its usual repose. His forehead, cheeks, and mouth were unruffled and smooth. His eyes were calm, wide open, just gentle deeps of impenetrable light, as they usually were. The compassion in them hit Carl like a whip. He did not want anybody's compassion. He took a step back, wanted to speak, but could not get any word out of his throat. He backed away another step, half-turning away, then another step and another half-turn, until he literally *found* himself moving away. He told himself he had walked away, but deep in himself he knew he had been repelled, had been turned around and propelled away.

Apparently Olde too had his own protectors.

His association with Olde had important effects on Carl. Given his psychic gifts, it was almost inevitable that Olde's introduction to Eastern mysticism, with its emphasis on the parapsychological, would impel Carl down a road of research in the then relatively fresh field of parapsychology and the paranormal elements of human consciousness.

Over and above all else, Carl's time with Olde had sharpened his extrasensory ability to perceive other people's thoughts. Before his instructions from Olde, Carl did not always know each and every thought of those around. More generally, he knew very accurately their state of mind—worry, happiness, fear, love, hate, and so on; and, on occasion, he knew precisely what they were thinking. Olde's discipline had brought that more precise part of Carl's extrasensory perception into greater use and control. He found it working more frequently with everybody. And soon he was exercising it at will.

After his "training" with Olde, there were apparently only two people during Carl's university career who remained peculiarly "opaque" for him. He could never read their thoughts, and he rarely knew their inner condition. The first was a onetime girlfriend, Wanola P. The second was Father Hartney F. ("Hearty"), a priest who was sent by his bishop to study parapsychology.

In 1954, one year after his break with Olde, Carl met Wanola P., a graduate student in psychology. A tall, blonde, attractive Midwestern girl, Wanola was a good sportswoman, socially quite popular. Curiously, it was none of these things that attracted Carl, but rather a mixture of her unusual intelligence, her point of view regarding his work on religion and the psyche, and, most of all perhaps, his own inability to get any clear extrasensory perception of what she thought or felt.

As they began to date, Wanola got to know something of Carl's psychic gifts. She was fascinated by them, by his novel concepts, and his brilliant attack on various puzzles and problems of psychology. But as she got to know him, her fascination turned to compassion, and then to a fear for Carl's own sanity and for his religious beliefs. It was like a curious echo of Olde's reaction a year before, but it all went much more swiftly this time. And his rather brief association with Wanola left Carl puzzled.

At times, Wanola spoke to Carl at length about some seemingly offhand remarks he made about "finding" Christianity in its "true" or "original" state. She remarked on his growing opinion of Jesus as a simple Galilean fisherman who had been powerfully changed by God and by his taking over of God's spirit. But mainly she grew to be disturbed by Carl's ambition to subject the very spirit of religion to controlled laboratory experiment.

Finally one day, just back from a short vacation home to the Midwest, Wanola came to Carl's room straight from the airport. She had a simple bouquet of wild flowers she had picked herself before catching her plane. Curiously, Carl remembers those flowers in every detail, although he says that at the very moment Wanola entered his room and started to talk with him, his interest and attention were elsewhere. He does remember blue gentians, dogtooth violets, little-boys' breeches, starflowers, and Queen Anne's lace.

But when Wanola walked in with them, Carl did not give her even a smile or a hello. He was brandishing a small book just published: *The Doors of Perception*, by Aldous Huxley. She remembers him blurting out the title. Then: "Huxley knows all about it! Mescalin! And I don't need mescalin!"

Wanola listened to his long sermon on Huxley; and when she left, she took the bouquet of flowers with her.

Carl had made a delicate choice; he had taken a step away from simple human tenderness. This he understood only after the exorcism. Wanola had understood at that moment. He called her from time to time after that day, but to his confusion she never would see him again.

Carl's excitement over Huxley's book was enormous. He grasped immediately the central point advanced by Huxley: that the mind and

psyche are capable of a knowledge and a breadth of experience of
which men in our civilization have rarely dreamed. Living in our
urban society, the human psyche has learned to siphon its energies in
one direction—coping with the material and tangible world. Huxley
made a plea in his book for the development of a psychedelic (literally,
a psyche-opening) drug, nonaddictive and harmless in its side-effects,
by which men and women could free their psychic energies and enjoy
the full range of their potential.

Carl, in the middle of his studies on dual personality, suddenly
found in Huxley a window opened for him onto a new horizon.
Perhaps, he now saw, what is often called a multiple-personality
problem really was a case of psyche freed—particularly at least—from
conventional bonds? Perhaps at least some so-called schizophrenics
were really enlightened people for whom the shock of enlightenment
has been too much? And perhaps such people exist in an altered state
of consciousness with which they could transcend the material and
tangible world around them, leap over the barriers of space and time,
and enjoy genuine liberty of spirit?

This was an important moment in Carl's development. What Huxley
had attempted and, with the aid of mescalin, achieved piecemeal, Carl
now aimed at achieving by developing and controlling his own psychic
gifts.

Thinking back, as he sometimes did, about the vision he had had as
a boy in his father's study, he now saw that vision as a foretaste of
what he could and should achieve: a perception of spirit, a participation in spaceless and timeless existence reached by a parapsychological
path. The aim of all Olde's instructions now appeared to Carl to be
simply a liberation of the mind and will from any involvement with
sensory experiences and material trammels. It was no wonder that
Wanola's disappearance from his personal life gave him no sense of
loss. In effect, she would have had to go, he concluded. There was no
room in his life now for a personal attachment that would involve
emotions and the physical presence of another human being.

Although Carl's study of parapsychology had begun in 1953 through
his association with Olde, it was about five years later that this interest
took on a consistently religious character. After two years of study and
research in Europe, he returned to the United States at the end of
1957, in order to take up a post as lecturer in the Midwest at the
beginning of 1958.

It was an attractive appointment for Carl: it gave him a good deal of latitude for research. He found a small apartment not very far from the campus and was given perfect space for his professional needs in the department of psychology. There his life would be centered. He had a reception room, a study for himself, and, opening off his study, there was a room large enough for seminars, private lectures, and experiments.

By the following year, Carl was well settled and had attracted a small and enthusiastic group of assistants from among his better students.

One evening, quite unexpectedly and while alone, Carl had the first of what he and his associates later called "trances." He had just returned to his office from dinner at a colleague's house. It was about 7:30 P.M. He had a great sense of tranquillity and confidence.

When he entered his study from the reception room, his eye fell on the window facing west. The sun had not yet set, but there were incandescent patches and streaks to be seen in the sky. The whole window space looked like a two-panel canvas painted in reds, oranges, blue-grays, gilded whites.

Carl crossed to the window, and as he gazed at the sunset, there was a gentle but rapid transformation in him. His body became motionless, as if held painlessly immobile by an unseen giant hand. He was frozen, yet without any sensation of cold or paralysis.

Then the living scene outside took on the same odd aspect of immobility and frozenness for him. Next, parts of the scene started to disappear. First of all, everything in the intervening space between the window where Carl stood and the sunset disappeared: quadrangle, buildings, lawns, the road, the trees and shrubbery. It was not as if they just remained on the periphery of his seeing. They altogether ceased to be there for him. If he were to look for them, he knew at that moment, he would not be able to find them. All seemed to have been plucked out of sight. And their disappearance seemed to him to be more normal than their permanency there in front of his eyes. For a moment he felt very much at ease, for all the bizarre nature of what was happening.

And, of course, the *distance* between him and the sunset was now a formless vacuum after the disappearance of the objects on his landscape. There was nothing "between" him and the sunset, not even a gap, not even emptiness. He was no nearer to the sunset physically, yet now he was knowing it intimately.

Finally the window itself faded. Carl, meanwhile, had been looking less and less at the colors and hues of the dying sun; and, when the window frame faded, he was "looking merely at the sun," although he cannot express clearly in words the difference between those two sights or the obvious importance it had for him at that moment.

Finally the viewed—what he was viewing—seemed to loom larger and larger in his consciousness, but he himself seemed to be diminishing correspondingly. Smaller. Smaller.

A sudden panic arose in him that he, too, might "disappear" from his own consciousness, just as all the landscape had disappeared. That, he was sure, would mean nothingness for him. And, as the viewed loomed larger and more gargantuan in its weird nonphysical way, the more miserable and expendable he felt.

At this low ebb in his feelings Carl experienced the initial stirrings of what he later came to call "my friend." He always insisted that this "friend" was personal—a person, but not a physical person. "It was a personal presence," he maintained. It did not seem to "come" to him, but to have been there all along; yet it was unexpected, and he had never noticed it before that moment.

No words passed "between" Carl and his "friend," and no concepts or images that he was aware of. But he knew with absolute certainty he was being "told" that, unless he "nodded" or "gave approval," his progress into nothingness would be a fact.

The anguish this possibility caused him was awful. Still, some aspect of that personal presence seemed "deficient," seemed to leave him with an option to say no. He had one brief, strange impulse to challenge the absolutist demand for consent now being made upon him. But a rapid confusion as strange as the whole incident dulled the impulse to fight: *he did not know how to issue the challenge.* In the name of what power would he "speak"? In whose name would he bear the consequences, and how could he survive them? He says now for a long time he had nourished no idea of aid or help or salvation, and he had "no one or nothing to turn to or call upon." He had been brought to nearly total aloneness, indeed, to the brink of nothingness.

Easily, therefore, and with relief, he "nodded." He gave his interior approval. He still did not know exactly what this approval concerned.

Immediately the sense of being reduced to nothingness ceased. Relief flooded his consciousness. Almost simultaneously he heard a voice calling from a great distance.

"Carl! Carl! Are you all right? Carl!"

The window "reappeared" and the landscape. The sunset "withdrew," and his vision was normal once again.

He stirred and looked around. Albert, one of his young assistants, had a hand on his shoulder. Neither of them said anything for the moment. They waited until the sun was completely down. Then, while Albert listened, Carl sat down and dictated into his recording machine.

What now emerged surprised even Carl. He spoke of the entire trance as God-manifesting, as a religious experience. Turning to Albert at one stage, and still dictating, he declared that he now saw his life's work to be the finding of true spirit-life and an accurate knowledge of God and his revelation—all by means of parapsychological research.

Carl's course was set. For the next five years he would work steadily and methodically, building his theories, testing and developing his own psychic powers, nourishing a group of students and assistants around him.

In 1963 Carl became acquainted with the second person in his university career who remained "opaque" to his psychic perceptions. Father Hartney F. came into Carl's orbit almost ten years after Wanola P., almost eleven years after Olde.

It was in the fall semester. Carl had just been made a full professor. Father Hartney F. (or "Hearty," as he was called by his friends) was the one member of the new class whom Carl could not quite understand or "grasp" psychically. As had been the case with Wanola P. a decade before, Carl's inability to get any "inner perceptions" of Hearty intrigued him.

Hearty, however, looked completely normal, even innocuous. A large, bony man rapidly going bald at that moment of his life, and wearing thick-lensed spectacles, Hearty sat in the second row, looking at Carl intently and taking notes from time to time. He always wore a Roman collar and an impeccably clean black suit. During lectures he rarely stirred, looked around him, or asked a question.

After Hearty's first term paper, which was no better and no worse than average, and would not normally have provoked special interest in Carl, Carl took the occasion to interview his "opaque" student.

He found the priest to be at heart a very simple man with a better than average memory, robust health, thorough grounding in the basics of psychology, and an ambition to study parapsychology for what he called "pastoral purposes." Apparently he had convinced his bishop that a knowledge of parapsychology would be particularly helpful in working with his co-religionists and for understanding some of their problems.

Offhand and, as it were, by the way, Hearty mentioned to Carl some cases of diabolic possession. And he also spoke of Exorcism. At the time it seemed to arouse very little interest in Carl's mind. He brushed the topic aside into the back of his mind, so to speak, with some remarks about the need of updating beliefs and rites in the Church.

Apparently having observed as much as he could or cared to after a fairly short time, Carl ended the interview with a brief criticism of some technical points in Hearty's term paper.

But Carl remained intrigued, and he was not unsympathetic when two of his students, Bill and Donna, who were later to go with Carl to Aquileia, suggested that they bring Hearty into a special study group Carl had formed. Their argument was that the group needed a trained representative of some Christian community because one of the group's deeper objectives was to experiment with Carl's psychic powers and gifts in order to probe the past of Christianity. Now, Hearty was the only student in the department at that time who was a cleric and who was trained in theology.

Carl decided to have another interview with this opaque cleric before inviting him into the study group. He asked his two assistants, Albert and Norman, together with the student members of the special group, to be with him.

Hearty was a very easygoing man, very affable, a little slow to make up his mind. As Albert and Norman listened to Carl's questions and Hearty's answers, they had a growing persuasion that Carl was getting nowhere. Hearty was not resisting. He was not even being evasive or vague. It was just that, in spite of his perfectly frank answers to all the questions put to him, Hearty seemed to be immune to Carl's persuasion. And the reason for this was not any mental opposition on Hearty's part or any verbal clashes between the two men. It was something else.

All present would probably have put the problem down to a fundamental difference in temperament between the two if it had not been for one unfortunate turn in their conversation, when Hearty seemed to take over the direction of the interview. Hearty wanted to understand what basis there was for assuming, as Carl seemed obviously to be doing, that psychic knowledge and psychic activity inevitably led to spirit.

Albert conceded that it was a presupposition, but an acceptable one.

Then Hearty wanted to know if that meant that psychic knowledge and psychic activity were under the direction of the spirit?

Again, the answer was yes.

Well, then, it seemed Hearty had still another problem: unless they claimed prior knowledge—which they didn't (of course not, they all acknowledged; wasn't that, after all, why they *had* study groups: to find out what they didn't know?), how could they be sure they were under the direction or influence of a *good* spirit? Or did they presume that all spirit was good? And if so, on what basis?

These questions represented such a fundamental doubting of the position Carl shared with his group that the peace of the meeting was shattered. As one of those present recalled, up to that moment in the meeting "we had not known how pervaded our minds were with one outlook [Carl's]." It felt, for Albert and Norman, as if some accepted guest or some presence accepted among them had been insulted and had started to grumble in resentment.

All of them started to question Hearty at one and the same time. Carl held up his hand for silence. He was perfectly calm, but his eyes were glittering and his face was very pale. Hearty's "opaqueness" had become transparent to Carl, for only that time and only for those moments. Hearty was deeply opposed, Carl now understood, to all that Carl stood for.

But Carl was cool; he was composed and self-controlled. All students, he admonished his assistants, were free. And all points of view were allowed. Moreover, Father F. (he stressed the "Father") had a professional basis for his opinion.

Hearty quietly broke in to add that Carl, too, had a professional basis for his position. There was an unexpected silence. For that moment, some of the opaqueness of Hearty's psyche had been dispelled, but Carl could not quite make out what he perceived dimly in Hearty. Then Hearty "closed" up on him. He was "opaque" once again.

Carl gave a deprecating smile and made a little gesture, as if to go on to explain the professional basis of Hearty's opinion. But he stopped and knitted his eyebrows. Every member of the group felt a new tension in that silence. Hearty looked steadily at Carl.

Carl recomposed himself and looked pleasantly at Hearty. "And what, Father," Carl finally said, "is your professional basis? In short, I mean."

"Jesus. Jesus Christ, sir. As God and as man." Then, without pausing, Hearty asked lightly: "And yours, Professor?"

Carl dismissed the query. Perhaps, he said, Father F. would become a subject for group study some day as he, Carl, had already become. In the meantime, they would table for the time being the motion of his entry into the special study group.

The tension was gone.

From time to time during the remaining two years of Hearty's studies, Carl racked his brains as to the "opaque" character of Hearty's psyche. What did Hearty and Wanola P. have in common? Suppose, indeed, that there was both good and evil spirit? But no sooner would he put himself that question than the entire panorama of his life would flood his mind; and always he ended with what was for him an unacceptable alternative. A doubt of the fundamental point as to what kind of spirit was leading him would mean a total revision of his work. How could he do that? It could even mean resigning his professorship and renouncing his parapsychological research.

In June 1964, after his final exams and thesis, Hearty had a short farewell talk with Carl. He said he would like to stay in touch. It was a pleasant moment for both of them. Carl felt good about his departing student, in spite of his failure to pierce Hearty's psyche.

When Hearty departed, Carl found he could not work any more at that moment. Something Hearty had said or, perhaps, done—Carl could not quite tell—had struck an unaccustomed chord in Carl. He sank his face in his hands and found himself crying unaccountably. He remained sobbing for about ten minutes, and felt intense relief.

Then a slackened wire in his mind suddenly jerked tight and stiff again. He sat up straight in his chair. His tears dried. The old mood was back. There was work to be done.

It would be almost ten years before Carl and Hearty met again.

In the next eight years Carl experienced an almost permanently altered state of consciousness. He received a similarly permanent perception of what he called the "non-thing" aura (what Huxley had termed the Non-Self aura) surrounding all objects. He had various trances. And, above all, he underwent his "exaltation."

The first few times that Carl noticed the alteration in his consciousness, he put it down to a complex of physical causes. The atmosphere of a particular day when he sensed some change had been very clear, he thought; it had rained for four days previously, and there was a strong, blustering wind. On another occasion, he felt, the new sensation was due to a great physical well-being and deep satisfaction over the way some experimental work had gone. On still another occasion, he put it down to an exhilarating discussion with some colleagues.

Gradually, however, he acknowledged quietly to himself that some deep alteration was taking place within him.

First of all, it had to do with what he sensed—saw, heard, felt, smelled—but the newness and surprise of what he felt really lay in the fact that it seemed to *originate* and *reach* "beyond" his senses. It was "trans-sense." Second, it concerned people, animals, plants, and inanimate objects. And, most importantly for Carl, it was theophanic. He maintained it was a *manifestation* of deity. (Carl in those days never spoke of "God" or of "the deity," but only of the "divine" and of "deity.")

The earliest stages were simple, but very perplexing. Walking in the street during the daytime crowd of shoppers, for example, or in more solitary walks away from town, he would somehow switch his consciousness away from eyes or hands or trees or the ground. Some totality of individual traceries and patterns and meanings emerged, instead, and became the center point of his consciousness.

In the street crowd he would suddenly stop seeing eyes or faces or clothes; he would see, instead, a sort of pattern all the people traced as their heads bobbed and moved toward him, or receded behind him, or passed in the same direction as he was going.

But the sensation was quick, subtle as mercury. At first, when he tried to seize it by his full attention, he chased it away, instead. Then, when he went about his business again, it thrust itself back into his consciousness.

After a number of experiences, Carl began to realize that the traceries he saw were not bobbing heads or swaying tree branches, and he was not seeing with his eyes. He was watching something with his unaided consciousness. And what he saw was the buoyancy and fluidity and free-streaming verve of spirit. Just spirit, untrammeled by the chains of physicality.

After one of these experiences, Carl rushed back to his laboratory and scribbled an excited record of the event: "It's theophanic! I've done it! I've found the relation between psyche and spirit, between consciousness and belief, between deity and human beings. I've found it! I've found it! It's theophanic!" This entry in his notes is dated March 1965.

In the following two years, the frequency and intensity of such experiences increased. Sometimes it was the eyes of people, sometimes it was the onward movement of their feet, sometimes it was their heads. The meaning in each case was different; yet all the meanings coalesced into an awesome totality.

Eyes were of a particular pattern. Over and above their color, brightness or dullness, shape, individual expressions, every pair of eyes seemed to constitute one reflection of a total seeing, an enlivening and quickened sight. And all the pairs of eyes he saw were a unified reflection of that totality, and at the same time completely individual. The pattern they traced was not of one huge eye, but of *one sight*, of *one seeing*.

It was in the same manner that in the onward movement of feet he saw the *power* of that one being—he now called it "spirit" in his notes. In the working of hands—holding, gesticulating, waving, pointing—it was the spirit's subtlety. In the sound of voices it was not the accent, the pronunciation, or the pitch of the voices that struck him. It was what he called the "tonality." Each voice reflected a certain total harmony, as water, without becoming light, *reflects* light; or a valley wall, without becoming sound, *reflects* the sound of a shout; or colors, without becoming a mood, *reflect* a mood; smells, without being touchable, *reflect* surfaces and substances we have touched.

At the beginning of the following year Carl began to notice two new elements in his constantly altering state of consciousness. There was a great sense of "being with," of "being together with." What he was "with" or "together with" on these occasions he dared not think out too clearly, because he knew that would be the death of it all. But it was a personal "being with." What he was "with" was intelligent, free, supreme in scme awesome but not frightening way. Slowly, over a period of time, when note-taking or recording on his machine, he came to refer to "my friend."

The second element was that the fits and starts of his experiences were over. Now all was coalescing. All the traceries and patterns, all the aspects of meaning and significance and existence seemed to come as one. He realized after a brief spell that all the traceries had always been one. But, he also realized, he could have started to know that oneness only through those initial fits and starts. Theophanic happenings thus became a theophany, and everything now was seen by him as united. Everything was an aspect of the one being.

Then subtly, simply as a suspicion at the beginning, Carl started to feel some basic differences between what he called "my friend" and this one being, this all-pervasive, free-moving, and independent spirit in which all things were, but which was not itself just one of all other things.

Whenever he "perceived" the slightest smidgeon of difference between the "friend" and the "one," some sadness he could not control entered him. He felt again as if he were going to be deprived, as he had been at sixteen when his first vision had ended. He took even more copious notes and made long recordings in order to catch and retain everything he could.

In the last days of 1965 Carl began to perceive what he called the "non-thing" aura of all objects and people around him. Until that moment, and even when he was absorbed by that totality of being in which all things were now bathed for him, Carl still did always see them as things. Their "thingness" still was a basic characteristic.

Very early one morning he was walking the short distance from his apartment to his office on campus. There was still some of the night chill in the air, but a brisk wind moving the trees and rifling the grass promised one of those zesty, sunny days Carl liked so much.

The last stretch of the walk was a path lined on the west side by a row of poplar trees. On the east side there was a wide expanse of grass sweeping away for about 200 yards to a row of buildings used by the agricultural department. Behind the buildings there was a ridge of high ground.

As he walked, Carl glanced eastward at the ridge, his eyes traveling leisurely over the trees, shrubs, buildings, and grass, taking in the fresh light that was creeping over everything.

He was so attuned and attentive to his own perceptions that he immediately noticed a qualitative change. Each thing had something more than mere thingness. It was that each one existed on the edge of an abyss all its own, a vast chasm of "non-thingness," of what it was not.

This experience was far more absorbing than even Huxley had intimated in his lyrical description of the "Non-Self"; and its beauty was more authentic and filling than anything expressed in each physical object.

This "non-thingness" was an actual aura around every object. It was dim and shallow and pale nearest to the object, but as Carl's eye drew away from the object and into the object's aura, the aura deepened and heightened in appearance and meaning.

Nothing, no object, Carl felt, would ever be banal anymore: it would never again be merely itself, have only its own self, for him. The aura of its non-thingness, its "Non-Self," glowed always and *made the thing possible.* Carl made the quiet discovery that in the aura of each thing there was no difference between appearance and meaning.

As his eye traveled and the "non-thingness," the "Non-Self," of each object glistened and signified for him, he began to hear a vaster and vaster choir of soundless voices, and to see a greater and greater multitude of participants in worship. Each blade of grass chimed its silent "Holy! Holy! Holy!" Every tree bowed and swayed in obeisance to the supremacy of all existence, and each building stood in reverence before the mystery of allness.

All this produced no shock in Carl. He did not even stop walking. He seemed to be ready for it all. As he swung into the pathway to his office, he felt in his mind one desire: that he be once and for all exalted—even if just for a short time—to see and know that supreme existence of all things and to see the holiness of its mystery that gave all things meaning.

That exaltation would eventually come for him, but only four years later.

It was in May 1969 that possession seemed to have been extended further and deeper in Carl's life than ever before. That possession was effected through his professional interests. His attention for about two years previous to this date had concentrated on two aspects of psychic development: astral travel and reincarnation. Both were in direct relationship to Carl's all-absorbing aim of "finding out" the "true and original Christianity."

By astral travel he hoped to transcend the boundaries of space and time, and thus to "revisit" the locales where Christianity existed before it was corrupted. By his researches in reincarnation—he believed fully in it—Carl hoped to relive some ancient experiences of his own, possibly even around the birth of Christianity.

In his researches, studies, and experimentation into astral travel, Carl had by 1969 some proficiency in this psychic capability, but his achievements had remained within traditional bounds. He usually remained in sight of his own inert body and of locales known to him in his physical life. And in some definite way he remained tied to the time frame of the present moment. His immediate goal now was to find a way out of that time frame. There must be, he maintained, some "gate" through which he could pass to freedom.

With his two closest associates, Albert and Norman, and the student members of his special study group, he now proceeded to launch a series of experiments. He himself was the guinea pig; and, each time, one of his trances became the starting point for an experiment. Carl had apparently an enormous fund of psychic energy and was immune to the injury that others sustained in such experiences.

The experiments took place in the audition room of his campus offices. There he had had installed various machines for recording voice and actions, and for monitoring his vital functions—heart, pulse, respiration, and brain activity.

Albert functioned as chief monitor, with Norman as his immediate assistant. Albert would interrogate Carl at key points in each experiment. Until the last stages of this series of experiments, Carl answered only direct yes-or-no questions put to him by Albert. The other members of the group took on various assignments in operating the machines.

Carl's optimum time for "trancing" was in the early morning, an hour or so before sunrise. At the end of each trance session, the assistants withdrew on Carl's instructions, and he was left alone to recover his normal composure. Recovery periods lasted for any length of time between ten and forty minutes depending on the length of the session and Carl's psychic condition. When the assistants returned, they usually found Carl sitting at the table recording his memories— sensations, thoughts, feelings, intuitions.

By repeated experiments, starting always with one of Carl's trances, they found that astral travel was not to be accomplished in one step. It was not a question of one, but rather three "gates." These he termed "low-gate," "mid-gate," and "high-gate." Carl had to pass through them all in order successfully to achieve full freedom of astral travel.

Low-gate was, more or less, the initial condition of trance: an absence of all sensory reaction and feeling on Carl's part. Mid-gate implied that Carl himself felt no relationship to his body; but, nevertheless mid-gate still implied "immobility" on the part of his psyche. High-gate, Carl figured, would mean that his psyche escaped from that peculiar "immobility" of mid-gate and depart "freely" on astral travel. The rest was discovery and revelation.

The verification of Carl's passage to low-gate and mid-gate positions was accomplished by a series of laboriously conducted experiments, repeated and repeated, until they were all satisfied that objectively Carl could be said to have reached these different positions. To help our understanding of how these experiments went, we have the films, tape recordings, and the minutes of the laboratory log, together with Carl's own recordings made after each session. Some members of the group have also contributed their recollections of what happened.

Once Carl was in a trance and all physical feeling (say, a pin stuck in the sole of his foot) was negative for him, the assistants proceeded to change the objects around Carl's inert body. They introduced objects he had never seen—usually placards inscribed in another room by one of the assistants. They placed them face up and face down; they moved them around. They proceeded thus through a series of experiments, testing Carl until they were sure that his responses identifying the objects previously unknown to him were accurate and were coming from the low-gate position.

As Carl recorded it, in low-gate position he was perfectly conscious, but not through his senses. And he was observing from a position outside his own body, at every side of it as well as beneath it and above it and the couch upon which his body lay.

Mid-gate was the next goal. In all low-gate positions there always persisted in Carl some instinctual relationship to his own inert body, as he viewed it from "outside." They understood that this instinctual relationship was a "given" of normal human conditions. The aim was to get rid of it.

All knew that there was a risk involved in shedding something so basic and instinctual as the feeling for one's own body. What guarantee was there that one could resume it, how could one "return" to normal body living? Did one just escape from the relationship, leaving it intact, and then return to its bonds? Or by leaving it did one destroy it? No one knew. "But we must find out," insisted Carl.

In late 1968 Carl had the beginnings of mid-gate: in his trances now, the relationship to his body was weakening; and, as the weakening progressed, a strange, dimensionless condition of mind and will began to fill his consciousness. Great caution was exercised by the assistants and by Carl at that stage. Carl allowed a certain degree of weakening of that instinctual bond, then returned again to full immersion in his bodily senses. He then repeated the operation several times, until he felt sure of his psychic energy and resources to help him back to psychic normalcy and then, down past low-gate, back to physical normalcy. Eventually, in the early summer of 1969, he fully attained mid-gate.

At the end of the summer it was decided that they should aim for high-gate. It was a Saturday morning. All proceeded in the orderly and controlled manner adopted from the beginning. Carl passed into low-gate and, without much delay, into mid-gate. At this point, according to the plans made at the previous night's preparatory meeting, there was a three-minute regulatory pause while they waited for Carl to attain control of his psychic energy for the next and difficult step.

When the three minutes were up, they started again. But quickly Albert found he could get no answers or reactions from Carl. After a sudden racing, pulse, heartbeat, and respiration had slowed down to the pace "normal" for mid-gate. Physically Carl was "in normalcy." Norman and Albert looked at each other and at the rest of the group; there was nothing to do but to wait and keep monitoring Carl's vital signs. It was a risk Carl had insisted be taken, and they had all agreed.

When Carl had reached mid-gate and Albert's interrogating voice had ceased for the regulatory pause, Carl's progress had not stopped. The diminishing relationship to his body had melted into nothing. And he was suddenly within another ether or state: neither far from nor near his body, neither light nor heavy, his whole self wholly transparent to himself, desirous neither of death nor of life, neither remembering anything nor forgetting anything, neither realizing anything new nor ignoring anything old. In that state he had neither past nor future. He was past mid-gate and into the high-gate position.

Albert, Norman, and the others were seriously worried at first when the monitoring machines ceased to record any brain activity in Carl's body. But Carl had forewarned of this also and told them that perhaps on the threshold of high-gate, and most probably in the high-gate position, there would be no apparent brain activity, certainly none that could be picked up by machines. But Carl had not been able to predict anything more. His assistants had no inkling of Carl's experience at that moment.

Quickly and simultaneously he surveyed an entire panorama. As he tells it, it was a medley of faces and places and animals which he had seen before either in real life or in books, faces such as the Ramses II colossus at Abu Simbel in Egypt, a Minoan goddess from the sixteenth century B.C., a lute player from ancient Tyre; places such as the Nike

temple in Athens, the baths of Mohenjo-Daro, the early buildings of
Jericho, sheets of ice-capped land, swamps, swirling gases, deeps of
blackness; objects such as a sycamore tree in Pharaonic Thebes of the
eighteenth century B.C., the high places of Machu Picchu.

It was not a question of images or pictures; it was the actual places
and objects themselves. And an added peculiarity was that to Carl
they did not come singly, one after the other or separated in space and
time. He was ranging far above them, and they were simultaneously
present to him.

The recordings taken during this portion of the session are silent
except for the whispers of his associates. Carl was silent throughout
high-gate.

After 25 minutes Albert and the others were beginning to become
alarmed, when the pulse and heartbeat monitors began to record a
faster pace. Carl must be "returning," reviving, they knew. He was
beginning to respond to Albert's direct commands and suggestions. In
another ten minutes it was all over. Carl opened his eyes slowly and
blinked in the electric light.

They all filed out, leaving Carl his accustomed time to recover.
When they returned some 15 minutes later, he was dictating into the
recording machine as much as he could recall of that high-gate astral
travel. The elation of the group as they listened was understandably
high. They still had to devise some method of verifying the data of his
high-gate travel, but they had full confidence that such controls could
be devised with repeated experiments.

Albert, Norman, and Carl were the last to leave the audition room.
Their path lay across the campus to the dining room. As they walked,
they discussed the salient points of Carl's trance. There were two or
three aspects of Carl's astral travel that Norman was sure were unique,
even in the low-gate and mid-gate states. He mentioned especially the
peculiar time frame within which Carl seemed to move during the
trance, and he remarked on the bodiless experience of Carl at certain
moments of his experience: not only had Carl felt as if he was looking
at his own inert body; he felt as if he had been definitively separated
from it.

As they continued to talk, Albert and Norman were what they now
call "taken over" or "totally dominated" by some psychic dimension of
Carl.

Carl was just explaining the absence of distance during astral travel. They both recall his saying: "Take, for example, that ridge over there." He indicated the high ridge that flanked his favorite walk. "You see it as a vertical dimension, some distance from you, on your horizontal plane."

At that point, their perception of the ridge itself was no longer as of an obstacle on their horizon. The ridge was as much there as it had been the moment before this peculiar change. But now they were neither distant from the ridge nor near it, neither level with it nor lower in level, nor above it. They had, in other words, no sense of distance. In their description of it, the experience seems something like Carl's experience the evening when all distance had disappeared between him and the sunset outside his study window.

And the same change affected their relationship to each other and to Carl. Without any perception of distance or space between them, they were "with" him, "with" each other. The only material relationship that remained was that of presence: they were present to each other.

They were also aware of another change, this time in Carl. He was present to them and they, to him. But he was *more* present to, more "with," something or someone else. And they were not so present to or "with" that something or someone else as Carl was. They witnessed his "meeting" with that other being, as it were, and heard strange words of conversation they did not understand. At times it seemed Carl was "talking" with more than one, with two or three "persons." They could not make out exactly how many. And, while the dominant emotion of both Norman and Albert was one of fear and of nostalgia for a normal physical stance and posture, Carl seemed to be in ecstasy and wholly absorbed in his "meeting."

Their memories become jumbled at this point. They remember speaking but in a wholly undeliberate way, as if some power in them was producing the words they pronounced. Several times they were saying the same things in chorus together; at other times they were talking almost at cross-purposes. They do remember hearing each other say: "Surely, we must make a special place here for Carl and his companions." And they have only the dimmest memories of who or what those companions of Carl's were during these experiences. They have no recollection of human forms.

At a certain point, they remember, their vision was obscured by a blackness they could not understand or see through. Their hearing

358 THE CASES

grew fainter. After that, Albert and Norman say, they seemed to become numbed or drowsy, and that numbing seeped through them both, lulling their senses.

Then they each felt a hand on one shoulder and heard Carl's normal voice.

"Albert! Norman! Do you hear me! Wake up!"

Albert describes himself as opening his eyes. Norman's description is of blackness melting from his vision. Both of them saw only Carl standing between them, a hand on the shoulder of each, and looking as normal as always. He was smiling at them and telling them by that smile that he knew what they had experienced. Nobody said anything. But Carl pointed to the ridge.

They looked over. The ridge was now flooded in sunlight, and so were the buildings at its base and the green expanse of grass between them and the ridge. They looked back at Carl.

He only said: "This exaltation is something people will not easily understand."

They both nodded. They would themselves spend many hours discussing and trying to understand what had happened.

This experience made a huge difference in Carl's life. After some discussion, it had been decided to communicate to all the members of the special student group what Albert and Norman had experienced that morning. All now accepted Carl as a guide and guru. They referred to his guruship openly when speaking to others of their studies, although it was agreed that no public mention of Carl's "exaltation," as he called it, should be made until all their findings were published. But from then on until after the Aquileia incident, Carl was revered by each individual of his special group not merely as a parapsychologist but as a personal guide in their progress of spirit and in true religious belief.

Inevitably word spread beyond Carl's in-group. And before long, Carl had a much greater following. He attained particular notoriety following a lecture he gave shortly after his "exaltation." It concerned religion and Christianity. In it, Carl announced the goal of his studies and research to be a rediscovery of what Christianity truly meant, what Jesus had wanted it to be before Jesus' message had been corrupted by other men.

As time went on, Carl's following grew fairly large. More people began coming for guidance in their personal spiritual growth. But even as the group grew in number, Carl's influence over the group became more profound. He imposed very severe exercises on each of the participants, disciplining their imaginations and schooling them in control of their mental processes in a way and to a degree quite beyond anything Olde had put him through many years before.

Carl began to lead special spirit-raising sessions for his growing group. They were held in the large room off his private study where he also held seminars and did so many of his experiments.

During these sessions, Carl stood at one end of the room, while all the "participants" sat on the floor in a semicircle around him. He spoke slowly and deliberately, instructing his listeners. His psychic abilities seemed to be at their most powerful during these sessions. With every sentence his control seemed to become more concentrated, and everyone gradually fell into a very quiet, yet alert state of body and mind.

Finally they all seemed to feel not only a special presence "with" them, but an overwhelming inclination within themselves to "bow" (or, as some said, to "annihilate" themselves) before that presence. A few participants withdrew from the group at one time or another because, they said, they felt the strange presence that was "with" them to be "unloving" or "cold" or "nonhuman." Most, however, persevered. The few who talked with me about that presence which they felt during Carl's spirit-raising sessions stressed the peculiar control or "grip" which they found holding their inner feelings. It did not frighten, but it gave no impression of being benign or loving. It overawed, as one of them commented; but it did so much as an enormous skyscraper might overawe somebody standing close to its base and looking up its entire length. Overawing, it numbed the feelings. And, as it numbed, it seemed to control.

It was at the very end of one of these spirit-raising sessions in September of 1971 that the first signs of possession became outwardly apparent in Carl. Nobody, however, in Carl's immediate entourage was equipped to read these signs for what they were. They all took them as awesome manifestations of what they called Carl's "other and more real world."

On that particular occasion, Carl had just finished his commentary, and the participants in the session were all returning to a normal state of consciousness, slowly being set free from that numbing "control."

As they returned to ordinary perception of things around them, they became aware that Carl was having difficulties in breathing and standing up straight. He was in a peculiarly bent position. With his soles still flat on the ground and his knees bent, the upper part of his body up to his shoulders was being bent precariously, as if he was falling backward. His chin was sunk in his chest in his effort to straighten up. Only his head moved in that effort.

The rule at all sessions had always been clear: no hands on Carl during the session. So nobody moved to help, but everyone watched.

Norman and Albert, who knew Carl more intimately than the others did, felt that Carl was in some unusual difficulty. Something was wrong. Glancing at each other in agreement, they moved quickly about the room and whispered to the participants to rise and leave them alone with Carl. When they had all gone, Norman opened the shutters, letting in the light of day.

Carl's face was clearly full of pain and rage. He was muttering some words such as "Latter," "truly," "won't," "will," "faithful," "forever," "prime." But they could make out only a jumble of words that conveyed no sense.

Gradually Carl straightened. He took one or two deep breaths, then stumbled to a chair, sat down, and covered his face with his hands.

"Leave me be," Norman and Albert heard him say in a muffled voice. "I'll get to you later."

They left him alone.

The next day, when all three met, Carl was composed, smiling, and as masterful as usual, until Albert mentioned the previous day's happenings. Carl's face clouded over. He would not look at either of them. He only said: "We too have our enemies. Our enemy. The *Latter*" (he gave a special emphasis to this word) "would disturb all harmony of psyche and reality, of mind and body." He repeated these phrases over and over as if repeating a ritual recitation, until he began shaking and perspiring.

When Norman suggested that they put off that afternoon's session, Carl was vehement. To delay was to give in to the *Latter*. They must at all costs keep on, Carl said. They were on the brink of a history-making breakthrough.

The "breakthrough" took place in the late autumn of 1972.

Once Carl attained the first proficiency in astral travel, his next aim was to use that skill in order to attain at least one of his former incarnations.

Reincarnation, for Carl, was a very definite reality. He believed that the psyche of each person had multiple "layers" or "tiers." Each "layer" or "tier" was evolved during one of several successive lifetimes, and every human being was composed of such "layers." He also believed that the unifying factor for all such "layers" was one particular "layer" in which the person in question had received a direct light from "divinity." For, at that precious moment, the reincarnating psyche became perfectly human. And, for Carl, to be perfectly human was to be indestructible. He called this unifying "layer" the "alpha layer."

Carl theorized further that, in the freedom of astral travel, that alpha layer would come to the fore; but only the forceful action of one's will, prodded by the intelligent interrogation of a monitor, could help bring it out. If there never had been an alpha layer in the evolution of a psyche, then such a psyche would merely enjoy astral travel, but obviously never attain a reincarnation in the full sense of the word.

Carl's progress in reaching his alpha layer or principal incarnation was relatively slow. He began by studying the audio and visual tapes of his astral-travel sessions. He was searching for clues in words and actions. A special language, specific names and places, gestures that had a cultural, ethnic, religious, or even geographical connotation—these could be clues to the emergent alpha layer he was seeking.

From looking at fragmentary shots of his assistants taken occasionally and accidentally by the cameras as they panned over the entire scene at the sessions, Carl detected traces of what he felt was an astounding phenomenon: at times one or another of his assistants unconsciously made a gesture or took up a momentary attitude which corresponded to his own words and/or actions at that particular point in the session. Some of his own psychic ambient was obviously affecting those witnessing and assisting at the session. He did not know what this meant, but it all helped, with fresh indications of where to search for his alpha layer.

It was by the coordination of all these clues that Carl finally uncovered his own alpha layer: an incarnation back in the early days of Christianity in Roman times. His own mind and memory were like a sieve through which bits and scraps of perception were being shaken and sifted; they all concerned scenes, names, objects, actions, and events which, during the group review of the sessions, were determined to be identifiably of Roman and early Italian origin. Most of the jumbled words and phrases he used in session were classical Latin.

The name Petrus kept returning again and again. At first, they thought that this referred to Peter, the Apostle and Bishop of Rome. But, although Roma (Rome) did come up in connection with Petrus, together with other names historically connected with Peter, it became clear that the Petrus in question had something to do rather with Roman Italy, with the East, and with the sea.

What intrigued Carl and the others as they went over the tapes after each of the sessions was that, whenever the name Petrus was mentioned by Carl, one of his assistants would—apparently without realizing it—do one of two things. Either he raised his hand momentarily in the old Roman salute: outstretched arm, upraised hand, fingers together and pointing upward, palm turned outward. Or he would crouch momentarily, as if he were about to get down on all fours.

Bit by bit, Carl and his associates honed and refined the method of conducting the sessions. Albert, the chief monitor, developed a technique of interrogation. Carl's power of recollection subsequent to each session increased. They became more expert in reading the tapes of the sessions. It was only a matter of time and of the right occasion, Carl kept telling them. One day they would hit the target.

An offhand remark by a colleague who inquired how his work was going gave Carl a small but valuable clue. At the end of the conversation, the colleague quipped that, if his sainted Irish grandmother were alive, she would tell him to hold special sessions on the feast day of All Souls. She had always said that the souls of the dead returned to earth on that day. Carl always considered his friend's remark as a "message" from the world of spirits.

On November 2, 1972, Carl held an unusual session of his special student group. With the help of Albert and Norman and his closest associates, he was going to make another astral bid to reach one of his reincarnations—the one he always seemed to be striving for but had never successfully achieved.

As was customary, the group met in the audition room an hour before daybreak. Carl seemed in fine form. He was tranquil and happy-looking as he greeted each of his group affectionately. He was in full command of the situation. He lay down on the leather couch and was connected to the various monitoring machines. The audio and visual recorders were started. Then all recited together the prayers Carl had written.

Carl's speech throughout this session was almost completely in Latin with an occasional Greek word or phrase and some expressions in a language they ascertained later to be a form of Coptic.

Carl apparently had no difficulty in attaining the high-gate position for his astral journey. Once he passed into high-gate, the anticipation among the onlookers became extreme. They sensed that this was one of the rare occasions in their lives when they might witness a genuine scientific breakthrough. They knew by now that in his former reincarnations, Carl had belonged to the ancient Roman world in early Christian times. But he had not, up to this point, found out where he had been living, the identity he had assumed in that reincarnation, and the events that had marked his life in those ancient days.

As Carl had continued over the months searching for his alpha layer by means of high-gate astral excursions, levitation of his inert body began to occur, but only in association with the ancient Roman incarnation for which he was now purposely searching. His body lifted off the couch ever so slightly; it remained suspended in midair without touching the couch, and returned by itself to the surface of the couch as Carl returned to normalcy. There was no regularity to the occurrence of this phenomenon of levitation, except as it was associated with his chance excursions to Roman Italy, and there were never any side effects apparent in Carl's physical well-being.

The videotape made on this particular occasion shows Carl lying motionless on the couch. Donna and Bill are sitting at the foot of the couch; both have an intent look most of the time. But the same changes pass over their faces as over the others around the couch—Albert and Norman sitting at the head of the couch, Keith and Charlie at the far side, and the two technicians attending the monitoring machines. If one did not know better, one would be tempted to say that all present were brothers and sisters. For the intensity of the emotions portrayed on their faces produced such a similarity in looks that it is as though an invisible wash painted on them mysteriously had made all one family.

With Carl's passage beyond high-gate, everyone leaned forward, eyes wide open, faces drawn, completely absorbed in and concentrating on Carl's face and words. As Carl's body, still supine, rose slightly from the couch, all sat back in their chairs, a gaze of awe and reverence sweeping across their faces.

Albert's voice took up the interrogations. "Who are you?"

There is a small pause. Then Carl answered. "Peter, a Roman citizen."

"Where do you live?"

"In Aquileia."

"What day is it?"

"The feast of Lord Neptune."

"What are you about today?"

"We are celebrating the mystery of salvation."

"Who is with you?"

"Those of the sacrament."

"What sacrament?"

"The sacrament."

"Why here?"

"This is where the Tortoise confronts the Rooster."

"Where?"

"In the secret oratory."

"How do you celebrate the mystery?"

"We adore the Tortoise. We curse the Rooster."

"Why?"

"The Rooster has corrupted the salvation."

"How?"

There was no answer from Carl, but the expression on his face changed several times. What looked like indignation, pain, anger, fear, joy skimmed across his features. His pulse and heartbeat quickened. Albert waited for five minutes, then tried again.

"Where are you now and what is happening?"

"Beside the Rooster facing the Tortoise."

For the first time Carl's body stirred—ever so slightly, still in levitation. Donna noticed it immediately. She glanced at Norman, who shook his head: no need for alarm, he was indicating. Carl's body then began to vibrate all over. The look on his face was one of effort.

Albert reflected a moment, then made up his mind.

"Are you continuing with the rite of the sacrament?"

Carl made no answer. He was going limp and quiet. His pulse and heartbeat were back to normal. His body lowered gently, imperceptibly back onto the couch. He was returning to high-gate obviously, and the session had to be almost over.

When this much was clear, they all acted out their parts. The monitoring machines and recorders were turned off. As usual, everyone stood up then and filed out. Norman, the last out the door, paused to switch off the light, then stepped outside and gently pulled the door to.

He had closed it and was about to join the others when his nerves were jangled. They all heard laughter, a sardonic cackle, a peal of mockery and vicious amusement coming from the audition room.

They looked at each other incredulously, fully persuaded that it could not be so, that there must be some explanation. The tone of the laughter was so outrageously out of keeping with their mood of reverence and gratitude that everyone grimaced with disgust and a little grain of fear.

As the last notes of derision and sneering amusement died away, Albert turned the handle of the door and opened it. They all looked at the blackness of the open doorway. Donna, nearest to Albert, craned over his shoulder. There was no sound, no light. Dimly, Albert made out Carl's inert form. He was still asleep. Albert shrugged his shoulders in puzzlement and pulled the door closed quietly.

Donna said nothing. But while the door was open, she had noticed a strange smell in the room. She looked at Albert, then finally asked him if she was crazy or if anyone else had smelled it, too.

No need to be alarmed, Albert told her. He and Norman had noticed the smell after several experiments and had discussed it with Carl. They did not understand it yet. But that, he said, was why they were scientists—to find out what happened and why it happened.

Donna still has a clear memory of that smell. It was not unpleasant. It was strange. Neither of any animal nor of any plant nor of any chemical she had ever known. A deep sense memory of it remained with her for many weeks.

Between this moment and Carl's exorcism one year later, Donna was to experience that smell again and again. Part of her later distress came from the fact that, by the time of the exorcism, she had come to like it.

From the data of the sessions two things became obvious: Carl's former incarnation had been localized at some special place in the Italian town of Aquileia; and the high point each year in that former life had been the feast of the ancient Roman god, Neptune. This feast day in modern calendars would be July 23. They resolved, therefore, to be in Aquileia on July 23 of the following year.

During the intervening months between the All Souls session and their July trip, Carl took to wearing the two emblems of Neptune, the dolphin and the trident, on a chain around his neck. He also became more abstracted than ever before from his physical surroundings and spent a great deal of time listening repeatedly to the recordings of his trances. He tried on several occasions to write about it all, but he never got beyond a few paragraphs. The word spoken to him in his teenage vision, "*Wait!*" seemed to be his watchword.

Meanwhile, he made one further advance in his psychic accomplishment. He claimed several times to have acquired a new power: to be able to be in two places at the same time because, he said, of a psychic "double" he could project forcefully into visible reality some hundred miles from where he was.

During these months Carl's directions for the personal life of his associates got much more dogmatic and absolutist in tone. They were always given in gentle terms. It was merely that, as one of them remarked, Carl no longer gave them any alternatives. There was no "either/or." They all had to be "purified," Carl said. They must be cleansed of any stains attaching to their minds and wills, stains which came from previously accepted lies about Jesus and Christianity.

Most of his followers found the regimen Carl established for them to be a healthy one. They slept better, studied with deeper concentration, and ceased to be disturbed and distracted by inconsequential matters.

Now and again, some of them felt that they were abdicating some secret part of their being. Some felt vaguely disturbed, but it was hard to pin that disturbance down. And, anyway, the whole venture with Carl was exciting and new, and promised to lead them beyond the matter-of-fact horizons of ordinary daily existence.

Carl put no difficulty in their way when Christmas 1972 came; and they all went to their own homes to celebrate. But when Easter approached, he insisted that they spend it with him.

They did not attend any church or religious service. Instead, on Easter Saturday evening they all met beneath the ridge overlooking Carl's favorite walk. From there they watched the sun go down while Carl maintained a running commentary on "true spirit."

He had chosen as his subject the eternity of spirit. And, using the symbols of the tortoise for spirit's eternity and of the rooster for the rising and setting sun of man's intellect, he preached vehemently against "the mental corruption that destroyed the beauty of God's word." The sun, he said, would rise on the morrow and set on the morrow. So with every human resurrection. It was a constant rising and falling. Only spirit remained forever, like the ocean, like the tortoise, like the sky, like man's will. There was much in the same strain, all very mystical and exultant.

Afterward, he left them and returned to his office. Nobody dared go with him. He was in one of those "states" which they all venerated.

On July 15, their plans as carefully mapped out as possible, the small group left the campus by car for the airport.

About an hour after their departure, Hearty arrived at the psychology department. He was looking for Carl. No, he told Carl's secretary, he had no prior appointment with the professor, but he had a vitally important message for him and his companions.

It took some time before he learned the news of Carl's departure and about the proposed visit to Aquileia. He sped by cab after Carl's party to the airport, but arrived as the plane taxied for takeoff.

Hearty looked for some time into the evening sky as it swallowed up Carl's plane. He could only guess at Carl's condition of mind. But he knew rather exactly how the whole Aquileia venture would end. He was not guessing.

FATHER HARTNEY F.

When Hartney F. was born in Wales in 1905, his parents had been living there for almost 18 years. He was a late child. His mother was Welsh, his father, an Englishman from Northumberland.

Hartney's hometown, which he called Casnewydd-ar-Wysg but which is shown on English maps as Newport, stands on the banks of the river Usk in Monmouthshire. He was baptized in St. Woolos parish church.

When Hearty was one and a half years old, his father, a general medical practitioner of the old school, came into a substantial inheritance from his father. Up to that point, the family had struggled to make ends meet. Now, with the sudden affluence, his father gave up his city dispensary and practice. The family moved out of the town to a small village near the confluence of the Usk and Severn Rivers.

There, Hartney spent the next twelve and a half years. His father maintained a small private practice. At their home on the Severn, his first ideas and emotions were formed by his mother and aided by the ambient of Welsh tradition in which the neighborhood—its people, history, monuments, and communal life—were bathed. At the age of six he was sent to grammar school. His daily language was Welsh, but his father tutored him in English from the age of seven.

Up to that time his mother, an ardent Welsh nationalist, steeped in Welsh history and literature, would not allow any English to be spoken in her child's presence. Only after he was fourteen did she consent to send him to a British public school, where he acquired a thorough grounding in English and developed a deep interest in science. But his English never quite lost the Welsh lilt and cadence.

His parents were Methodists and worshiped each Sunday at the little stone chapel in their village. Between his mother's fixation with the Welsh soul or spirit, the attractiveness and beauty of their hymn-singing Methodism, and his immersion in the folklore of village and country, Hartney's mentality was early on soaked in that peculiarity of all Celtic peoples which the Welsh developed to a very particular degree.

The best name for that peculiarity is style, style, as distinct and different from all other humanly valued qualities or powers, and not encompassed by or to be equated with intelligence, cunning, artistry, money, land, blood.

The soul of the Celt has a particular universality of its own: all of life and the world is interpreted in terms of light and shadow. But that innate generalism of their souls has never enabled Celts to achieve military conquest, imperial possessions, huge wealth, or cultural predominance. Early in their history, they were confined to the extremities of France (Brittany), of England (in Wales and Scotland), and in Ireland as the outermost tip of the European continent, dominated by Romans, Vandals, Franks, English, Normans, Danes, and others.

Celts developed the only power that remained: verbal expression and a corresponding mercurial agility of spirit. Oralism, not mentalism, is the mark of the Celt. The aspect of their peculiar style that became most noteworthy and most celebrated was their remarkable verbal expression of emotion.

At that one thing the Celts excelled. The Irish turned their style to express the Celtic twilight: the two dusks of birth and death. The Scots concentrated on the play of light and shadow, never clearly happy, never undoubtedly sad. The Bretons took refuge in the shadow as a covert for their perseverance.

But the Welsh took up the light in style and developed the distinct colors of their singing into a Pindarism all their own; and the clarity and brilliance of their language became a more powerful factor of identity than their nationalism or their religion. They maintained the Celtic shadow as a secret background in which to treasure their emotions. The great presumption of "Welshism" was that the visible and material world was merely a clothing or garment thrown over the living heart of sublime and beautiful reality.

It was this peculiarly Welsh style of thought, feeling, and expression that deeply characterized Hartney through the various stages of a life spent far from his native Wales.

Hartney's psychic powers were part and parcel of this "Welshism." Among his fellow countrymen there was no prurient curiosity as to his psychic ability—"Half of the people I knew had it, the other half presumed they had it," Hartney remarked once. Nor was there any mystery attached to it. Consequently, he did not grow up with a feeling of being abnormal or out of the ordinary. And the security he enjoyed was a distinct advantage.

Only when he went to public school and thence to Cambridge did he realize that his psychic power was a rarity and usually regarded as an untrustworthy abnormality. The English, permissive though they might be about their own emotions and peculiarities, tend to regard emotions or psychic abilities in non-English people as evidence of primitive conditions.

Hartney's latent psychic perception was mellowed at an early age by three prime, never-forgotten influences: the folklore of his people, the physical countryside, and his family's Methodism.

Before he knew one rule of English grammar or how to use a test tube, Hartney's memory was filled with the deep stuff of Welsh folklore that placed him in a living continuity with the "spirit" or "soul" of the land and the people. His mind was filled with the names of romantic Welsh princes such as Rhun ab Owain, Llewellyn, Owain Glyn Dwr, and of poets such as the fifteenth-century Tudur Aled. His mother recited the odes of the sixth-century Taliesin and Aneirin. And his speech was modeled after the metrical forms of the Welsh Middle Ages, the cywydd and englyn. He learned to avoid mentioning the year 1536 (when the infamous Act of Union abolished Welsh national independence).

The Welsh countryside that grew to be a part of Hearty's inner man was and still is of a special kind. There was a living magic about its whitewashed houses, its stone chapels, the intimate play of light on running water, the aloneness of mountain and valley, the perpetuity of pastureland, the merciless maw of mines where men grew black and sick working beneath the earth but returned to sing in chapel and go home to their wives and children. As Owen M. Edwards wrote, "The spirit of Wales is born in the mountain farmhouse, in the cottage by the brook, in the coal miner's home."

This entire complex of nature's face and men's haunts was taken as a living thing. Years later, in the jungles of Burma and in postwar Japan, when waves of nostalgia hit him now and then for the Vale of Usk, Bala Lake, the Swallow Falls, Llyn Idwal, or for the north beach of Tenby Bay, where he spent all the summer vacations of his childhood and youth, Hearty saw himself once again in the long straw-thatched, small-windowed cottages, smelling the flitches of bacon hanging from the kitchen rafters, and eating hot "shot"— ground oatcake and milk. Such a memory was as mystical as a poem about the Vale of Avalon and as faery as the cuckoo's song in Merion.

Methodism was the third great developing influence on Hartney. The meaning of Methodism was holiness. Not that the chapel was holy, or the singing sacred. (The minister, indeed, used to preach that it was the adjoining graveyard that made the chapel holy, not vice versa). But it was holiness in expression: the hymnal. Worship of God and Christ, performed according to rule and with the characteristic Methodist regularity and rhythm. This expression was holy because it was believed to be a conversation with the spirit of Christ and God. And more than once in his early youth, as Hartney stood between his parents during the soaring phrases of the chanting, the gabled roof of the chapel would no longer be a thick shield against the sky. It was for him a sacred mountaintop opening on to Heaven through which the angels of song descended from God to men and ascended back to God.

The extent of Hartney's psychic power became clear to him at a young age. He could and did receive clear—often literally accurate— inner intimations of what other people, near him and far away from him, were thinking and—on rare occasions—what they were suffering. It was thus in a Burmese jungle clearing late in 1943 that he knew the exact hour when both his parents died in the German blitz of London.

In 1924 Hartney chose to follow lectures in physics at Cambridge. While at the university, he became interested in Roman Catholicism. When he graduated in 1929, he had already been received into the Roman Catholic Church and had his mind made up to become a priest.

Ordained in 1936, he served in a succession of parishes in the London area, until he joined the British Army as a chaplain in 1941. Shortly afterward, his unit left for India and within a few months of his arrival there was sent into the Burmese jungles to harass the Japanese forces. During this part of his career Hartney was nicknamed "Battling Hearty" by his men. The shortened form, Hearty, stuck to him ever after.

He had his first experience of possession by Evil Spirit during the Burmese campaign. The small force of men with whom he traveled as chaplain had halted for the night in a small clearing. All was quiet and tranquil. But Hearty woke up at about 2:00 A.M. with a strong feeling that other human beings were moving near or around their encampment. He tried to fall asleep again, but the idea would not go away.

He finally sat up and listened for a few minutes. He crawled over to the commander of the unit, woke him up, and told him of his fears. It was not the first time Hearty had had these experiences. And he had always been right. The commander waited a while, talked with the posted sentinels, and finally decided to send a mortar barrage in the direction Hearty indicated. After five minutes, when there was no answering fire, they settled down to watch for the rest of the night.

In the faint light of the new day, scouts were sent out. One was back in minutes. The mortar barrage had found its target. Their night barrage had taken a Japanese hospital unit by surprise. When Hearty and the others arrived, all Japanese personnel, except for one soldier, were dead; the sole survivor was unconscious. Hearty's unit commander wanted him for questioning. He was brought back to the encampment, and his wounds were tended. When he regained consciousness several hours later, the unit commander knew he would not live very long. He had the poor fellow interrogated by his intelligence officers.

Late that afternoon Hearty went over to talk with the prisoner. He wished to find out if he was a Christian, possibly a Roman Catholic. If he were, Hearty wished to give him the last rites of the Church.

It was at the time of the short Burmese dusk that Hearty approached him. Hearty wore battle fatigues like all the members of his unit. He wore no sign or badge indicating that he was a chaplain. As Hearty approached, the prisoner's eyes flickered and then opened wide; he was looking straight up at the overhanging foliage and at the sky. Hearty expected a look of fear mixed with hate to appear in his eyes. But what he saw there was neither fear nor hate. It was some other emotion he could not recognize: inimical, yes but with an added trait he could not grasp immediately.

Still interpreting all this as a natural reaction to the sight of an enemy uniform, he drew nearer. The dying man grew more and more agitated; his limbs and torso shook; his eyes rolled around in their sockets; even his short-cropped hair seemed to stand up on his scalp. For all the world, he was like a helpless animal bristling in defense.

Hearty stopped and waited.

He had begun to perceive a very unaccustomed "mental" message. He had approached Japanese prisoners before and he knew their mentality. Hearty did not speak Japanese, but the language difference between him and them created no barrier for mental communication; that communication was not by words, verbal or mental. This dying man's mentality had some curious trait in it which Hearty was perceiving for the first time in his life in a human being.

Years before, when he and his father with some local hunters had cornered a fox that had been devastating the chickens in the farms around their home on the Severn, Hearty had killed the fox. As he took aim and was about to pull the trigger, his eyes had caught the direct glare of the defiant, snarling animal. Now, in the jungle clearing, looking at that prisoner, he had a similar feeling.

Still thinking that he had been misunderstood, Hearty pulled a small crucifix from his breast pocket and held it up so that the dying man could see it. The effect was instantaneous and catastrophic. By this time, one of the intelligence officers who spoke fluent Japanese had joined Hearty. He and Hearty heard strange guttural sounds coming from the man's throat.

"My God! Padre, he's cursing your cross," the officer said. But already Hearty was "receiving." His mind became full of a strange perturbation; and the wordless message was clear: *Go away. Take yourself and all you signify away from us. You serve what we hate.*

"Ask him a question for me, Captain," Hearty said to the officer. "Ask him why does he hate the cross."

The officer had no sooner put the question than the prisoner started to rise. His right hand flashed up to the bandages covering his chest wounds, tearing them off in a convulsive movement.

"Himiko! Himiko!" was as much as Hearty could catch of his shout before the man fell back. The intelligence officer could not understand the curious word, but thought it must be a name of some sort. In a matter of seconds, the prisoner's eyes opened with the sightless stare of the dead. Blood flowed for a few moments from his wounds; then it stopped.

It was not until later that Hearty found out what Himiko meant. But, in the jungle, he had a dawning realization that the man who had just died had been dedicated to some spiritual power from which his hate of the cross had come. Obscurely, without fine lines or definitions, Hearty understood the raw elements of possession.

At the end of the war, in 1946, Hearty volunteered for a vacant chaplaincy in occupied Japan. He was posted to the city of Kyoto and settled into his new quarters in April of that year.

Untouched by war and deliberately preserved from bombing by the Allies, Kyoto had been the imperial capital of Japan until 1868. It was the one city of Japan that had been laid out geometrically in rectangular shape, every street running north-south or east-west. In Japan of the postwar period, Kyoto sank deeper and deeper into its traditional past while attracting radical politicians and thinkers. Its Buddhist and Shinto shrines were magnificent, and Hearty spent his spare time visiting them all.

It was during a conversation in 1947 with a teacher named Obata at the Ryukoku, the Buddhist school, that he learned about Himiko. Himiko had been, it appeared, a shaman queen in very ancient times, and a modern sect still existed that worshiped her as a devil-goddess. They believed she lived and ruled from among the snow-covered mountains behind Kyoto.

Hearty and Obata became good friends. Obata had graduated from the Sorbonne in 1938. His chosen field was mysticism; his thesis had been a comparative study of Dervish knowledge and Buddhist enlightenment. With the facts he had researched about the dance and rhythms of Dervishes and his own native knowledge of Buddhism, Obata gave Hearty a systematic perception of a type of human knowledge not based on scientifically controlled and verified facts.

Hearty's scientific background began to fall into a new perspective. He started to realize the meaning of mysticism in his own religion. And very soon, also, he began to see that whatever psychic abilities he had should be carefully distinguished from spirit and the supernatural. For this was the central lesson of Buddhist and Dervish beliefs and practices.

(Here was the distinction that Carl V. had never really understood, indeed had lost almost from the start of his parapsychological career. If any one factor in Carl's mental makeup had helped preponderantly to his being possessed, this failure was it. Failing in this vital distinction, Carl inevitably took spirit, or soul, and psychic activity as one and the same thing. Any change produced in the psyche was taken by him as a change in spirit; and any illusion imposed on the psyche was taken as an ultimate truth of the soul.)

With Obata, Hearty explored the basic ideas of telepathy and telekinesis as well as bilocation; all these had been current coin over one thousand years before the words "parapsychology" and "extrasensory perception" had been breathed on a Western campus.

Obata used simple expressions and some current terms to instruct Hearty. Hearty's psyche, he said, was a "screen" on which some powerful psychic sender could flash images. Hearty had, however, a "censor bond," a faculty with which he could make his psyche opaque to the psychic probe of any "mind reader."

Obata assessed Hearty as a "receiver." And, concluding one of their discussions on the subject, he added, "Be thankful." He would only grin good-humoredly in the Japanese fashion when Hearty asked why he should be thankful that he could not also "send" messages or move objects by telekinesis.

Hearty got only one clue, though a very dramatic one, as to why it was better thus. Once on their way home from an early-morning walk, the two men passed by the edge of the Geon, Kyoto's renowned geisha district. Obata pointed this out to Hearty, and they stopped a moment. Without any forewarning, Obata suddenly fell forward on his face and rolled over. He was up in a flash, his eyes narrowed with apprehension.

"Hearty-San, they don't like me to be with you here. Hurry." He was bleeding from a cut in his forehead where he had struck the pavement.

Hearty was too dazed by the bizarre experience to say anything. But as Obata left him at the gate to his quarters, he said to Hearty, again with good humor, but with a faintly grim note: "You see, my friend, it's better you be only receiver. But watch. They know you already. And they know always for future time."

Only by reflecting on this incident did Hearty begin to understand why it was better not to be able to "send" messages or move objects at a distance. To have those abilities apparently laid one open in some mysterious way to assault by others—human beings or spirits—who enjoyed similar powers. To be on the same plane as they was somehow to be vulnerable to them.

By the time Hearty's enlistment as chaplain came to an end in 1949, the Himiko incident in the jungle as well as Obata's fall near the Geon had receded in his memory. He had already applied for and received permission to transfer himself to the United States. A bishop on the East Coast was more than willing to accept Hearty into his diocese.

Hearty had been living and working in Newark, New Jersey, for two years when the bishop called him and asked him to assist the diocesan exorcist. There would be nothing to it, the bishop assured him. Hearty had nerves of steel, and the bishop felt anyway that nine-tenths of all these things "are simply bad nerves or bad faith or both."

The exorcism proved to be neither bad nerves nor bad faith. As far as Hearty could see, the exorcee—in this case, a middle-aged man—was afflicted with some peculiar disturbance and anguish that ceased once the exorcism rite was completed. He reported back to the bishop, adding a request to be included in future exorcisms. The bishop remonstrated; no one, absolutely no one, wants any truck with these matters. "Well, I do. And I don't know why. But I do," had been Hearty's answer.

In the next six years Hearty was assistant at more than 17 exorcisms.

When the diocesan exorcist died unexpectedly after a long and exhausting exorcism, Hearty was clearly the strongest and most experienced man to replace him. When he was approached by the bishop, he did not hesitate for a moment.

In that same year he took his one and only holiday vacation: two weeks in his native Wales. He wandered once again around the countryside he had loved, visited the cottages of the ordinary people, ate great meals of bacon, potatoes, buttermilk, cheese, and oatcakes. He spent evenings reminiscing with old friends around open fires and tasting the fire in *cwrw*, the Welsh national liquor.

For the next six years or so after his return from Wales, Hearty served as an assistant priest with several assignments in the diocese. He remained diocesan exorcist. In 1963 the bishop offered Hearty his own parish. Hearty took this rather important occasion to sit down for a long and serious conversation with his bishop. With six years as exorcist behind him, as well as broad day-to-day experience with normal parish problems, Hearty had begun to see a subtle but already pervasive change.

There was, he said to the bishop, a new situation rapidly developing which the Church had not yet recognized. It concerned a new direction of psychology and psychiatry; but it seemed to Hearty that it also involved popular devotion and piety. Several times when putting candidates for exorcism through psychological and psychiatric tests he had found the experts talking of parapsychology. They seemed to look forward to some future date when all religious phenomena would be easily and understandably taken as the *products* of the human psyche as the psyche somehow passed through hitherto unknown altered states of consciousness. It bothered him a good deal, he told the bishop, because the new study, parapsychology, tended to displace religion altogether and to empty it of its significance.

There was a sabbatical coming to Hearty. If it was all right with his bishop, he could take a two-year sabbatical and do some private research on the subject. He would, of course, maintain his activity as diocesan exorcist; for anything of that nature he would return home, he said. The bishop gave his consent and promised Hearty the necessary financial support. Only later did Hearty tell him of his intention to follow courses at a university.

Hearty thus came to study on the campus where Carl V. had already made his name. At that point in his life, by the time Hearty started to attend Carl's lectures, he had developed a very strong instinct in matters concerning diabolism. He knew almost immediately that Carl V. was in trouble. How deeply he could not make out in the beginning. But after three semesters and various conversations with Carl and his group, Hearty was convinced that Carl was heading for serious disturbance and possibly was already well into the first stages of diabolic possession.

In the last few months of his stay at the university, Hearty was somewhat puzzled by Carl's effect on him. On the one hand, Carl took no pains to hide from him and the others that he regarded Hearty's clerical profession a definite hindrance to Hearty's full potential as a parapsychologist. On the other hand, time and time again Hearty "received" subtle "messages" from Carl, messages that were appeals for help.

The process of receiving "messages" always followed a pattern. The "messages" came as little chunks of knowledge suddenly appearing in Hearty's consciousness, always preceded by a short blank period when, it seemed to Hearty, his mind stopped thinking but he remained conscious. Immediately after that, he knew something without knowing what he knew. And then there was a sudden realization of what he knew; images appeared for what he knew; and after that he attached words to the images.

Hearty finally realized that, if part of Carl was already under the domination of an evil spirit, nevertheless another part of him was still free and as yet unpossessed. It was this profound part of Carl's being that was appealing for help. In a somewhat disconcerting moment, Hearty realized that Carl must be aware that he, Hearty, knew of the possession.

It was quite a while before Hearty got used to the idea of such a fission in a human personality with whom he was in contact several times a week. But Hearty had already learned enough over the years to realize that evil spirits do not always know everything—they do not necessarily know accurately even what they already possess. He had more than once taken hope from that very fact.

The last three "messages" Carl sent him occurred at some distance apart both in terms of time and space. One came to him on the day of his farewell to Carl at the end of his studies. When he looked back at the office building where he had just left Carl, the message came loud and clear for Hearty's psyche: "Help me! Come when I am just about to be completely taken." Hearty dropped into the college chapel and said some prayers. He had to believe and trust that he would arrive in time for that moment when Carl was about to be "completely taken."

The next message came to him one morning in Newark in late 1972: Carl was about to take some final step; he needed now to be pulled back, but he was helpless. Left to himself, he had to go on and perform the final act of submission to the spirit that had taken possession of him. Hearty came as fast as he could to the university campus, but he missed Carl both at the campus and at the airport.

The last message came to him at the end of July that same year. He knew Carl was home in Philadelphia and that he needed him. Again Hearty set out without delay in order to get to Carl. Hearty lost no time in beginning the examinations and study that were needed in advance of any expected exorcism.

His first undertaking was to acquaint himself with Carl's life and to test the validity of Carl's supposed psychic powers. He spoke with all those who had known Carl intimately. He tracked down both Olde and Wanola P. in different parts of the country. They both came to see Hearty; and Olde in particular was an enormous help. Carl's mother, now divorced from his father and remarried, lived in Malta. But his father and two brothers gave Hearty all the help they could.

The best parapsychologist Carl knew, a Swiss-born German, was in New York for a lecture series. Carl and Hearty spent three weeks there; and the parapsychologist completed his examination of Carl between his lecture commitments. His verdict on Carl: positive. That is, the man possessed extraordinary extrasensory powers, but he was suffering from some deep trauma which was out of the parapsychologist's reach. Neither hypnosis nor pharmacological treatment was of any avail.

Hearty and Carl returned to Philadelphia, but Hearty was not yet satisfied. He distrusted parapsychologists.

While maintaining a home base in his own diocese in Newark, he went to New York several times with Carl. After a thorough physical examination, Carl was put in the hands of two psychiatrists who put him through a battery of tests. In substance, their verdict was the same as that of the parapsychologist: Carl V. was normal and sane by any standard acceptable to their profession. He had suffered, they said, from a good deal of nervous tension during the previous summer. But they could uncover no abnormality.

One of them urged Carl to return to Aquileia and finish the rite he had gone there to perform. Hearty vetoed this suggestion.

The other suggested mildly that Carl "go easy on the religion bit" for a couple of years, to give himself a chance to recuperate lost ground and gain self-confidence. As Hearty was leaving his office, the second psychiatrist became a little more expansive. He felt a lot of people were crazy on account of religion, he said. All that guilt. "Get him to go out and lay broads, Father. That'll do the trick."

"God bless such salutary broads, Doctor," Hearty said, tipping his hat as he left.

As his investigations progressed over the weeks and months, Hearty was increasingly certain. Carl had to be exorcised. All this while, and right up to the exorcism, Carl was completely docile. He urged Hearty to hurry up. "I haven't much time, Hearty," he used to say wistfully.

But Hearty felt he had to be thorough. He had never been involved in an exorcism of a person as psychically gifted as Carl, and he did not know how this unusual element might be used, even against Carl's will, as a serious weapon against them both. He insisted on covering every inch of ground Carl had traveled in parapsychology since his student days. Only in this way would Hearty be at least reasonably well equipped to follow and deal with any vagary through which Carl might pass during the exorcism.

In addition, Hearty had one profound doubt. For the first time he foresaw the possibility that in an exorcism the exorcee might die or go insane because of the exorcism.

Hearty was rather sure of a few things: that Carl's claimed perception of the non-thing aura as well as his professed astral-travel trances and his knowledge of former reincarnations were deceptions induced by the evil spirit. And he guessed the only tangible proof that the spirit had been expelled would be the cessation of these effects in Carl.

Hearty felt that, if he was correct in his basic analyses, then the final and possibly the greatest danger to Carl would lie in his reaction to the sudden exposure of how he had been deceived over and over and had consented to each deception. The bottom would fall out of his life. Could he take the strain? Disillusionment or disappointment as profound as Carl would likely undergo in this exorcism could, as Hearty knew from his studies and experience, render a human being not merely catatonic, but in extreme cases suicidal.

Right up to the last moment, in spite of the assurance that every precaution and test he could devise showed Carl to be strong and sturdy, Hearty could not rid himself of this idea of extreme danger for Carl. Finally he gave Carl the option to withdraw or to go ahead. He warned him of what he felt to be the risks if he chose to go ahead.

Carl insisted on going on with the exorcism. "If I live as I am, I will die a real death of soul. If I die under exorcism, I may be saved. If I go insane, perhaps God will take this into account when judging me."

The choice of locale for the exorcism was easy. Carl wanted it to take place in his childhood home out beyond Chestnut Hill among the hills of the Piedmont plateau, and in the place where he had had his teenage vision—his father's library-den.

Hearty, going against the practice of many exorcists known to him, had nothing removed from the place except breakable objects such as desk lamps, vases, ashtrays, light tables, glasses, statuettes, and pictures. He had the carpet taken up. Books and bookshelves he left in place.

He had a reason for this which was part of his guessing game at this point. He assessed—rightly, as it turned out—that any special difficulty in unmasking the evil spirit in Carl would arise because its possession of Carl was so subtle and so bound up with his psychic forces.

Carl did possess a power of telekinesis. It was theoretically possible that Carl would use this power to make the exorcism difficult, if not impossible. But Carl, relying on that still-intact part of him with which he had signaled to Hearty before for help, now reassured Hearty that he, Carl, would not use, and could refrain from using, that telekinetic power. Hearty felt, therefore, he could be practically certain that, if there were telekinetic disturbances during the rite, they would be signs of the evil spirit's displeasure. And in that case, he could follow that clue and seek the further discomfiture and final expulsion of the spirit.

Hearty was ably aided in the exorcism by four men whom he had trained over the years as assistants. They never failed to come to him whenever he was performing an exorcism. One was a doctor; two were businessmen; the fourth was a factory foreman.

The exorcism of Carl V. lasted for five days. It was very unusual in that its course was largely determined, as Hearty had been certain it would be, by the exceptional psychic gifts Carl possessed. Hearty had to deal with Carl not only as possessed, but as a medium in the psychic sense. Indeed, there were brief silences throughout part of the exorcism when only the looks of Hearty and Carl indicated to the assistants what was going on. At those times, the quick interchange of challenge, threat, command, and insult between Hearty and the evil spirit possessing Carl were telepathic. Hearty's notes serve us well for these verbal blanks.

A dangerous, complicating problem, in addition, was that Hearty could not always determine whether it was Carl or the possessing spirit that was producing psychic effects. In this case above all others in Hearty's career, all care and alertness had to be maintained. There was no shortcut. As exorcist, Hearty had to get to the core of the possession and make sure that the evil was expelled in its vicious essence.

Hearty also realized his own danger in such an exorcism. He was moving on a slippery psychic plane, where thought and memory and imagination are peculiarly naked and open to aggression. His friend in Kyoto had shown him that many years ago. He had had occasion to learn it again since.

Curiously, but briefly, the one great advantage Hearty enjoyed at the beginning of the exorcism was precisely Carl's power as a medium. With Carl disposed to help, Hearty had little difficulty in ferreting the evil spirit out and compelling it to identify itself. Therefore, Confrontation with Tortoise, as it called itself, was achieved quickly. But, by the same measure, the Clash between Hearty and Tortoise was immensely painful.

Carl's cooperation with Hearty was cut off abruptly when the Confrontation took place between Hearty and Tortoise. Carl became helpless and unhelping. In his struggle alone, the wrenching of Hearty's will and the wound to his mind were acute, sharp beyond words, and irreparable.

In excerpting the exorcism transcript, therefore, choice has been made of passages concerning the identification of the evil spirit, the unmasking of the deceptions Carl had accepted, and the effect of that unmasking on Hearty and on Carl himself. The transcript contains many more details (omitted here) about Carl's supposed reincarnation in the ancient Roman, Petrus, about early Christian rites, and about Carl's own psychical development from teenage on.

TORTOISE

"Do you feel all right, Carl?" Hearty's voice at the opening of the exorcism is full of feeling. But Carl is perfectly calm.

"Yes, Father. Don't worry anymore. Let's get going."

Carl is lying on the couch in his father's den. Hearty's four assistants are kneeling around the couch. Hearty, flanked by his assistant priest, stands at the foot of the couch. It is 4:30 A.M., the beginning of the first day of the exorcism.

Hearty takes up the opening words of the rite. His chanting stops after the first three sentences.

He looks at Carl. He is motionless. Something alarms Hearty.

"Carl! Carl! Answer me! Don't slip away, Carl! Answer me!"

Carl stirs and speaks uneasily. "It's hard, Father. It's hard."

"Carl, what's happening?"

"Low g-g-ga-gate . . ." Carl stumbles off into silence.

"Carl, before you slip into high-gate, tell me. Just before. Do you hear me? Carl! Do you hear me?"

"Ye-e-e-e-e-e-es, Fa-a-a . . ." Carl's voice trails off.

Hearty continues for a minute or two with his monotone chanting of the exorcism prayers, then the chanting stops. Carl's mouth is opening and shutting. His fists are clenched.

"High-g-g-g-g-g . . ." Hearty can hardly hear his voice.

He motions to the assistants to take hold of Carl's legs and arms. Hearty speaks.

"Spirit of Evil, you are commanded in the name of Jesus: Do not cloud the mind of Carl. Do not enslave his will. There is to be no deception. In the name of Jesus, stop."

Hearty looks at Carl: his face relaxes; his fists are unclenched. After a few moments, Carl speaks slowly without opening his eyes.

"I cannot hold against them . . . him . . . them, Father. I cannot hold much longer. Too habit . . ." His voice breaks.

"In the name of Jesus . . ." Hearty breaks off. The strain in the faces and arms of the assistants is a warning to him. Carl's body is struggling to rise.

"Speak, Evil Spirit! Speak and declare yourself," Hearty commands. He sprinkles some holy water and holds up the crucifix. Carl struggles for about a minute or so. There is silence in the room, except for the rustling and heavy breathing of that struggle.

Finally, all signs of life disappear from Carl's face. Carl's body ceases to move. His lips open. Hearty hears the voice of Carl, but silken, smooth, ingratiating in tone, without any accentuation; it speaks in short broken sentences. It is like a slowly turning record. Clearly Carl is now a medium for the evil spirit.

"I am the spirit. Of Carl. We are ascending. Into high-gate. And beyond. I am the spirit. Of Carl. We are ascending. Into high-gate. And beyond. I am . . ."

Hearty decides to break in. "You are not the spirit of Carl. You are the spirit of Satan, the evil spirit who possessed him. In the name of Jesus, cease your deception. Declare yourself. Who are you? What name do you go by? Why do you possess God's creature, Carl? In the name of Jesus, speak. By the authority of Jesus and his Church, I command you. Speak!"

All present now notice a sudden change in Carl's body. In some way or other, it seems to shrink or diminish in size or bulk. The assistant priest afterward described it "as if his body caved in on itself." The luster goes out of Carl's black hair, even his curls seem flat. The skin on his face is drawn taut. They see the stretched tendons and veins in his neck clearly. His trunk, arms, and legs look as if a huge, invisible weight rested on them, pressing them down but not flattening them. There is no sound. The silence becomes oppressive.

Hearty decides to speak again. "Evil Spirit, you are commanded. In the name of Jesus, speak!"

Silence ensues. Everyone becomes aware of the slightest sound—the breathing of the others, the scuffing of a shoe on the wooden flooring, the sound of someone swallowing hard, the intake of breath in a quick sigh. But Hearty is not discouraged. It is the Tortoise to which Carl was drawn; and the progress of a tortoise is slow but sure. Hearty is fully confident. He waits.

Then, without warning, a minor bedlam breaks out. Every book on the shelves lining three walls of the den come toppling down pell-mell on the floor, their pages opening, covers flying, book after book toppling off in no order, pages fluttering, onto the floor with dull thuds and tearing sounds. It is as if two pairs of hands attack each shelf simultaneously. The sudden sound unnerves one of the assistants; in sheer surprise and fright he half-screams.

Hearty has not moved even his eyes. They are on Carl's face. His gamble has paid off. The only thing Hearty does is raise his hand for calm; he knows exactly what is happening. The tortoise is "approaching."

There is silence once again. They wait. Carl is still sunk into himself.

Hearty has almost made up his mind to take up more exorcism prayers when he feels the first internal pressures. He finds it increasingly difficult to keep his eyes on Carl's face. His vision keeps fading as his imagination fills with curious images.

"Jesus, Lord Jesus," Hearty prays silently. "Save me. Help me now. I cannot resist this if you leave me to myself. I believe. Lord Jesus, help me."

The others know by Hearty's appearance that something is happening to him. His eyes blink open and shut. He sways slightly on his feet. His knuckles show white as he holds the crucifix.

The assistant priest understands. Hearty has instructed him well; and he, too, has worked frequently with Hearty at exorcisms. He folds his hand over Hearty's around the crucifix. With the other, he makes the sign of the cross on Hearty's forehead, saying out loud: "Lord Jesus, have mercy on your servant." The four assistants take their cue and repeat the same prayer.

Slowly Hearty's imagination clears. But pain is now his adversary. His head is racked by a shooting migraine. Every look he gives Carl is full of an ache he never felt before. This crisis passes, but like all attacks in exorcism, it has taken its toll.

When he speaks again, Hearty's voice has changed from a deep vibrancy to a strained and choking tone. His Welsh lilt has thickened.

"In the name of the Savior, the Lord Jesus, you will declare yourself, Evil Spirit!"

They all look at Carl. His head has moved. His mouth opens and they hear a voice that this time in no way resembles Carl's. It is like the thin falsetto produced by a deep-voiced man as a mockery of somebody else. It rings with a note of falsity, but is quite defiant. It irritates and frightens.

"We will do the bidding of no being but Carl's friend. We will answer to . . ."

"You will answer in the name of Jesus," Hearty shoots back vehemently, his voice cracking under the strain of this effort.

"Hear, then, our voice, and see if you, a miserable, two-legged piece of slime, can command the Lord of Knowledge, the Unconquered."

Before Hearty gets in a reply, Carl's voice changes. Hearty looks quickly at his assistants: "Brace yourselves, boys! This is going to be tough on all of us."

Their ears are suddenly filled with sound. As long as they could concentrate on Carl, it seemed to them that the sound was coming from his lips. But now the force and peculiar quality of that sound rapidly distracts them. They cannot bear to look at Carl or at anything else, so violent is that absorption of their attention. Carl starts to thrash around. The assistants barely succeed in holding his arms and legs.

It is not so much how loud or piercing that sound is. Rather, it is the quality of sound each one hears. For, as they find out by comparing notes later, the sound is tailored to each one's feelings, experience, and character. Each one is treated to a replay of all past pain made more agonizing now than when it had happened. Each feels the pain of every heartbreaking cry, of every lonely tone of voice, of every harsh piece of news he has experienced during his past life. The doctor hears again the dying breath of the first patient he ever lost—a young mother in childbirth crying as she died, "Let me see my son! Let me see my son!" And together with that, his own crying as a child; and the shout of a man who was knocked down and killed in front of his eyes a year before. Another hears the last crying of his own child, who had died of a brain tumor; another, his own betrayal of his employers at a private meeting with a competitor company. And so on for all. That voice is duplicating and reproducing for each one all those now-remembered sounds of pain, regret, guilt, despair, sorrow, disgust, anguish that make up the sum of his life's experience of suffering and human weakness.

When one listens to the taping of this part in the exorcism, all one hears is an uneven series of groanings and heavy breathing.

Hearty's experience is different. The voice does not affect his imagination. It seems to twist his mind. He becomes full of a quietly running commentary: whole sentences are scurrying through his mind—"The Lord of Knowledge must be adored. . . . With knowledge one can be sure. . . . Surety only comes from a clear vision. . . . Clear vision comes from clear thought. . . . Feelings and beliefs are a travesty. . . . The Lord of Knowledge gives possession of the earth. . . . The earth is all one, all one being. . . ."—until the harangue seems endless. Hearty cannot remember it all. When it finally seems to reach an ending, it is only to start again from the beginning, going faster and faster, as it repeats itself over and over again.

Hearty can manage no word, verbal or mental, on his own. But instinctively he presses the crucifix to his lips and holds it there. The gesture is seemingly enough. The grip on his mind eases. The logic countdown stops. He is free again.

"In the name of Jesus, the Savior, you are commanded to declare yourself clearly. Speak, Evil Spirit!"

Hearty's assistants are recovering. They renew their grip on Carl.

Carl himself is still. But his face is lit up with color. He looks alive, well, just like somebody lying down with his eyes closed as he talks calmly. It is not Carl's voice, however. All present hear it, but each one's description of it differs from the others. All agree it is calm, almost superior in tone, neither slow nor fast, with just a little suspicion of a laugh or sneer in it. But some of them hear a young person speaking, some a very old man, some a mechanical voice, still others hear that voice as a distant echo. On the tape today, the sex of the speaker is indistinguishable—it could be male or female. To this writer it brought back memories of the tone of voice used by announcers in the music halls of the 1930s: affected, openly artificial, always with a note of laughing ridicule, loaded with suggestive undertones.

"We come in the name of the Tortoise. Tortoise. Call us Tortoise. We have the eternity of the Lord of Knowledge."

Hearty feels thankful: he has gained a point. But almost immediately he regrets that distraction.

The voice speaks again. "Thankful, eh? Don't you know what we've prepared for you, rooster-lover? Cock-lover?" Hearty concentrates again, restraining his impulse to ask what. The evil spirit may be constrained to Confrontation; but any opening he, the exorcist, affords it can be turned in a flash and fatally to the spirit's advantage. Hearty swings into his main interrogation.

"Tortoise—"

"Yes, cock-lover—"

"You will speak only in answer to the question put you in the name of Jesus." No rejoinder to that one, but Carl tries to turn over on his face. The assistants hold him firmly. He struggles a little, then is still.

"Were all Carl's psychic powers due to your intervention, or because he was so gifted by nature?"

"Both." At this answer, Hearty concentrates again. Some force is attacking his mentality. His mind is like a barred door with strong hands beating insistently upon its panels.

"Let us take his reincarnation, his supposed reincarnations. Was this your work?"

"We, belonging to the Tortoise, existing in his eternity, have all time in front of us as one unceasing moment."

"But Carl spoke to people long dead. He knew their thoughts and their surroundings."

"The living are surrounded by their dead. Those of the dead who belong to us, they do our bidding. Everyone in the Kingdom does our bidding."

"And those who don't belong to you—"

"The Latter." It comes as a snarl, but also, Hearty feels, with a certain note of craven fear. That fear impresses Hearty. Again he is distracted, and again he pays the price.

"You too, cock-lover! Priest! You too will be afraid when you get what's coming to you." The door of Hearty's mind is giving way. That force is battering at him. He falters a moment, then regains concentration in an immense effort. He goes on questioning.

"The astral travels of Carl? Did you engineer that?"

"Yes."

"How did you get him into such delusion?"

"Once spirit is confused with psyche, we can let anybody see, hear, touch, taste, know, desire the impossible. He was ours. He is ours. He is of the Kingdom."

Carl is not moving, but his entire body lies once again in the crushed position. The pathos of his captivity makes Hearty wince. He prays quietly, "Jesus, give him strength." Then he tries to continue his interrogation, but the voice interrupts, this time screaming in unbelievable despair.

"We will not be expelled. We have our home in him. He belongs to us." Hearty waits as the scream dies away in gurgles. Carl's own throat is visibly moving.

"Are you the maker of the Non Self aura?"

No."

"How did you use the Non Self aura in Carl's case?"

"The aura is there for all who can perceive it. Only humans have learned to unsee it. If they saw it continually, they would die."

"How did you use it?"

"We didn't."

Hearty now flings concise questions, most of which need only a yes or no as answer. His aim is to expose the evil spirit, to make it tell its own deceptions.

"Did Carl see it?"

"Yes."

"Did you make it clear for him?"

"Yes."

"Why?"

"He wanted it so!"

"Did he ask you?"

"We offered."

"Did he know who you were?"

"He knew."

"Clearly?"

"Clear enough."

"Did he bilocate?"

"No."

"What happened?"

"We gave him knowledge of distant places as if he was there."

"Had he a double, a psychic double?"

"We gave him one."

"How?"

"Gave him the knowledge a double would have."

"When did you start at Carl?"

"In his youth."

"Did you give him his early vision?"

"No."

"Did you interfere with it?"

"Yes."

"Why?"

"He wanted us to do so."

"How do you know?"

"We know."

"By what sign?"

"We know."

"What did he do that let you know?"

"We know."

"In the name of Jesus, I command you: Tell me how you knew."

There is a long pause of about two minutes. Hearty waits patiently, all the while looking at Carl, keeping his mind on the question.

Then the trap comes for him.

"There is no word for it."

"Is there a thought for it?"

"Yes." Hearty, his concentration failing momentarily, caught up in his interrogation, does not see the trap opening in front of him. He asks simply:

"What is that thought?"

And immediately he and the assistants notice the change in Carl. The crushed and lifeless look is instantaneously gone. His body relaxes beneath the hands of the assistants. He draws in a long, deep breath and stretches himself like a man coming pleasantly out of a deep sleep. His eyes start to open. He moves his head gently from side to side. The color is back in his cheeks, his lips are smiling, and his eyes are quizzical with good humor.

It all happens so unexpectedly that everyone is taken by surprise. The assistants who have been holding him in grim determination and fear up to this moment now feel embarrassed. Carl is not even offended. He seems to be amused but tolerant.

"Hey, guys, can I sit up? It's okay. It's okay."

The voice is Carl's. His behavior is normal.

Hearty is the only one who realizes what has happened. But too late! He is trapped. He is getting the "thought." Before he feels the full force of that invasion in his mind, he sees the four assistants on their feet looking at him for some explanation or instruction. Carl has sat up on the couch, one leg thrown easily over the side. He also is looking at Hearty. All five wear the same quizzical expression: they seem to be surprised at Hearty's behavior.

The assistant priest also has turned around to look at Hearty. He, too, has a questioning look. The look is an appeal to Hearty, but Hearty is helpless at that moment.

His chief feeling is one of horror: horror at what he sees happening, horror at his own imprisonment in his mind. The "thought" is now clear to him in a way he never dreamed: he sees it concretely in his four assistants and in Carl. They are completely at ease, their only emotion is wonder that Hearty is not at ease. He wants to scream at them, to shout: "Watch out! Watch out! They have played on your desire for normal behavior. They are making it all normal for you." But he cannot open his mouth or produce a sound.

As his helplessness grows, he sees more and more clearly what is happening. No one wants to believe in evil, really, above all, not in an evil being, an evil spirit. Everyone wants to abolish the idea. To admit the existence of evil means a responsibility, and no one wants that responsibility. That is the opening through which Tortoise crawls, stilling all suspicions, making everything seem normal and natural. This is the "thought," the unwariness of the ordinary human being which amounts to a disinclination to believe in evil. And, if you do not believe in evil, how can you believe in or ever know what good is?

Inside in his mind, this realization begins to inflate like a rubber balloon, widening and swelling in its intensity, increasing his helplessness side by side with his new understanding.

Now all looking at him are smiling, Carl included. All they see is Hearty's long, bony face, his lips split in what they take as a grimace of embarrassment. And the more effort he makes, the more he seems to grimace.

Hearty's torture is at its peak, and his endurance almost ended, when the assistant priest notices one thing: Hearty is pressing the crucifix to the side of his head. The younger priest stops: something must be wrong. Something *must* be wrong. Otherwise, Hearty is striking a comic pose using the crucifix, and Hearty would never do that during an exorcism or at any other time. What can be wrong?

Then, turning to the others, the assistant priest says: "Something's wrong with Hearty. Look!"

It is Carl who answers, evenly and in apparent good humor. "Look yourself, Father. He's trying to crucify himself. A bald-headed Christ with spectacles." And he bursts into a peal of laughter.

The effect is like a gunshot. Everyone suddenly stops. An eerie note has been struck. Five heads turn around and five pairs of eyes stare at Carl incredulously.

The assistant priest takes over. "In the name of the Church and of Jesus who founded it . . ."

But he is interrupted. Carl begins to protest, apparently in good humor still. "Father, look!"

"Hold him down!" the priest orders the four assistants. Then to Carl: "In the name of Jesus, I command you to desist."

This delay is all Hearty needs. The pressure relents; the "thought" deflates inside his mind. He is free again. He almost lost, but he has learned two things. He knows the ruse of normalcy that this spirit has used to work in Carl for his acceptance, step by step, year by year. He knows the "thought." And, second, he knows for certain now that Carl's psychic powers, and his own, will be used as a weapon against him at the slightest opening. His careful preparation may at least be some defense.

Carl is lying down again, wide awake, under the control of the assistants once more, his eyes narrowed to slits, his face a sheet of white anger.

As Hearty gazes at Carl, his mind races back: somewhere he has touched a raw nerve. Somehow he has almost found the central weakness of the spirit that calls itself Tortoise. He has to pursue this line. His next question is peremptory.

"Where were you leading Carl?"

"To knowledge of the universe." The words come out from between Carl's tightly clenched teeth.

"What knowledge?"

There is no answer at first. Then slowly and grudgingly the words come. "The knowledge that humans are just a part of the universe."

"How do you mean a 'part' merely?"

"That they are parts of a greater physical being."

"What being?"

"The universe."

"The universe of matter?"

"Yes."

"And of psychic forces?"

"Yes."

"And that this was creator of humans?"

"Yes."

"A personal creator?"

"No."

"A physical creator?"

"Yes also."

"A psychophysical creator?"

"Yes. Indeed, yes."

"Why did you lead Carl in this way?"

"Because he would lead others."

"Why lead others in this way?"

"Because then they belong to the Kingdom."

"Why belong to the Kingdom?"

Those looking at Carl begin to feel that he is about to explode in some way. The words are coming out of him with greater harshness. He draws a breath for almost every word, so that each word comes out on a blast of breath. His arms, legs, and torso are writhing more and more. The assistants hold him down, but cannot hold him still. Now with that last question, all see the explosion coming. It starts building with Carl's response to Hearty's last question.

"*Why*, Priest? *Why?* You stand there with your bald head, your scorched testicles, your smelly clothes, your yellowing teeth, your stinking guts, and you ask us *why? Why? Why? Why? Why?*" The word comes out on the crest of ever-louder shouts.

"*WHY?*" he finally shouts at the top of his voice, his head raised to stare at Hearty. "*Why?* Because we hate the Latter. We hate. Hate. Hate. We hate those stained with his blood. We hate and despise those that follow him. We want to divert all from him and we want all in the Kingdom where he cannot reach them. Where they cannot go with him. And we want you, Priest! Because we have Carl. He is ours. And no power can undo our hold on him. No power. No power!"

Carl falls back, his eyes bulging, sweat pouring down his face and body.

Hearty all this time remains utterly still. He yet has to maneuver the spirit into a direct clash.

He now plays his trump card; he addresses himself to Carl.

"Carl, in the name of Jesus who saved you and who will save you, I command you, listen to me."

Carl's body begins to go cold. The assistants tell that to Hearty. He shakes his head and goes on.

"Carl! We know you are prisoner. We know that. But a part of you is free and has never been touched. Speak to us. Communicate with us."

Hearty is gambling on the same telepathic power in Carl that had called to him for help, to reach out now in some crucial sign of cooperation with good, a sign of his deepest will turned against evil.

"Carl, I never told you all the years of my student days. I never told you. I am a receiver. I can receive. You can communicate with me now. Please. We need your cooperation. Just one clear effort and the whole thing is over. Please, Carl! Please!"

Carl's body is now quite calm, his head thrown back on the couch, his arms and legs limp, his body soaked with perspiration. Hearty looks at him, waiting, voiding his own mind, hoping and waiting.

Then the message starts to come. It wisps across Hearty's "screen," at first in vague waves, then in clearer outline. It is an experience of emotions and emotional ideas each entwined with the other. It invades Hearty's psyche, stealing into all the nooks and corners of his conscious being. It is unlike any message he could have imagined. He is undergoing the feelings and desolation of ideas that beset someone exiled to a baleful land, no warmth, no love, no togetherness, no home, no smile, only the automatic gyrating of controlled beings. Animals frozen by blinding light or tumbling into a private abyss where their free-fall scream never meets its own echo and from which their desires never escape to fulfillment.

It is Carl's message, his picture of what his bondage is like. He is faced with the suicide of those who die denying they want to live on, or were ever made to live by love. It is an instantaneous tale of sadness in living and utter misery in dying.

Carl has done the trick. Translated into words he is saying to Hearty: "See! This is my exile from love, my slavery to a degrading psychism, and my final tumbling into the aloneness of Hell forever."

"Jesus can save you, Carl," Hearty begins. "Jesus . . ."

He gets no further. The "message" stops abruptly. Hearty shakes his head. A warning word from his assistant priest makes him focus his vision on Carl. Carl has opened his eyes and speaks in a gentle whisper to the two assistants holding him by the arms. Apparently he asks them in a normal voice to let him sit up and "watch the Father." The two release his arms. "It sounded so normal," one of the assistants said regretfully later.

Carl fixes his eyes on Hearty, a slow grin of delight comes over his face. Hearty is no longer "opaque" to him. For the first time, he is looking into Hearty's mind.

In retrospect, it now seems to Hearty that Carl's minimal freedom from constraint and his telepathic communication with Hearty, while he was not yet free of possession, provided an ideal avenue for a direct attack on Hearty.

Carl is now to be used as a medium for the final Clash. Against Tortoise, Hearty now has no ally. He sees the purpose in Carl's life. He knows. He braces himself.

Hearty's first, frightening realization is that his "censor" bond is gone: he cannot block at will, as always before this, any message from the outside or any perception by an outsider into his mind and inner condition. Now, for the first time in his life, he is an unwilling "receiver." This he has not foreseen. He has thought that as long as his will was free his censor bond would be at his disposal. But his protection is gone. He is naked. And each part of his inner man is successively invaded, seized, and polluted. A malevolent intelligence is scanning the innards of his very self. That attack finally wells up and pours over him. Hearty is filled with a disgust and loathing he cannot control. He starts to retch.

In the Clash of his will with the evil spirit, he is whipped with a ferocity he could never have imagined. Hearty's torture comes from himself: he seems to be an onlooker watching his own punishment. According to the tape and the accounts of his assistants, this crisis of Hearty's lasts from three to five minutes. To Hearty it is an age. As he looks into Carl's eyes, he no longer sees their color, shape, or expression. Carl is in every sense the medium of evil. Hearty becomes a passive one, the "viewed." He "stops seeing" for that time and "is only seen."

The keynote of that Clash is an "either/or." From the beginning it is conveyed to Hearty subtly that, if he submits, if he renounces his opposition to the evil spirit, all will be well; the attack will cease. If not, he will be destroyed.

Now, in one hurting glare of exposure, he sees his weaknesses laid bare: the tawdry logic he received in his philosophy training, the self-confident and ignorantly treated facts of theology, the self-indulgence and onetime hypocrisies of his piety, the useless pride in his priesthood—all is so much drivel and dross, a dump of human trash that withers under the fire of that gaze looking in at him and probing every darkest cranny of his weakness.

"For as long as it lasted," Hearty relates, "it was a brutal partial possession of me. All that remained finally free was my will. And even that . . ." Hearty always leaves this thought unfinished.

The searching gaze continues like a filthy and malicious hand pawing each of his faculties contemptuously. Even his will is fingered and stripped of the motives he had always relied upon. His will is the last bastion. It holds. But now he sees all its apparent strength torn from it like so many cardboard coverings from an inner treasure: his sensuous enthusiasm for beautiful ceremony, his esteem of good people, his compassion for the sick and the helpless, his pride in being a priest and a man, his satisfaction in his Welsh culture, his reliance on the approval of parents, teachers, superiors, his bishop, the Pope, the consolation of prayer and submission to law. All are torn brutally aside. And only his willing self holds at last. His soul as a willing being stands naked of all the supports and reasons of a lifetime, scrutinized by the unwavering gaze of high, unlovely, and unloving intelligence.

"But this was all by the way," Hearty explains in the offhand way survivors of terrible sufferings speak of certain indescribable moments. "The aim was to make my free choice impossible."

The only external sign of his experience is seen by his assistants in the way Hearty holds his crucifix between him and Carl: his two arms straight out in front of him, his eyes level with the crossbar of the crucifix, so that he is looking past the head and over the arms of the crucified. In the beginning of Hearty's agony, the crucifix faces Carl. After about two minutes or so, Hearty turns the crucifix around so that the crucified faces Hearty himself. We can only guess that then his real crisis starts. It lasts only a moment, a never-ending moment in which he knows no time, and suffering seems eternal.

For the onlookers, meanwhile, Carl never seems to change. He sits upon the couch, his eyes fixed on Hearty's, his body immobile. "His eyes were like hollow blanks," said one assistant. And several of them are reminded of ancient statues in which soulless eyes of antiquity turn upon the banality of life with a barren gaze.

Hearty is reduced by that gaze to an effort of sheer survival, holding on fiercely to his will and resolve. The worst is just beginning. His mind, imagination, and memory are now out of his control. He thinks, he remembers, he imagines what the "others" want him to think, remember, and imagine. He is now treated to himself in a humiliating way. He sees his world as a globe dotted with lands and oceans, with cities and houses and people, covered with vegetation and sand and animals, the whole hanging in an atmosphere; and "above" it, somehow or other, "God" or "Jesus" or "Heaven," with little tenuous lines running down to each human being. It is all now so laughable, so childish, so contemptible, so superstitious—this is conveyed to him like a cosmic joke turned on him with a cackle of superior intelligence.

And in that sound he feels all meaning to his life is flowing away into derisive nothingness. What he had ambitioned to be, what he had become, the values he had lived by—all now seems an ugly, useless comedy of illusions. "I never meant anything, never came to anything, never was anything." Hearty's mind drummed with the words.

And what now seems the core of that childish view is the way he always saw Earth as a collection of things, of separate and disparate little objects, men, animals, plants, stones. "Wrong! Wrong! Wrong!" are the echoes in his mind. "Wrong and childish from the beginning." The sadness and chagrin at his weakness and childishness are about as great as he can bear, when that vision is swept away and a new series of images is presented to him in an aura not of ridicule, but of approbation and applause. The aura of untruth.

It is the globe again, together with all the objects in it—men, women, animals, plants, cities, oceans. But now all exist in an organized system. Everything is interconnected. There is really no difference between one thing and anything else. From the mitochondria in cells that convert oxygen into energy up to the largest land masses, the most complicated systems of living societies. He is shown it all. And all, land, oceans, animals, humans, plants are one living organism clad in the shell of breathable atmosphere. Psychic forces bind it all together, like ethereal blood running in the veins of some unimagined giant. It is a self-creating, self-protecting, self-developing thing. A unique being. Earth as mother, as womb, as god, as tomb, as a whole unity protected by its own shell and its own strength, as all there is.

Now and again that globe's outlines swirl into the form of a snail or a tortoise clad in its own protective hard and furrowed shell. This sight swamps Hearty's mind with intellectual satisfaction and clothes his imagination with images of harmony, freedom, truth.

His memory is in abeyance. He is only in the present moment, and he can anticipate no future. It is irresistible for all his powers—except his embattled will. Naked and, as it were, standing alone in the shadow of its own unfulfilled desire, his willing self remains aloof—brooding, wavering, doubtful—but aloof, not yet committed.

Only one element in that vision of human life keeps him from embracing it. It is its loveless character. Something inside him keeps crying out, "I need love. I won't take less." At the last central pinpoint of his free being Hearty stands and holds, rejecting the ultimatum, the "either/or" thrown at him.

But immediately some physical strength starts giving way in him under a series of shooting pains that jab at the muscles in his arms and legs. The strain is unbearable. His fingers are loosening their grip on the crucifix. He ceases to hold it rigidly upright with the crucified facing him. It wavers and swings a little to the left, a little to the right. The light glances off the metal head of the crucified and off the small notice over it which carries the letters "INRI" ("Jesus of Nazareth, King of the Jews").

In Hearty's world at that moment there is no such thing as an accident. The apparently accidental shining of the metal sparks a deep instinct in him. He begins to say, at first internally, then audibly: "Jesus . . . Jesus . . . Jesus . . . Jesus . . . Jesus . . . Jesus."

When his words become audible, he is already over the worst. A new force sweeps across his mind and imagination, blowing to nothingness the entire fabric of loveless belief thrust at him as his guarantee of peace. Hearty feels for an instant some crushing pain within him: in his success he has had to sacrifice something—he does not yet know what—some intimate joy of being human, some one personal desire or inclination, some indulgence in the comeliness of human beauty and symmetry, some happiness he otherwise would be able to have legitimately in his human living. Some deeply personal fiber of his will has been seared.

The switch of Hearty's concentration from himself to Carl is instantaneous and "murderous"—his own word—in its intent. He now wants to murder that which holds Carl. The assistants see his head lift and his eyes burn with some fire of anger and willfulness. "I honestly thought for an instant that he had gone mad," the assistant priest relates frankly.

Hearty's first words after the Clash still sound vicious today on the tape.

"Murderer! Be murdered now! In your turn!"

Carl falls back on the couch. The assistants hold him, but Carl's struggle is not physical now. In a weak and pathetic voice he says only: "Opaque . . . opaque . . . opaque . . ."

"Evil Spirit," Hearty continues, "you will go away from this creature, Carl. You will cease to possess his soul and body. In the name of Jesus you will cease. Now."

Then he turns to Carl in his remarks. "Carl, you have to pay the price. But Jesus is with you. Insofar as you are not under the control of evil, you will renounce step by step each of your former consents. Each one of them."

Carl shakes with terror. He has begun to perspire. He says nothing.

"The vision, Carl! You will see it again. You will see it."

Carl's eyes are fixed now on Hearty's own. They bulge with fear and loathing.

"You will see it. You will reject it!"

"N-n-n-n-n-n-no!" Carl suddenly stutters. "No. Please! No . . ." The words on the tape trail away incoherently.

"Renounce it, Carl," Hearty says sharply, "even though you cannot say so in words."

Carl begins to babble and moan, then stops. Foam seeps out of his mouth.

Hearty goes on mercilessly.

"Carl! Your psychic powers! Carl! Renounce them, insofar as they are products of the Evil One. In the name of Jesus, Carl! Renounce them!"

Carl is no longer looking at Hearty. He has turned his head to one side and keeps looking at the wall to his far left.

"Turn his head around." Hearty's command is curt. The assistants do so. Carl's head is boiling hot and bathed in sweat.

"Now, Carl! For the final renunciation. Look at Tortoise, Carl!" The assistants feel from now on that they are listening to a verbal description of an invisible scene. Only Hearty and Carl seem to be in view of it; both are looking over toward the wall of the room.

"Look at that Evil One, Carl! The Tortoise, your all, your friend, your master, your devil, your death, that Evil One is about to be destroyed for you by Jesus."

Hearty stops. The others see him turn his head aside, as if listening to some instructions; they see a wave of new light shine in his eyes. Then he looks steadily at Carl again.

"You will see that Evil Spirit for what it is, Carl!"

Hearty pauses abruptly as if he has been interrupted. Then: "No! Not in anybody's name, anybody who merely lives and dies." Another pause. Then: "Only one who lives and dies and lives again. Only in his name, Carl."

Carl's eyes are now full of some scene which only he sees. He is not focusing on Hearty. And even though Hearty is looking straight at Carl, he is obviously watching something more than Carl. The assistants can only guess at its identity, but they are as sure as people watching a theater audience that Carl and Hearty are watching something they cannot see.

At a certain point Hearty draws near the couch. Hearty speaks in a low, confident tone. He is praying:

"Lord Jesus Christ, who said, 'I and the Father are one,' act now to purify your servant, Carl, and save him from the Pit and all those who fall into it in everlasting death."

Carl's attitude has changed. He is relaxing. The tension is being wiped off his face. A faint smile of recognition creeps over his mouth and eyes.

Hearty bends low over Carl and whispers in his ear: "Carl! Carl! Look at me, if you can."

There is a small wait. Then Carl turns his head and looks at Hearty. His eyes are warm. And even though they are bloodshot and tired, behind them Hearty can read Carl's look, his personal regard.

"Carl, repeat these words after me. As much, as quick as you can. Put your heart into them. It's the last help before your final struggle."

Carl is looking at him steadily. Hearty says quickly, pausing after each phrase so that Carl can repeat it:

"Lord Jesus, if I must die, let me die. If I live, it will be your will. As long as I remain in life, let me abide in your presence, so completely that, despite my sins and my enemy, when I die, I merely go from your presence to your presence. Amen."

Carl repeats every word. But at the "Amen," his eyes are glazing over. His face is hardening. His head jerks back on the couch.

"Hold his head," Hearty tells the assistants.

He stands up and takes his place at the foot of the couch, holding the crucifix up in front of him. This is the last stage of the exorcism.

Hearty today is loath to go into details of what Carl and he saw at that moment. Clearly from the tapes, it was some vision of Tortoise, but not as in the Aquileia mosaic medallion, and not simply as the animal whose name Tortoise took as his own. Hearty gave the nearest measure I could get of the character of what they both saw when he commented that only because something of human joy had been seared in him was he able to see Tortoise, and, to use his words, "not have a brainstorm or a heart attack or go into permanent shock."

It was apparently some view of Tortoise as a mass of suffering and punishment illuminated and glowing with a hatred and vicious contempt. It was Tortoise as an angel who had been damned to eternal pain by love itself and who only increased in hatred of love according as his pain increased with the infinity of eternity. "Damnation unrelieved in any way," Hearty commented in one of our meetings.

Hearty viewed Tortoise as a threatening enemy, but Carl was now seeing Tortoise, his master, who held him in his actual condition of damned misery.

After a little waiting, Hearty speaks with evident urgency.

"This is Tortoise, Carl, your friend and master. This is the world our enemy would have us accept." He stops and waits.

Carl never takes his eyes off Hearty now.

"Enclosed and shut up within its hard shell, Carl. Imprisoned in Hell. It's the same. Only—" Carl interrupts with a choking sound. Hearty goes on: "Only multiplying its own shape in endless succession, soul-killing succession, banal as graves in a row, Carl."

Carl is beginning to shake again. Hearty assures the assistants with a look, then he continues:

"This is our enemy, Carl. The one who possesses you and has fascinated you and wills you to die the death of the Pit."

If Carl is listening and taking it all in, he is far from uneasy or fearful. His eyes are full of the old fire. There is a look on his face that reminds Hearty of the "twist" or askewness that Carl used to acquire during his trances in his heyday as a psychic.

Hearty's voice gets a special edge to it. "It is all deception, Carl. And it is all about to be destroyed."

Hearty is interrupted by a sound that shakes him severely. Carl has started to cry in sobs. For that moment, Hearty recalls, "I felt like the most uncouth and cruel person that ever existed. I was hurting a baby, it seemed to me."

He forced himself to go on.

"It must be destroyed, Carl. And your Non-Self aura, your non-thingness, your voices, your visions, all will go into the Pit of Oblivion with that Tortoise."

Carl is beginning to struggle against the restraining hands of the assistants.

Hearty grits his teeth for the last effort. He has been on his feet now for over 21 hours. His legs are tired. He has shooting pains across his back. His chest is stiff. His arms and fingers ache from holding the crucifix. His voice is hoarse. The migraine is splitting across his forehead still. Within him, the strange, deep wound in his soul bleeds. All his physical pain is only a dull accompaniment in the background of that inner agony so sharp and present and intimate to him. He will not recover from that wound for a long time.

Carl is trying to get up, to stretch out his arms.

"Nothing can save you, Evil Spirit. And nothing can hold you against the power of Jesus. As you took the form of Tortoise for this creature of God, so as Tortoise depart and fall back where you belong, with your Non-Self aura, with your deceptions, with your lies, with your death."

Hearty makes the sign of the cross over Carl slowly and very deliberately three times.

"Sink into the primeval slime of your punishment where God thrust you after your own rebellion. Be dissolved in the mud and waters and air and fire of that Hell from which Jesus saved Carl and all human beings. Depart!" Hearty pauses. Then in a loud shout: "Depart! Unclean Spirit! In the name of Jesus, depart! Go!"

"DON'T GO!" Carl screams. "Don't leave me now. I cannot live without you. Don't go! Please! My friend! Master!"

Hearty's voice breaks in sharply.

"Look at it, Carl! Look at this chair!"

Carl swivels around, twisting his head. Then he starts to groan: the chair, he sees, has no aura. The Non-Self glow is gone. The chair is there. That is all. Simply there. In all its *isness*. Just a thing. Just a chair. Frantically he looks around the room. As he sees it now, all the lights are out. Things. Things. Things. Things. Among more things. Yellowed ceiling. Faded rose-colored wallpaper. Oaken door and windowsill, parquet flooring. The table with candles and crucifix. The bodies of the assistants and of Hearty. Six brutish lumps. Clods of flesh standing in a darkened world of crass things.

Carl screams and screams until darkness and unconsciousness smother him.

When he forced Carl to look at the objects around him—chairs, windows, flooring, people—Hearty already knew he had vanquished Tortoise. As with any crisis that has carried with it the threat of death, there had been at its ending an abrupt sense of a "lifting off" of stifling oppression; it was the same sudden relief that Father Gerald and his assistants described when Girl-Fixer was beaten and Richard/Rita was freed. It was something akin to the feeling so often recalled by those who were in London the morning everyone expected the final wave of Hitler's blitz that would crush London altogether. In previous weeks, the whining rain of bombs had brought unending destruction, death, mutilation, and growing helplessness. But on that morning of expected horror the eastern sky was empty, tranquil. There was a lifting off of dread. There was the sound of silence. It was over. They had defended and persevered and survived. They knew.

Hearty knew.

And when he forced Carl to see it too, the rest of Hearty's fears for Carl were in large measure justified again. When Carl screamed as Hearty showed him all the things in the room, Hearty knew that, along with Tortoise, the more spectacular elements that had gilded Carl's real psychic abilities had left him. The "Non-Self" aura was gone, as Hearty knew it would be.

With it, Hearty was sure, had gone all those elements that Tortoise—under Hearty's relentless prodding during the Confrontation—had admitted to producing: astral travel, bilocation, and all the rest. Remaining were only those more modest talents Carl had possessed since his early childhood and which he still possesses today.

So desperate was Carl's fear to let go of those privileges and of all his life structure built around them that he cried in pain at the departure even of purest evil. He screamed in horror as all that he had been convinced was "normal" left him forever. He saw again only what everyone sees. Carl in that moment knew with his heart and soul that every warning Hearty had given him was accurate. He had listened to Hearty's warnings before the exorcism only with a cool and detached mind, because with his will he had chosen to follow the fascinating secrets Tortoise offered to share with him.

Now, with Tortoise expelled and the truth of Tortoise's identity crystal clear and admitted by him, a frightful disillusionment ran through Carl with the speed of an electric shock, searing and twisting all his thinking and remembering. This was the shock Hearty had tried to warn Carl of, the shock he was not sure Carl would survive with his sanity, perhaps not even with his life.

The doctor who had assisted at the exorcism continued with Carl's case. Carl remained unconscious for several hours. When he came to, he was unable to converse. He barely reacted to any stimulus and was seemingly alienated from his surroundings. He seemed to recognize no one. But there was no trace of violence.

Carl was transferred to a private clinic, where he remained for just over 11 months. At first, he was not able to care for himself at all. He remained in bed all the time, motionless and apparently caring about nothing. Little by little, he regained awareness of his surroundings. But, even with returning awareness, it was quickly evident that, if he had not lost his memory, it was blurred and incomplete.

During the first few months of his convalescence, Hearty spent hours sitting by Carl's bedside. Sometimes he read excerpts from the daily newspaper, or a chapter from some book about current events, or prayers from the ritual book. At other times, Hearty talked to Carl, for all the world as if the sick man were listening and understanding every word, even though for quite a while there never was the slightest sign or response from Carl.

All this while, as he read or talked by Carl's bedside, Hearty was probing psychically for some stirring in Carl, some little break in the congealed immobility that now enveloped Carl's spirit, some motion out of that deadening passivity he "felt" held Carl captive now that he was free of Tortoise. Each time he left Carl, Hearty carried away with him to haunt his waking hours the memory of that still, drawn face and Carl's staring eyes.

One afternoon at the end of a short visit, as he opened the bedroom door to leave, Hearty turned back to wave goodbye to the man he left each day lying inert, impassive on his bed. But what he saw now held him rooted in the doorway. Carl had turned his head. He was returning Hearty's look. His eyes shone with meaning and recognition and intention.

Hearty remained still for some silent seconds, receiving the first weak but unmistakable indication that Carl would mend. He said Mass in Carl's room every two or three days after that. Speech and movement came back slowly to Carl. It was some weeks before he could receive Holy Communion. And it was still longer before he would venture out into the sunlight.

Today Carl is well, but so changed in appearance and so frail that no one who had seen him on that sunny road to Aquileia would easily recognize him now as the same man.

"I want to tell you the truth as I now see it," Carl wrote° later to his

_____

° Here, this letter is condensed from its original version. Omitted are some of the long, technical discussions with his students and colleagues, as well as personal references that concern former students and colleagues. "I was wrong in my personal instructions to each one of you about your lives.

"All through my childhood and youth, I had an affinity with God. Especially after my first vision.

"I'm certain God was there. Somewhere. But then came Princeton. Stanford. Tubingen. Cambridge. London. After that, my guruship and the efflorescence of the gifts I had. I became confused. Somehow I lost God. At the same time, I wanted to help. Really to help. To be of service. All around me, I could see floating neon images of pain, of putrefaction, of illness, of corruption and decay. I saw strange people who did not give a damn. Give a damn, please, I said. They took God's name in vain. As I did. They were bright and cold and hard as storage ice. They liked gratuitous evil and upholstered innocence.

"I signed a moral contract to change all that. I was young, eager-beaver. I was determined to succeed. All up-tight, you might say. I was going to be a good psychologist, an honest and conscientious and understanding servant of mankind. Servant. Not slave. And then I was going to be a good parapsychologist. And then a thoroughgoing guru.

"I groped, even prayed, searched, never took no for an answer. And I found that lyrical liar, the Devil.

"I knew with whom I had to deal, of course. But, first of all, the Devil was not the Devil preached by the Churches. There was no room in my universe for a principle of Evil. Not at that time of my life. And, I thought, the bond and contract would be, could be temporary. Of course, it could not be. But when pride gets hold of your mind and heart, you cannot see clearly.

"Solemnly and of my own free will, I wish to acknowledge that knowingly and freely I entered into possession by an evil spirit. And, although that spirit came to me under the guise of saving me, perfecting me, helping me to help others, I knew all along it was evil.

"After my conversations with Father F. [Hearty], I put everything into perspective intellectually. And I must ascribe my liberation, or, to speak correctly, my desire to want to be free (because I was not allowed any simple desire to be free) I must ascribe all this to what Father F. calls the grace of God and the salvation of Jesus.

"I never enjoyed astral body-travel, only the illusion of it. I never

---

them alone. In every other respect, the condensation is complete and maintains the meaning and intent of the full version.

achieved the privilege of a double—if that be a privilege. Bilocation never succeeded, never was a fact for me. Of myself, I could not see things happening hundreds of miles away, read the future, see the past, peer with minute detail into people's minds. I could give the illusion of these only by being prompted by someone who could see from a great distance, could read the future, had a detailed knowledge of the past, could peer into people's minds. Any idea of reincarnation I championed was an attempt to trick. I was not a shaman. Just a sham.

"I never willed to be rid of possession until the day that Father F. explained my basic error about consciousness and spirit.

"My central error, which was both intellectual and moral in character, concerned the nature of ordinary human consciousness. Like many before me and many others nowadays, I found that with rigid and expert training I could attain a fascinating state of consciousness: a complete absence of any *particular* object (in my awareness). I found I could attain a permanency on this plane of consciousness. It finally became a constant environment within me, during my waking hours, no matter what I was doing. It seemed to be pure and therefore sinless, undifferentiated and therefore universal, simple and therefore without parts—and therefore incorruptible and unchangeable, and therefore eternal.

"My error started when I took this psycho-biological condition of life as the life of *spirit*. Consciousness basically means awareness, being alert. And such awareness can be measured by certain physiological data. It can be phenomenally described, because it is a phenomenon.

"If it were not for one further mistake, that initial error would, I believe, have been corrected as time went on—simply because finally the scientific imperative would have taken over and forced us to look at the facts in the face.

"With the passage of time, I began to experience a further state of consciousness. It is difficult to put it into words. Before that, I was in a sort of state of suspension about my aware state. I was aware that I was in awareness. One day, I realized through a faculty which I have not been able to identify, that there was some other activity taking place which was so refined and subtle that, while I was dimly aware of it, I knew absolutely nothing about it—what it was, where it was, what it accomplished, whether it began and ended, or whether it had always existed, did then exist continuously, and would go on existing—whether I was aware of it or not.

"It lay beyond all my developed capacity to reach. It was utterly transcendent. Indeed, this was its mark; and this is how I realized its differentiation from my other levels of consciousness. They, no matter how subtle, were subject finally to my senses—at least to representation in images drawn from my sense-life. This further state of consciousness was not so subject.

"But this was sufficient indication for me, I thought. I took this as *the absolutely spiritual* state of my being. I took it for granted that religiously speaking I was out beyond that Dark Night of the Soul described by John of the Cross and well into something the Eastern mystics had called by various names like *satori* and *samadhi*. The fact that, at least in afterthought and reflection, I could measure and quantify this state of consciousness never struck a warning note. And that was crass enough on my part. What confirmed me in my error was that I refused to take into account the fact that this state was in complete disjunction from all historical religion—and without any chance of linking up with historical religion. It was, in other words, pure subjectivism. And from then on, the door was open to any influence and any distortion. What crawled through that door was Evil Spirit. Tortoise.

"I did arrive at part of the truth about spirit—the nether part, the negative part. But in the flux of spirit life, that was the only part it uncovered. And it necessarily attacked the human in me. For it is not that I am part animal, part human. I am not a human animal. I am a human spirit. We are of the spirit in its fluid, non-static, non-quantifiable existence. And, in matters of spirit, nether and upper, bad and good, these are terms that refer to its approximation to or distance from the source and sum of all spirit.

"I have been the subject of the cleverest of illusions: that spirit was a static quantum of more or less determinable dimensions; that Christian authorities had obscured the truth about the spirit; and that only by parapsychology and preternatural gifts could one arrive at the truth.

"The truth is that all along, despite my triumphal career until Aquileia, since the advent of possession I had a sorrow I could not shake. Such a deep sodden sadness. I looked for joy everywhere and lived beneath a winter moon that made a carcass of all my days.

"My advice for all who engage in the study and pursuit of the parapsychological is simple but vitally important: do not confound effects with causes, or systems with what maintains the systems. Do not take it that a photograph of Kirlian dots or auras is a photograph of spirit. Do not accept the feats of seance mediums as results of spirit from God. But do not, on the other hand, tamper with or treat of parapsychological phenomena as if you could do this without ultimately impinging upon spirit. You cannot. And that fact will, depending upon what you do, be to your detriment or to your betterment—in spirit."

Manual
of Possession

Good, Evil,
and the Modern Mind

The surest effect of possession in an individual—the most obvious and striking effect common to all possessed persons, whether observed in or apart from Exorcism—is the great loss in human quality, in *humanness*.

Curiously enough, the difficulty in talking nowadays about possession and in describing its progress and effects in those attacked does not come from the weird, bizarre, or "unimaginable" happenings that may accompany possession.

The difficulty comes, instead, from the insistence of latter-day opinion makers that the religious view of good and evil is outdated; that the personality of each man, woman, and child exists only as a cross section of single traits and attributes best revealed in scores we achieve in psychological tests; that the truest and purest models for our behavior come from "lower animals" and from "natural man"—a mythical invention that has never existed and that we cannot imagine.

The difficulty is increased by additional factors. There is an ongoing insistence that religion and any form of worship and all ideals based openly on Christian morality should be banished from public, tax-supported institutions—and that this is "objective" and "democratic." In our mass entertainment—motion pictures, television, novels, theater—there are no hero figures and no concept of right and wrong, of good and evil. We are shown human life as alternating between a bleak despair and a desperate struggle with banal forces against which our only allies are ourselves and our own resources.

But the Christian viewpoint is still the viewpoint of the majority. It still guarantees that we are, each of us, whole persons, not bundles of separate reactions to be studied in cross sections and pushed to the outer limits of our endurance in a topsy-turvy world.

The core of the Christian view of individual men and women is that our humanness—our essence and value as separate and whole people—is treasured and protected by the spirit of Jesus. It is, in fact, to reestablish that humanness and its integrity that an exorcist presents himself freely in the name and with the power of Jesus. He makes himself a hostage—as Jesus presented himself as hostage for each one of us—in a battle for one person's humanness. He will win that battle only by the strength of his faith in Jesus and with the fiber of his individual will attached to Jesus' salvation.

In common sense and in the popular mind, a distinction is always made between *human being* and *humanness*. We find a universal agreement about the general appearance and the functional capacity that indicate human being. A certain physical form derived from another human being with the same general form. Certain normal functions: eating, sleeping, walking, talking, laughing, thinking, willing, dying. Certain capacities: learning, growing, inventing, planning, sympathizing, and so on. One or more of these may be lacking or in a reduced state. But a certain number of them enable us to describe their possessor as human.

As is clear from some of the cases reported in this book and from many others known, possessed people can and do, at least for a time, function reasonably efficiently as human beings, in their jobs and in society in general. Actually, the more perfect the possession, the less likely any disturbance in one's functioning on the level of human being. Jay Beedem, whom Father Mark seemed to uncover as one perfectly possessed, was a model of cool efficiency.

But between that condition of human being and what, for want of a more accurate name, we call humanness, we always make a distinction.

In humanness we include qualities that adhere to the inner self and are interconnected with an appreciable outer way of living and doing. These qualities, taken together, confer a commonly recognized aura, a decor, a configuration of winsomeness and worth on the whole person. The quality of humanness reaches a striking degree of fullness in some of us; when it does, it seems to give a shimmering tonal halo to our communication with those around us, and others feel in such a person a temperament that eagerly responds to fragile but intimately precious values.

Humanness is a grace, not necessarily graceful but never ugly; not necessarily holy—in the religionists' sense of that word—but never obscene; not necessarily sophisticated by "higher culture," but always with its own refinement; not necessarily dominant or predominant or dominating, but in itself indomitable. It makes its possessor a connected human being, lovable to some, alive to all others, yet with a personal regnancy; he loves himself but no genuinely vile egotism blinds him to others; he loves others, but no hatred of self makes him a pawn or a plaything for them.

We always see humanness as a variable quality. Sometimes we think not all have it. Some seem to have little of it. All who possess it, have varying degrees of it, are never constant in it, and from time to time fail in it completely. And, in ourselves, even when we have done "as well as we can" and console ourselves by saying that "under the circumstances we could not have done better," we are sensible of how much better, how much more perfectible we are, how more perfectly we could have acted.

For Christianity, the source of humanness in all individuals, past, present, and future, is Jesus of Nazareth. All forms of possession, from the partial to the perfect, are clearly seen as an attack simultaneously on the souce of humanness, Jesus, and on the humanness of an individual man or woman. The process of possession in any individual consists of an erosion of the humanness Jesus confers.

To explain how possession develops, therefore, one must answer several questions. What is Evil Spirit in relation to Jesus and in relation to us all? What is the humanness of Jesus? How is Jesus the source of humanness for all individuals? How do we explain this in relation to all men and women who lived historically before him and after him? Concretely, how do ordinary men and women attain or miss the humanness of Jesus? And finally, how is this humanness of Jesus eroded—what, in other words, is the process of diabolic possession?

Some of the greatest minds in our history have asked and pondered these questions. Some of those minds have gone a good deal of the way toward answering them—as far, it is fair to say, as minds in science have gone in answering questions proper to their domain.

Even though our coverage of these questions concerning Jesus and Lucifer must be brief due to limitations of space, we are not merely indulging in a comforting cliché when we make one observation: the best that latter-day prophets and modern doom sayers seem able to do with these matters is to ignore them and tell us to do the same. They cannot prove them false, but only increase their efforts to persuade us so. And for all their mighty efforts, they cannot repair the damage they do in this way to our humanness.

Human Spirit
and Lucifer

In the history of Exorcism there is constant reference to evil spirits: to Satan (or Lucifer) as the head or chief of those spirits, and to an entire world of being inhabited by such spirits.

In the preceding five exorcisms, that world inhabited by evil spirits is most often described as "the Kingdom." Christianity would be unintelligible if we were to omit or deny belief in that world of evil spirits. In the New Testament and in Christian tradition salvation by Jesus is presented as a victory over an opposing and baleful intelligence belonging to a bodiless being. It is never simply and primitively the subduing of blind material forces. Nor is it merely the setting up of ethical examples and moral rules. And the "Kingdom of God" is always juxtaposed to the "Kingdom of Evil" or of Satan.

We cannot speak in any ordinary sense of the "history" of these spirits. For their existence did not begin with and is not confined to the space-time continuum in which history's events must take place. Yet it is clear from tradition that the entire existence and fate of these spirits lies in a very intimate and intricate relationship to the human universe we inhabit.

Tradition speaks of a primordial sin of rebellion against God by some of the spirits, and led by one particular spirit symbolically named Lucifer ("the Son of the Dawn," to indicate supreme qualities) or Satan (to indicate a function as chief adversary of God). From the sparse items of information in the Bible, from stray remarks made by Jesus himself during his lifetime, and from continuous traditional

Christianity, the general "history" of these spirits and their relationship to Jesus and to our world would seem to be the following.

God's decision to create intelligent beings—spirits and humans, free to love him and free to reject him—was intimately linked with his decision to become a human being.

But in speaking of that decision of God, we have to make a distinction between the way we understand and talk about it and how God made and implements it.

Our understanding of and speech about this decision is a step-by-step process. First, creation of spirits. Then, their rebellion. Then, the creation of mankind. Then, mankind's revolt. Then, the conception and birth of Jesus. Then, the sacrifice and resurrection of Jesus and the consequent salvation of mankind. Then, the life of men and women beset by those spirits who revolted. We have to think in this way. But that is *our* limitation.

For God there was and is no step-by-step process. He did not, as it were, first decide to create the spirits, then, as an afterthought, to create humans, and then, on further reflection, to become a man. Creation did not proceed like Topsy. It was one decision englobing spirits, humans, and God-made-man. And it was a decision not made at any given point in time but in eternity. God was never without decision.

This means that his decision was integral in cause and effect from the start. His view of what everybody would do at any given moment was identical with his view of what everybody did, does, and will do until the end of all time and space. That view was complete always. And every detail of the decision was taken integrally and wholly from eternity in view of every possible human action and reaction and result.

The centerpiece of that decision was God's own choice to become a man. Just as his own divinity was, to speak in a human fashion, turned in this one definite direction, so all the "pieces" of God's decision—spirits included—were created and ordained in this direction. God was to enter into an intimate relationship with matter—place, time, objects, humans.

So also his creatures, the spirits, were made by him and ordained by him to be in an intimate relationship with matter—place, time, objects, humans. The destiny, powers, personal interest of these spirits, their very being, in its deepest instincts and ramifications were and will remain forever intimately focused on this human universe, on all this universe contains, and—above all—on Jesus as the source of that universe's meaning.

Christian tradition thus assigns to these spirits the role of intermediaries. They were and are bodiless—like God. They were and are creatures—like humans. In the piecemeal working out of God's overall decision through time and space, and in the individual minds and hearts of billions of human beings surrounded by material things, the spirits were given functions at which we can only guess. These functions were related to the human universe and to God's decision to become a member of that universe.

At this point of our understanding about spirit, we are somewhat helped by side-comments of Jesus. He spoke once or twice rather mysteriously but quite succinctly about the important personage among those created spirits who revolted, Lucifer.

Rebutting those who harassed him on the streets of Jerusalem and who reviled him as an evil man, Jesus said fiercely: "You belong to your father, Satan. And you are eager to gratify the appetites which are your father's. He, from the beginning, was a *murderer*. And, as for truth, he has *never taken his stand on it*. When he utters falsehood, he is only doing what is natural to him. He is *all false*. And it was he who *gave birth to falsehood* [emphasis mine]."

On the lips of a Jew of that period, the term "murderer" did not have the legalistic meaning we have attached to it. The word had more the connotation of our "blasphemy" or "desecration."

The second aspect of Lucifer's rebellion, Jesus adds, was one of falsehood. Again, on the lips of Jesus, this word referred not so much to lying by words, to fibbing, as to what we call "pretense," "deception," "false claims."

The emphasis of Jesus is quite clear. Lucifer was and is the *originator* of all blasphemy and deception in the universe of spirit which God had created—to the point that all those who practice deception and who commit the ultimate blasphemy are merely reproducing Lucifer's appetites for falsehood and blasphemy. In some mysterious way they share in and augment Lucifer's falsehood and blasphemy. "You belong to your father, Satan."

Jesus adds a few more details. "From the beginning" seems to indicate that the rebellion was instantaneous with the creation of Lucifer's intelligence. There never was a fraction of his existence when Lucifer opted for God. Furthermore, Lucifer is "all false." It is "natural" for him to deceive and blaspheme. These are stark and simply effective terms used by Jesus to describe *total evil*. Not merely a totally evil being, but a being who is the *source* of *all evil* in the world of mankind.

From these few details we can only guess at the nature of Lucifer's rebellion in which he was joined by unnumbered other spirits. It involved blasphemy and deception. It concerned Jesus as God and as the savior of mankind; and it concerned men and women as participants in the fullness of Jesus' humanness.

Did Lucifer falsely claim to be higher, more noble than the man Jesus? And, in doing so, did he blaspheme by claiming that he, Lucifer, a bodiless spirit, the supremest angel, should be regarded as higher than Jesus, who, like all humans, was part spirit, part matter? He, an angel, worship a mewling baby at Bethlehem and a bleeding half-animal groaning in death throes on Calvary?

Or did Lucifer revolt because he and the other angels were destined to help elevate human beings beyond the merely material and human, beyond even the status of the angels, right to the status of sharing God's life?

Or did Lucifer reject God's decision integrally? That is to say: did he reject God's decision to ordain and relate everything—God's own being and the spirits God created—to a human universe? And, if so, was this because Lucifer rejected the prime trait of that decision, a universe of beings—humans—who would need compassion, and mercy and help and sustainment? The spirits were to be servants of that compassion and instruments of that help to an unmerited glory for those creatures.

Or did Lucifer, with angelic intelligence, foresee a destiny of human beings yet hidden from our human eyes—that after eons of development, when outer space is colonized in billions of galaxies, mankind will progress and evolve in *spirit* to a status we now know nothing of, and in which men and women will enjoy a freedom from matter but still be able to enjoy the beauty of this material world?

Jealousy? Ambition? Pride? Scorn? We can only surmise.

Whatever Lucifer did, he blasphemed against God's unique divinity, and he made false claims. Punishment was immediate. Jesus, in an overt reference to his personal memories of this revolt, spoke of that one quick, terrible moment of degradation and punishment of Lucifer and of those spirits who followed his lead. Jesus said: "I saw Lucifer falling like lightning from heaven." Again, in the style of Jesus, we have a stark evocation of the sudden flash of Lucifer's brilliant intelligence in the clean skies of creation's dawn; then the moment-long glare of Lucifer's claimed glory; and, finally, the immediate humiliation of utter defeat and rejection by God, as Lucifer plummeted from the clarity and brightness of love and changeless beauty down past the rim of happiness into the pit of eternal exile from all good and all holiness.

In this revolt and punishment, the natural orientation of Lucifer and of those spirits who were part of his rebellion remained. They were by their very essence in intimate relation with the human universe. They were powerless to free themselves of it. Their powers of will and intelligence remained. Only now, those wills and intelligences were twisted by revolt and their unchangeable state as the condemned ones. Their love for God, for Jesus, and therefore for mankind became hate. Their need to move in a human universe and to be in relationship with matter remained; but it now became a need to disrupt, to soil, to destroy, to make ugly, to deform.

Their knowledge of truth became solely the means for an exercise in distorting the truth. Their reverence became mockery and contempt. Their lovely desires became gross threats. All their light became a confusing darkness. And their primordial destiny to be the helpers of Jesus became a living and baleful hate of him, of his love, of his salvation, and of those who belong to him.

They were, in other words, conditioned through and through by the diabolic "twist," that peculiar upside-down, disjointed, askew existence, covered in deception and falsity, which we always detect in the morally evil person, in the war-filled world of a Michael Strong, and in the frightful topsy-turvy world of every possessed human being.

The nearest we can come to gauging the degree of Lucifer's ugliness is in the overtones of the totally insane who laugh all day uproariously at their own dreadful aberrations—their spasmic violence, their treasured filth, their self-mutilation. We pity them as out of control, as beside themselves, as unconscious of their tragedy. But in them and in every grin of our own Schadenfreude we can detect an echo of Lucifer's very own accents, his signature, that uproarious burst of reasonless laughter mocking his own self-delusive and deliberately chosen state of absolute hate.

"Good" and "evil" as applied only to human beings, therefore, must bring us into *direct*, daily, practical relationship with the influence of Jesus and the influence of Lucifer. Furthermore, "good" and "evil" as applied only to human beings must bring us into direct recognition of our own individual wills. For whatever the invitations offered by Jesus, whatever the blandishments offered by Lucifer, we each make our choices, even as Jesus, even as Lucifer. We choose.

Much of what we know from our direct experience with evil spirits dovetails with what we would expect, based upon what we know or can glean of their origin.

The most notable and, for many modern minds, contradictory aspect of such spirits is that each spirit seems to be a personal and intelligent being, but that it has no physical existence. It is bodiless. This is a constant and primary datum of Christian belief about such spirits and is borne out by evidence from exorcisms.

In modern psychology the terms "personality" and "person" have been tied to psychophysical consciousness. "Personality" is taken to be a complex of psychophysical acts—emoting, willing, desiring, thinking, imagining, remembering—and the exterior actions that are motivated or colored by such "internal" acts. All of them can be quantified. A "person" is somebody with a more or less consistent and definable complex of such acts and actions.

Thus, a "person" of unbalanced "personality" is one in whom that complex of acts and actions lacks the ordinarily observed and socially acceptable type, tension, and frequency. Of course, there is no room in our minds for any consideration of bodiless personal spirits if we accept this modern terminology as correct and all-inclusive. For "person" and "personality," in this terminology, are material, fractionated, dimensional, measurable, and finally perishable.

The classical Christian thought and belief about "person" and "personality" is very different. And it echoes the natural persuasion of most men and women.

"Person" in Christian thought is a spirit. As a spirit, it is imperishable and indestructible. It can will and think. It is freely *responsible* for what it thinks and wills and does. And it is capable of self-awareness. In Christian thought, "personality" is another word for the total individuality of the person. The diminution or reduction of this internal and self-aware center of responsibility of the self to a tidy bundle of arbitrary divisions—something called "thinking" and something called "willing" and something else called "acting," etc. etc.—is itself insanity. For these concepts of "person" and "personality" are applied to God and to bodiless spirits as well as to humans.

In our human condition the individual and personal spirit is destined to exercise its willing and thinking and all its power *by means* of psychophysical activity, rarely by passing that quantifiable arena.

The evil spirits in question are not personal *in that sense*. Being bodiless, their individual identities do not depend on a *bodily* identity. Christian teaching is that they think, will, act, and are self-aware and exercise their power purely, simply, and directly without the use of the psychophysical.

Experiences with evil spirits in exorcisms bear this out. In virtually every exorcism, at a crucial point, the possessing spirit will refer to itself interchangeably as "I" and "we," and as easily refer to "my" and "our." "I'm taking him." "We are as strong as death." "Fool! We're all the same." "There's only one of us." All this was hurled at Michael Strong by the one spirit at *Puh Chi* in Nanking—"I," "me," "all," "one," "us." Individuality in any human or even remotely bodily sense is not operative here.

The fact that the spirits described in the exorcisms of this book finally responded to names ("Girl-Fixer," "Smiler," "Tortoise," etc.) is no indication of separate identity. They are names assumed apparently in view of the means or the strategy used by the spirit as it possessed the person in question. When Father Mark pressed Ponto's "superior" for its name, the response was "We are all of the Kingdom." "No man can know the name." When Mark insisted, the spirit replied: "Multus, Magnum, Gross, Grosser, Grossest. Several times. Seventy-seven legions." The names they give are clearly *ad hoc* names and, for all we know, may change for the same spirit in relation to different victims. What the exorcist is after in pushing for such names is not personal identity, but a name the spirit will respond to. "In Jesus' name, what name will you obey?" was Mark's crucial question in this regard.

Nevertheless, the behavior of spirits, in endless variations, in exorcism after exorcism, does suggest some coagulating common identity of a kind that leaves evil spirits distinct in their personalities while unified and, indeed, one in their responsibilities and intentions.

Somehow closely linked to this identity of spirits and contributing to it is the obvious gradation of intelligence that one observes in different possessing spirits. Jamsie's "familiar," Uncle Ponto, for example, was clearly of a lesser intelligence than Tortoise, who possessed Carl, or then Smiler who held Marianne captive. Ponto's gimmicks never went beyond the grotesquely comic. He never showed the subtlety of Smiler or the sophistication of Tortoise. Each of these used clever arguments and intricate games to further their purposes and in general displayed a penetration of mind absent in Ponto.

Yet, while Ponto was deferential in the extreme in front of his "superiors," Girl-Fixer, who possessed Richard/Rita, and Mr. Natch, who possessed the two priests, David and Yves, also showed a marked deference to "superiors."

At one point in the exorcism of Marianne, when Smiler was losing the battle, Father Peter began to feel the change in level of intelligence of his enemy, as "another" (to use our human terminology of separateness) spirit came to Smiler's aid in the final attack on Peter.

Father Gerald felt the opposite in his exorcism of Richard/Rita. As it became clearer that Gerald was going to be successful and that the end of the battle was near, Gerald felt that some strand of evil had faded and·that he was suddenly dealing with a lesser intelligence.

In this most intimate of all confrontations, with mind pitted directly against mind, will against will, a sudden shift in the intelligence of one's adversary is unmistakable—more so than in a confrontation so unsubtle that words are needed.

· This difference of spirits from one another on the basis of intelligence seems to culminate in the servile, almost wooden allegiance of all to "the Lord of All Knowledge," as Tortoise called him. "Those who accepted, those who accept the Claimant, have his will," Uncle Ponto's superior, Multus, told Father Mark. "Only the will. The will of the Kingdom. The will of the will of the will of the will of the will."

This servility and allegiance to Lucifer among evil spirits is matched in constancy and overshadowed in intensity only by their craven fear of and hatred for Jesus, freely and undisguisedly displayed at any mention of his name or at the sight of objects and people associated with Jesus.

A possessing spirit of whatever skill and intelligence will pronounce the name of its leader repeatedly, and the sense one has is of obedience, fear, and recognition of a superiority that will not be questioned. But no evil spirit seems able to bring itself to pronounce the name of Jesus. "The Other," he will be called, or "The Latter," or "That Person," or "The Unmentionable," or any of a whole dark litany of such names.

Nor will an evil spirit hear the name of Jesus without protesting. Knowledge of this fact can be a principal weapon for the exorcist, for the evil spirit will often be forced to answer questions or tell its "name" out of an obvious desire not to have to hear again the phrase of total faith, "In the name of Jesus," from the lips of the exorcist.

The curious quality of unity, almost a coagulation, which one sometimes feels can be glimpsed in these areas of personality and intelligence of evil spirits, also gives us an interesting perspective on another constant among spirits—their attachment to place.

Again, it is clear from experience that possessing spirits are intent on finding a "home" (as Ponto put it simplistically) in the possessed person. But it is not a question of one lonely and homeless spirit. For the possessing spirit, the "home" or person belongs to all the "family" of that spirit—the coagulated mob of evil spirits, headed and governed by the shadowy leader, "The Claimant." It is a macabre version of *"Mi casa, su casa"* hospitality, and was mirrored long ago on the lips of Jesus when he told of "the unclean spirit which has possessed a man and then goes out of him, walks about the desert looking for a resting place, and finds none; and it says: 'I will go back to my own dwelling from which I came out.' And it comes back . . . and brings in seven more other spirits more wicked than itself to bear it company; and together they enter in and settle down there." Seven is the biblical formula for any multitude.

We will always have intense intellectual difficulty understanding how we can talk of personality or intelligence when there is no physical brain, or of hearing a voice when there is no throat to produce that voice, or of seeing a flying plate when there is no hand to throw it and sustain it in midair. But these are problems that will be doubly perplexing so long as the modern mind-set holds sway with its insistence on the materiality of all that exists.

All in all, for example, it is very bothersome that we cannot speak of these spirits as having gender, sexuality, or individuality like that of human beings. Individuality alone is a terrible problem for the computer society. Identity for us is *always* linked to *physical separateness*. If we say there are 217 million Americans, we mean 217 separate and *therefore* distinct bodies.

But, from all we know, it seems obvious that trying to number or count spirits on the basis of physical separateness is not going to get us very far. And our denying that spirits exist because they literally will not "stand up and be counted" does not seem to impress them.

Even when we get past all those difficulties and *can* begin to think about the identities of these bodiless creatures, there is another problem. We tend to think all the bizarre and violent happenings that occur at exorcisms *are* somehow the evil spirit. In our understandable fascination with the screams and the flying objects, with the smells, the tearing wallpaper, and the banging doors, our tendency is to mistake those events for the spirit itself. That is a little like mistaking the baseball for the pitcher.

Better clues to the identity of *individual* spirits seem to be based and rooted in the strongest quality we can discern among them: that curious and undulating hierarchy of intelligence and power of will that links even the lowest "familiar" to Lucifer himself.

Because of these different powers of intelligence and will among spirits, their *activities* are different. They remain unified, as we said, in their responsibilities and their intentions. They remain always subordinate to "the will of the will of the will of the will of the will." But their activities—the way they go about what they do—seems directly related to their differing levels of intelligence and the differing force of their single-focused wills.

In the mere five cases reported in this book such difference in activity is borne out dramatically; in each case there is a feel for the subtlety or lack of it, the degree of predatory intelligence being challenged, and the degree of irresistibility of the will that struggles in contention with the exorcist.

Paul of Tarsus was referring to this kind of differentiation when he used the concepts and terminology of Alexandrine Gnostics and theosophers, and spoke of "powers," "principalities," "thrones," "dominations," and again when he used such biblical terms as "cherubim" and "seraphim."

All of this information, elaborated by painful experience, detailed and extended through years of offering themselves as hostage for the possessed, is of prime interest and value to the exorcists. But the most important fact about evil spirits is that none of their faculties or powers is divine. Evil spirits are forever excluded from God's life and the vision of God's truth.

Their knowledge and foresight, then, are based only on what they can know by their native intelligence. They are not, in effect, supernatural, but merely preternatural beings.

In traditional usage, "supernatural" *means* divine: *of God*. The supernatural is therefore totally separate from, superior to, and in no way dependent upon what is created—what is "natural" in that sense.

Only God is supernatural in his very being. He can act with

supernatural power upon all "natural" (that is, created) things and beings. He can communicate his supernatural life and power to what is created, thus elevating it. But the distinction always remains between what is created and what is supernatural.

Supernatural power can affect all that is at the disposal of the preternatural; but one essential difference between the supernatural and the world of evil spirits is that supernatural power can bypass all natural modes of operation. The supernatural can act directly on spirit. It need not pass via the senses, or through the internal powers of imagination, mind, and will in order to reach the soul of a human being.

Only God and those who share in his supernatural power can do this.

Preternatural power is superior to human power in its abilities. That is, evil spirits, by virtue of preternatural power, are not bound by laws of physical nature and of matter that govern all our human exercise of power in the physical and psychic orders. But they do appear to be bound by other laws of nature (because they, too, were created) beyond which they cannot exercise any power at all.

We do not know all that preternatural power can effect, but we do know some of its abilities and some of its limits.

By virtue of preternatural power, evil spirits can manipulate psychic phenomena and produce psychic states. That is to say, psychic powers are at their disposal. Psychic powers (telekinesis, telepathy, astral travel, bilocation, second sight, etc.) do not themselves become preternatural (any more than that baseball becomes the pitcher), much less supernatural.

Evil spirits, then, are able to produce fascinating effects in our human fields of perception and behavior. They may not be and probably are not responsible for all psychic phenomena, but they have not only mastery of this sort of behavior but the ability to pique the human imagination with a wondrous gamut of enticements. Carl, who almost lost his sanity and his life in his struggle on this very battlefield, wrote in his letter to his former students that he had never, in fact, mastered astral travel or bilocation, "but only their illusion." And he was aware they were illusion—but so eager and so fascinated was he that he would not admit that awareness beyond the faintest far focus of his mind.

The point is that Evil Spirit can titillate and entice us through our senses and imagination with images of psychic wonders as easily as images of sex or gold. Whatever will work. But Evil Spirit can produce nothing in us that was not already there, actually or potentially.

God, for example, can "give" us grace, which is not ours of ourselves. Evil Spirit can only act upon what it finds and only within the limits of its knowledge.

For instance, preternatural power does not enable evil spirits to control or interfere directly with the moral behavior of human beings. They may be able to produce a pile of gold dollars at will by any of a number of psychic means, but they could not thereby force a person to accept them. They cannot interfere with our freedom to choose or reject, because that freedom is granted and guaranteed by the divine.

The inferiority of the preternatural power of evil spirits compared to the supernatural power of Jesus is clear and definite in many of its effects. There is an opaqueness that impedes and even stops Evil Spirit—its ability to act and its ability to know—everywhere that Jesus and his supernatural power extend, where the choice has been for Jesus and where the supernatural reigns, where the supernatural invests objects, places, and people.

The power of *symbols* of the supernatural (a crucifix, for example) to protect good and repel or control evil is such an effect. Objects used in and closely associated with worship (holy water), exorcists, any person in a state of supernatural grace (an exorcist's assistant who has been absolved of his sins), even houses, countrysides, whole areas, are protected in their essence from the freewheeling activity of Evil Spirit. This limitation of the preternatural and so of Evil Spirit extends to another important sphere as well, for it means that the reach of knowledge of Evil Spirit is severely limited. An evil spirit cannot, for example, foresee and therefore forestall the intent of an exorcist who is acting in the name and with the authority of Jesus.

When Father Gerald stepped out from behind the protection of Jesus to confront Girl-Fixer in his own name, he was immediately and horribly attacked, physically and emotionally. But for all the blood and pain and horror, that was no victory for Girl-Fixer. The spirit could not reach Gerald's mind or his soul. Gerald's will held firm. All the efforts of Girl-Fixer had been precisely to affect Gerald's mind, his will, and so ultimately his soul—where the spirit had not the power to reach directly. Girl-Fixer failed; and having failed, he stood at bay. Richard/Rita was ultimately freed to make his choice between good and evil.

Evil spirits have the power to know without reasoning, to remember what is available to their knowledge from eternity, and to use that knowledge to influence, cajole, frighten, and otherwise affect the minds and hearts of men and women so that they desert the plan of God and score another victory of rebellion against good. Their knowledge concerns every occasion where a choice is made against the supernatural. When spirits shout the sins of the people present during an exorcism, they are reaching as far as their natural power can take them.

Finally, those who are selected for possession may accede to possession and then quickly recant; or be deeply enmeshed and be freed only at great pain and risk; or be fully—perfectly—possessed. It remains completely unclear, however, why one person and not another is chosen for such direct and single-minded attack.

Ponto said to Jamsie as they drove along a highway near San Francisco, "All those homes up there . . . there's no welcome for me up there in spite of their boozing and bitching and despair."

But why not? Did that mean that those people too had been "invited," as Jamsie had and Carl and Marianne and David and Yves and Richard/Rita? And had they, whatever their smaller choices for evil, refused the gross invitation? Is everyone a possible target? Are only some "selected" for "invitation"? There is no way to be sure.

Human Spirit
and Jesus

Evil Spirit aims at attacking and destroying the humanness of each human being. This humanness is neither a physical nor a psychophysical condition. It is a spiritual *capacity* possessed by each man and woman and child.

Only because of this capacity in spirit are we able to believe in God and to attain unending happiness in our after-death condition. Only because of this capacity can we perceive beauty and truth in this human universe. And, perceiving it thus, we may reproduce it in our actions and our products. Diabolic possession negates this capacity.

The reason we have this capacity of spirit is Jesus of Nazareth. As a man, he lived for not more than 50 years, as close as we can calculate. But all of his achievements were his as God made man. Hence those achievements are timeless and affect those at the very beginnings of our species as well as all other humans until time ends. Every man and woman in all time, every human ever conceived had, has, and will have this capacity of spirit made possible by Jesus. All, therefore, are capable of humanness.

We know of this humanness only from the mortal life of Jesus. As our own lives proceed, we know only that by ourselves we become increasingly helpless in every way, that our human love which we desire so much seems to become vain and weak; and that all of us, with all our aspirations and hopes, must end in the silent darkness and the numbing secret of death. Jesus overcame the helplessness. He accepted human love. He died successfully. On this triad of helpless-ness, love, and death all humanness depends.

Jesus' experience of each one, and how he responded to the challenges of each—here is the central mystery of Jesus—made it possible for every other human being to respond successfully when faced with the same challenging experiences in the trial and develop-ment of individual humanness. Such was the means by which God from the beginning provided that mere creatures, tied to their physical bodies, might overcome their all too obvious limitations of time and physicality, and share, each one, in supernatural life. As with Jesus, it requires not only the desire, but the participation, the life action, the choice—in short, the will—of each.

Without any doubt Jesus spent his entire life attaining the perfection of his humanness. But in the historical records about him we find the ultimate steps in Jesus' achievement of humanness were crowded into a period of weeks prior to his execution. Because of variations between the different written records, we have to take the crucial period to be about four weeks in length, although it may well have been that all those steps were concluded within the last week of his life.

Nowhere is Jesus' victory over *helplessness* more clear or vivid than in the raising of his friend, Lazarus, from the dead.

Throughout his life as described in the records, Jesus displayed a constant mastery over people, events, and things. There was never any faltering or hesitation in his actions. He acted in his own name with an authority that never reeked of authoritarianism or arrogance, but at the same time brooked no refusal. "Amen! Amen! I say to you." All was decisive. He gave commands to men and women, to evil spirits, to friends, to enemies, to the elements. In confrontation with private people or public authorities, it was always the same behavior: he acknowledged no one as superior to himself, praised and blamed and condemned as he saw fit, never withdrew before any other man as his master or as greater than himself.

Whenever he worked miracles or ordered something done, his instructions and dictates were clear, concise, supremely confident, and direct: "Go out from this man." "Be clean!" "Arise and walk!" "Go show yourself to the priests!" "Be cured!" "Stand up and walk!" "Hear!" It was only at the raising of Lazarus from the dead that Jesus exhibited a dependency, a lingering hesitation, a doubt—and that he *acknowledged* his *helplessness*.

It is evident from the Gospel that at the tomb of Lazarus Jesus experienced a flood of helplessness. In fact, his behavior from the time Lazarus' two sisters, Martha and Mary, sent for him was so uncharacteristic as to be called indecisive. It was as if he were passing through a waiting time, a period of unknowing and apprehension we humans call doubt. First of all, he stated plainly that "the end of Lazarus' sickness is not death." Then, "Our friend Lazarus is sleeping. But I shall go and wake him up." Finally: "Lazarus is dead." He delayed his departure for two days. Then he spent two more days traveling.

When Jesus arrived at Bethania, where Lazarus, Martha, and Mary had their estates, Lazarus had been buried. From the moment of his arrival Jesus' behavior was peculiar and unwonted. When he met the weeping sisters, he was distressed, sighed, and wept openly. At the tomb itself he publicly stated his personal trust in and dependence on God—apparently a newly felt need of his at that moment.

Looking up at the skies, he said in a loud voice: "Father! I thank you for listening to my request. I myself know that you always listen to me. But I am speaking for the sake of the people standing around here, so that they may come to believe you sent me."

We can only imagine, and by comparison with our own lot, the trouble Jesus suffered. He who never hesitated, hesitated. He who personally commanded in his own name had to wait for approval before commanding. In the previous years of Jesus' life there may have been other such moments. But this experience at the tomb of Lazarus is the only one recorded in which Jesus' exercise of divine power within the human order was accomplished only after a short but intense experience of helplessness.

Without diminution of his divinity, and only so that his humanness would be achieved, Jesus was offered in this raising of Lazarus the human ridge of fears and probabilities. He had the same alternatives in that moment that all of us have at certain crucial moments throughout our lives. One alternative says: "Stay with your fears. With the probabilities. With your impotencies. Accept them. That's the way it is. That's life." Another alternative says: "Declare yourself helpless and incapable, *and* ask for help to transcend all your helplessness and impotencies. Say: 'I am helpless. Help me! Unsure as I am, help me to be sure!' "

The second key element in the fullness of humanness achieved by Jesus, and so guaranteed as a capacity in each of us if we choose, is human *love:* its acceptance, its felt sweetness, its celebration, the giving of it.

At first glance it would seem that there is no one who cannot love humanly, that it is "second nature" to do so. Yet experience has always told men and women that it is as hard to love as to be loved. For human love is never a matter of logical concepts or data matching. It implies no use of purposiveness. It is never a managed process of *quid pro quo.* Those who love each other, in the exercise of their love are enveloped in a transcendental atmosphere where they remain distinct, but no emphasis is laid upon one individual over another.

Richard/Rita's exorcist, Father Gerald, had learned one shining truth about human love through his ordeal with the evil spirit whose method of dehumanization was debasement of love itself. In the long conversation with him as we strolled in his garden some months before he died, Gerald sketched for me his realization that our need for sexuality in love is a result of our not possessing God—love itself; and that sexuality is valid humanly and ennobling only as a striving for and expression of the love we can achieve.

Our difficulty is that we cannot imagine a close and personal love between man and woman that is not sexually based and ultimately sexually expressed. But this is a limitation of our outlook, not a deficiency in Jesus.

Jesus, being God, did not need the vehicle of sexuality, nor did those who loved him. Yet who can doubt the tactile and warm love of that Mary who poured a "pound of pure spikenard perfume" over his feet and then dried them with her long hair? Her very gesture implied a tender affection for Jesus, together with a trusting presumption that what she did he understood, accepted, and, in his own way, reciprocated. Full of the power that love confers, she held captive the guests gathered around with the solemnity of love expressed, as surely as the breath of that perfume filled "the whole house," as the Gospel tells us.

This is the only recorded occasion when Jesus was proffered the beauty and intimate sweetness of human love by a woman, and Jesus insisted it be his. "Leave her alone!" he said to the grumbling Judas Iscariot. Jesus knew that human beauty and love was its own sanctification, because they were tangible blessings given only by God.

And he therefore insisted that they be received—uncovered except with their own inherent grace.

The Gospels make it clear that during the last days, when Jesus was waiting for the Passover feast, he was frequently near the Bethania family of Lazarus, Martha, and Mary. It is left to our imagination to portray his hours of companionship with this family, the happiness of being with friends and the object of their love, the gentle, probing conversations they carried on between them, the nearness, the warmth, the celebration of their unity in heart, and the sweetness of total acceptance.

In tasting such love, so Christianity teaches, Jesus made that love possible for each of us. Humanly. If we choose.

It is central to Christian understanding of the fullness of humanness achieved by Jesus that when, earlier, he overcame his human helplessness, and when he accepted human love, he was preparing his soul for his victory, not over mere dying, but over death.

For the victory over helplessness was only possible by trust, by relying on the power of God, by resting his hopes on something outside his human ambit. And the consent to love and be loved was made possible only because he recognized and accepted God's guarantee that all human love—despite its pathos and weakness—could be made eternal and divine.

In other words, to be humanly victorious in all three of these circumstances, Jesus relied on the more than human, and on what no human agency could tell him or effect for him.

For Jesus, as for us, dying was the ultimate and only surety. He himself did not escape dying. Nor has he made it possible for any other human being, even his own mother, to escape dying.

Jesus' experience of dying was colored by two opposites. On the one hand, his natural shrinking from dying and death as the summary evil, as that which ended his human integrity. On the other hand, his devotion to the purpose of his whole life, which could be accomplished only by dying.

In some mysterious way, Jesus was made to undergo the same agonizing natural fear of death that all humans have. Still at a distance from the hour of his death, the thought of dying made Jesus sad, almost querulous. "One of you is going to betray me," he revealed to his followers at their intimate supper. "Could you not stay awake this one hour with me?" he complained to his three companions who had dozed off. "Let this trial pass me by," he prayed in the Garden of Gethsemane as he writhed and sweated on the ground in sheer apprehension and loathing for his dying.

Whenever he confronted Judas, his captors, Caiaphas, Pilate, Herod, the Good Thief, the Women of Jerusalem, Peter, his mother, he was in command. His awareness was clear. His mission was firm.

It was only the black hand of death and the merciless coils of dying that frightened him. For he had to accomplish his mission in his identity as a man in order to break beyond the bonds of mere humanity. "My God! My God! Why have you forsaken me!" This was no questioning complaint. It was merely a human exclamation at the sharp peak of his physical torture. For the first time, mists of numbness were blackening and dulling all his psychophysical acts. He could not see or hear very well anymore. His control of his imagination was slipping. His memory worked in quick snaps, then went blank.

Yet he passed through this dying and out of all physical existence, preserving his hope and trust: "Father! Into your hands I commend my spirit." At that one moment all his psychic faculties—memory, imagination, feelings, sensations—were gathered into a hard ball of pain. He could not breathe anymore. His heart ached with effort, then stopped beating. His brain had no more blood. That quick dislocation we curtly name with an inert monosyllable, death, overtook him.

Jesus has not told us of the physical agony in that shuddering wrench, when he ceased to hear, see, and taste, and in a traumatic flash the human self he used to be was in a new dimension where all was clear, where there was no more doubt, where he could no longer be afflicted by material ills, and where his human soul existed in the undisturbable harmony of God. He had died. As all humans must. And he survived in spirit, as all humans may now do, because of Jesus' dying and death.

As the first human being to undergo dying and death perfectly, Jesus had to rise from the dead. He had to live again as a human being. His bodily death and his living again in the body are two phases of one integral act. Hence, what Christians have always called his Resurrection implies not only living again; but also dying, and surviving that physical death.

Jesus' message in the Resurrection accounts of the Gospels is clear: Do not simply accept that I survived death. For this is not a Christian idea. But it is: *Believe* I have transformed your dying and your death, making them a means of resurrection and ascension and an entrance into the Kingdom of God. For every man and woman.

This is why the witnesses to his Resurrection were not concerned with his bodily appearance or characteristics after death when he lived again, but with his person and his identity and his presence.

A real salvation from the pathos of being merely human, therefore, implies that not only does it become possible for us to live forever, but that we know and pursue this goal in a way that enables us to escape the confines of time and space. We must *know* with absolute surety. Such knowing is called belief.

Jesus effected that our act of believing give us knowledge of him and of our salvation; and, by that act of believing, we escape from the confines of our material world and of our own consciousness. And, after the first assent of belief, we have the quiet flow of certainty about each person as man, as woman, and about God as father, savior, and eternal joy.

Because Jesus completely fulfilled his humanness as regards helplessness, love, and dying, each one of us is capable of overcoming our helplessness; of achieving genuine love; and of living forever. This is the *capacity* Jesus won for us. It is a capacity that defines the largest outlines of what we experience as the potential humanness in each one of us. On this huge canvas are painted all the smaller details of what we may achieve in our individual humanness.

This capacity, our potential for humanness, puts all men and women into direct relationship with Jesus. It is not merely that our aspiring, our loving, and our dying is *measured* over against his. Nor that we receive from him parcels of *strength*, in order to be able to *imitate* him in these matters—much as we consciously or unconsciously imitate popular heroes, heroines, idols, and ideals, and so model our behavior on someone whom we esteem highly. Jesus does not help us merely in the same way as we assert from time to time that this or that great man or woman has helped us by their actions and their inspiring words.

The relationship is much more intimate. If our *choice* is to aspire, to love, and to die in the hope of living, then our aspiring and our loving and our dying in such a deathless hope *is* the aspiring and the loving and the dying Jesus performed so perfectly once for all time and for all humans. When we choose to achieve this humanness, then between our humanness and the humanness achieved by Jesus there is a *paradigm* of *identity*. Not a physical identity, but rather an *assimi-*

lation in spirit. The limited capacity of each mortal becomes a minor and partial participation in the divine fullness and rich overflow of Jesus' divine spirit. Each individual is destined to become a "Jesus self" in some degree or grade: to be a self with the humanness of Jesus.

It was this primordial function of Jesus that Paul of Tarsus summarized when he drew on the ancient Jewish myth of Adam as the "first man" and as "head of the human race" in physical generation and biological derivation. Paul called Jesus the "Second Adam" and the "head of all men and women" in the being of spirit. In the language of classical Christian piety and religion, each one becomes an *alter Christus*, another Jesus. They become part of that fullness of good in our human universe that God has foreseen and permitted.

In the Christian view, all of this is so because Jesus was God made man. All his human acts belonged to him as God. Their value and meaning shared in the eternity and total perfection of God. Jesus has a priority in that eternity that ensures his ever-presence and priority within all the changing time-space frames of our human history. As a mortal human being, he lived in one place at one time. Yet in humanness he was and is coexistent with and present to all human beings as the source and guarantee of whatever humanness each of us attains.

At the same time, Jesus was also a mortal man, a Jew who lived a certain number of years in and around Palestine; who had certain mortal limits of mind, culture, life experience. During his mortal lifetime Jesus could not achieve the full extent of humanness possible in billions of individual humans diversified by climate, language, culture, gender, and civilization. For this goal, God chose to need the participation of men and women.

In the Christian view, therefore, Jesus is the key to the fullness of our humanness, because he achieved that fullness for us *potentially*. It must be achieved *actually* in each man and woman, and can be achieved only by each one's choice and personal actions in the reality of the good and the evil present and possible to us all, and whether or not we have ever even heard of Jesus.

And the key to the fullness of evil—that which negates and kills humanness and achieves the opposite of God's plan—is Lucifer, the shining angel who chose freely to separate himself from God, but as God's creature could not separate himself from the human universe.

The Process
of Possession

We will never know in detail how evil spirits select a special target for possession or the details of how they set about their grim task in the earliest stages. "When did you start working on Jamsie?" Father Mark asked Ponto's superior. "He was chosen before he was born" was the chilling reply.

We can, nevertheless, trace the general lines along which possession proceeds, and sketch as well the broad stages of the development and success of possession in a victim.

From all five cases in this book, and from countless other cases, it is fair to say that usually before either the target of possession or those near him are aware of it, the actual process of possession has begun. In the cases reported here, the earliest lines of "invitation" can be followed back into childhood, except in the two priests, Yves and David. We find the first signs of diabolic attack only in their adult lives.

The beginnings of possession are generally traced only after the fact, in the memory of the one person—the possessed—who can tell us about those beginnings. Sometimes, during an actual exorcism, the exorcist can elicit from the possessing spirit some bare details about how entry of Evil Spirit was effected and possession became a fact. Father Mark, in particular among the exorcists in this book, believed strongly in pushing for such information. Perhaps as a consequence of that, Mark impresses one as having an extremely quick "feel" for the practicalities of dealing with evil spirits and exorcisms. It was clear that he understood Jamsie's predicament in considerable detail on the basis of a single long interview with Jamsie nearly two years before he was actually called upon to perform the exorcism in that case. Still, Father Conor, who taught Father Peter so well during his months in Rome, remains the exorcist of my acquaintance who seemed to have the broadest understanding of the stages and perils of the actual processes of possession and of Exorcism. Conor's general outlines of the process of possession ran as follows.

First, the actual *entry point*, the point at which Evil Spirit enters an individual and a decision, however tenuous, is made by the victim to allow that entry.

Then, a stage of *erroneous judgments* by the possessed in vital matters, as a direct result of the allowed presence of the possessing spirit and apparently in preparation for the next stage.

Third, the *voluntary yielding of control* by the possessed person to a force or presence he clearly feels is alien to himself and as a result of which the possessed loses control of his will, and so of his decisions and his actions.

Once the third stage is secure, extended control proceeds and may potentially reach the point of completion—perfect possession.

In any individual case, these four stages will dovetail and overlap differently. And, while the process may be swift, more often it seems to take years to accomplish. "We have the eternity of the Lord of Knowledge," Tortoise told Hearty arrogantly.

At every new step, and during every moment of possession, the consent of the victim is necessary, or possession cannot be successful. The consent may be verbal, but always involves choice of action. Once initial consent has been given, its withdrawal becomes more and more difficult as time goes on. In Jamsie's case, he was subjected to intense physical pain when he thought of ejecting Ponto. When Carl hesitated, he was threatened with vivid images of his own extinction. But whatever the pain or threat, it is wielded to retain the consent of the possessed for the continuing presence and power of the preternatural spirit.

Rather than being signs of the great power of preternatural spirits, these threats are evidence of their limitations, for they cannot attack and seize control of the will directly. They can only work through the senses (Jamsie's pain) or the imagination (Carl's fear was produced through the attack on his imagination), in order to assure the continuance of that most basic element of all human possession: the consent of the victim by his own will.

The first stage, the actual entry of Evil Spirit and the beginning of its personal influence *within* a person, appears always to be made by means of the spirit's knowledge of a trait of character or of some special interest or of some avocation of the victim.

It was Marianne's stubbornness of character that seemed to lay her open to invitation. It was Richard/Rita's unusual appreciation of femininity, Jamsie's loneliness, Carl's psychic gifts, David's intellectualism, Yves' esthetic instincts, personal charisma, and priestly avocation. By knowledge of these special traits and interests—none of them either good or bad in and of itself—and by clever appeal in special relation to these traits and interests, entry was made in every case.

All the exorcees here mentioned admit in retrospect that they knew—whether they acknowledged it vaguely (as, say, Marianne) or explicitly (as Carl did)—that the source of the offered help was neither a human being nor any religious source. The source was always vague, always reassuring. It always alienated them from their surroundings and from those nearest to them. The general feeling was that "great things could happen" to them (Yves), or "new developments could take place" in them (Richard/Rita), or that "special success" would be theirs (David) if they were to "listen" (Jamsie) or to "think along these lines" (Marianne) or "wait for more" (Carl). At this stage, there never appeared to be an overt suggestion against religion or religious faith, or against Jesus. At some point during this earliest stage there arrives a delicate moment when each person *chooses* to consider the particular *offer* made to him or her. The exorcees in this report agree individually that they made such a choice, and that they had a sense of violating their consciences when they made it, though at the time in some cases it seemed a fairly minor violation.

It also happens that places, objects, and even animals are used to arouse the attention and interest of the victim—in this book, Jamsie is a notable example; and, later in the process, Carl in another way, and Richard/Rita in still another way. But even when diabolic attack starts with some action or objects, places or animals, the aim is ultimately human beings: to impress them, frighten them, subdue them, fascinate them, to act upon their senses and imagination in order finally to elicit their consent.

Once the initial consent is given, there follows a period in which the victim makes a series of practical personal judgments that profoundly alter him and prepare him for the next critical stage, when he will yield control. This is the stage when *erroneous judgments* of a highly personal nature are made, generally beginning once again in the areas where the individual places the greatest value and enjoys the greatest sense of personal expertise and freedom. Through this process, the original strength, beauty, and idealism of the individual are slowly, piece by piece, turned upside down.

Thus Jonathan's original idea of a new priestly ministry to meet the new needs of the 1960s led him to adapt one after another of the traditional rites and teachings of his Church, until finally he had changed the supernatural meaning of sacrament to a social celebration.

Richard/Rita's initial erroneous judgment concerned his androgyny —he took it as real; and from that flowed a series of judgments about the sexual act, about woman, about marriage, and about the purpose of life that turned the meaning of each of these things into an Alice-in-Wonderland nightmare and led Richard/Rita to defile the very femininity he had so appreciated.

Marianne's judgments were primarily of an intellectual kind, but all of them had a concrete application. She made up her mind that freedom of thought meant you freed yourself of all moral obligations to God and to authority, and that you avoided those who would still inculcate those obligations. And, in quick succession: that others were fools; that freedom meant immunity to advice from those who disagreed; that immunity to advice meant finding herself; that finding herself meant being isolated; that being isolated meant retiring within herself; that retiring within herself meant total absence of initiative and of merely being oneself; that such a condition of "merely being" was the same as "not being at all"—just two facets of the same thing; that from this condition she would be open to an unheard-of secret which "the Man" would reveal; and so on.

We can trace a similar progress in David's judgments based on his anthropological studies and the methodology of his science. He was finally in a condition in which he was applying the norms of scientific method to the data of his religious faith.

Carl, in this respect, was the most disastrous and the most Lucifer-like. Each of his brilliant gifts became an avenue of a deception he refused to acknowledge. And, even to the end, he labored under the illusion that he, Carl, was about to "rediscover" the "true version of Christianity."

If the victim, by now partially possessed, does not withdraw consent and succeed in freeing himself, with help or by dint of his own strength of will and resistance, he will arrive at one sure, critical moment. He will be presented with an increasing and finally unremitting pressure to allow an "inner control" by an alien force. This control will affect thoughts, emotions, acts of will, intentions, likes and dislikes.

Each of our exorcees had this experience. Each felt an eerie "pressure" to allow "someone else" to give them directives; and that "someone else" was "inside" them in some way or other. The pressure was not physical, just as the presence inside them was not physical. There were physical results when they tried to resist that pressure, however.

Once they yielded, they started to receive "instructions"—ready-made judgments and attitudes arose in them, even words on their lips and actions in their limbs. Jamsie seems never to have passed as far as this point. He apparently refused to accept control in refusing Ponto's permanent presence within him.

In David the yielding was subtle, but he nevertheless did yield. There was in him some deep and covert lying to himself about his consent to be controlled. Yet, precisely because of this subtlety, which in turn indicates a wavering in his consent to be controlled, possession of him never progressed very far.

Yves yielded to the intensest pressure of "remote control," even as he looked for relief from that pressure by driving out to visit with friends. Richard/Rita seemed to yield as a young boy when he spent his first night alone in the wilderness of a campsite. Marianne experienced the entry of control almost physically as she sat on a park bench opposite "the Man." Carl's first moment of yielding may even be traced as far back as the moment when, as a teenager, he "agreed" to "wait"—with all its implications of future acceptance; but the intensest pressure on him came as he gazed at a sunset through his office window. Tortoise had prepared his victim well, for even as Carl thought of resisting, he knew he no longer had the means at his command; and he consented fully and with an unusual awareness.

For all the blandishments of success and happiness, for all the visions of special freedoms that may have led to this point, once control is yielded, virtually all personal freedom ceases from that point on. This is the most profound personal choice that can be made. Significantly, the option to relinquish all freedom of choice rests upon that very freedom guaranteed by God as long as the person chooses to be free. The choice can only be made *by* the person; it can never be made *for* him. If the fundamental option is made to relinquish that freedom of will, then possession has been accomplished in its most essential and conclusive step. The simultaneous decision is to reject God and Jesus and the humanness Jesus made possible. Divine light is no longer theirs. There is a vacuum of any such deep knowledge as contributes to that humanness. All luminosity for the soul is progressively snuffed out. Into that vacuum Evil Spirit pours its own light and knowledge.

When possession is achieved, expansion of diabolic control is dramatic and rapid. The light and knowledge of Evil Spirit has its own effects, striking, immediate, and self-protective. It puts the possessed on their guard against circumstances, people, places, and objects closely associated with God and Jesus. It will lead the possessed to avoid situations that constitute a threat to the possessing power of Evil Spirit. Ponto's injunction to Jamsie to keep away from women and alcoholic drink, and his influence on Jamsie's behavior that made it almost impossible for Jamsie to develop any normal human relationship with another person, not only furthered Jamsie's loneliness and increased his need for Ponto's companionship; it also kept him from any possible human love—because love is a positive good necessary to our humanness.

Some of the effects of this special diabolic light may help the possessed in their work. Ponto improved Jamsie's broadcasting style; Yves' charisma was heightened by Mister Natch; Carl's reputation in parapsychology soared with the help of Tortoise. Often the possessed are forewarned of physical threats of an ordinary kind (Marianne's repulsion of the mugger was the result of such protection); they are enlightened about opportunities to pursue their individual satisfaction or prosperity, are given additional weight, fresh information, mental energy, and added power with people.

But the most striking effect of the light and knowledge of Evil Spirit is the extraordinary and dramatic change it effects in the judgments, principles, and outlook of the possessed, together with an ever-growing sense of loss of self-control, even to the point of a loss of awareness of one's actions.

"I always knew, from that point on," Carl recounts today, "that I had consented to a rigid control, and that I would think and say and do things without being able to say why and without any prior reason or motivation."

And while Richard/Rita does recollect the scene with the dying girl in the snow, at the same time he remembers that he was totally beside himself. He was not in any common way aware of what he was doing. The most shocking incidents in this book, in fact, are in Richard/Rita's case, and they serve as tragic and dramatic counterpoint to the thing that Richard/Rita sought most earnestly from his consent to possession: to have tenderest love and to understand the meaning of maleness and femaleness, of masculinity and femininity.

Even though Richard/Rita's quest was genuine and sincere, for Richard/Rita femininity became odious. It became a baleful power to be conquered, even by necrophilia. His own body became a means of total defilement at the Black Mass.

Apparently that "control" changed all the judgments, principles, and outlook of Marianne. All the symbols of good and beauty became signs for panic and flight: the cross on the General Building, the Mass, sexuality, her own body, her parents. She chose to be wholly free and self-sufficient, but she ended a total slave—except for that pocket of resistance that allowed her to make use of help when it came through Peter.

For Yves the sacraments and his own priesthood came to mean merely material values with no referrent to God or Jesus or the supernatural. But apparently he, too, preserved a pocket of resistance on which he could rely when his friends initiated Exorcism.

If extended control continues unabated, if *total* consent is achieved, then total (or perfect) possession is achieved. Father Mark is certain he has met more than one such case—but only by chance, for no exorcism would be requested for such a person; and even if attempted, without at least the partial will of the possessed it probably could not succeed.

Though Mark had never met Jay Beedem, Mark was sure that Jay Beedem had played a part in such an odd, if small, way in Jamsie's troubles. Mark pursued his suspicion in the exorcism. But Multus, Ponto's "superior," would tell Mark absolutely nothing. "No," Multus responded peremptorily. "That Person has no authority over Jay Beedem. He is ours."

In Richard/Rita's case there must also be a question as to whether the psychiatrist, Dr. Hammond, was well on his way toward perfect possession. "He is ours! We needn't fight for him!" screamed Girl-Fixer. "You can't get him back. He is ours."

In every case of possession that comes to the point of Exorcism, the subject has reached a crucial crossroads. Some small corner of reservation remains, some glimmer or recollection of the light of Jesus still shines. Some iota of control is withheld by the possessed against the ever-increasing encroachment of all his being by that first fallen creature of God. Some area of revolt arises against the control originally accepted. The possessed become revolters; and insofar as they do revolt, they are attacked with increasing ferocity by the invading spirit, who, in its turn, protests any attempt to dislodge it from its "home."

Possessed people who have been successfully exorcised often recount how, at some point, they began to make an effort to control their thoughts, their wills, their memories.

It is that strange and terrible struggle between the rebelling victim and the evil spirit protesting the rebellion that, in a strange way, begins to produce the repulsive, disquieting, and frightening events so often associated with the possessed and which lead their families or friends to seek help on their behalf.

Many exorcists think that the majority of the partially possessed who rebel in this way never get priestly help. They are taken to doctors and psychiatrists, who never succeed in helping them. Through treatment with drugs, a temporary "remission"—a calming of the violence—may be achieved for a while, usually at the cost of some mental acuteness and physical energy. The subjects, these exorcists feel, may often spend time in mental institutions, and there they will become progressively worse as their awful battle goes on.

When the rebellion of the possessed person does lead to Exorcism, the bitter struggle is brought out into the open. The exorcist literally offers himself as hostage. He stands in for the possessed and fights for him the battle he cannot fight for himself—beyond his bizarre call for help.

The three principals, exorcist, exorcee, and invading spirit, are placed in jeopardy. The possessed must withstand excruciating and exhausting wracking of his body, mind, and emotions; and what small will remains free must not waver.

The exorcist will suffer all the pains and unimaginable penalties we have already described, and that each exorcist in this book graphically brings home to us.

The possessing spirit's anguish can be traced in the thumping, screeching, discordant wail that so often holds the exorcist's mind in thrall, as spirit after spirit is forced painfully to leave the human "home." This must truly be an echo of the eternal agony once and for all time experienced by Lucifer: the irremediable pain of sorrow undergone by that brightest of all created intelligences howling again in the voice of Smiler, Mister Natch, Ponto, Multus: "Where shall we go? Where shall we hide from God avenging?"

The End
of an Exorcist

Michael Strong–
Conclusion

They brought Father Michael back from Hong Kong to Ireland in early July 1948. For five months he stayed in a rest house with the Medical Sisters, in County Meath. By December he felt strong enough to make the trip to his hometown, Castleconnell, in County Tipperary. There he had flocks of married nieces, nephews, and cousins. And there he lived until his death in October of the following year.

Michael was extremely uncommunicative about himself. But the townspeople gradually got to know his condition and some general facts of his recent past. They took him for granted, as one of themselves who had come home from the big, unknown world "outside" where, as they put it, "those haythen Chinks and Bolshies had given Father Michael a rough time of it."

Michael never ventured out into the narrow streets of Castleconnell and rarely went into the garden surrounding his house. Morning and evening his housekeeper opened the French windows so that the old man could sit on the porch in the shadows and look out at the grass, the apple trees, and the trellised walls. Now and again he tended the Virginia creeper which he loved, or he puttered about the radishes, onions, and parsnips growing in the small vegetable patch that occupied a narrow space beneath the south wall. He slept lightly and very little at night, read only the Sunday editions of the newspapers, and seemed to be lost in thought and reverie most of the time.

A young curate said Mass in his bedroom at 6:00 A.M. every morning. Once a month or so Father Michael himself said Mass; but it took him almost two hours. The effort was an obvious strain. Other visitors were rare and stayed briefly: a niece or nephew with their children each Sunday, an old seminary friend, or the bishop. Yet none of them ever got to know anything precise of what he had been through and what was the reason for the peculiar lull, the hush of waiting, in which Michael obviously spent his last years. He seemed to be waiting for something, expecting something.

My uncle was resident G.P. of Castleconnell. And as a young seminarian I heard about Father Michael Strong months before I finally saw him face to face and started to visit him from time to time. My memories of him are fresh some 25 years later; certain phrases and words of his remain indelibly with me, together with his tones and expressions. When I met him, he gave the impression of a great fragility. Big and raw-boned, he had obviously lost much weight.

But the fragility was not chiefly the effect of his thinness, his mop of gray hair, his bony hands or hollow cheeks. It was a general appearance of delicate survival, as of a hair's-breadth balance in him, between life and disappearance from life. There was a transparency about his face and person that clothed him in a quiet tension. Imagined or not, a silent dialogue seemed to be always in progress between Michael and a world I was too crass and physically flesh-bound to perceive. Only its aftertones registered somewhere within me, cautioning me against any abrupt movement or aggressive way of talking.

He talked willingly and easily of China and of the work he had done there. Those in his small circle of acquaintances knew the general profile of his story. But of Thomas Wu he spoke sparingly and with difficulty, rarely in any detail. At first, I thought this was due to some repugnance in his memories of those times. But then, when we did speak of his recent past, I began to discount that reason for his reticence. When I put questions about his exorcism of Wu, he started to recollect and to answer, but then he trailed off, as if still waiting for some explanation, some finale, some bottom line to be written to his story.

There was a soft silence for ten or fifteen minutes. He stirred in his chair finally: "Well. All in God's good time. . . . The glass will clear. Must clear . . ." or some similar remark was all he would say.

And I learned that at such moments (not before) you rose and left Father Michael alone with his thoughts and his abiding presences.

He had characteristic gestures: the palm of his right hand on his forehead; rubbing his chin with the back of his wrist; holding the fingers of his right hand in the left hand. All the while his eyes looked straight out, not dreamily, not awake-looking, not blank and wide in remembering, but filled with narrowing details or a present panorama invisible to all others. This was why the few townspeople who saw him reported: "Poor Father Michael. Shure, he's waitin' for the good Lord."

Waiting was the keynote of his personality in those months, as if "waiting for the glass to clear . . ." When now and again he went as far as the gateway to say goodbye to a visitor, he had the same look on his face. He seemed to be scanning the road, the horizon, the sky, waiting for something or someone whom he would recognize the moment they came into view. An old acquaintance, I often thought in the beginning, a messenger. You never knew.

I got the same impression from his long vigils on the porch, and his hours spent sitting bolt upright in his study looking toward the door or the window.

The first breakthrough I had in gleaning some information about the Thomas Wu exorcism was in May 1949. A local farmer of Castleconnell, John Gallen, had killed his neighbor, Jim Cahill, with a billhook late one night. It had been just one more act in a long-standing family feud: either a Gallen or a Cahill died by violence in every generation.

Michael talked to me about Cain and Abel in a rambling fashion. Then he turned his head and asked me abruptly: "Has John Gallen got something on his chin?" Without waiting for my answer: "Anyway, what would you know about that? Thank God. For your sake."

But he had revealed something, I felt, and it was worth pursuing even with a guess. "Had Thomas Wu something on his chin, Father Michael?"

He looked around slowly. His eyes normally a faded blue, were burning: "Young man, there are things better learned by you only when they happen to you."

Then one of the long silences. I waited.

Finally, stirring, he said surprisingly: "Well . . . now that you've a little inkling, I suppose you'd better know something more. But not today. Some other day." After a pause, the inevitable, "Please God."

I did not get out to see Father Michael again until the middle of July. It was one of those long summer evenings rare in that part of Ireland, beneath a cloudless sky after a long day of dry heat. By the time I arrived, all brightness had gone from the sky. There was only a soft light streaked here and there with tiny broken lines of bronze reflections from the Western ocean where the sun was setting. A light wind was beginning to freshen everything after the hot day.

Michael was down by the trellis picking some leaves off the Virginia creeper. They had reddened prematurely. He placed each one carefully between the pages of his Bible.

"I'm glad you stayed away so long," he said. "Time is so necessary." He closed the Bible on the last leaf. We walked back slowly to his chair on the porch.

We chatted for a few moments about local news. Then I asked him about the mark on Thomas Wu's chin. He was very insistent: it was a personal mark. "Like what a potter would put on the bottom of a vase he made. Or a painter on his picture. *Satan me fecit* sort of thing." He added some details about Thomas Wu. Apparently Wu had spent some years in Japan in the early 1930s. When he returned to Nanking, he had completely changed: rabidly anti-Japanese, rabidly anti-Kuomintang, constantly talking about the Communist leaders in North China; and something else in him, all his friends felt uneasily, was now totally alien to them.

Wu, Michael added, had given himself body and soul to that old, old force, the one which led Cain to murder his brother, Abel, in the fields, the one that tried to impede God's creation of man's world. The oldest. The strongest. For all of them. "Them," in Michael's mouth, were the Japanese, the Chinese, the Russians, the Americans. They all acted as if death were the final arbiter and the strongest ally in all the universe. Cain's father was a murderer from the beginning, as Jesus was the first to state in the Gospels.

I wanted to know something of Michael's condition in 1948 when they brought him home. But at the mention of "home," he interrupted me saying he had not yet gone home. He couldn't, he said. Not before he finished the business he had begun at the exorcism in *Puh-Chi*. I noticed the tears at the back of his eyes, and looked away.

The wind was stronger now. We could hear the lowing of cows across the way and the barking of dogs as they herded them into the barn for the oncoming night. Michael called for a rug to wrap around his waist and knees.

There was another of his fifteen-minute lapses. It ended when the housekeeper brought out his supper on a tray. He ate in silence. When he had finished, the sun was below the trees, and the countryside lay in the half-light, half-darkness of dusk. Away to the northwest, a flight of wild geese was hurrying home to the fens and woodlands of Connemara. Michael pulled the rug tighter around him and filled his pipe.

"Home. Yes . . ." His voice died away into a mumbled hole of silence for another minute or two. Then, as if there had been no pause or interruption, he went on talking.

The tears I had seen earlier were not of regret or revolt, he said, just of homesickness. Since 1938, he had been alone and in the dark. Everybody else could go home, but he had to wait.

I looked at him. His gray hair and pale face were melting into the shadows. Only his eyes were clear, visible pools of light, looking toward the bottom of the garden.

"Believe me, once you mess with Exorcism, and above all if you don't pull it off, something departs from you. And the rest of you yearns to depart also."

It did not seem a good moment to pursue his "waiting" to "depart." So I asked him about the Confrontation with Evil Spirit in an exorcism. What was it like? What effects had it? It was a meeting, he said, a personal meeting. What the exorcist met in person was something that existed in a state where the all-important, the only, reality was a "living *not.*"

I wanted to stop and ponder that for a while, but he went on to talk of a reality that is *not* beautiful, *not* true, *not* holy, *not* pleasant, *not* bright, *not* warm, *not* large, *not* happy, *not* anything positive.

I started to say that all this sounded like Hell or how people used to describe Hell. "No," he interjected distinctly and firmly. "That *is* Hell. Just to be utterly alone and immutably without love. Forever." In the exorcism the exorcist knew that what he was up against existed in that state. He just knew it.

The effect of all this? I asked the question still very tentatively, not wishing to increase any pain he had. Did he feel he was in a box or a prison? Did it make him dispirited and lose initiative?

The effects were far deeper, he said. Years before in the seminary, he loved music, flowers, a good book. He could laugh the loudest of all; he enjoyed swimming, tennis, a good meal, and so on. He loved children. They made him happy, just to hear their voices. And many other things he liked also—singing and dancing and long walks, and the sound of waves on the shore, and smells such as new-mown hay, flowers and grass after a light shower, a turf fire in the early morning. And he slept like a top. Always he woke up ready for the world, rain, hail, or shine.

After Thomas Wu's exorcism was over, all that had changed. No, it wasn't age, he answered some unvoiced remark of mine, but something else.

The housekeeper appeared, and he nodded to her. It was time for him to turn in. She left.

I asked: "What does it really mean?"

He was standing up now. The moon had risen over the back wall of the garden. We both looked at it with upturned faces.

"You are never quite at home in this human world ever again after an exorcism," he said slowly. He sat down again and explained.

After an exorcism the exorcist hears and sees and thinks and talks as he always did. But now he perceives on two planes. Spirit is everywhere. Flesh and matter is only "our picture" of what's there. And it's not *all* good. There's evil *and* good hidden in that "picture."

After an exorcism you always know, if you didn't know it before. You are now walking with double vision, a second sight, as the old people used to say.

And the exorcist never really sleeps, not as he used to. He dozes off. Some deep part of him is keeping watch, always watching, and doesn't want anything to escape him even momentarily. All sleep is escape. And he knows that escape for him is impossible.

He eats, he must in order to stay alive. And he breathes. His heart beats on. But he has a terrible option always: not to breathe, to let his heart stop.

As we entered the house he said quietly: "Come back in a few weeks. I'm getting to the end now. There isn't much time."

Before his death in the following October, I saw Father Michael twice more. Once was in early September, and again a few minutes before he died.

"Yeh'll find Father is changed," the housekeeper whispered when I arrived in September. "He nivir goes out anymore."

Michael was in his study sitting in an armchair facing the door. The shutters were drawn, so the only light came from two candles that burned steadily on the mantelpiece. He did not look at me as I entered, but raised his hand in salute.

"Want me to let in some fresh air and sun?" I asked, after greeting him. I moved toward the window. For a minute there was silence.

"If you open those shutters," he said patiently, like a schoolmaster explaining a problem to a pupil, "you'll be blotting out the only light I have. Come, sit down and stay by me for a while."

There was no flurry or annoyance in his voice. It was even and factual. I crossed over and took a seat facing him. The candlelight fell directly on his head and face.

The change in him was devastating. His face had shrunk, not inward, but upward. All its form and character seemed to have departed and receded from the jawline, the mouth and lips, up past the nose to an invisible dividing line running through his cheekbones. There was no definite expression on the mouth. The jaw and chin had lost some firmity, some configuration that had made them his. Now they might have been anybody's or those of a lifeless statue. His complexion was not exactly a pallor, nor white. At first, it seemed colorless. Then, clearly I saw a tint of yellow and off-white, but nothing that belonged to a normally healthy face. It had too much transparency, too much glaze. The words "immobile," "immobility" kept jumping to my mind.

The right eye was permanently half-closed, like a shutter. Both eyes were overlaid with a filmy gauze of liquid that oozed gently from the corners. There was little or no expression in them.

Behind the apparent fixity of the staring eyeballs, I could see or feel a darting, lively presence, an intelligence alert and aware. His forehead was smooth and clear of all wrinkles. Michael had a domelike head with a hairline that had never receded. His gray hair had been cropped into a crew cut. He was cleanly shaven.

Breeda, the housekeeper, had told me not to talk too much.

"Father Michael, how are you?"

He said he was fine. He had a request to make. Before my visit ended, I should remind him of it. But he wanted first to say something further to me about the effects of the exorcism on him. "It helps me to talk about it all"—this by way of explanation.

It was the double vision: he had not defined it properly, he said. I waited, because, as Michael spoke, a wave of misery swept over his face. The veil of immobility was withdrawn for an instant, then fell back again. For that quick instant I had seen a load of pain and sadness framed in lines of a gently resolute hope. His whole expression said: I will not give up my trust, although I have nothing to rely on but that trust.

Then he went on to describe the double vision. It was not like seeing another table beside the real table or another wall beside the real wall. It was not a vision of eyes or a hearing with your ears or a touching with your hand. It was another level of reality. An exorcism sharpens your awareness of that reality, he said. You know what stands behind and around and beneath and above all that is visible and tangible. The intertwining cords of spirit appear everywhere. Good and bad spirit. Beauty and ugliness. Holiness and sin. God as a tremendous majesty. Personal evil is a formidable force. Nothing escapes those cords.

He fell silent at this point. After a pause, I could not resist asking him directly about his failure to complete the exorcism of Thomas Wu. Did it entail any special liability within this sphere of his double vision?

"Of course." The words were loaded with an ache and a distress which silenced me. Once pronounced, they hung in the air between us as silent signs of his suffering.

"I can now hate. I can choose to hate," he said drily. Before the exorcism of Wu, he had never even thought of hating. Now, to hate was a living option for him. Before the exorcism, he never even imagined what it would be like really to despair. Now it was a real option. "Real." "Real." He repeated the word several times. The idea of rejecting Jesus as a charlatan now came to him as a real choice.

All those choices and others too unspeakable to mention were like plates of food placed in front of him continually. His pain was that he was forced to consider each one as a possibility. Before, he had them all banded together and thrown into a box, and he had thrown away the key. Now he had to take a taste of each one. Slowly. Realistically. He stopped at a certain point, groping for an image. It was, he finally said, as if a mad wolf were allowed sniff and smell and nose around his naked body, always threatening to bite and crush, always moving, moving, moving. He bent his head on his hands. There was a pause of about five minutes.

And all the waiting, I finally asked, why all the waiting? He had failed in the exorcism, but he had not accepted Satan or evil or hate. Why, then, the perpetual waiting?

"Simply put, my young friend," he said thickly, "evil has power over us, some power. And even when defeated and put to flight, it scrapes you in passing by. If you don't defeat it, evil exacts a price of more terrible agony. It rips a gash in the spirit with a filthy claw, and some of its venom enters the veins of the soul. As a price. As a memory. As a lesson. A warning that it will return again."

It was time to go. I stood up. He said nothing. I touched him lightly on the forehead. It was cold.

As I went out, Breeda smiled at me: "Now, young man, don't worry about Father Michael. He knows what he's doin'." Somehow, this old woman understood more that I had ever understood.

Then I heard his voice calling after me: "Malachi! At the end, be sure and read Paul, First Corinthians, Chapter 15, verses 50 to 58. All of it."

I hurried back into the study. But he told me to go with the usual silent wave of the hand.

It was an early October morning when Breeda telephoned. The day was heavily overcast, and it rained continuously. A thunderstorm was moving in from the Atlantic. Michael had received the Last Rites of the Church, Breeda told me.

When I arrived at the house, all was quiet. The doctor had seen him that morning, had left, and was back again. He was an old friend of Michael from their distant schooldays in Castleconnell. Michael's relatives had come and gone. The bishop had sent a monsignor with a special blessing. Only Breeda and the doctor remained.

In his room, lit by two candles, Michael was supported by pillows in a half-upright position on the bed, his body slightly turned to one side. He looked as if he had fallen limply from a height. He held a crucifix between his hands. Both his eyes were closed. His mouth was open as he endeavored to breathe.

His face still had the devastated look. But now, as I tiptoed across the room, his face looked crooked to me, as if some hand had dislocated its general lines and destroyed its symmetry. The forehead was a mass of entangled furrows; the eyebrow line was crooked; one eyelid seemed more bulbous and puffy than the other; the nostrils flared irregularly; the nose and mouth were angular and seemed turned at the wrong place.

Almost immediately after my arrival a change came over Michael. Without a sound, he started to turn around facing front. His body grew stiff. The heavily labored breathing grew easy.

His lips moved; and, bending down close, I heard him say faintly: "Over there. In the corner. By the window. The candle. Please . . ."

I moved one of the two candles to the top of a low bookcase and returned to his side.

"It's all very black, my friend," he whispered as I bent down, "and . . . it stings."

The rest was lost in a moaning that streamed from between his teeth. Still bent over him, I opened Paul's first letter to the Corinthians and started reading the verses he had requested, reciting them from memory as I looked at him, now and again glancing at the text.

" 'We shall all be changed . . . in the twinkling of an eye . . . the dead shall be raised incorruptible . . . and this mortal must put on immortality . . .' "

Michael was still moaning as if a great weight lay on him, holding him helpless.

" '. . . then shall be brought to pass the saying that is written: Death is swallowed up in victory . . . the sting of death is sin. . . . Thanks be to God who giveth us the victory through our Lord Jesus Christ . . .' "

I stopped and waited. Michael's chest had risen as he managed a large intake of breath. He seemed to be holding the air in his lungs, fearful to let go.

"I'll open the window," said the doctor. As the two shutters swung in, the room was suddenly flooded with the grayish white light of the sky. There was a rush of cold air and the drumming sound of rain falling on the trees, the grass, the stone garden path, the roof, and the special sound of gutters running with water. An occasional gleam of lightning lit the gloom. The storm was not very distant and was moving quickly in over us.

Michael, still holding his breath, clearly a man in great distress now, seemed to be trying to get something out of his throat or chest. His whole frame vibrated without moving from its place. His head shook sharply up and down in a little nodding motion. He raised his right hand slightly and pointed to the far corner: the candle had been blown out by the fresh air that had entered the room.

I hurried over to relight it, but was only a few feet from his side when I heard a sharp sound like the opening of a tightly closed door. Michael released his breath; and as he did, it began to resound in his chest and throat louder and louder. As he exhaled, the sound it made grew to a small crescendo. It was not a shout or a scream, nor was it simply escaping air. It was a tremulous pronouncement as near words as such a sound could be without using words. A death song sung with the only accents his dying permitted him.

I came back and knelt beside him. "His victory, Michael. His victory. Believe it! His victory!" I whispered.

The sound of his breath died away gently like the most finalizing of final statements ending all discussion, completing all expression. He lay there utterly still. Then both his eyes opened. The gaze in them held me hypnotized. Gone was the filmy gauze which had clouded them. There was no trace of the ooze and deformity that had distorted them in previous weeks. An invisible hand had wiped away the disfigurement and agony lines from all over his face. It was now smooth. Between his eyes and his mouth a triangle of joy shone in his smile and in his look. The faded blue his eyes had aquired in latter years was now luminous, not deep and sharp, but soft and glowing. All that I had ever known, read about, heard of, imagined of human happiness and of unalloyed joy in peace, and peace in joy shone out for that brief interval.

Then there was a tiny rattle in Michael's throat. The lips smiled faintly. The eyes lost all light. I felt sure Michael had partaken in Jesus' victory over death and that he had escaped death's sting. But he had, indeed, paid the price for his failure of years before.

We will never know the exact note of suffering such a man as Michael Strong must undergo at dying, for it lies in the spirit unattainable by our logic, unimaginable by our fantasy, impervious to any clever methodology we can devise. But each exorcist could well have as his epitaph the most noble phrase Jesus ever pronounced about human love: "Greater love than this no man hath: that a man lay down his life for his friend."

APPENDIX ONE

The Roman Ritual
of Exorcism

PRELIMINARY NOTE

The traditional text of the Roman Exorcism Ritual, which follows here in translation, has a long history of development. Starting with the explicit command and example of Jesus to "drive out devils," continuing through the age of the Apostles, and the century following their death, on through the centuries of the early Church Fathers (200–600 a.d.), and into Medieval Times, there is an unbroken tradition of belief and Church practice in this matter of Exorcism. Some parts of the present text are identifiably of the late 3rd and early 4th centuries. Others certainly predate the year 1000 a.d. Much of the text was developed in the centuries leading up to the Renaissance. The text finally reached its present format in the 17th century.

The Roman Ritual is divided into three *Chapters*. In *Chapter One*, there is a series of general instructions for Exorcism and exorcists. There follow two versions of the Rite. One version *(Chapter Two)* is for the exorcism of people; the second version *(Chapter Three)* is reserved for the exorcism of places.

In the Latin, these *Chapters* are not subdivided. In presenting an English translation of the text, however, I have divided each *Chapter* into numbered parts, and have supplied descriptive titles for each part, so that the sequence and logic of the Rite would be more apparent to the reader.

It is important to remember that the Exorcism Ritual is not a Sacrament. Its integrity and efficacy do not depend, therefore, as in Sacraments, on the rigid use of an unchanging formula or on the ordered sequence of prescribed actions. Its efficacy depends on two elements: authorization from valid and licit Church authorities, and the faith of the exorcist.

This nature of Exorcism as a Church rite rather than as a Church Sacrament has an important consequence. Church authorities have always insisted on a structured text to ensure that the essentials of Exorcism (the summoning and expulsion of Evil Spirit solely in the name of Jesus) are maintained in each exorcism. Yet, in spite of traditional formality, great freedom is allowed and practiced in the use of the Ritual text. The very nature of Exorcism makes this a necessity: in the turbulent and changeful atmosphere of an actual exorcism, it would be impossible to adhere rigidly to a given text and ceremonial.

In practice, the flow of the text is broken by dialogues between exorcist and Evil

Spirit. Exorcists, according as they judge fit, omit certain parts, repeat others, substitute their own Psalm and Gospel readings, have their own favorite prayers, always use at least the Second Exorcism Address to Evil Spirit, give blessings with relics, add further Signs of the Cross, and otherwise vary the printed Ritual, as they would and could never vary the official text of a Sacrament.

Nowadays, parts of the text—especially well-known prayers—are sometimes prayed or recited in the vernacular (German, English, French, etc.). But, among exorcists as a class of Church ministers, there seems to be a persuasion born of experience that the Latin text has some special unction and disruptive value for Evil Spirit. This may be part and parcel of the peculiar bond between spirit and material or human things which is one of the most consistent traits displayed by spirit in exorcisms.

The main parts of the Ritual are performed, of course, by the exorcist alone. His assistants (indicated in the text by the letter A) join him in Psalm and Gospel readings and in responding Amen to nine Prayers and Addresses. Some exorcists add two or three assistants to the usual four; and the additional assistants recite the Rosary or chant hymns right through the exorcism.

Whenever a printed cross appears in the following text, the exorcist makes the Sign of the Cross in the general direction of the exorcee, unless the text indicates a precise place or direction (as, the forehead of the exorcee, the assistants, or etc.).

CHAPTER ONE: INSTRUCTIONS FOR EXORCISING THOSE POSSESSED BY EVIL SPIRIT

1: The priest who with the particular and explicit permission of his Bishop is about to exorcise those tormented by Evil Spirit, must have the necessary piety, prudence and personal integrity. He should perform this most heroic work humbly and courageously, not relying on his own strength, but on the power of God; and he must have no greed for material benefit. Besides, he should be of mature age and be respected as a virtuous person.

2: To perform his task correctly, he should be acquainted with the many practical writings of approved authors on the subject of Exorcism. These are omitted here for the sake of brevity. He should, in addition, carefully observe the following few rules which are of major importance.

3: Above all, he must not easily believe that someone is possessed by Evil Spirit. He must be thoroughly acquainted with those signs by which he can distinguish the possessed person from those who suffer from a physical illness. The signs of possession by Evil Spirit are of a peculiar genre. Among others: when the subject speaks unknown languages with many words or understands unknown languages; when he clearly knows about things that are distant or hidden; when he shows a physical strength far above his age or normal condition. These manifestations together with others of the same kind are major indications.

4: To be all the surer, the exorcist should interrogate the subject after one or two exorcism addresses, asking him what he feels in his spirit or in his body. In this way, also, he will find out what words disturb Evil Spirit more than others; and thus he can repeat such words and have greater effect on Evil Spirit.

5: Let the exorcist note for himself the tricks and deceits which evil spirits use in order to lead him astray. For they are accustomed to answering falsely. They manifest themselves only under pressure—in the hope that the exorcist will get tired and desist from pressuring them. Or they make it appear that the subject of Exorcism is not possessed at all.

6: Sometimes, Evil Spirit betrays its presence, and then goes into hiding. It appears to have left the body of the possessed free from all molestation, so that the possessed thinks he is completely rid of it. But the exorcist should not, for all that, desist until he sees the signs of liberation.

7: Sometimes, also, Evil Spirit throws up every possible obstacle in order to stop the possessed from submitting to Exorcism. Or it tries to persuade him that his affliction is quite natural. Sometimes, during Exorcism, it gets the possessed to go to sleep; or it shows him some vision. But it hides itself, so that the possessed appears to be freed from it.

8: Some evil spirits reveal an occult spell and by whom it was made, and the way in which it can be loosened. But the exorcist must beware of having recourse in such matters to witches or warlocks or sorcerers or to any others beyond Church ministers. And let him not rely on any superstitious practice or any other illicit method.

9: Sometimes, Evil Spirit leaves the possessed in peace and even allows him to receive Holy Communion, so that It seems to have gone away. In sum, innumerable are the stratagems and deceits which Evil Spirit uses in order to deceive men. The exorcist must practice caution in order not to be deceived by any of them.

10: He must remember, therefore, that Our Lord said there is a species of Evil Spirit which cannot be expelled except by prayer and fasting. Let him make sure that he and others follow the example of the Holy Fathers and make use of these two principal means of obtaining divine help and of repelling Evil Spirit.

11: If it is convenient, the possessed can be exorcised in a church or in some other religious and appropriate place apart from the public eye. If the subject is ill, or if there is any other good reason, he can be exorcised in a private house.

12: The possessed must be encouraged to pray to God, to fast, and to get spiritual strength from the Sacraments of Confession and Holy Communion, if he enjoys mental and physical health.

13: The possessed should hold a Crucifix in his hands or have it in front of him. Wherever available, the relics of the saints can be placed on his chest, or on his head. They should be appropriately and safely covered. But let care be taken that these holy things are not treated irreverently and damaged by Evil Spirit. The Holy Eucharist should not be placed on the head or anywhere on the body of the possessed. There is a danger that it will be treated irreverently.

14: The exorcist must not make great speeches or put superfluous questions out of vain curiosity, especially about future events and hidden matters which have nothing to do with his work. He should command the unclean spirit to keep silent and only to respond to what is asked of it. And he must give no credence to Evil Spirit, if it claims to be the soul of some saint or of a dead person or to be the Good Angel.

15: Questions he must ask the possessing Evil Spirit are, for example: the number and name of the possessing spirits; when they entered the possessed; why they entered him; and other questions of the same kind. Let the exorcist restrain the other vanities, mockeries, and foolishnesses of Evil Spirit. He should treat them with contempt. And he should admonish those who are present—who should be few in number—not to take any notice of what Evil Spirit says and not to put any questions to the possessed. Let them pray humbly and fervently to God for the deliverance of the possessed.

16:   The exorcist should perform and read the exorcism with command, authority, great faith, humility, and fervor. And, when he sees that the possessing spirit is being tortured mightily, he should multiply all these efforts at pressuring it. Whenever he sees some part of the possessed person's body moving or pierced or some swelling appearing, let him make the Sign of the Cross and sprinkle Holy Water.

17:   Let him pay attention also to the words and expressions which disturb Evil Spirit most, and repeat them very often. And when he arrives at the point of Expulsion, let him pronounce that Expulsion again and again, always increasing the punishment. And, if he sees that he is succeeding, let him persevere until he is finally victorious.

18:   Finally, let the exorcist beware not to offer any medicine to the possessed or suggest any to him. All this he should leave to the medical doctors.

19:   If he is exorcising a woman, he should have with him some reputable women who will hold the possessed when she is tormented and shaken by Evil Spirit. Such women should be of great patience and belong to the family of the possessed. The exorcist must be mindful of scandal and avoid doing or saying anything which could provoke ill for himself or for others.

20:   During Exorcism, the exorcist should use the words of the Bible rather than his own or somebody else's. Also, he should command Evil Spirit to state whether it is kept within the possessed because of some magical spell or sorcerer's symbol or some occult documents. For the exorcism to succeed, the possessed must surrender them. If he has swallowed something like that, he will vomit it up. If it is outside his body in some place or other, Evil Spirit must tell the exorcist where it is. When the exorcist finds it, he must burn it.

21:   If the possessed person is freed from Evil Spirit, he should be advised to be diligent in avoiding sinful actions and thoughts. If he does not, he could give Evil Spirit a fresh occasion for returning and possessing him. In that case, he would be in a much worse condition than before.

CHAPTER TWO: RITUAL FOR EXORCISING THOSE POSSESSED BY EVIL SPIRIT

1:   PRELIMINARY INSTRUCTIONS

Before starting the exorcism, the priest appointed by the Bishop should make a good Confession—or, at least, renew in his heart sincere contrition for all his sins. He should say Mass, and ask for God's help. Then, wearing a surplice and purple stole, he should stand in front of the possessed. The possessed should be tied down, if there is any danger of violence. The exorcist is then to invoke protection on the possessed, on himself, and on his assistants, by making the Sign of the Cross and sprinkling Holy Water.

2: INVOCATIONS

Then, kneeling down, he is to recite the following invocations, to which his assistants respond:

Exorcist: (The Litanies of the Saints).
Do not remember, O Lord, our sins or those of our forefathers.

Assistants: And do not punish us for our offences.

E: (Pater Noster)—silently until the last part:
And lead us not into temptation.

A: But deliver us from evil.

E: (Psalm 53)
Save this man (woman) your servant.

A: Because he (she) hopes in you, My God.

E: Be a tower of strength for him (her), O Lord.

A: In the face of the Enemy.

E: Let the Enemy have no victory over him (her).

A: And let the Son of Iniquity not succeed in injuring him (her).

E: Send him (her) help from the Holy Place, Lord.

A: And give him (her) Heavenly protection.

E: Lord, hear my prayer.

A: And let my cry reach you.

E: May the Lord be with you.

A: And with your spirit.

E: Let us pray.
God, it is an attribute of yours to have mercy and to forgive. Hear our prayer, so that this servant of yours who is bound with the chain of sins, be mercifully freed by the compassion of your goodness.

Holy Lord! All-powerful Father! Eternal God! Father of Our Lord Jesus Christ! You who destined that recalcitrant and apostate Tyrant to the fires of Hell; you who sent your only son into this world in order that he might crush this Roaring Lion: Look speedily and snatch from damnation and from this Devil of our times this man (this woman) who was created in your image and likeness. Throw your terror, Lord, over the Beast who is destroying what belongs to you. Give faith to your servants against this most Evil Serpent, to fight most bravely. So that the Serpent not hold in contempt those who hope in you, and say—as It said through the Pharaoh: I do not know God, and I will not let Israel go. Let your powerful strength force the Serpent to let go of your servant, so that it no longer possess him (her) whom you deigned to make in your image and to redeem by your son, Who lives and reigns with you in the unity of the Holy Spirit, as God, for ever and ever.

A: Amen.

3: SUMMONING OF EVIL SPIRIT

E: Unclean Spirit! Whoever you are, and all your companions who possess this servant of God. By the mysteries of the Incarnation, the Sufferings and

Death, the Resurrection, and the Ascension of Our Lord Jesus Christ; by the sending of the Holy Spirit; and by the Coming of Our Lord into Last Judgment, I command you:

Tell me, with some sign, your name, the day and the hour of your damnation.

Obey me in everything, although I am an unworthy servant of God.

Do no damage to this creature (the possessed), or to my assistants, or to any of their goods.

4: GOSPEL READINGS

John 1: 1–12; Mark 16: 15–18; Luke 10: 17–20; Luke 11: 14–22

E: Lord, Hear my prayer.

A: And let my cry reach you.

E: May the Lord be with you.

A: And with your spirit.

E: Let us pray.

All-powerful God! Word of God, the Father! Christ Jesus! God and Lord of all creation! You gave power to your Apostles to pass through dangers unharmed. Among your commands to do wondrous things, you said: Drive out Evil Spirit. By your strength, Satan fell like lightning from Heaven. With fear and trembling, I pray and supplicate your Holy Name. Pardon all the sins of your unworthy servant. Give me constant faith and power; so that, armed with the power of your holy strength, I can attack this cruel Evil Spirit in confidence and security. Through you, Jesus Christ, Our Lord God, Who will come to judge the living and the dead and the world by fire.

A: Amen.

5: LAYING OF HANDS ON POSSESSED

The exorcist then invokes divine protection on himself and on the possessed by making the Sign of the Cross. Then he places the tip of the stole on the neck of the possessed and his right hand on the head of the possessed. He intones the following with great conviction and faith:

E: Behold the Cross of the Lord. Depart, Enemies!

A: Jesus, with ancient strength, with noble power, is conqueror.

E: Lord, Hear my prayer.

A: And let my cry reach you.

E: May the Lord be with you.

A: And with your spirit.

E: Let us pray:

God, Father of Our Lord Jesus Christ, I invoke your Holy Name and suppliantly request you: Deign to give me strength against this and every other unclean spirit which is tormenting this creature of yours. Through the same Lord Jesus.

A: Amen.

6:   EXORCISM ADDRESSES TO EVIL SPIRIT

(1) *Serving notice on Evil Spirit:-*

E: I exorcise you, Most Unclean Spirit! Invading Enemy! All Spirits! Every one of you! In the name of Our Lord Jesus + Christ: Be uprooted and expelled from this Creature of God. + He who commands you is he who ordered you to be thrown down from the highest Heaven into the depths of Hell. He who commands you is he who dominated the sea, the wind, and the storms. Hear, therefore, and fear, Satan! Enemy of the Faith! Enemy of the human race! Source of death! Robber of life! Twister of justice! Root of evil! Warp of vices! Seducer of men! Traitor of nations! Inciter of jealousy! Originator of greed! Cause of discord! Creator of agony! Why do you stay and resist, when you know that Christ our Lord has destroyed your plan? Fear him who was prefigured in Isaac, in Joseph, and in the Paschal Lamb; who was crucified as a man, and who rose from death.

(Then making the Signs of the Cross on the forehead of the possessed): Retire, therefore, in the name of + Father, and of the + Son, and of the Holy + Spirit. Give way to the Holy Spirit, because of this sign of the Holy + Cross of Our Lord Jesus Christ, Who lives and reigns as God with the Father and the same Holy Spirit, for ever and ever.

A: Amen.

E: Lord, hear my prayer.

A: And let my cry reach you.

E: May the Lord be with you.

A: And with your spirit.

E: Let us pray:

God, Creator and Defender of the human race; you who made man in your own image: Look on this, your servant (the exorcist names the possessed) who is assaulted by the cunning of the unclean spirit. The primeval adversary, the ancient enemy of Earth, surrounds him with the horror of fear, paralyzes his mind with darkness, strikes him with terror, agitates him with shaking and trembling. Repel, O Lord, the power of Evil Spirit! Dissolve the fallacies of its plots! May the unholy temptor take flight. May your servant be protected in soul and body by the sign + of your name (on the forehead of possessed).

(Then he makes three signs of the Cross on the chest of the possessed, while pronouncing the following words):

+ Preserve what is within this person.

+ Rule his (her) feelings.

+ Strengthen his (her) heart.

Let the efforts of the Enemy power be dispelled from his (her) soul, Lord, because of this invocation of your holy name. Grant the grace that he who has inspired terror up to this, now be put to flight and retire defeated; so that this man (woman), your servant, be able to worship you with a firm heart and a sincere mind. Through Christ Our Lord.

A: Amen.

(2) *Enjoining of Evil Spirit:-*

E: I enjoin you under penalty, Ancient Serpent! In the name of the Judge of the Living and the Dead! In the name of Our Creator! In the name of the creator of the world! In the name of him who has power to send you into Hell! Depart from this servant of God *(the exorcist names the possessed)* who has had recourse to the Church. Cease to inspire your terror in him (her) I again enjoin you solemnly + *(on forehead of possessed)*, not because of myself who am weak, but because of the strength of the Holy Spirit: that you go out from this servant of God *(name of the possessed)* whom the all-powerful God made in his own image. Surrender, not to me, but to the minister of Christ. His power forces you. He defeated you by His Cross. Fear the strength of him who led the souls of the dead to the light of salvation from the darkness of waiting. May the body of this man + *(on the chest of possessed)* be a source of terror for you. May the image of God + *(on forehead of possessed)* be a source of fear for you. + God the Father commands you. + God the Son commands you. + God the Holy Spirit commands you. + The faith of the Holy Apostles, Peter and Paul, and the other saints commands you. + The blood of Martyrs commands you. + The purity of the Confessors commands you. + The pious and holy intercession of all the Saints commands you. + The strength of the mysteries of the Christian faith commands you. + Get out! Offender! Get out! Seducer! Full of guile and falseness! Enemy of virtue! Persecutor of the Innocents! Give way, most despicable being! Give way, most impious! Give way to Christ in whom you did not find any of your own doing! He destroyed your kingdom. He bound you up in defeat. He broke your strength. He threw you out into the exterior darkness where destruction was prepared for you and your followers.

But why are you resisting truculently? Why do you dare refuse? You are condemned by the all-powerful God whose law you broke. You are condemned by his son, Jesus Christ, Our Lord. You dared tempt him and you dared to have him crucified. You are condemned by the human race to whom you offered the deathly poison of your suggestions.

I, therefore, charge you solemnly under penalty, Most Evil Serpent, in the name of the Lamb + most immaculate who walked unharmed among dangers; who was immune to all Evil Spirit: Depart from this person + *(on forehead of possessed)*. Depart from the Church of God + *(over the assistants)*. Fear and take flight at the name of Our Lord whom the powers of Hell fear, to whom the Powers and Virtues and Dominations of Heaven are subject, whom the Cherubim and Seraphim praise with unceasing voices, saying: Holy! Holy! Holy! Lord God of Hosts!

The Word made Flesh + commands you. He who was born of a Virgin + commands you. Jesus + of Nazareth commands you. When you ignored contemptuously his disciples, he ordered you broken and humiliated to get out of that man. And when he tore you from that man, you did not dare in his presence even to enter the swine. Now that you are enjoined in his name +, depart therefore from this person whom he created. It is impossible for you to will to resist. + It is impossible for you to refuse to obey. + Because the more you delay, the more punishment you will get. It is not men you are disobeying. It is he who rules the living and the dead. It is he who will come to judge the living and the dead and the world by fire.

A: Amen.

E: Lord, hear my prayer.

A: And let my cry reach you.

E: May the Lord be with you.

A: And with your spirit.

E: Let us pray:

God of Heaven! God of Earth! God of Angels! God of Archangels! God of Prophets! God of Apostles! God of Martyrs! God of Virgins! God who has the power to give life after death and repose after labor: There is no god but you. Nor could there be a true god but you. Creator of Heaven and Earth. You are a true king. Your kingdom is without end. Humbly, I supplicate your majesty and your glory: that you deign to free this your servant from unclean spirits. Through Christ Our Lord.

A: Amen.

(3) *Second Enjoining of Evil Spirit:-*

I, therefore, enjoin every unclean spirit, each devil, each part of Satan: In the name of Jesus Christ + of Nazareth. After his baptism by John, he was led into the desert and he conquered you on your own ground. Desist from attacking this man (woman) whom Jesus formed from matter for his honor and his glory. Shake with fear, not at the human fragility of a miserable man, but at the image of the all-powerful God. Surrender to God, therefore, +, who put you to flight from King Saul by the spiritual songs of his faithful servant David. Give in + to God who damned you in Judas Iscariot, the traitor. For he touched you with divine punishment and, shouting, you exclaimed: "What is there between us and you, Jesus, Son of the Most High God? Have you come here before the proper time to torture us?" He who drives you now into perpetual flames will say at the end of time to Satan and his angels: "Leave me, Cursed Ones! And go into eternal flames which have been prepared for the Devil and his angels." Death is your lot, Impious One! And for your angels there is an endless death. For you and for your angels the unquenchable flame is prepared, because you are the Prince of cursed homicides, the author of incest, the head of all the sacrilegious, master of the most evil actions, the teacher of heretics, the inventor of all obscenity. Go out, therefore, + Impious one. Go out + Criminal! Go out with all your falsehoods! God has willed man to be his temple. Why linger any longer here? Give honor to God the Father + the all-powerful, to whom every knee will bend. Give place to Our Lord Jesus + Christ, who poured out his blood for man. Give place to the Holy + Spirit who through the Blessed Apostle Peter defeated you manifestly in Simon the Magician, condemned your falsehood in Ananias and Saphira, frustrated you in the magician Elymas by afflicting him with blindness. By the same apostle, he ordered you to depart from the

Prophetess of Python. Leave therefore now +. Go away + Seducer! The desert is your home. The serpent is your dwelling. Be humiliated and cast down. The time cannot be put off. Behold the victorious Lord is near and quick. The fire is burning before him and devours all his enemies. For, even though you have deceived men, you cannot make a mockery of God. From his eyes nothing is hidden: he has ejected you. All things are subject to his power: He has expelled you. The living and the dead and the world will be judged by him with complete discernment: He has prepared Hell for you and your angels.

7: FURTHER INSTRUCTIONS AND PRAYERS

When all has been recited, it can be repeated as often as is necessary, until the possessed is completely free.

It will help, besides, to repeat with devotion the Pater Noster, Ave Maria, and the Credo over the possessed, as well as the Magnificat and the Benedictus Canticle (ending the last two with a Gloria).

8: PROFESSION OF FAITH (ST. ATHANASIUS)

Whoever wishes to be saved, must above all other things, hold firmly to the universal belief. If anyone does not preserve this in its integrity and purity, he shall without doubt perish forever. This universal faith is as follows.

We adore one God in the Trinity and the Trinity in one God, without confusing the Persons or dividing the substance of God. For the Person of the Father is different from the Person of the Son. And both are different from the Person of the Holy Spirit. But the divinity of the Father and the Son and the Holy Spirit is one and the same in equal glory and coeternal majesty.

What the Father is, that the Son is, and the Holy Spirit is. The Father is uncreated, the Son uncreated, the Holy Spirit uncreated. The Father is immeasurable, the Son is immeasurable, the Holy Spirit immeasurable. The Father is eternal, the Son eternal, the Holy Spirit eternal. Nevertheless, there are not three eternal beings, but one eternal Being. There are not three uncreated beings, nor three immeasurable beings, but one uncreated and immeasurable Being.

Similarly, the Father is omnipotent, the Son omnipotent, the Holy Spirit omnipotent. But, still, there are not three omnipotent beings, but one omnipotent Being.

Thus, God the Father, God the Son, God the Holy Spirit. And, nevertheless, not three gods, but one God. Thus, the Father is lord, the Son is lord, the Holy Spirit is lord. But, nevertheless, not three lords, but one Lord. Just as we are compelled by our Christian truth to confess that each Person is God and Lord, so we are prohibited by the universal faith from speaking of three gods and lords.

The Father was made by no one: neither created nor generated. The Son is from the Father: not created, but generated. The Holy Spirit is from the Father and the Son: not made, not created, not generated, but proceeding. There is one Father, therefore, not three fathers. And there is one Son, not three sons. And there is one Holy Spirit, not three spirits.

And in this Trinity, there is no prior or posterior element, no greater or lesser. But all three Persons are coeternal with Each Other and coequal. And, thus, in all things, as said above, we adore unity in the Trinity and the Trinity is unity. Whoever therefore wishes to be saved, must believe this about the Trinity.

But it is necessary for eternal life that you also faithfully believe in the Incarnation of Our Lord Jesus Christ. The correct belief, then, which we profess and believe, is that Jesus Christ, Our Lord, is the Son of God and is man. He is God from the substance of the Father, and generated before all time. And he is man from the substance of his mother, having been born from his mother in time.

Perfect God. Perfect man subsisting with a rational soul and human flesh. Equal to the Father in divinity. Less than the Father according to his humanity. Although he is God and man, he is not two but one. He is one, however, not because his divinity is changed into humanity, but because his humanity is assumed by his divinity. He is integrally one, not because his divine and human substances are fused and made one, but because of the oneness of his person. For, just as the rational soul and body make up one man, so God and man make up Christ.

He suffered for our salvation, liberated those already dead and waiting, and rose from the dead three days later. He ascended into Heaven and sits at the right hand of God. Afterwards, he shall come to judge the living and the dead. At his arrival, all human beings must rise again with their bodies and they must give an account of all their own actions. And those who have done good, will enter eternal life. And those who have done evil, will enter eternal fire.

This is the universal faith. If you do not faithfully and firmly hold on to it, you cannot be saved.

Gloria.

A: Amen.

9: PSALM READINGS

E: Psalms: 90, 67, 34, 30, 21, 3, 10, 12.

10: CONCLUDING PRAYER OF THANKS

E: We pray you, all-powerful God, that Evil Spirit have no more power over this servant of yours (give name of possessed), but that it flee and not come back. Let the goodness and the peace of our Lord Jesus Christ enter him (her) at your bidding, Lord. For through Jesus we have been saved. And let us not fear any ill, because the Lord is with us, He who lives and reigns as God with you in the unity of the Holy Spirit, for ever and ever.

A: Amen.

CHAPTER THREE: EXORCISM OF SATAN
AND APOSTATE ANGELS

1:   INSTRUCTIONS

The following exorcism can be recited by Bishops and also by priests who have received authorization to do so from their own Bishops.

2:   INVOCATION OF MICHAEL THE ARCHANGEL

E: Most glorious Prince of the Heavenly Army, Holy Michael the Archangel, defend us in battle against the princes and powers and rulers of darkness in this world, against the spiritual iniquities of those former angels. Come to the help of men whom God made in his own image and whom he bought from the tyranny of Satan at a great price. The Church venerates you as her custodian and patron. The Lord confided to your care all the souls of those redeemed, so that you would lead them to happiness in Heaven. Pray to the God of peace that he crush Satan under our feet; so that Satan no longer be able to hold men captive and thus injure the Church. Offer our prayers to the Most High God, so that his mercies be given us soon. Make captive that Animal, that Ancient serpent, which is enemy and Evil Spirit, and reduce it to everlasting nothingness, so that it no longer seduce the nations.

3:   ANNOUNCEMENT OF EXORCISM

E: In the name of Jesus Christ, God and Lord; through the intercession of the Immaculate Virgin, Mother of God, Mary, and Holy Michael the Archangel, the Blessed Apostles, Peter and Paul, and all the Saints; and relying on the holy authority of our office, we are about to undertake the expulsion of diabolic infestation.

4:   PRAYER

E: (Psalm 67)
May God rise up, and may his enemies be dissipated.
A: And let those who hate him flee before him.
E: Let them be dissipated like smoke.
A: As wax flows before fire, so let sinners perish before God.
E: Look on the Cross of the Lord. Be defeated, all enemies!
A: The ancient strength will conquer, the King of Kings!
E: Let your mercy be with us, O Lord!
A: According to our hopes in you.

5:   EXORCISM ADDRESS TO SATAN AND TO APOSTATE ANGELS

We exorcise you, each unclean spirit, each power of Satan, each infestation of the Enemy from Hell, each Legion, each Congregation, each Satanic sect! In the name and by the power of our Lord Jesus + Christ! Be uprooted and put to flight from the Church of God; from the souls that were made in the image of God and redeemed with the blood of the divine Lamb.

+ Do not dare further, most cunning Serpent, to deceive the human race, to persecute the Church of God, to strike and shake the chosen of God like chaff +. The Most High God orders you +. It is he whom you, in your gargantuan pride, emulated. He wishes all men to be saved and to come to the acknowledgment of the truth.

God the Father + commands you. God the Son + commands you. God the Holy + Spirit commands you. Christ orders you, he who is the eternal Word of God become man +; he who destroyed your hateful jealousy against the salvation of our race; he who humiliated himself making himself obedient to death; he who builds his Church on a firm rock and provided that the strength of Hell would never prevail over that Church; he who will remain with his Church for all days even up to the end of human time.

The Sacrament of the Cross + commands you. The virtue of all the mysteries of the Christian faith commands you. The most exalted Mother of God, Mary the Virgin, + commands you. She, though lowly, trampled on your head from the first instant of her immaculate conception. The faith of the Blessed Apostles, Peter and Paul, + commands you. The Blood of Martyrs and the pious intercession of all the Saints + commands you.

Therefore, Accursed Serpent, and all the power of Satan! We enjoin you under penalty, through the living God +, through the true + God, through the holy + God, through God who so loved the world that he gave his only son so that all who believe in him should not perish but should have eternal life:

Cease to deceive human beings and to offer them the poison of eternal perdition.

Cease to injure the Church and to set traps for the Church's liberty. Go, Satan! Inventor and master of all falsehood! Enemy of human salvation! Give way to Christ in whom you could find nothing of your own evil. Give way to the Holy, Catholic, and Apostolic Church which Christ himself created by his blood. Be humiliated under the powerful hand of God. Fear and take flight, when the holy and terrible name of Jesus is invoked by us. For he is feared by Evil Spirit, and to him all Powers and Virtues and Dominations of Heaven are subject. And the Cherubim and the Seraphim praise him with unfailing voices, saying: Holy! Holy! Holy! Lord God of Hosts.

Lord, hear my prayer.

A: And let my cry reach you.

E: May the Lord be with you.

A: And with your spirit.

6: PRAYER

E: Let us pray:

God of Heaven! God of Earth! God of Angels! God of Archangels! God of Patriarchs! God of Prophets! God of Confessors! God of Virgins! God who has power to grant eternal life after death and rest after labor! There is no god but you. Nor could there be any other god. Creator of all visible and invisible beings! Your kingdom is without end.

We humbly supplicate you in your majesty and glory: Liberate us, through your power, from all the power of Evil Spirit, from its traps, deceptions, and treachery; and deign to keep us safely. Through Christ Our Lord.

A: Amen.

7: INVOCATIONS

E: From the ambushes of Evil Spirit,

A: Free us, O Lord.

E: When we ask you to help your Church to serve you securely in liberty,

A: We pray you: Hear us!

E: Humiliate the enemies of the Holy Church,

A: We pray you: Hear us!

8: BLESSING OF PLACE OF EXORCISM

The place is sprinkled with Holy Water

APPENDIX TWO

Prayers Commonly Used in Exorcisms and Mentioned in the Exorcisms of this Book

PATER NOSTER

Our Father Who art in Heaven: Hallowed be your name! May your kingdom come! May your will be done on Earth as it is in Heaven! Give us this day our daily bread. And forgive us our offences, as we forgive those who offend against us. And lead us not into temptation. But deliver us from Evil. Amen.

AVE MARIA

Hail Mary! Full of Grace! The Lord is with you. Blessed are you among women. And blessed is the fruit of your womb, Jesus. Holy Mary, Mother of God! Pray for us sinners, now and at the hour of our death. Amen.

GLORIA

Glory be to the Father, and to the Son, and to the Holy Spirit. As it was in beginning, is now, and shall be, for ever and ever. Amen.

ANIMA CHRISTI

Soul of Christ, sanctify me. Body of Christ, save me. Blood of Christ, exalt me. Water from the side of Christ, wash me. My Good Jesus, hear me. Within your wounds hide me. Never permit me to be separated from you. At the hour of death, call me. And bid me come to you. So that with the angels and saints I may worship you. For ever and ever. Amen.

SALVE REGINA

Hail Holy Queen! Mother of Mercy! Hail! Our life, our sweetness, and our hope. To you do we cry, poor banished children of Eve. To you do we send up our sighs mourning and weeping in this valley of tears. Turn, then, most gracious mother, your merciful eyes towards us. And, after this our exile, show us the blessed fruit of your womb, Jesus. Clement, loving, sweet Virgin Mary, Pray for us, most holy mother of God, that we may be worthy of the promises of Christ.

Index

About the Author

Malachi Martin, a former Jesuit professor at the Pontifical Biblical Institute in Rome, was trained in theology at Louvain, specializing in the Dead Sea Scrolls and intertestamentary studies. He received his doctorate in Semitic languages, archeology, and Oriental history. He subsequently studied at Oxford and at the Hebrew University, concentrating in knowledge of Jesus as transmitted in Jewish and Islamic sources. Among the many exorcists of his personal acquaintance was the redoubtable Father Conor, who figures importantly in the first case in this book. Dr. Martin is the author of *The New Castle, Jesus Now, Three Popes and the Cardinal, The Encounter, The Scribal Character of the Dead Sea Scrolls,* and *The Pilgrim,* and many articles for magazines and newspapers, and is Religious Editor of *The National Review.*

Malachi Martin's fourteen books include *The Final Conclave, The Jesuits, The Encounter* (winner of the Choice Book Award of the American Library Association), and *Vatican.*

Dr. Martin has been described as "a weaver of spells with words" (*San Francisco Sunday Examiner & Chronicle*), "one of the finest writers alive" (*Psychology Today* Book Club), and "the most fascinating writer in the religious field today" (*The Sunday Houston Chronicle*).